"This is an important exposé of America's meat industry, which has only gotten more cruel and dangerous since Upton Sinclair penned his original exposé, *The Jungle*, nearly a century ago. Today, industrial meat barons are engaged in a destructive war against America's health, our environment, our national security, our values, and our democracy."

—Robert F. Kennedy Jr., president of Waterkeeper Alli

D0506535

"*Veggie Revolution* takes us into places that very few of us ever see: the factory farms where most of America's chicken, pork, eggs, and milk are produced. Read it, stop buying factory-farmed animal products, and use the helpful advice and great recipes to change your life and make a difference."

—Peter Singer, author of *Animal Liberation* and Ira W. DeCamp
professor of bioethics, University Center for Human Values,
Princeton University

"A lively and festive paean to our colorful friends that celebrates their vital role in the food chain. ... The Kneidels understand vegetarianism to be more than a diet, but a political and ethical statement borne of a broad understanding of our place on Earth."

—*Kirkus Reviews*

"This account of how one family has explored the connections between food, health, community and the environment may inspire others to look beyond stereotypes to discover the many dimensions of a vegetarian lifestyle. ... Best suited for young adults who are vegetarians or considering a vegetarian lifestyle, this work may also prove useful to parents of young vegetarians who want a more complete understanding of vegetarian nutrition and menu options."

—*Publishers Weekly*

"*Veggie Revolution* is *the* book for anyone who gives a thought to animals, the environment, and the impacts of what we eat. Of all the veggie books, this is the most witty, savvy, and sensible. Help yourself and the planet: get with the veggie revolution."

—Jim Mason, author of *An Unnatural Order* and coauthor with
Peter Singer of *Food Matters: The Ethics of What We Eat*

"Wondering about going vegetarian? The authors present the most disturbing material in the gentlest, most matter-of-fact way. In reporting that digs deeper than a farmer's plow, they examine every alarming angle of our contemporary eating habits, yet inspire us with hope for change. Turn to this feast of vegetarian recipes and begin to grow younger, healthier, saner."

—Dannye Romine Powell, award-winning news columnist for *The Charlotte Observer*, author of *Parting the Curtains: Interviews with Southern Writers*, and winner of a National Endowment for the Arts fellowship

Veggie revolution

Smart Choices for a Healthy Body and a Healthy Planet

Sally Kneidel, Ph.D., and Sara Kate Kneidel

Fulcrum Publishing
Golden, Colorado

Library of Congress Cataloging-in-Publication Data

Kneidel, Sally Stenhouse.
Veggie revolution : smart choices for a healthy body and a healthy planet / Sally Kneidel and Sara Kate Kneidel.
     p. cm.
Includes bibliographical references and index.
ISBN 1-55591-540-X (pbk.)
1. Cookery (Vegetables) I. Kneidel, Sara Kate. II. Title.
  TX801.K57 2005
  641.6'5—dc22

                                        2005019745

ISBN10 1-55591-540-X
ISBN13 978-1-55591-540-7

Printed in the United States of America
0 9 8 7 6 5 4 3 2 1

Editorial: Katie Raymond, Faith Marcovecchio, Haley Groce
Cover image and design: Jack Lenzo

Fulcrum Publishing
16100 Table Mountain Parkway, Suite 300
Golden, Colorado 80403
(800) 992-2908 • (303) 277-1623
www.fulcrum-books.com

This book is dedicated to all the farmers

who work long hours to fill our plates

for little pay and even less recognition.

Contents

Preface
(Sally)

Researching and writing this book has changed me as much as any project I've ever done. I've felt like Alice tumbling down the rabbit hole into a strange new world, where nothing is as it seems.

When I set out to do this book, I was working as a writer in a private high school. My husband, who holds a Ph.D. in ecology, was working in the same school as a biology teacher teaching conservation, nutrition, population ecology, and other topics relevant to a sustainable future. As vegetarians ourselves, we both knew a large number of vegetarian students at the school, and that number was growing. We knew their parents too, and the parents were often hungry for information about vegetarian recipes and vegetarian nutrition for their families. I often found myself photocopying our home collection of vegetarian recipes and handing it out to friends and parents, so one of my motives in writing this book was to share our recipes and the basic facts about vegetarian nutrition.

But I also wanted to pull into one volume all the possible reasons for choosing a vegetarian diet. Our own two kids, both in college, had many friends who were vegetarians too, or were thinking about it. Most of the students I knew who were considering a meatless diet seemed to have one particular reason for it—ranging from animal welfare to health to the environment and sustainability issues—but they didn't have a grasp of the whole picture.

And neither did I. I thought I did, and that was one of my reasons for deciding to do the book. But as we began making phone calls and talking to farmers and food workers, I realized how complex the topic truly is.

My daughter, Sara Kate, was interested in working on the project with me. As a student who has been a vegetarian for many years and has also worked in a vegetarian restaurant for years, she would bring a student's perspective to the work. She's passionate on the subject of food. My son, Alan, also wanted to help; he is one of the many college students whose voices can be heard in the "student voice" pieces throughout the book.

When we pulled on our boots and actually started visiting farms, we learned pretty quickly that factory farms live up to all the rumors we'd heard about them. The animals we saw on these huge farms were indeed caged, crowded, smeared with feces, and treated as brainless production units. But we also learned that not all meat is produced on factory farms. We easily found at least four farms in our area that raise animals humanely at pasture. What about that meat? Should we view that meat differently?

Then there was the farmer who asked us about the pollution generated by the trucks that bring our tofu from California to the grocery in North Carolina. Could we really argue that eating tofu produced far away is better than eating meat raised from humane and environmentally responsible farmers in our own community? Maybe it's more important, he said, to support our own community, to buy from farmers we know. Neighbors can hold neighbors responsible for growing food in a humane and environmentally sustainable manner.

Those were interesting points, but what does *humane* really mean?

And just in terms of buying local produce, were we really making full use of our nearby farmers' markets? Or were we choosing supermarket vegetables shipped here from Texas and even Holland?

While struggling through all these questions, we've made some changes. Our trips to farms big and small have cemented our resolve to remain meatless, even though we saw many comfortable animals on the small farms. After our trip to a nearby egg factory, we can no longer buy eggs from caged hens. We've found a powdered egg replacement that works great in recipes, including omelets. And we're making more of an effort to buy local produce.

Most of all, I have enjoyed meeting the farmers in our area, including the factory farmers—maybe especially the factory farmers. They're fascinating to me because they all have a blend of qualities and opinions that can't possibly coexist, yet do. They've all been kind and generous with their time. They are all sensitive people who originally got into farming because they like animals and nature. At one time, they enjoyed being their own bosses. Yet now, with such irony, they find themselves cogs in a powerful and cruel machine, with less and less control over their own livelihoods. And whose fault is it? This is a complex question that we'll address later in the book.

Sara Kate and I have both been inspired by the small farmers we've met who are committed to a sustainable future and are struggling to put their ideals into practice. It's not easy to put principles above dollars when you have families to raise. Even though we both remain vegetarian and dream of a meatless future for all, we've been impressed with the ways these small farmers have found to protect the environment, to create comfortable living conditions for their animals, and to develop connections and trust within their own communities.

We've also been impressed with the number of students we interviewed who feel strongly about taking a stand, refusing to participate in the corporate meat industry. It's encouraging to see so many young people determined to change the world, one forkful at a time. With these students, there is hope.

I invite you to hear the voices of the students throughout this book and to share our visits with all the farmers as described in chapters three, four, and five.

I hope you enjoy the book. I hope you find some surprises here. I did.

—Sally Kneidel, Ph.D.

If I've learned anything during my years in college, it's that passion cannot be controlled. Once upon a time, I thought I could choose what captivates me. But a few quirks along the way have taught me that a budding interest—in an idea, a person, a hobby, a song—has a mind of its own. It either grabs me or it doesn't. And if it does, I've got to go with it.

One of my greatest passions, one that chose me, is food. It's an ardor with a thousand forms. Most enticingly, there's the simple joy of cooking food. Then there's the joy of sharing of it, building bonds dish by dish. Just think of all the interchanges that take place over shared dishes, the connections made by gifts of food, the rituals and traditions based on what we eat. Food connects and binds us, from the childhood comfort of Grandma's homemade soup to a romantic box of chocolates to the friendly sharing of movie popcorn. Those interchanges are what make food so meaningful in our lives.

Interaction centered on food seems to be the common thread in my life. From my job as a vegetarian cook to my immersion in a new culture to my residence in a vegetarian co-op, again and again I've seen food build community. The passion for food that these experiences have cultivated in me resonates throughout this book.

My love affair with food blossomed during the years I've worked as a cook in a small vegetarian restaurant. It was there that I discovered the simple joy inherent in the mechanical steps of cooking. I learned to relish the feeling of a sharp knife biting through fresh peppers and eggplants. I learned to pick out the smells of tarragon, basil, and oregano sizzling in a stir-fry. I learned to cook with an adventurous streak, brewing strange concoctions to coax the most savory flavors from my ingredients.

And most of all, I learned to love our customers. I never tire of watching people realize that eating well makes them feel good. Every time a new customer gets excited about eating a tofu dog for the first time or is thrilled to find out that the salad they're eating is not only organic but also locally grown, I feel the thrill all over again too.

I love our regulars, the ones who have been eating lunch at our restaurant for two or five or thirty years. They'll keep coming back until they die or we do, because who needs McDonald's when we've got one eye out the window as they pull up and have their special order made just right before they're even in the door? Our customers' loyalty to us—and ours to them—meant we survived when a Baja Fresh opened next door ... and when it closed only three months later. When we ask our customers about their pets and admire pictures of their grandkids, we're doing more than just chatting. We're building relationships, community.

This trend, born in the restaurant, has spread like wildfire throughout my life. It traveled with me to Mexico, where I spent a semester with a grassroots organization working for social change. As I joined this community, so different from my own, I was welcomed with hot tamales and soothed with steaming *atole*. I learned the subtle social cues: to bring gifts of sweet bread or fruit when I was invited to dinner, to always accept a snack when offered, to eat and praise my way into the hearts of the families that sustained me. In that culture, eating food that's offered to you is a crucial symbol of acceptance. Eating the meal means thank you for welcoming me; I respect and honor you and your home.

As an outsider, it was easy for me to objectively observe the importance of food in Mexican culture. But what role did it play in my own? On our long morning walks to school, my friend Matt and I puzzled over this. When the time approached to return to our Quaker college in North Carolina the following year, we knew we needed to carry on the lessons we were learning in our Mexican community, from the dedication to social change to the way community members devotedly took care of each other. On one early morning's walk, as we dreamily recollected happy memories of the American foods we missed, the solution became suddenly apparent.

Our college owned a number of houses that groups of project-minded students could apply to live in. We would apply to form a Food Ethics House, a place focused on examining the ethics of our food industry. Our lifestyle would require taking social change into our own hands. And as a center of student life on campus, our house would promote a sense of community with open dialogue and space for change, just as we were experiencing in Mexico.

But why focus on food, of all things? Well, for starters, nothing is more fundamental to our lives than food. Everyone must eat, and the food we consume has a tremendous impact on the world around us, as well as on our own bodies. Being conscious of what and how we consume is the most basic way of taking control of how our daily choices affect others.

In addition, our international experience was making the reality of our complicated and damaging modern food industry unpleasantly clear. From across the border, we could not ignore how the globalization of our food market is hurting not only the people of developing nations such as Mexico, but Americans too.

Our proposal was accepted and we moved into our house, along with twelve other students committed to ethical food choices. As a group, we pledged to cook and eat together; to prioritize eating vegetarian, organic, local, and sustainable foods; and to act on our food ideals in the greater community. Once a week

we cooked with Food Not Bombs, a roving soup kitchen that salvages food that would otherwise be wasted and serves it to hungry folks. We salvaged for ourselves as well, and what food we actually bought came from Eastern Carolina Organics, an organization of local organic farmers that delivers boxes of produce fresh from the fields right to our door.

We had potluck dinners, monthly gatherings where everyone brings a dish and tries a bit of everyone else's. You end up with a plate of tofu chili heaped over falafel with roasted peppers from the school's organic fair-share garden peeping out from under your crumbling apple pie. Other times we hosted bigger, schoolwide events where we got people talking about food-related issues.

For me, food and community are inseparable. My experiences as a cook, in Mexico, and in my home have all come together to convince me that sharing food is a fundamental way of building community. That includes sharing food as a family as well as trading food as a producer and consumer. Buying and eating food grown by our neighbors keeps both buyer and seller personally accountable for the quality and integrity of the product.

Community means real connections. It means caring about other beings, caring about where our food comes from, and caring about how we nourish and sustain others. I believe that when the production and sharing of food stays within the community, food is grown more responsibly.

I hope that this book will be a guide to people who are interested in exploring the role of food in their lives. Food is essential. It is what ties us together. It is community. It is both how and why we live. Understanding this has changed my relationship with food forever. I hope it does the same for you.

—Sara Kate Kneidel

Acknowledgments

When we embarked upon this project, we had no idea what we were getting into. Little did we suspect that a few months down the road we would be trucking through fields and feedlots alongside helpful and informative folks we never would have encountered otherwise. Little did we imagine how the information we gathered there would affect the other people in our lives, not to mention ourselves.

First and foremost, we would like to thank all the people who allowed us to interview and observe them as they went about their busy days. These include a number of farmers who wish to remain anonymous, but may recognize themselves in these pages. Thank you for being honest and giving us a glimpse into the reality of your situation.

We would like to thank those who are mentioned by name in our text: Chase Hubbard and his student helpers at Warren Wilson College Farm; Amy, Jamie, and Cyrus Ager of Hickory Nut Gap Farm; Sammy, Melinda, Benjamin, and the Koenigsberg family of New Town Farms; and Tom and Linda Trantham of 12 Aprils Farm. To all the farmers we met, we appreciate your patience as we stumbled after you in our city shoes, mistaking steers for heifers, confusing broilers and breeders. If you saw through half of our bluffing, you'll realize how much we learned from you and how much you inspired us.

We would also like to thank the many faces of the food industry who spoke with us so candidly. The cafeteria managers, store managers, farmers' market vendors, university professors, and county agricultural representatives offered us perspectives we never could have envisioned on our own. Glimpsing your point of view was invaluable to our understanding of the system.

In addition, the professionals who helped us fact-check and clarify were profoundly important. When we doubted our perspective or the veracity of our findings, you helped set us straight. Despite all the assistance we received, any errors in the text are purely our own.

On the consumer end, we are deeply grateful to our friends and family for facilitating and patiently supporting us and for enduring our obsession with this project. From sampling endless recipes to posing for photos, our loved ones made this book possible. Thanks to Ken for support and encouragement, for so much cooking, and for spreading the word. Thanks to Alan for his uncensored and sassy comments and for his brilliant photos of Costa Rican wildlife. And thank you to all the residents of Hildebrandt House for some fantastic Sunday brunches and potato pancake extravaganzas and for never giving in.

We are grateful to all the students at Guilford College, Charlotte Latin School, and other schools and universities who agreed to be interviewed and who provided recipes and youthful insight. It's so important to feel supported by our target audience.

Finally, we are very grateful to our agent, Sally McMillan, and to everyone at Fulcrum Publishing, particularly Katie Raymond, Sam Scinta, Catherine White, and Jack Lenzo, for their painstaking attention and suggestions along the way.

Introduction

If you picked up this book, chances are you have some questions about the typical American diet, the one that includes meat at nearly every meal. Maybe you've heard that a steady diet of burgers and chicken fingers is not necessarily the best choice for your health. Or maybe you feel kindly toward animals and you have a nagging, uneasy feeling about how the animals we eat are raised. Or perhaps you've seen disturbing reports on the news about pollution from factory farms. Whatever the case, in these pages you'll find an easy path to understanding all of these issues and more.

We Had Questions Too

We set out wanting to write a book about vegetarian nutrition, cooking, and recipes, along with environmental concerns related to meat production. We already had a firm understanding of vegetarian cooking and nutrition and a good start on the environmental aspects, so we thought the book would be fairly straightforward. But as we started interviewing college students, high school students, and parents about their diets, the plot began to thicken. New questions piled up, questions about hormones in milk, hog waste lagoons, and sows in narrow gestation crates. These issues were troubling. We searched for answers in written material, but what we read we could hardly believe: chickens debeaked and crammed in tiny cages, single farms with more than a million animals, hog waste spilling across neighborhoods ... Was this stuff real?

We Went Straight to the Source

So we got on the phone and started calling people. We called factory farmers and asked if we could come visit. Given that some investigators have spent years trying to get inside one of these huge confinement facilities, we were surprised when they said yes to us. But they did, so we were able to visit four factory farms. We interviewed the farmers at length and took lots of pictures of their warehoused animals, stunned by what we were seeing. These experiences changed us ... profoundly so.

To balance things out, we called four small family farms too. They were happy for us to come visit, so we interviewed them and took more pictures there.

In chapters three, four, and five, through our words and photos we walk you through each of our farm visits, showing you everything we saw in the way the animals are treated on both kinds of farms. See for yourself. As much as anything else, this book is an account of discovery and transition—our own.

We Kept on Calling

We didn't stop after the farm visits. Once we started peeling back the layers, we realized farmers are just one small part of our complicated food industry. And so we went deeper. We interviewed environmental scientists, agricultural scientists, supermarket managers, workers at health food stores, a school cafeteria manager, and government workers.

We investigated every angle. We wanted to know the truth about how our dietary habits—particularly our meat consumption—impact the world at large. How do our food choices affect our land, our rivers, the contract farmers, the farmed animals themselves, our health, future generations? We dug, we read, we asked, and we got answers.

From scientists, we learned that the thriving meat industry is the second biggest cause of environmental damage in this country, second only to travel. And the implications for the future are scary.

Who's to Blame? It's Not a Simple Story

When we first began learning about factory farms, we thought the farmers themselves must be responsible for the miseries of the animals and laborers on these industrial-sized farms and responsible for the environmental costs too. But the more we stirred, the more the whole story began to stink. We've learned that in many ways, factory farmers are just pawns in a system they did little to create. The real culprits are the corporations whose ads tell us we need animal products at every meal, corporations that profit by providing these products to us. But the corporations aren't in it alone. We, the American public, drive this ugly machine with our demand for meat and more meat. We're responsible too. And yet, at the same time, we're victims, because we have to deal with the health problems caused by high-fat diets and with the pollution and land-use problems caused by massive numbers of livestock.

Solutions: How to Make More Ethical Food Choices

Before we started writing, we knew the obvious solution to problems caused by the meat industry: to eat less meat. But we became aware of other solutions as well.

We learned about a growing alternative market for livestock raised humanely in pastures. Owners of small farms told us about their Community Supported Agriculture programs, groups of farmers who believe strongly in selling their products directly to their local communities. In chapters five and six, we explore these different priorities.

Nutrition

But no matter where the food comes from, your diet affects no one more than you. For this reason, in chapter six you'll find a complete guide to getting all the nutrients you need without animal products. We explain how to make sure meatless meals include enough protein, calcium, iron, vitamins, fiber, and everything else you need for optimum health. With a little practice, you'll find that cooking without meat actually opens the door to more variety at mealtime. Meat is just a habit, but with a little guidance, it's a habit that's easily broken. If you decide to take this route, we think you'll soon wonder why you ever thought meat was necessary.

Cooking

In chapter eight, we get to the cooking. That's the really fun part. Before you turn to the recipes, however, we've described special techniques for preparing vegetables, beans, grains, soy products, spices, and herbs—tricks of the trade that will show you how easy vegetarian cooking can be.

And the recipes, well, they speak for themselves. Gathered from family members and friends, from recipe boxes and our own experimentation, we have included a variety in every category—breakfasts; breads; salads and side dishes; main dishes; spreads, sauces, and dips; and desserts. We've selected only the very best friend-tested and family-approved recipes.

What We've Learned Has Changed

What is the transition we've undergone? For me, the biggest change is my firsthand awareness of the billions of sentient animals living in desperate misery in order to provide us with food that none of us need. Millions of these animals live within an hour's drive of my home, while I sit here in comfort at my computer. I regret the many years I kept their flesh in my refrigerator.

I also know more about the environmental havoc wrought by keeping too many animals in too little space. I see now that the responsibility for the disaster that is the American meat industry rests with corporations more than farmers, and it rests with the American public for the vast quantities of meat we consume.

I've learned there are solutions other than total abstinence. Just eating less meat can make a huge difference. Every individual meal matters.

For those who choose to eat meat, pasture-based meat is a viable option. We can choose to support farmers who treat the environment and animals with respect. By doing so, and by buying locally produced food, we're both protecting the environment and promoting a healthy, interactive, and mutually responsible community.

Who Is This Book for?

This is a book for people who want to learn more about eating less meat. Is it for vegetarians? Yes, but not exclusively. It's about eating more plant-based food that's grown locally and how to choose healthy alternatives to meat. That could mean a vegan diet, or it could mean a few meatless meals each week—that's up to you.

It's also a book for anyone who cares about the environment or anyone who loves animals. It's for anyone who is concerned about our future as occupants of this planet with its finite resources.

The book is also for readers who want to learn more about health and nutrition. And with dozens of meatless recipes, it's for people like us who enjoy cooking exciting and scrumptious new foods to share with friends and family.

When someone asks me why I've given up meat, it's hard to give a short answer. A vegetarian diet is more healthful, especially when care is taken to seek out protein, calcium, and all the other essential nutrients.

A vegetarian diet spares the wretched lives of animals on factory farms. I don't want any creature living a life like that on my account.

A vegetarian diet protects the environment too. Massive amounts of manure and chemical fertilizers used to grow food for livestock pollute our air and water.

The more obvious question would be, Why eat meat? Because we're used to it? I can't think of a single good reason.

—Sally Kneidel

Be the change you wish to see in the world.

—Gandhi

Change is possible. Change starts in our communities. Taking control over the food we eat is a simple route to larger-scale change. In the process of creating this book, we have ended up with a very different final product than we originally set out to write. But as my mom says, "If you know exactly what you're going to say before you sit down to write, then there's not much point in writing it."

In researching and writing this project, both of us have become much more aware of how we, as consumers, interact with the modern food industry and how complex that interaction is. In the end, however, my message is simple: whatever your reasons for being vegetarian—be it your own health, animal rights, the environment, or social values—your food choices have a huge impact on the world around you, particularly on your community. Through this book, this is what I hope to communicate: change is possible. Making intentional choices about the food we consume is a simple, practical step toward larger-scale social change.

Why food? You may ask yourself, How can my choice between a pork chop and a veggie burger possibly affect huge problems such as global warming or world hunger? Well, as you'll see, that personal choice not to eat meat *does* affect those larger issues, both directly and indirectly. As you will read in this book, the consumption of meat contributes directly to environmental destruction, to issues of world population sustainability, to human health concerns, and to the welfare of millions of animals, both domestic and wild. By choosing not to eat meat, you are choosing not to participate in a system that abuses and damages these parts of our world. And indirectly, your mindful food choices positively impact the world in a more subtle way. When you choose produce from the farmers' market instead of the grocery store, food grown by a farmer in your own county rather than from a corporation thousands of miles away, you are supporting your local economy, building a relationship with members of your community, and encouraging a sense of responsibility and stewardship between vendor and customer.

Every farmer or food producer we've interviewed has said the same thing: food production is driven by customer demand. As long as customers buy cheap food that is produced through a system of abuse, someone will continue to sell it to them. Only when customers demand healthy, responsibly made food will it be profitable, and therefore possible, to produce it.

And thus, the power is yours. Each time you choose vegetarian, organic, or local food, you are taking a stand for change. I hope that this book informs you of the ways in which your choices matter and that it equips you to go out into the world with a better idea of how the small choices in your life affect the billions of beings on this planet. I hope that it leaves you feeling empowered and hopeful, because that is how I feel.

—Sara Kate Kneidel

Chapter One

How Many People Can Earth Feed?

Hunger in the Land of Plenty

During the past ten years, we've taken trains across the United States on several family vacations. It's cheaper than flying and a lot more fun than car travel. And not much is more impressive than the absolutely tremendous size of our country as it unfolds, day after day, from an Amtrak train.

On the first full day of the ride west from Philadelphia, you wake up as the sun is rising somewhere in eastern Illinois. Peering out the giant windows of the observation car, you're startled by the unexpected feeling that you've somehow stumbled into infinity. As far as the horizon in either direction, there are nothing but endless fields of soy, corn, wheat, and oats nodding gently in the breeze. The undulating amber waves of grain are boundless.

As the day continues, you chug doggedly past Chicago, meander through Iowa, and finally drift off to sleep as darkness falls in Missouri. When you wake up in the morning, you're *still* only in Kansas. The landscape is flatter than it was the day before, if such a thing is possible. But other than that, the scenery hasn't changed much. You're still surrounded by farmland that won't end for hours more, until you begin the long, slow climb into the mountains of Colorado and New Mexico.

WHO EATS THOSE GRAINS?

With such bountiful space, it seems impossible to have a shortage of land, food—or anything at all—here in the land of plenty. And yet we do. More than two-thirds of those amber waves of grain never reach our plates. They are fed to cattle, pigs, and other livestock, which are sliced up and *then* put on our plates.

In America, that is. But not everywhere. The United Nations estimates that one-fourth of the world population—that's 1.5 billion people—are severely malnourished. But this isn't because we lack the space to grow food. Even though the human population is skyrocketing, it is still possible to grow enough food for everyone in the space we have. Or at least it *would* be possible if we made better use of our land—if we used it to grow food for people instead of livestock. The grain and soybeans that we grow and feed to our livestock here in the United States could feed more than a billion people instead.

AMERICANS TAKE UP A LOT OF SPACE WITH OUR MEAT DIETS

Because it takes so much food to feed cows, pigs, and chickens, the average meat-eating American is responsible for the consumption of about 2,000 pounds of grain a year. Most of that is not consumed by the person, but rather by the animals that the person eats. In contrast, the average Indian consumes only 400 pounds of grains a year, most of which goes directly into his mouth.[1]

AMERICANS USE A WHOLE LOT OF WATER TOO

Raising livestock also requires massive amounts of water to irrigate the corn and grains for the animals. While it takes 300 gallons of water to grow a day's worth of food for a vegetarian, it takes 2,500 gallons to raise a day's worth of food for a meat eater![2]

Student Voice: William, Age 18

I don't have a problem with people eating meat, but you've got to be responsible. There's not enough room for everyone on Earth to eat a Big Mac for every meal. Americans eat more meat than most countries. The oceans have been really overfished. Any time you have to stock fisheries, you're taking more than nature is providing. No matter how efficiently you use stuff, you have a set amount of resources to work with. It's our Earth. We have one Earth. We've got to take care of it.

How Come Land Produces More Veggies than Meat?

JUST LIKE RABBITS

Have you ever heard the phrase "multiplying like rabbits"? That's not really fair to rabbits. If any living thing deserves to be the symbol of reproducing too fast, it should be humans. We are rapidly engulfing the planet with our offspring. The current human population is more than 6 billion, and it is projected to grow to 9 billion in the next fifty years.[3] We've managed to survive on the Earth for thousands of years so far. But if we continue to reproduce at the current rate for another 600 years, there will then be 170 quadrillion people alive. That would put one person on every square meter of the whole land surface of the Earth! A little cramped, to say the least. Clearly, the Earth could not support such a ridiculously large population.

So how many people *can* the Earth support? That number, whatever it is, is called the "carrying capacity." Nobody really knows what the Earth's carrying capacity is for humans, because it depends on how we use the land. It depends mainly on how livestock fit into the picture.

SHANGRI-LA

Let's imagine a fictional place to help understand why livestock make such a big difference. Imagine a small planet called Shangri-La. Let's say all the people on Shangri-La are vegetarians. All the available land on Shangri-La is devoted to growing human food. In this situation, let's say Shangri-La can support 1,000 people; in other words, the planet's carrying capacity is 1,000 people.

Now let's imagine an alternate picture: that people on Shangri-La are meat eaters whose diet consists of 50 percent animal products such as beef. You would think that in order to get half their nutrition from eating animals, they would have to devote half their land to animals. Seems logical enough, right? But this is not the case. In fact, the citizens of Shangri-La will have to devote a huge amount of their land to growing food for the cows, not to mention space for the cows themselves. Now the planet Shangri-La can grow only enough food to support 180 people. By making their diet half meat, the carrying capacity of the planet has been reduced by more than 80 percent.[4]

Not So Fast—
What about Those Calculations?

How is it that eating meat reduces the carrying capacity so much? It goes back to that old food chain you learned back in fourth grade.

Let's think for just a minute about two different roles that animals can play in a food chain: herbivore and carnivore.

Herbivores are animals that eat plants. Examples are cows, rabbits, squirrels, deer, beavers, elk, antelope, woodchucks, gophers.

Carnivores are animals that eat other animals, or meat. Examples are wolves, cats of all kinds, snakes, sharks, eagles, frogs, eels, spiders, praying mantises.

When a deer eats leaves, it takes about ten pounds of leaves to produce one pound of deer. In other words, when an herbivore eats plants, the herbivore is able to convert only 10 percent of the energy in that plant into body mass or energy for daily life.

Now let's say a mountain lion attacks the deer and eats it. Again, it takes ten pounds of deer to produce one pound of lion. That is, the lion is able to convert only 10 percent of the energy in the deer into its own body mass or energy.

In general, this "10 percent rule" applies to any food eaten by an animal. Because animals are able to convert only 10 percent of the energy from their food into energy stored in their bodies, 90 percent of the available energy is lost with every step along the food chain.

Now here's the crucial part: what is the relationship between the mountain lion and the leaves? The lion is getting 10 percent of the deer's energy, and the deer is getting 10 percent of the leaves' energy. Ten percent of 10 percent is 1 percent, so the lion is getting only 1 percent of the leaves' energy! Using the deer as a middle step, that means it would take 100 pounds of leaves to produce one pound of lion.

What if the deer disappeared and the mountain lion just ate the leaves directly? Then, following the 10 percent rule, 100 pounds of leaves would produce ten pounds of lion.

Of course, that isn't going to happen. Mountain lions can't eat leaves. Their bodies are designed and genetically programmed to eat meat. They have no choice.

Humans, however, have a choice. We are omnivores, which means we can eat the leaves (meaning vegetables and other plant food) and get 10 percent of the energy in the plants. Or we can eat the deer (meaning cows, pigs, and chickens) and get only 1 percent of the energy in the plants. This means that choosing the leaves gives us more energy from the same amount of growing space.

Thus, if we choose to eat the plants directly, then the land we have can support five times more people than if we choose to eat meat. (It's not ten times more because human meat eaters don't eat purely meat-based diets.)

WE CAN GET THINGS UNDER CONTROL … AND STILL EAT MEAT AT EVERY MEAL, CAN'T WE?

Someone might argue, well, let's just have fewer people so that we can still have meat. If the human race would cooperate, that would be an option. But our population is booming, and most people aren't aware of the consequences.

The fact is, starvation does not stop people from having children. In fact, starvation and poverty are linked to *higher* birth rates.

Why is this so? In countries where women have few rights, little access to education, and little opportunity for employment, women tend to be poor and they tend to have big families. Motherhood may seem like their only option, or they may have no access to birth control. When those same countries introduce programs to educate and employ women, the birth rate drops. In this situation, women have more resources to control and improve their quality of life. The majority of women still have children, but they have two or three instead of six or seven. Iran is an example of a country that has been very proactive in improving opportunities for women, and one result is a decrease in average family size. Other benefits include an increase in literacy and in the general standard of living for everyone.

Web Sites for More Info

For more information on factors that affect human population growth, do a Google search for Population Connection or International Data Base (IDB). Population Connection is a nonprofit organization that has dozens of links to articles about the factors that affect human population growth and how the growth is affecting our world. IDB is a fascinating computerized data bank of census information from every country. Among other things, it has animated graphs showing changes in population over time.

Measure Your Ecological Footprint

It's amazing that we still have millions of hungry people here in the United States when you consider how much of the world's resources we are using to support ourselves. Have you ever heard of an "ecological footprint"? Here's how it works: if we add up all the usable land in the world and divide by the number of people, we find that there are about four and one-half acres per person. Your share of the land includes the land your food is grown on, the land that grew the tree for your desk and the cotton for your shirt, the land that provided the gas and oil for your car, the land your house stands on, and so on.

BUT WAIT! HOW CAN THAT BE?

Considering all these demands, it's easy to see how the average American uses a whopping twenty-four acres. Unfortunately, that's five times more than our four-and-one-half-acre share. Such an overuse is only possible because most people on the planet are using far *less* than their share. An average person in Bangladesh, for example, is using only 0.5 acres. If everyone on Earth were living an American lifestyle, eating what we eat, then it would take four more Earth-sized planets to support us all.

Go to www.earthday.net or www.re definingprogress.org and see how much land *you* are using. What is your ecological footprint? Is it more or less than the average American? Taking the quiz is interesting. When we did it, we learned that our travel choices have a huge impact on our use of the world's resources. We saw that our diet choices also play a major role in determining how much land is needed to support our lifestyles. The test made both of us think about how to reduce our use of resources. Changing what we eat is one of the easiest ways.

Globalization: What a Tangled Web We Weave

Smothering the planet with livestock is one of the problems causing world hunger now and into the future. Another major problem is unequal access to the food we do have.

The next time you're in the grocery store, take a look at some stickers and labels. Where does the food you buy come from? You might be surprised—your lunch has probably traveled farther than you have. In fact, the average distance that food travels from farm to fork is *1,500 miles*.[5] The most popular fruit in the United States today is not Washington apples or Georgia peaches—it's Costa Rican bananas. Tomatoes, meanwhile, often come from Mexico. Beef, from Australia. Sugar, from Brazil. In fact, these days America imports more food than it exports.

But wait! Why do we—the land of plenty, after all—need to import food from anywhere else? Aren't those the very countries with all the starving children who would supposedly be grateful for the leftover food on your plate? Yes, they are. So if they're starving, well, why don't they just eat all this fancy food that they're sending to the United States?

RICE IN ASIA, CORN IN MEXICO

Well, they would if they could. But they can't.

It works like this: not long ago, there used to be more trade barriers between countries. That means that if one country wanted to buy a product from another country—for example, if the United States wanted to buy grapes from Chile to sell in U.S. grocery stores—they would have to pay a big tax. That made it very expensive to import products from other countries. Therefore, because it was so much cheaper, most countries ate the food that they produced themselves. In Asia, they ate lots of rice because that's what grows best there. In Mexico, they ate lots of corn because that's what they could produce easily and cheaply.

AND THEN … GLOBALIZATION

And then in the 1980s, a process called globalization began to have a major worldwide impact. Basically, globalization means uniting the entire globe, breaking down barriers between countries. Sounds like a good idea, right? Well, the basic principle of globalization is free trade, or trade without taxes between countries. Countries with free-trade agreements can import and export each other's products with no extra tariffs or fees. This means that for a person in California, rice imported from China is almost as cheap as rice grown ten miles away.

To the governments of poorer countries, this new system seemed like a great deal. Now, instead of growing cheap crops such as beans, they could grow expensive, exotic products and sell them in the United States for a big profit.

THE SHORT END OF THE STICK

A good example of this is Mexico, a country more integrally linked to the United States than any other. You've probably heard of NAFTA in the news, right? Well, NAFTA stands for the North American Free Trade Agreement. It's an agreement between Canada, the United States, and Mexico that eliminated all taxes and trade barriers between the three countries. When it went into effect on January 1, 1994, groups of Mexicans called the Zapatistas staged a huge protest because they knew they were getting the short end of the stick. And they were right.

Until then, much of the agricultural land in Mexico was devoted to corn, beans, and traditional foods that were produced and sold within Mexico. But after NAFTA, these lands were converted to grow expensive specialty foods such as strawberries, which are shipped to the United States and sold for $4 a pound. That's much more money than beans and rice could ever bring.

This is good for the Mexican economy because the government and the big companies that ship the strawberries are earning more money. But it's bad for the Mexican people. If you go to a grocery store in Mexico that's next door to strawberry fields, there are no strawberries on the shelves. They are too expensive. No one there can afford them at the prices Americans pay.

The beans and rice have grown more expensive too. Because it no longer has space to grow them at home, Mexico has to import these basic staples from other countries. And because the imported products cost more, fewer people can afford to buy them. As a result, 90 percent of rural Mexicans are malnourished. And because Mexico now depends on the United States for basic staples, the country is now less self-sufficient, less stable, and more dependent on the United States.

HEY! TOO MUCH FREE TRADE!

This is a sad story, and, unfortunately, it's happening all over the world. NAFTA was just the beginning. In 2005, a new treaty called the Free Trade Agreement of the Americas turned all of North and South America into one big free-trade zone. This has made Argentinean beef and Nicaraguan pineapples cheaper here in the United States and it will send more profits in U.S. dollars to the big companies and governments of those countries, but the people of Latin America will become poorer and will have less access to the food they need.

So, what all of this means is that food consciousness isn't just about eating meat. Even if the whole world went vegetarian, there would still be hungry people. It not only matters what you eat, but where it comes from. People must have access to food that is grown locally, by their neighbors, for their neighbors. Please turn to chapters four and five for more about eating locally grown food.

IT'S ABOUT MORE THAN JUST FOOD

But globalization is about more than just food. It applies to all kinds of products. Free trade means that many of the goods in American stores, from socks to stereos, are produced

elsewhere. Converse shoes, for example, were made in North Carolina for almost 100 years before their factories moved to China in 1999.

This company, like many others, made this switch because in other countries there are fewer regulations on salaries, workers' rights, and environmental damage. This means that when American industries build factories in developing nations, they can cut corners and save money. They can pay the foreign workers less than twenty cents an hour without benefits or health insurance; they can condone safety and health hazards in the workplace; they can ignore pollutants the factory may produce. All of this allows them to produce a much cheaper product that is then sold on the rich American market.

Factory workers in developing nations are making goods for us that they could never dream of owning. The factory owners are growing rich, while the environment is polluted, the local people struggle to survive, and we save pennies at Wal-Mart.

BUY LOCAL AND MAKE A DIFFERENCE!

This system is ugly, but you are not powerless. You can do your part to resist the unhappy side effects of globalization. Check tags and stickers. Make an effort to buy products that were made in the United States, and buy food that was grown close to home. Find out about farmers' markets or co-ops in your town. Many greengrocers or markets sell local produce, grown by farmers in your county or state. Buying American products boosts the American economy, supports American workers, saves the fuel required to ship food hundreds or thousands of miles, and strongly states that you refuse to participate in this system of exploitation.

Chapter Two

What Does Meat Have to Do with the Environment?

Small Farms versus Factory Farms

Small family farms still exist. We visited several and they are just as charming as the farms in *Babe* and *Charlotte's Web*. Compared to factory farms, they are rare, but they're out there. You can read detailed accounts of our visits to these farms in chapter four.

The small farms we visited raise small numbers of animals that can be carefully managed. We saw cows, pigs, turkeys, chickens, and sheep, all free to roam in spacious pastures. They were not fed hormones, antibiotics, or animal products. Meat from pasture-based farms such as these sometimes costs more than meat from factory farms, but not always. When the meat is more expensive, these farms gain customers by developing relationships within their community. They are supported by people living close by who know how the animals are raised and how the environment is protected and are willing to pay more for their products because of it. For these small farms, community support and interaction are vital to their survival.

We also visited huge factory farms. We visited a pork facility with 40,000 pigs and

two big Tyson chicken farms, one with more than 170,000 birds. We visited an egg factory with more than a million hens. The vast majority of meat sold in the United States is produced by factory farms such as these. Four giant meatpacking companies—Monfort, Excel, National, and IBP—slaughter and market 80 percent of the beef cattle born in this country. Four other corporations control 50 percent of the hogs slaughtered in the United States. And as of 1998, eight chicken-processing companies controlled 62 percent of our poultry production.[1] The biggest of those by far is Tyson, the largest chicken processor in the world.

On factory farms, everything is designed to cut costs and maximize profit. On big hog and chicken farms, the animals are usually owned by a big corporation, such as Tyson or Smithfield. The farmer owns the buildings and the land and has a contract with the corporation to raise the animals through one stage of production. The corporation delivers the animals to the farm, provides feed and medicine for the animals, and comes to get them when their time is up. The corporation in this arrangement is called a "vertical integrator." In the case of Tyson chickens, farms with broiler sheds are arranged in a complex, all within fifty miles of a central Tyson feed mill, hatchery, and processor that slaughters and packages the broilers. Drivers from the Tyson hatchery deliver chicks to all the farms along one route at more or less the same time. The chicks stay in the broiler sheds on the farm for seven weeks. When they are big enough for slaughter, the Tyson crew comes back to get them. A Tyson breeder farm provides fertile eggs for the hatchery.

Hogs owned by a corporation are divvied up according to age. One farm might have only a farrowing operation, keeping the sows during the time they are delivering litters and nursing the piglets. When the piglets are weaned, at about three weeks, a crew employed by the corporation (which, again, might be Tyson) may collect the piglets and take them to another farm for the nursery stage, where they are raised in group pens indoors to an age of ten to eleven weeks and a weight of forty-five to sixty pounds. Then a crew returns, taking all these feeder pigs to another farm for finishing. The finishing operation feeds them to a market weight of 250 to 280 pounds at about twenty-five weeks of age. Then they are trucked off to the slaughterhouse. The big hog farm we visited was a farrow-to-finish operation, covering the whole hog life cycle, but that's unusual these days.

The vertical integrators, such as Tyson or Perdue, sell the meat to mass markets, such as Wal-Mart or grocery store chains. The integrators compete with each other for these markets. The stores too want to sell the meat as cheaply as possible in order to compete with other stores that are also selling meat cheaply. For everyone to sell cheap and still make a profit, the meat must be produced at the lowest possible cost. So factory farms are all about efficiency, cutting corners to save money. That's why pregnant sows on factory

farms are kept in tiny "gestation crates," stalls too small for them to even turn around in or to lie down in comfortably. (To see photos of these stalls, Google "gestation crate.") That's why the cages of laying chickens are stacked on top of one another: to save money on heated space. That's why beef cattle spend half their lives in crowded feedlots, standing in their own manure and eating unnatural diets that make them gain weight faster. That's why dairy cows are injected with growth hormones to make them produce more milk.

A curious dairy cow.

Small farmers are much more likely to provide humane housing for their animals and to farm without pesticides, hormones, and antibiotics. They're not competing for Wal-Mart's business. Instead, they often sell directly to local families that are willing to pay more for meat they know is produced humanely, safely, and with careful consideration of the environment. If all farmers practiced this type of farming, then the environmental and health complaints related to livestock farming would greatly diminish, or perhaps vanish altogether.

So why don't we just do away with factory farms and return to the small, pasture-based farms that used to be standard? Well, because Americans eat *so much* meat. Small farms may not have the capacity to crank out the great volume of meat that Americans consume.

We create a huge and irresistible market for the giant meatpacking corporations that control America's meat industry. In order to develop a more humane system, we, as a nation, will have to consume less meat. As long as we keep demanding meat two or three times a day, there will be corporations competing with one another to provide it.

What can we do? We can reduce our consumption of meat and make an effort to buy our animal products from pasture-based providers. You can find one in your area by checking www.eatwild.com.

AS CONSUMERS, WE ARE IN THE DRIVER'S SEAT

We are bombarded almost daily with distressing news about the environment. Global warming, destruction of the rain forest, water pollution, air pollution, erosion—the list can seem overwhelming. How can we, ordinary people and families, have any effect on all of these problems?

Although our environmental problems may at times seem hopeless, we are actually much more powerful than we think. As consumers, we are in the driver's seat. We control industries with our buying selections—they make products that they know we'll buy. This includes the giant meatpacking corporations. And according to the Union of Concerned Scientists, one of the most important things we can do to solve our multitude of environmental problems is to buy less meat.[2]

Americans buy twice as much meat per person as the rest of the world. By doing so, we are shooting ourselves in the foot. Sure, we can blame factory farms for causing environmental problems. We can ask them to change their methods. We can ask our government representatives to make them stop. But as long

as factory farms turn a profit and are allowed to continue, they will continue. Another approach is to take matters into our own hands more directly by choosing other foods instead. Just by buying less meat, we are protecting the Earth in numerous ways. See what scientists and researchers have had to say:

Nothing will benefit human health and increase chances for survival of life on Earth as much as the evolution to a vegetarian diet.

—*Albert Einstein*

Meat and poultry consumption has a large impact on common water pollution, water use, and most important, land use ... making food second perhaps only to transportation as a source of environmental problems.

—*Union of Concerned Scientists*

A reduction in beef and other meat consumption is the most potent single act you can take to halt the destruction of our environment and preserve our natural resources. Our choices do matter. What's healthiest for each of us personally is also healthiest for the life support system of our precious, but wounded planet.

—*John Robbins, nominee for Pulitzer Prize, President of EarthSave Foundation*

DATA ARE DIFFERENT FOR PASTURE-BASED LIVESTOCK

In chapter six, we talk about some of the health issues related to eating meat. Some of these issues may be different for pasture-based livestock as opposed to animals from feedlots and factory farms. Grass-fed cows tend to be much healthier than cattle fed an artificial diet of corn and protein supplements, which may consist of ground-up chicken litter, chicken feathers, or other animals. Pigs, chickens, and beef cattle in big operations are usually given antibiotics to speed growth and prevent the spread of disease in crowded and dirty pens.

Beef and dairy cattle are given hormones to spur weight gain or milk production.

In chapter three, we talk about how animals are treated in large operations. Other than slaughter, very little of this section applies to animals raised in pastures on small farms. From what we have seen, most aspects of animal care are different on small farms. It's important to remember this distinction when learning about farming practices.

This chapter is about the environmental problems caused by the huge numbers of livestock raised in this country. Most of these problems did not exist when all livestock lived on small farms in modest numbers. Moderation is the key word here. Problems occur when massive numbers of animals are concentrated in a small area or when livestock invade every corner of the outdoors, as sometimes seems to be the case with grazing cattle. A small amount of manure can be useful fertilizer on a pasture or a prairie. Huge quantities of manure become a waste-management problem.

When reading this chapter and chapters three and six, keep this in mind: because the vast majority of livestock in the United States are raised on factory farms, most of the data published on current farming practices and meat consumption consider only factory and feedlot animals.

Raising Livestock Uses Half of Our Water

**MEAT, WATER—
WHAT'S THE CONNECTION?**
In your local newspaper you've probably seen suggestions for saving water: water the lawn after dark, turn off the water while you brush your teeth, put a brick in your toilet tank, limit your shower time, and so on. All of those things are well and good, but they're just a drop in the bucket compared to the amount

of water we use to raise animals for our dinner tables. Almost half the water consumed in the United States is used to grow food for cattle and other livestock.

Take a gander at the amounts of water required to produce one pound of vegetables versus one pound of meat: [3]

- 1 pound of lettuce: 23 gallons
- 1 pound of tomatoes: 23 gallons
- 1 pound of potatoes: 24 gallons
- 1 pound of wheat: 25 gallons
- 1 pound of carrots: 33 gallons
- 1 pound of apples: 49 gallons
- 1 pound of chicken: 815 gallons

Raising crops for livestock uses huge amounts of water.

- 1 pound of pork: 1,630 gallons
- 1 pound of beef: 2,500 to 5,214 gallons

Another source reports even higher estimates: [4]

- 1 pound of potatoes: 60 gallons
- 1 pound of wheat: 108 gallons
- 1 pound of corn: 168 gallons
- 1 pound of beef: 8,449 gallons

To help put this in perspective, consider that a typical American household uses 16,000 gallons of water in their washing machine each year for the whole family's laundry. With the 2,500 gallons of water required to grow one pound of beef, this typical family could do eight weeks' worth of laundry.

Why Is More Water Needed for Cows than for Pigs and Chickens?

Cattle are concentrated in the dry Midwest. Cattle on feedlots are fed corn, and in the Midwest, cornfields need a lot of irrigation.

Remember that 2,500 gallons is just the amount of water required to produce *one pound* of beef. A typical steer at slaughter weighs more than 1,200 pounds. After his head, legs, tail, organs, and skin are removed and his body is sawed into two "sides of beef," he still weighs more than 700 pounds as he's shipped off to the grocery store.[5] How much water is required to produce 700 pounds of beef? You do the math.

The amount of water that goes into a 1,000 pound steer would float a destroyer.

—Newsweek[6]

These cows are thirsty. But growing food for cattle uses much more water than they drink.

WHO'S THE BIGGEST USER?

Who needs more water to supply his or her daily diet, a vegetarian or a meat eater? It takes more water to feed a meat eater for one month than to feed a vegetarian for a whole year.

McDonald's Is Still Cranking out Burgers, So We Must Have Enough Water, Right?

So what's the problem? If we need water to grow cattle, and we apparently have the cattle, then the water must be available. Yes, that would make sense ... except for the part everybody's ignoring.

At the beach, have you ever started digging a hole in the sand only to have the hole fill in with water from underneath? That water is held in the ground in most places, if you dig deep enough. The level of water underground is called the water table. If you dig a well in your front yard and after only six feet you hit water, then the water table is very high. If you dig for 100 feet and it's still dry, then the water table is very low. A body of water underground is called an aquifer. Some places have an aquifer near the surface and another one deeper down.

In regions without much rain, water from underground is often used for crops or livestock. This is not a bad practice, as long as we don't take too much. In the Midwest, there's a huge underground lake called the Ogallala Aquifer. It stretches all the way from South Dakota down to Texas, underneath eight states! This vast aquifer is more than twice the size of all five Great Lakes combined—or at least, it used to be. In the early 1900s, farmers began digging wells and tapping into the aquifer to water their crops and livestock. This was a convenient arrangement for such a dry area. With water from the aquifer, the land became much more productive and towns were able to grow into cities. Still, the amount of water drawn from underground was so small that the aquifer stayed more or less the same.

New Inventions
Led to More and More Cows

Then, in the 1950s, new developments such as chemical fertilizers, advanced water pumps, and antibiotics changed everything. When modern pumps became available, ranchers and farmers and towns were able to pump water out of the Ogallala Aquifer and other underground water sources at a much faster rate. Farmers produced more and more crops and ranchers began feeding the extra corn to their cattle to fatten them up faster for slaughter. Feedlots evolved, where more and more corn-fed cattle were brought together for fattening. Antibiotics helped keep ailments related to the corn diet under control. As the number of cows increased sharply, the demand for corn increased sharply and the amount of water drawn from the Ogallala Aquifer increased sharply. In fact, the land watered by the Ogallala Aquifer now supports 40 percent of the feedlot beef in the United States. And the aquifer is shrinking. By 2020, one-fourth of the aquifer will be gone.[7] In the southern states, where it's shallower, the water is disappearing even faster than that.

The Ogallala Aquifer can refill on its own somewhat, but very slowly. It will take thousands of years to regain the water that has already been removed.

Ah, the Land of Plenty, Bread Basket of the World

You've probably heard the United States called "the bread basket of the world." It's because of the Ogallala Aquifer that the United States is by far the world's largest producer of grain. But America's grain belt produces much more grain for feedlot and factory farm animals than bread for people. More water is pulled from the Ogallala Aquifer for beef cattle than we use to grow all the fruits and vegetables in the whole country.

California's Aquifers Are in Trouble Too

California is another big agricultural state. They too depend on an aquifer that's getting sucked dry. The ground in some parts of California is actually sinking because so much water is used for irrigating pastures for cattle. Growing crops in the desert uses far more water than would be needed in a naturally rainy area. Livestock use more water than Los Angeles, more than California's famous grape vineyards, more than all other California agriculture and industry. The single biggest cause of the West's water crisis is livestock.

Most beef cattle are fed corn, which needs a lot of irrigation.

SO WHEN WE RUN OUT OF WATER, CAN WE JUST GIVE UP THE BURGERS THEN?

When our aquifers run dry, we will be up the proverbial creek without a paddle. Ninety-six percent of rural drinking water comes from aquifers, plus 20 percent of urban drinking water and 43 percent of irrigation water.[8] In some states, more than 90 percent of the population depends on groundwater for drinking.[9] Groundwater also feeds our streams and rivers, so wildlife and natural systems will be profoundly affected as aquifers are depleted. We need to protect our aquifers and stop pouring them into corn-fed beef.

How Mountains of Manure Pollute Our Air and Water

MANURE HAS ITS MERITS

Back in the days when we had modest numbers of livestock spread out over spacious pastures, manure was a good thing in many ways. It fertilized and enriched prairies and pastures and may have even improved the health of native grasses.

Home gardeners can pay a wad for a big plastic sack of manure to put on their gardens. It's full of organic matter that adds nutrients and also improves the texture of soil. Organic matter helps soil to absorb water and hold onto it, with very little runoff. It also keeps soil from becoming too compacted and hard.

But while a little manure can be beneficial, too much of it becomes a waste-management problem, and sometimes a disaster.

Do Diapers Come in Whopper Size?

Most beef cows have a better life than factory pigs or poultry—at least in the beginning. The calf's first half-year is spent outdoors with his mother, nursing and grazing on grass and bales of hay. Whatever manure they produce is spread out over a big area. But at six or seven months of age, the calf is weaned and separated from his mom. If he is extremely lucky, he may live on a small farm and spend the rest of his life at pasture. More likely, though, he is sent by truck to a feedlot, a huge and sprawling operation with dirt roads and pen after crowded pen of young steers. There he learns to eat corn and protein supplements from a trough as he is fattened for slaughter, which takes place at the ripe old age of fourteen months.

One feedlot steer generates fifty to sixty pounds of urine and manure every day. Good thing they don't wear diapers, because that'd be a whole lot of changing! A feedlot may house as many as 100,000 steers at one time, which explains the stink and the open sewers that are

a staple of feedlot life. But wait, where does all that waste *go*? The feedlot operators must come along every evening with a big pooper-scooper, right?

Some feedlot pens have paved or slatted floors, but most are just soil. The cattle in these pens spend a good bit of their time standing in mud mixed with urine and manure. This explains why their fur is matted with manure when they are slaughtered, why they are hung by one foot after slaughter to avoid fouling the assembly line, and why the industry likes to irradiate meat to kill the fecal bacteria in it.

The mucky mud does get scraped up periodically, pushed into mounds in the pens. Then, anywhere from once a month to once a year, the mounds are removed. Removed to where, exactly?

The Blue Lagoon—Uh, Make That Brown

One steer makes fifty to sixty pounds of waste each day, but dairy cows make even more: about 120 pounds a day, because they're older and bigger. So how much does the whole gang make? The problem of manure is huge, literally. According to the Environmental Protection Agency (EPA), livestock in the United States produce about 291 billion pounds of wet manure each year—six times more than the amount of human sewage in this country.[10] But livestock waste doesn't go through sewage treatment plants, even though it is much more toxic than human waste.

Factory farms and feedlots have only two ways to get rid of the waste they generate. They can store it in open-air pits, deep pools of poop that the industry calls "settling basins" or "lagoons." These storage pits may be twenty-five feet deep and as large as several football fields.

The other legal option is to spray the liquid manure into the air over crops or farm fields. Since manure does contain nitrogen and phosphorus, nutrients that plants can use, this is viewed as fertilizing the crops. Spewing waste into the air under high pressure causes a host of environmental problems, though, which we'll get to in a moment.

Imagine a city as big as New York suddenly grafted onto North Carolina's Coastal Plain. Double it.

Now imagine that this city has no sewage treatment plants. All the wastes from 15 million inhabitants are simply flushed into open pits and sprayed onto fields.

Turn those humans into hogs, and you don't have to imagine at all. It's already here.

A vast city of swine has risen practically overnight in the counties east of Interstate 95. It's a megalopolis of 7 million animals that live in metal confinement barns and produce two to four times as much waste, per hog, as the average human.

These were the opening remarks of a Pulitzer Prize–winning series of articles in the Raleigh *News and Observer* entitled "Boss Hog: North Carolina's Pork Revolution."[11] A great many of us in North Carolina were shocked by the series because we really had no idea. The number of hogs in the state quadrupled in the 1990s while no one was paying much attention. All of a sudden, we were swamped with thousands of industrial-sized hog farms cranking out huge amounts of waste in a state with very few laws to control how the waste was disposed of.

What kinds of problems are caused by 10 million tons of hog waste each year? Lagoons leak. Some lagoons are lined with either a thick layer of clay or a synthetic liner, but many or most of those built before 1992 or 1993 are not lined. That would be a problem anywhere, but it's especially troublesome on the coastal plain of North Carolina, where the vast majority of the state's hog farms are located. The sandy soil of the coastal plain is

easily penetrated by water and the underground water table is close to the surface, so the contents of unlined lagoons seep into the water table. In fact, the government allows a certain amount of seepage. From a three-acre hog waste lagoon, 1 million gallons of seepage per year is permitted. Many hog farms have lagoons as big as ten acres.

Untreated hog sewage is stored in huge open pits and sprayed on farm fields.

LAGOONS AND HURRICANES— NOT A GOOD MIX

Open-air lagoons can overflow; they can empty out entirely if a wall breaks down. If you watch The Weather Channel, you'll notice that during late summer and fall, the southeast coast is a frequent target of hurricanes roaring in from across the Atlantic. Hurricanes can bring torrential rain. When rain fills a lagoon to the top, the contents can spill over and travel downhill to streams, rivers, and eventually to coastal estuaries. Floods are common in the low-lying coastal counties, which is where most hog farms are, and floodwaters can flush a lagoon out completely. In the summers of 1996 and 1997 alone, more than thirty North

Carolina hog lagoons spilled their toxic brew into nearby streams and rivers.

One hog farmer we interviewed acknowledged that his lagoons have spilled during storms but said, "We can't help that. We can't do anything about the rain."

When lagoons leak into groundwater and rivers, what is the problem, exactly? One problem is fecal bacteria that are carried downstream to wildlife and to recreational areas. The nitrates and phosphorus in manure are another huge problem. Plants and ecosystems need a certain amount of these nutrients, but too much of them causes serious trouble. High levels of nitrates in drinking water are dangerous to human health, and can even be lethal to babies. Nitrate or phosphate pollution also disrupts aquatic and coastal ecosystems. High concentrations of these nutrients in lakes and rivers can cause algae to grow out of control. As the algae dies, the bacteria feeding on the dead algae use up all the oxygen in the water and the animal life in the water suffocates and dies. This is called eutrophication, and it's bad.

High levels of nutrients are also associated with a very dangerous microscopic organism called *Pfiesteria*. It attacks and kills fish and causes frightening health problems in humans who come into contact with it. See more about *Pfiesteria* on page 21–22.

Another serious problem from lagoon leaks and spills is fecal bacteria that get into rivers and travel downstream to wildlife and recreational areas. Just what kinds of bacteria? Here's a sampling: *Salmonella*, *E. coli*, *Campylobacter*, *Enterococci*, *Streptococcus*, *Cryptosporidius*, and *Giardia*. After the rupture of a hog waste lagoon in North Carolina, bacteria were found in nearby streams in concentrations up to 15,000 times higher than the level considered safe for human contact.[12]

The Official Said …

We called a county official in charge of hog waste management and asked him about the problem of leaking or spilling hog lagoons. He spoke with us on the condition that we not use his name.

He said, "Lagoons never overflow, that's a bunch of baloney. There are thousands of lagoons in North Carolina and I only know of two cases of that happening. One was a brand-new lagoon and it had hardly anything in it."

"Then why is there so much in the media about lagoons spilling?" we asked.

"Well, it's just people unhappy with their neighbors, because of the smell. Or because the hog farmer is making a good living and driving a Cadillac, while the fella down the road is driving a beat-up old Chevy. You know what I'm saying?"

But in Reality …

Although the problem has been getting better very recently, lagoons do still leak and overflow. A former hog farm manager for Carroll's Foods quoted in one of the "Boss Hog" articles in the *News and Observer* said that hardly a week passed that there wasn't some kind of leak or overflow. "There are so many ways to have a spill that it's impossible not to have one. Pipes fill up with leaves. Drains get stopped up." The workers clean it up as best they can, then "it's just pray and keep your mouth shut."[13]

According to a 2001 report from the Environmental Protection Agency, catastrophic spills occur through overflow following large storms or by intentional releases to reduce the volume in overfull lagoons. Other causes include pump failures, malfunctions of manure irrigation guns, breakage of pipes or retaining walls, and washouts from floodwaters when lagoons are on floodplains.[14]

They Followed the Brown Plume

When a North Carolina hog waste lagoon ruptured in June of 1995 following a heavy rain, Dr. JoAnn Burkholder and other aquatic biologists decided to track the flow of 26 million gallons of hog poop. The stinky waste of 12,000 hogs flowed overland for a third of a mile, across the lawns of indignant neighbors who called the news media. Leaving a thick puddle on the lawns, the waste oozed into a stream feeding the New River. Over a period of sixty days, the scientists measured and monitored the brown plume of manure as it moved downriver. Once it reached a coastal estuary, where the New River meets water from the ocean, the plume hovered for more than a week. It coated the marinas of Jacksonville with brown, foul-smelling goop. Tourists and fishermen fled, costing the city millions of dollars in lost income. During its journey, the soup of waste carried huge concentrations of nitrogen and phosphorus that caused algal blooms and killed fish and other aquatic animals. It also carried high densities of fecal bacteria that settled into the estuaries. Plumes of poop may come and go, but this one achieved immortality in several academic research papers.

SPRAYING MANURE OVER CROP FIELDS

Dr. Joe Rudek, a pollution specialist with Environmental Defense, says that there are fewer spills from lagoons in North Carolina as the industry has become more aware of the consequences and that leaks are not as bad as they were twenty years ago. But what about spraying hog waste from lagoons onto farm fields and crops? That is a bigger problem, and one that is not improving.

Three of the factory farmers we interviewed talked about spraying manure over their fields as fertilizer. They are not supposed to spray more nitrogen, or nitrates, than the plants in a particular field can absorb. But as a rule,

farmers spray the highest possible amount. They have to get rid of it. There is nowhere else to put it legally other than in lagoons. To maximize the amount they're allowed to spray, farmers often plant crops that use a lot of nitrogen, such as Bermuda hay.

Is high-pressure spraying of animal wastes a safe practice for humans and for the environment? No.

That Brown Stinky Stuff Will Find a Way Downhill

We asked Dr. Rudek about the environmental consequences of spraying waste. He said that in spite of application based on plant needs, the nitrates in sprayed manure are not all taken up by plants and the nitrates do find their way into groundwater and rivers. Samples of groundwater under a typical North Carolina vegetable farm might have nitrate readings of ten to twenty parts per million, or ppm. Under hog farms, the readings are usually ten to fifty ppm of nitrate, often as high as 100 ppm under sprayed fields. The drinking water standard is ten ppm. Nitrates from sprayed manure are getting into our shallow groundwater that drains into ditches, streams, rivers, and eventually to the nitrogen-sensitive coastal waters. These coastal waters are being overloaded with nitrogen pollution from many sources (hog and chicken production, agriculture in general, sewage treatment plants, runoff from city streets, and heavily fertilized suburban yards), often leading to massive fish kills.[15]

Manure also contains a lot of phosphorus. This nutrient doesn't move through the soil as freely as nitrogen or nitrates do, and phosphorus is not hazardous to human health in the way nitrates are. But like nitrogen, phosphorus pollution of waterways wreaks havoc on ecosystems. It too contributes to algal blooms and eutrophication, which kills fish.

North Carolina is not the only state with a massive burden of hogs. Most states have significant livestock populations of some kind, whether it's hogs, chickens, turkeys, beef cattle, or dairy cows. A lagoon can be used for the waste of any of these animals, and any lagoon can leak or spill. According to the U.S. Environmental Protection Agency, agriculture is by far the biggest source of pollution to our streams and rivers, and a significant portion of that is runoff from hogs, poultry, and cattle waste.[16]

These breeder chickens generate tons of waste.

LAGOON LEAKS, RUNOFF FROM SPRAYING—IS THAT ALL?

There's More—Evaporation

In a waste lagoon, the solids settle to the bottom and the liquids rise to the top. As any pool of liquid will, the lagoon liquids evaporate into the air. In addition, there is evaporation from the spraying. Any time a liquid is sprayed into the air, especially under high pressure, a lot of it is going to remain in the air as tiny droplets, or vapor.

The viruses and bacteria in sprayed animal feces can travel in air. The ammonia in the waste also takes to the air. Ammonia is very volatile, meaning that it evaporates easily. Then the ammonia falls to the earth as rain.

When it falls on soil, it washes downhill into streams and rivers and groundwater. Ammonia is mostly nitrogen. When it falls on water or winds up in water, it contributes to the same nutrient overload that leads to algal blooms, eutrophication, fish kills, and dangerous drinking water.

Ammonia enters the air from the animal sheds as well. If you read the accounts of our visits to factory farms in the next chapter, you know that the piled-up waste in animal sheds reeks of ammonia.

Have you ever sniffed ammonia from a bottle? Don't. It will knock you backward—it's powerful stuff. Neighbors of animal factories complain of headaches, nausea, and other ailments from the air pollution. The stench often keeps them indoors, and many have trouble selling their homes. Who wants to live with a constant stink, unable to ever open their windows?

As one farmer with tens of thousands of chickens told us, "People move in next to us thinking the country is all wildflowers and honeysuckle. Then they complain about the smell. We've been here thirty years. What did they expect?"

Dr. Rudek of Environmental Defense told us that ammonia also forms fine particulate matter in the air. This particulate matter is a suspected cause of respiratory ailments of neighbors near factory farms. He says there are no laws at present to deal with the evaporation of ammonia.

Yet another pollutant from factory farms is methane, a gas in cow farts. Sounds minor, but it's not. Methane is one of the major greenhouse gases that are causing global warming. You can read more about methane on page 35.

Poultry Waste

Chickens and turkeys on factory farms generate tons of waste too. The litter in broiler sheds is turned over periodically to let ammonia escape, but it's removed from the sheds only once every twelve to eighteen months.

Poultry litter is already mixed with sawdust when it is removed from the poultry sheds. It's often stored in lagoons too, to decompose a bit before being sprayed onto fields. When it's sprayed, again there is a problem with runoff of excess nitrogen and phosphorus and evaporation of ammonia. There's also an odor issue. Poultry sheds stink just as much as pig sheds. The stink is magnified on days when the poultry sheds are scraped out and when the litter is sprayed on fields.

Broiler chickens in a crowded shed on a factory farm.

One chicken farmer we interviewed said, "When you're spraying litter, naturally it's going to smell for a few days."

There is one more use for chicken litter. According to a professor in the animal science department at a local state university, chicken litter and chicken feathers are fed to cattle for protein. It's not legal to give these materials to cows producing milk, but it is legal to feed it to cows that are growing.

Hormones Given to Livestock Wind up in Manure and Then in Our Water

Cattle on feedlots are routinely given a slow-release hormone implant behind the ear. Revlar, a synthetic estrogen, is a common choice. It increases the growth of steers by forty or fifty pounds. Laws permit measurable residues of these hormones in beef we eat, although the hormones may be to blame for premature adolescence in some human girls. The estrogens are in the cattle's manure as well, and, like the other components of manure, they wind up in streams and rivers. There have been reports of fish abnormalities in affected waters.

Dairy cows are often given a growth hormone that's called either bovine somatotropin (BST) or bovine growth hormone (BGH); they are the same thing. It's given by injection every two to three weeks to increase milk production after production has begun to wane. Again, laws allow BGH in the milk we drink.

As far as we know, pigs are not given hormones.

Everyone we asked, from poultry farmers to government officials to animal science professors, said that no hormones are approved for routine use in poultry. But a 2001 Environmental Protection Agency document reports that "poultry manure has been shown to contain about thirty ng/g of estrogen and about the same levels of testosterone. Also, estrogen was found in concentrations of up to twenty ng/L in runoff from fields fertilized with chicken manure."[17] (Ng means nanogram; g means gram; L means liter.) Well, then. Either someone is mistaken, or there's something fishy goin' down. Is it possible these are naturally occurring hormones in chickens? We're not sure.

It's the Same with Antibiotics

Most pigs and poultry on factory farms and beef cattle in feedlots are given constant doses of antibiotics in their food and sometimes in their drinking water too. The EPA reports that 60 to 80 percent of livestock receive routine antibiotics.[18] One pork producer in Nebraska reports using sixteen different antibiotics in his pigs' feed and drinking water. According to the Union of Concerned Scientists, farmers in one year routinely feed 25 million pounds of antibiotics to pigs, poultry, and cattle in the United States—but not because they're sick. No, these tons of antibiotics are fed to *healthy* animals. Why? Either to promote weight gain or as a precaution against potential ailments. This is 70 percent of all antibiotics used in the United States, far more than the 3 million pounds of antibiotics prescribed for people![19]

What about sick pigs, cows, and poultry? They get an additional 10 percent of our country's antibiotics.[20] Not that anyone begrudges medicine for a sick animal. But if we didn't have all these warehoused animals, then we wouldn't have so many sick ones.

Not surprisingly, antibiotics do turn up in the manure of livestock, and, as you might guess by now, these residues find their way into our streams and rivers.

BACTERIA RESISTANT TO ANTIBIOTICS—LIVESTOCK ARE A BIG PIECE OF THE PROBLEM

Scientists are concerned about the development of bacterial populations that are resistant to overused antibiotics. When a population of bacteria is constantly exposed to an antibiotic over a long period of time, especially at a low dose, the bacteria that are vulnerable to the antibiotic die out and disappear, leaving behind only the bacteria that are immune or resistant to the antibiotic. Then the antibiotic no longer has any effect on that bacterial population or their descendants. If a doctor then prescribes that antibiotic for a person with an infection, the medicine may have no effect. That's scary. Back before we had antibiotics, people often died from bacterial infections that would seem minor today.

We called a professor in the department of animal science at a nearby state university to ask him about this. Animal science is a discipline that prepares students to study or work with agricultural animals and the meat, egg, and milk industries.

"Do pigs routinely get preventive antibiotics?" we asked him.

"A few antibiotics are approved for use in pigs on a preventive basis. But they are not the same antibiotics that are approved for people. The FDA [Food and Drug Administration] saves the best ones for people," said the professor. That was January 5, 2005.

On the other hand, Dr. Margaret Mellon of the Union of Concerned Scientists said on NBC-TV, "The antibiotics given to animals are exactly the same antibiotics that are given to patients in doctors' offices. They are the penicillin, the tetracycline, erythromycin, the sulfa drugs that we're all familiar with and depend on. So the problem is, if the antibiotics are used on the farm, they lose their efficacy when those same antibiotics are given to patients in doctors' offices. In other words, the antibiotics won't work."[21] That was January 4, 2005.

Not only do pigs and other animals receive the same antibiotics that we take, but numerous studies have found tetracycline and other antibiotics in surface water and groundwater around hog lagoons. What is more frightening, an increasing number of recent studies are finding bacteria that are resistant to human antibiotics in waters near hog lagoons and in the air inside hog-confinement buildings![22] Yikes!

Do we really need to be giving healthy animals all these preventive antibiotics that are creating resistant populations of bacteria and turning up in our water? No. Both Sweden and Denmark have banned this practice with no ill effects to their meat industry.

For an impressive collection of current research-based articles on the subject of antibiotics and resistant bacteria, go to the Web site Keep Antibiotics Working, www.keepantibioticsworking.com.

The factory farms themselves produce huge amounts of air and water pollution on their own, the way they store large amounts of waste. It's stored in these open-air lagoons, and when it rains, they sometimes overflow into the river. They contain nitrogen, phosphorus, bacteria, and it's bad news for the rivers. Have you ever read *And the Rivers Turned to Blood*? It's about *Pfiesteria*, a dinoflagellate that feeds mostly off of phosphorus pollution and causes fish kills and degenerative nervous diseases in people. It wouldn't be such a problem if the hogs weren't contained in such large numbers in such small areas. That's the main problem, the size. My dad, who's been an environmental activist for a long time, always says that bigness is a big problem.

WHAT CAN BE DONE?

One thing you can do is reduce your meat consumption. In addition to that, you can write to your governor, state representatives, representatives in Washington, and the agricultural commissioner of your state. You can suggest these recommendations from the Natural Resources Defense Council and the Clean Water Network for reducing air and water pollution from livestock waste:[24]

- Ensure that local citizens are able to participate fully in the decision as to whether a factory farm is allowed to locate in their community.

Give citizens the opportunity to help decide what pollution controls are needed on factory farms to protect their communities.
- Ban massive open-air manure lagoons at animal factories and the spraying of manure and urine into the air. Encourage environmentally friendly farming practices that do not rely on these technologies.
- Prevent manure from running off the land.
- Establish a moratorium on Clean Water Act permits for new and expanding factory farms until all existing facilities have effective permits in place and standards are upgraded.
- The nation's water must be protected from poultry manure. Regulate chicken factories under the Clean Water Act in the same fashion as other animal operations.
- Hold corporations that own livestock animals responsible for paying the costs of waste disposal and cleanup.

Water Pollution from Growing Crops for Livestock

GOOD-BYE MANURE

Raising livestock hasn't always caused pollution. Before 1950, farmers usually raised a variety of things: crops as well as a modest number of animals. They could use the manure from their animals to fertilize their fields and improve the texture of the soil. Soil with lots of organic matter lets water soak in rather than run off.

But as you now know, small farms are no longer the norm. Nowadays, factory farmers with thousands of animals either have nowhere to put their waste or they dispose of it in environmentally damaging ways. Because livestock and crops are often raised separately, waste is, well, being wasted. Cattle feedlots may sell manure to nearby residents, but moving manure long distances to crop-growing areas is too expensive.

PFIESTERIA: AN ANCIENT AND DEADLY "CELL FROM HELL" REAWAKENED BY FARM POLLUTION

And the Waters Turned to Blood by Rodney Barker is a book about a bizarre microorganism that kills fish and can cause persistent, serious health problems in people. *Pfiesteria* is a one-celled creature first discovered in 1988 in fish cultures at North Carolina State University's School of Veterinary Medicine. It was killing the captive fish at the veterinary school. A professor of aquatic botany at the university, Dr. JoAnn Burkholder, and her colleagues were called to help identify the strange organism that was attacking the fishes' skin, causing open sores, hemorrhages, and death. The scientists figured out that the microscopic organism was an undiscovered species of dinoflagellate, but it was so different from any known dinoflagellates that they had to create a new species, genus, and family classification for it—a rare event in science. They named it *Pfiesteria piscicida*—*Pfiesteria* after Dr. Lois Pfiester, who contributed much of what we know about other dinoflagellates, and *piscicida* because the word means "fish killer."

Before long, the investigations of Dr. Burkholder and her fellow scientists linked *Pfiesteria* to massive fish kills in the coastal waters of North Carolina and then Maryland. They found that the microbe has many distinct life stages, most of which are harmless. Much of the time it lies dormant on the ocean floor. Large numbers of fish nearby can trigger a dormant phase to transform into a more toxic swimming phase with two tail-like flagella. These tiny cells swim toward the fish and give off toxins that make the fish dopey and unresponsive and cause bleeding sores. Once the fish are unable to swim, *Pfiesteria* feasts on the blood and tissue leaking from the wounds. After the fish die, depending on the environmental conditions, the microbe may change to an amoebalike crawling stage that can eat the fish down to the bone.

But *Pfiesteria* attacks more than fish. After researchers began studying it in the lab, thirteen lab workers had strange symptoms that were eventually traced to *Pfiesteria*. Those symptoms include a couple of the same symptoms fish have after contact: lethargy and open sores. Other symptoms were even more troubling, such as bad headaches, blurred vision, vomiting, asthmalike trouble with breathing, kidney and liver problems, memory loss, and mental impairment, as in difficulty reading or dialing a phone number. Not only researchers, but also people wading or swimming in waters with *Pfiesteria* have been affected with these symptoms, which are similar to those of Alzheimer's, multiple sclerosis, and AIDS. The microbe has been called "the cell from hell."

But some of the sickened researchers had not touched any water containing *Pfiesteria*. How were they affected? We know now that the toxins produced by this cell can aerosolize, or travel through the air.

Burkholder believes that *Pfiesteria* has always lived in the coastal waters of North Carolina, but that something in the past two decades has changed to encourage its growth. At first she didn't know what that something might be. Then she read the "Boss Hog" articles in 1995 (see page 14). One article made such an impression on her that she memorized the first few lines. The words made her think about all the examples she had heard and read from around the globe about pollution causing the emergence of organisms previously unknown and harmless. Was this another example? Was pollution of the coastal waters causing a shift in the ecology of this frightening organism—pollution from the hog industry in particular?

Dr. Burkholder and her colleagues in aquatic ecology published paper after paper documenting the increase in nutrients in coastal waters and in waters around hog farms. They documented that increases in nutrients, from sources ranging from hog waste to cropland fertilizer to human sewage, can foster the growth of *Pfiesteria*. But her discoveries were largely ignored. For years, government officials refused to even acknowledge that *Pfiesteria* existed. Her credentials were attacked by those in charge of protecting coastal waters, which raises questions about the powerful agricultural industry and its ability to sway state officials in its favor. If nutrient pollution was demonstrated to be associated with *Pfiesteria*, then runoff from livestock waste, chemical fertilizers, and human sewage would have to be controlled and more regulated. This might prove to be expensive for farmers, meat producers, and towns and cities, so most commercial interests were not enthusiastic about Dr. Burkholder's research. But she persisted.

Finally, in 1997, the North Carolina legislature imposed a two-year halt to construction of new factory hog farms and passed new regulations on waste disposal. Lagoons are now inspected twice a year for leaks, soil is tested for nutrients, and spraying of waste onto fields is limited by the amount of nitrogen the crops or grasses can absorb. Treatment of human sewage was also upgraded. In addition, indoor research with *Pfiesteria* and fish must now be done in specialized limited-access laboratories called biohazard level III containment systems. The government has formally recognized *Pfiesteria* for the dangerous microbe it is.

Were these actions enough? Scientists who study aquatic ecology say they weren't. Streams, lakes, rivers, and coastal waters continue to be polluted by the excess nutrients that foster *Pfiesteria*'s growth. Most of those nutrients are from agriculture, a combination of runoff from sprayed manure, lagoon leaks, chemical fertilizers, and the settling of ammonia clouds from livestock waste. We still have no laws whatsoever to address the ammonia problem.

What does the future hold for *Pfiesteria*? Who knows. Although several hurricanes that struck the North Carolina coast in the mid- to late 1990s caused severe flooding and economic hardship for people who live in the area, fortunately they also had the beneficial effect of scouring the estuaries and washing out most *Pfiesteria* populations. The floodwaters carried the dormant cysts into salty waters, where *Pfiesteria* can't grow well. As a result, Dr. Burkholder predicts that toxic outbreaks of this organism won't occur again for a decade or more, which is indeed good news.[23]

So if farmers no longer use manure to fertilize their fields, what do they use?

These days, most farmers use chemical fertilizers to grow crops. These chemicals add nutrients to the soil but do nothing to improve the texture. Chemical fertilizers actually degrade the texture of soil by feeding and increasing soil bacteria that then consume the organic matter, or humus, in the soil. This leaves the soil compacted and lifeless so that water runs off and the soil erodes.

Most water pollution from chemical fertilizers is due to growing crops for feeding livestock.

Another downside of chemical fertilizers is that, carried by rainwater and eroding soil, they find their way into our drinking water. This happens especially on sloped land near lakes and streams.

The most common nutrients in chemical fertilizers are nitrates and phosphates. As you read in the previous section about manure, high levels of nitrates in our lakes, rivers, and groundwater are toxic to humans, especially babies. In many states that produce a lot of livestock, such as Iowa, Nebraska, and Kansas, one in five wells are contaminated with nitrates.

In addition, phosphates and nitrates from chemical fertilizers cause the same problems in lakes that we see due to runoff from manure. Again, phosphates and nitrates cause algae to reproduce too much. As the dense algal blooms die and decompose, the resulting bacteria use up most of the oxygen in the water. Fish and other aquatic creatures can't breathe and then die. Their dead bodies, along with the dying algae, coat the lake with fermenting muck.

So Farmers Use Chemical Fertilizers. What Does That Have to Do with Livestock?
Livestock are by far the biggest consumers of our crops in the United States. More than 80 percent of U.S. corn is eaten by livestock. If we didn't have the livestock, we wouldn't be using fertilizers to grow so much food.

If we used chemical fertilizers to grow crops only for ourselves and not for livestock, then the water pollution from chemical fertilizers would drop by at least 60 percent.

WHAT CAN I DO TO FIX THIS MESS?
Eat less meat. Americans eat more meat than we need to and more than our share, if viewed in terms of world resources. If we reduce our demand for meat, then fewer cattle, pigs, and chickens will be raised and less fertilizer will be used to grow their food. Reducing the demand for meat is the easiest and broadest solution to all these problems.

We in the United States comprise 6 percent of the world's population. But we eat 23 percent of the world's beef. Think about it.

Land Use and Habitat Destruction in the United States

AH, THOSE PEACEFUL, PASTORAL HILLS …

I remember as a teenager riding through the mountains of Virginia and North Carolina near my home, oohing and aahing over pastoral scenes of cows on grassy hillsides. They seemed so peaceful, so poetic. Back in those days, I preferred the grassy hills of Allegheny County to the dense forests in other parts of the Blue Ridge Mountains. It took me many years to realize that those "lovely" grassy hillsides were at one time forests teeming with wildlife until someone cut down all the trees, until cows displaced the wildlife. Now the grassy hillsides don't seem so lovely. The cows are no more appealing to me now than a gas station or a Wal-Mart. But more and more of our forests are giving way to cow pastures.

It's not just near my home, but everywhere I travel—in the United States, in Latin America, in Europe—I see cows on hillsides that used to be forests, cows in muddy streams that used to be clear streams, cows in places I thought were protected for wildlife. Cows have become so much a part of our landscape, it's easy to think of cows as a natural part of our outdoor scenery.

—Sally

COWS ARE NOT PART OF A NATURAL ECOSYSTEM

Cows are animals, so they're part of nature, right? They belong in natural places. *Don't they?*

Cows are animals, yes, but they are not natural animals—they have been bred selectively by humans, just as dogs and house cats have. Cows descended from a wild cowlike animal, just as dogs are all descendants of wolves.

But the modern cow is as different from its wild ancestor as a terrier is from a wolf.

Let's think about food chains and food webs for a minute. A food chain shows the relationships between living things in a certain habitat, such as a pond, desert, or forest. For example, a butterfly feeds on flower nectar, a praying mantis munches the butterfly, a mockingbird swallows the praying mantis, and a hawk

Cows are common in natural places, but they don't fit into natural ecosystems.

eats the mockingbird. Animals and plants that interact with each other in a balanced way in a healthy and natural ecosystem are usually animals and plants that evolved together. Their interactions developed over millions of years of fine-tuning. They work together like a well-oiled machine, like a clock with dozens of tiny gears that fit together perfectly.

Living Out of Whack

Cows, pigs, and all other domestic animals do not live in harmony with any natural environment on their own. They survive only because humans support them, feed them, and protect them from predators and disease. If cows were set free, released from human care anywhere in this country, most would be sick or dead in short order.

Living things that can't live in harmony with their environment are usually weeded out by natural selection. Animals that destroy their environment or their food source will die out sooner or later—although they may destroy everything around them first. In the mountains of North Carolina and in some other places, there are populations of wild pigs that have descended from domestic pigs. They are surviving, but they are wreaking havoc on their environment.

Okay, So Cows Are Not Natural. But What's the Harm?

Sixty years ago, when each farm had no more than a few hundred cows, there really was no problem. Trees were cleared for pastures, barns were built, cows were grazed—all in moderation. That is the key word: moderation. The cows could move from pasture to pasture so that no one place was grazed too much, no ground was trodden too much.

When cows graze in a pasture, they crop the top off of each plant, leaving a few inches still growing. But when there are too many cows in a pasture, they go over the same grass again before it grows back, this time cropping it down to the ground or even yanking the roots out. When the grass dies, there are no roots to hold the topsoil in place.

Hey, Watch Yer Big Feet!

Overgrazing due to too many cows isn't the only problem. A grown cow is extremely heavy—about 1,200 pounds. Their big, broad hooves trample the soil, packing it down tightly, like the hard, bare ground between the bases on a baseball diamond. Too many feet continuously on top of it keep plants from growing. Land that has too many cows is too compacted for plants to grow.

The impact of countless hooves and mouths over the years has done more to alter the type of vegetation and land forms of the West than all the water projects, strip mines, power plants, freeways, and subdivision developments combined.

—*Philip Fradkin in* Audubon *magazine*

SOMEBODY STOP THAT TOPSOIL!

When rain falls on compacted soil, it tends to run off rather than soak in. As the rain runs over the top of the land, it carries away the topsoil bit by bit. The streams of water cause gullies to form. The topsoil clouds up streams, rivers, and lakes as tiny particles of dirt called sediment. Sediment suspended in water is a major pollutant—the biggest single contaminant of drinking water.

The Great Plains or The Great Desert?

Over the years, in areas that are overgrazed and trampled too much, the topsoil disappears completely. Plants need topsoil to grow because it holds water, supplies nutrients, and provides an anchor for their roots. Underneath the topsoil is hard mineral soil, with little or no organic matter. When this is all that's left, few kinds of plants can survive and, essentially, you've got a desert. That's why this problem is called desertification.

For every pound of beef sold in a grocery store, thirty-five pounds of topsoil are eroded by overgrazing and trampling.[25] According to the National Resources Conservation Service, one-third of our original prime topsoil has already been washed or blown into streams, lakes, and oceans, mostly as a result of overgrazing, overcultivation, and deforestation.[26] New topsoil does form naturally, but not nearly fast enough. It takes up to 100 years to form just one inch of topsoil—under normal conditions. Topsoil is formed when dead plants and animals decay, as on a forest

floor. Pastures and fields don't have lots of those ingredients, so it's important to conserve the topsoil that's already there, because that's all there's gonna be.

As the U.S. population increases, desertification will become more of a problem here. In many smaller and poorer nations, such as Kenya, desertification from overgrazing and from the plowing of marginal, easily erodable land is already a major crisis, contributing to hunger and poverty. The world continues to lose about 7 percent of its topsoil from actual or potential cropland each decade.[27]

COWS ARE GRAZING ON "PROTECTED" LAND!

About 40 percent of all land area in the United States is used for grazing livestock that we will eat. In the western states, make that 70 percent. It's logical to think that the grazing land must belong to ranchers, since the cows belong to ranchers. But that is often not the case. More than 23,000 ranchers in the United States hold federal permits to graze their livestock on public lands. Those lands include many of our national wildlife refuges whose purpose is to provide habitat and breeding areas for wildlife. Grazing lands also include many of our national forests and even some of our national wilderness areas. On many of our family's camping and hiking vacations in the national forests adjoining Yellowstone National Park, Grand Teton National Park, and in Arizona, New Mexico, and Colorado, we have discovered that we were sharing our recreational space with cows. Personally, we would prefer fewer cows and more cow-free wild places.

Cows Enjoy Streams, and That Ain't Good

Cattle need lots of water. But most cattle ranches are in the Midwest and western states, where water is not plentiful. Whenever a cow pasture has a stream running through it, you can be sure the cows make good use of the stream. If I had those huge feet and weighed more than 1,200 pounds, I guess I'd like to cool my heels in the water too.

A stream is much more than just a flow of water across the ground; it's an ecosystem. Certain plants, such as cattails, reeds, and willows, grow only near or in water. They form a lush strip of vegetation along stream banks. Many species of insects, frogs, and salamanders live and breed in streams. They depend on the particular plants that grow in and around the water. Turtles, snakes, birds, and other animals depend on the stream environment too for food, shade, shelter, and water. In the West, most wildlife depend on streams for drinking water. A stream is a finely tuned system of interdependent plants and animals, as long as nothing disturbs it.

Grazing cattle wreak havoc on streams and native plants.

Now imagine dozens of half-ton hoofed animals strolling along a delicate stream bank every day, each one dropping fifty pounds of urine and cow pies. Cows will churn the streambed and the stream bank into a muddy, mucky mess. The willows, reeds, and sedges diminish, as do the birds, animals, and insects. Not much but algae and bacteria can grow in churned and fouled mud.

Sadly, 80 percent of our stream ecosystems in the United States have been damaged by grazing livestock.[28]

WHAT CAN BE DONE?

It's distressing, but there are solutions. One solution is to fence off streams to keep livestock away from them. Some of the farmers we talked to have plans to do this with help from a cost-sharing government program. Another solution is to develop other water sources for livestock to use.

You can probably guess the other solution we're going to suggest, the ultimate solution: that's right, reduce our demand for beef. Less beef means fewer cows. Fewer cows mean healthier streams, less trampling, less sediment in our drinking water, more forests left intact.

Cows in moderation are okay. But the number of cows in the United States is causing environmental devastation.

WOLVES HELP STREAMS RECOVER IN YELLOWSTONE

I have always been fascinated with wolves and was thrilled when gray wolves were reintroduced to Yellowstone National Park. They were brought in from Canada in the 1990s to replace those that had been shot and removed in earlier decades. I've spent a couple of summer vacations camping with my family at Yellowstone, enjoying the wildlife, the beautiful landscape, and the hiking opportunities. But my true reason for going has been the wolves.

The Yellowstone wolves have done quite well since their reintroduction. Several packs now roam the hills and valleys of the park.

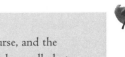

Wolves are predators, of course, and the Yellowstone wolves feed mainly on elk, but also on young bison, pronghorn antelope, deer, and the occasional smaller animal. Elk are abundant in Yellowstone. We have sometimes seen large herds in the valleys of the park.

Before the wolves returned to Yellowstone, the elk had only one predator there: grizzlies sometimes catch and eat elk calves. But only a pack of wolves is powerful enough to bring down an adult elk. During the decades when wolves were absent from the park, the elk became so numerous that they altered the ecology of the streams in the park. Their trampling of the streambeds was not enough to kill all the stream vegetation, but it was enough to change the type of plants growing there. More-sensitive plants disappeared, replaced by hardier types. I'm not sure researchers realized this had happened until the wolves returned in the 1990s. But careful monitoring of streams has found that since the wolves' return, the stream vegetation has shifted back to its more natural state: plants that existed a hundred years ago are growing again.

This has happened because the wolves have reduced the number of elk and thus have reduced the amount of trampling. As the streams have recovered, many animal populations have reappeared or have increased in number too. Reducing the amount of trampling in the park has had many beneficial effects that no one predicted.

—Sally

Land Use and Habitat Destruction in the Tropics

You've just read about how forests are cut to make pastures and how cows trample stream habitats and wildlands in the United States. It's a sad and frustrating topic, the squandering of our most valuable national treasures.

But one encouraging aspect of habitat loss in the United States is that temperate forests can grow back from pastures when given the chance. We are losing topsoil in this country, but not yet on the massive scale that's occurring in many tropical countries around the globe.

What if beef consumption dropped in the United States in the next few decades and some of our cattle pastures were allowed to

A tropical rain forest in Costa Rica, bathed in moisture.

regrow into prairies, or forests, or wetlands? That could happen. Would wildlife recover? Would species that have been edged out by people and domestic animals come back? Some of them would, others would be lost forever. But there is room for optimism that many of our damaged habitats in the United States could be restored, at least in part. We have hope for that.

In the Tropics, it's a different story. The loss of tropical habitats is more frightening and more disturbing—they are far less likely to recover.

WHAT'S ALL THE HYPE ABOUT TROPICAL RAIN FORESTS? WHY ARE THEY SO SPECIAL?

One of my main goals in life is to visit tropical rain forests in Africa, Asia, and South America—one of these days when my finances allow it. But so far, I have had the good fortune to visit the closer rain forests of Costa Rica a few times. I knew before I went that Costa Rica would be a peak experience, but I had no idea just how powerfully it would affect my life. On more than one occasion there, I have been so moved, so thrilled by wildlife encounters that I was left trembling. As I write this, I am surrounded by my photos of monkeys, sloths, huge iguanas, boa constrictors, colorful poison dart frogs, red-eyed tree frogs, parrots, and giant butterflies. There is no ecosystem on the planet that offers greater diversity or a happier experience to wildlife fans like myself. But who knows how long the forests will be there? I'm afraid when my kids are my age, almost all the tropical rain forests will be gone. Unless we stop destroying them right now.

WHAT IS A TROPICAL RAIN FOREST, EXACTLY?

Tropical rain forests are defined by their location, which is in the Tropics, near the equator, and by the amount of rain they get, twelve to twenty-four feet of rain per year. They have no cold seasons: under the tropical sun, they are warm and wet year-round. Because of the constant heat and moisture, they are incredibly productive. Tropical rain forests hold *more than half of the animal and plant species on Earth*, even though they cover only 6 percent of the Earth's landmass.

These forests are the Earth's oldest living ecosystems. Fossil records show that the rain forests of Southeast Asia have existed in more or less their present form for 70 to 100 million years!

A violet sabrewing, one of dozens of species of colorful tropical hummingbirds.

It's So Wet, the Trees Grow Fins

Because of the constant heat and moisture, the forest floor in tropical countries is rich with insects, bacteria, and other decomposers. Dead plant and animal matter decomposes quickly and is sucked back up into the living forest layers. Since soil is made of this dead matter, there isn't much soil in the Tropics. The top layer of rich organic soil is very shallow, so the roots of rain forest trees don't grow deep enough to anchor the trees. To steady themselves, these trees have aboveground fins that make them look like rocket ships. These fins, called buttresses, keep the huge trees from falling over.

Tropical trees grow buttresses like spaceship fins to steady themselves in shallow soil.

The tree cover is so thick in the Tropics that the daily heavy rains never actually strike the forest floor. Instead, rainwater runs down the tree trunks and drops are broken up by the leaves into a mist that slowly settles over the forest. Everything gets soaked, but little washes away.

Okay, the Wildlife Is Great and the Trees Are Like Rockets, but What Else?

For us, the number-one reason to value rain forests is the wildlife that live there and nowhere else—as mentioned above, more than half of the planet's animal and plant species. But the rain forests are important for other reasons too.

What Does Meat Have to Do with the Environment?

Cancer Drugs and Other Medicines Are Found in Rain Forests

Maybe someone you love has struggled with cancer. Did you know that 70 percent of the plants identified by the National Cancer Institute as useful in cancer treatment are found only in rain forests? Drugs used to treat leukemia, Hodgkin's disease, and other cancers come from rain forest plants, as do medicines for heart ailments, high blood pressure, arthritis, and birth control. Yet less than 1 percent of tropical forest plant species have been completely studied for their chemical compounds, so you can imagine what else might be found there.

Our Food Comes from Rain Forests

Rain forests provide popular foods too. About 90 percent of today's food crops were domesticated from wild tropical plants. Agricultural scientists say that modern crops need continual crossbreeding with their wild ancestors to help keep them resistant to new diseases and new insect pests and to keep them healthy and productive. For crops that were originally tropical, these wild strains for crossbreeding must come from the Tropics—usually from rain forests.

What are some of these tropical plants we eat? Avocados, bananas, black pepper, Brazil nuts, cayenne pepper, cassava, cashews, chocolate, cinnamon, cloves, coconuts, coffee, cola, corn, eggplants, figs, ginger, guavas, herb tea ingredients, jalapeños, lemons, oranges, papayas, paprika, peanuts, peppers, pineapples, rice, squash, sugar, tomatoes, turmeric, vanilla, and yams are just a sampling.[29] Many additional rain forest plants have great promise to become familiar foods in the future.

Yikes! Put Down That Chain Saw!

As you probably know, rain forests are in danger. In fact, they are being destroyed at a staggering rate. According to the National Academy of Science, at least 50 million acres a year are lost, an area the size of England,

Wales, and Scotland combined![30]

All of the primary rain forests in India, Bangladesh, Sri Lanka, and Haiti have been destroyed already. ("Primary" means the original unaltered forest, as opposed to "secondary" forest, which has been previously logged and has regrown to some degree.) The Ivory Coast rain forests have been almost completely logged. Many other countries have lost the majority of their forests to logging.

Why? Why are forests that are so precious and irreplaceable being destroyed at such a mind-boggling rate?

A green-and-black poison dart frog, one of many colorful tropical frog species.

WHAT'S THE PROBLEM? AND WHAT DO RAIN FORESTS HAVE TO DO WITH MEAT?

Cattle are a major piece of the picture, especially in Latin America. Norman Myers, one of the world's premier rain forest researchers, says that we are losing our Latin American rain forests to "hamburgerization."[31] In other words, tropical forests are being cut to create pastureland for cows who will become fast-food hamburgers, many of them eaten in the United States.

Don't we value the wildlife, the medicines, and the tourist potential in rain forests? Why are we cutting forests to raise cattle?

Too Many People
Living on $2 a Day, or Less

Poverty and population growth play a big part in the destruction of rain forests. Half of the 6 billion people on Earth are trying to live on less than $2 per day. The most extreme poverty and the countries with the highest population growth are in the Tropics. In some of these countries, the human population has doubled in the last twenty-five years! More and more desperately poor people are vying for limited amounts of land. Owning a piece of land is a way to make a living. A family with a little land can sell timber until it is all gone. Then they can grow food to feed themselves and perhaps sell a few crops. Temporarily, anyway.

Because tropical soil is so thin, it quickly loses its nutrients after the trees are gone and the heavy rains bombard it. When the thin soil is exhausted, the plot is abandoned or sold to ranchers for raising cattle. Then the family needs to clear a new plot of land for farming. The nutrient-poor soil on an abandoned farm can still grow enough grass for livestock, for a while. But eventually, the soil washes away completely, leaving an eroded wasteland. Then the ranchers must move on to another new plot. Sometimes, rather than using abandoned farms, ranchers cut and burn rain forests to provide pastures for cattle.

The continual need to abandon cleared and wasted land and clear more is a major cause of the rapid deforestation occurring in the Tropics. Two-thirds of Central American rain forests have already been cleared, and most of this land is used to raise cattle for the U.S. food industry.

What Happens to Rain Forest Beef?

Most rain forest beef from Latin America is exported to the United States, even though it is not considered top quality by American standards. Because it's not the fat-marbled corn fed beef we're used to, the fast food

**Student Voice:
Alan, Age 18**

Stepping foot into a rain forest and sharing space with another species is an emotional experience for me, whether it's with a miniscule hummingbird or a howler monkey. This feeling is one I get in no other way, the feeling that we are not alone in this world. I learn that we have a place in the family of living things and a duty to uphold our part of that relationship. The rain forest animals may not be able to speak to us verbally, but I think we can all understand what they need. We may be the cause of their demise, but we can just as easily be the cause for their survival. It is all of our duties; it is your duty. Your worth in this world is not determined by the money you have or what you own, it is how you treat others of all species.

I can't bear to think of a life without these natural places. Even though our future generations can't speak to us right now, we know what they need from us: they need for us to protect the natural places that are left. The cattle that provide that greasy fast-food hamburger took their last steps on land that once grew rain forests.

companies that buy it will mix it with fat that's been trimmed from U.S. cattle. Then it winds up in fast-food hamburgers and packaged foods, such as hot dogs, lunch meat, canned chili and stew, frozen dinners, and pet food.

McDonald's and Burger King claim they no longer buy beef from tropical countries, but these claims are hard to verify. Once imported beef is inspected by the U.S. government, it is no longer labeled with its country of origin. The amount of beef imported from Central America has decreased in recent years, but it still approaches 100 million pounds yearly.

Student Voice: William, Age 18

As for the standard reasons for being a vegetarian, land use is the main one for me. The world is getting pretty darned crowded, and it takes ten times as much land to raise cows as soybeans. They're cutting down a lot of rain forests to do it. A lot of our beef is from Latin America. I happen to think it's important to preserve rain forests. They're unique environments, with species that exist nowhere else.

Some of the ways animals adapt are pretty cool, the way they specialize to live in one environment. We have a lot to learn from animals. We gotta keep 'em around.

WHAT CAN WE DO TO SAVE RAIN FORESTS?

One thing we can do to save rain forests is to eat less beef. Rain forest beef is usually found in fast-food hamburgers or processed beef products, not at the fresh meat counter at your grocery. Reducing your consumption of beef will reduce demand for it, cutting back on pressure to clear more forests for cattle. An area of tropical forest the size of a small bedroom is destroyed for the production of every fast-food hamburger made of rain forest beef.

As a consumer, there is much more you can do to reduce the demand for American products that come from tropical rain forests, but that is beyond the scope of this book. For more information about how to become a rain forest activist, do a Google search for any of these organizations. On their Web sites, you'll find much more information.

• Conservation International
• The Jane Goodall Institute
• Natural Resources Defense Council
• The Nature Conservancy
• Rainforest Action Network
• Wildlife International
• World Wide Fund for Nature

Global Warming: Cows and the Greenhouse Effect

WHAT IS THE GREENHOUSE EFFECT?
You've heard plenty about global warming in the last few years. Maybe you've seen the movie *The Day after Tomorrow*, in which the planet is rocked by storms, floods, and a new ice age, all caused by greenhouse gases and global warming. But you've probably never heard that cows are partly to blame.

The warmth we enjoy in our atmosphere is created by a process called the greenhouse effect. Solar radiation, or solar energy, passes through our atmosphere and warms the surface of the Earth. Heat radiates outward from the warmed planet and some of it escapes back into space. But some of it is absorbed by greenhouse gases in our air—mainly water vapor, carbon dioxide, methane, and nitrous oxide. These gases then release the energy as longer-wavelength radiation, which warms the air.

Brr! We Need Those Gases!
As you can imagine, the more of these gases there are in the atmosphere, the more heat that is released into our air. And the more heat that stays, the warmer our air is.

TWO WORLDS COLLIDE
IN THE TWILIGHT ZONE

I remember a couple of years ago walking through a dense and extensive primary forest in a protected area in Costa Rica, a biological station owned by the Organization for Tropical Studies. One day, the narrow forest trail I was following took me along a big stream that formed the boundary of the protected forest. On the other side were no trees, only grass and dozens of cows. It seemed so bizarre—on my side of the stream were monkeys, sloths, toucans, and parrots and on the other side were future hamburgers. I knew that not long ago, the pasture had been forest too. I also knew that, were the forest not protected, it would be producing hot dogs and lunch meat for U.S. grocery stores as well, and all the wildlife would be dead or struggling to survive.

THE LOSS OF A FOREST BEGINS
WITH A ROAD

The destruction of a tropical rain forest in Africa, Asia, or South America often begins when an international logging company cuts a dirt road into the heart of a forest. The purpose of such a road is to provide workers and logging trucks access to the trees deep in the forest. Once trees are cut, trucks must be able to haul them out.

The road is the beginning. With the road, local people as well as the loggers have access to the forest. Local men use the road to penetrate the forest for hunting. With modern rifles, which they often get by trading cattle, they can shoot wildlife much faster and more efficiently than by traditional hunting methods. The hunters can sell the wildlife, including monkeys and exotic birds, as "bush meat"

A white-faced capuchin, a tropical rain forest monkey of Latin America.

If the people of Costa Rica ate as much beef per person as the people of the United States eat, then every bit of Costa Rica's forests would have to be cleared in the next year for beef cattle. I'm glad they prefer rice, beans, papaya, and fried plantain, with an occasional small bit of meat on the side.

—Sally

at local markets. The result? An eerily silent forest, devoid of wildlife. (Do a Google search for "bush meat" or "bush meat + silent forest" and learn much more about this problem.)

But the loss of wildlife is not the only problem. Local families begin to settle along the road. Some of them clear a small patch of land to grow crops. The shallow tropical soil, without tree roots to hold it in place, soon washes away with the heavy tropical rains. When farming is no longer possible, this cleared land may still grow enough grass to support cattle for a few years, but eventually, overgrazing and heavy rains make the land unusable for any purpose.

The companies that construct these roads are seldom local companies. They are companies from the industrialized, developed countries of the world. Japan accounts for 53 percent of the world's tropical timber imports, followed by Europe at 32 percent and the United States at 15 percent. This just means that impoverished tropical countries are losing their most precious resource to rich foreign businessmen who are making huge profits. These corporations have already had their way with most of Asia's tropical forests—what little remains is in small forest fragments that are of little use to wildlife populations.

Companies from industrialized countries such as the United States also clear large areas of tropical forest for plantations. The Tropics are attractive sites because of the year-round growing season, abundant rain and sunshine, and the low wages of tropical workers—which keeps the owners' operating costs very low. Large tropical plantations grow crops such as sugarcane, bananas, pineapples, peppers, strawberries, cotton, tea, coffee, palm oil, and rubber, mainly for export to the United States and other industrialized countries. Next time your family buys one of these products from the grocery, check the label to see where it came from. The bananas at our nearby Harris Teeter supermarket are from Costa Rica. I'll bet yours are too.

—Sally

This has to happen—if it didn't, the Earth would be as freezing as the rest of space. But it can't happen too much, or the Earth will get too hot. Unfortunately, human activities in the last few decades have created more and more greenhouse gases. The extra carbon dioxide comes mainly from burning tremendous amounts of wood and fossil fuels. Fossil fuels include natural gas and oil for heating homes and businesses, coal used in industries, and gasoline used for cars and trucks and farm machinery.

Surely, Burning Fossil Fuels Has Nothing to Do with Livestock, Does It?

Actually, it does. A lot of farm machinery and vehicles are used to grow and transport the corn that cattle are fed in feedlots and to ship food and build housing for pigs and poultry and dairy cows. Fossil fuels operate the trucks used to transport animals from one stage of production to another, to carry their milk, eggs, and meat to distributors, and so on. Also, fossil fuels are used in the manufacture of chemical fertilizers, which are used to grow corn and other crops for livestock.

That may sound trivial, but food products from animals require massive amounts of fossil fuels compared to vegetable food products. In fact, it takes *twenty-seven times* more fossil fuels to produce 100 calories from beef than it takes to produce 100 calories from soybeans. Meat production is an incredibly inefficient way to use fossil fuels for creating our food.

Burning Tropical Forests Is Part of the Problem Too

The burning of trees and other plants is a major contributor to greenhouse gases because it's occurring on such a massive scale in the Tropics, around the clock. When ranchers slash and burn patches of rain forest to create pastures for livestock, it has the same effect as burning fossil fuels: carbon dioxide is released, which is a major greenhouse gas.

Then There's Methane

Another abundant greenhouse gas is methane. A lot of the methane in the atmosphere comes from coal and from oil and gas production, but about 20 percent of it comes from cows—from their rears, to be specific.[32] Cow farts are made of methane. Sounds silly—how can intestinal gas have such a major effect? An adult cow weighs more than half a ton. Consider that there are more than one and a half billion cows worldwide. That's a whole lot of rear ends crankin' out gas. One single molecule of methane can trap as much solar heat as twenty-five molecules of carbon dioxide, so it's very powerful as a greenhouse gas.

Nitrous Oxide

Nitrous oxide is another gas that's increasing in our atmosphere and causing global warming. Like carbon dioxide, nitrous oxide is released when fossil fuels are burned.

Another major source of nitrous oxide is the use of nitrate fertilizers. When nitrate fertilizer is applied to crops, some of it evaporates into the air and forms nitrous oxide. A lot of the nitrate fertilizer used in the United States is applied to corn and other crops eaten by livestock.

BUT ISN'T GLOBAL WARMING JUST A THEORY?

Twenty years ago, maybe. But it's not a theory anymore. Most scientists consider global warming from excess greenhouse gases to be a fact. The majority of Nobel Prize–winning scientists believe that global warming is one of the most serious threats to the Earth and to future generations. Environmental Defense calls global warming "the most serious threat to our planet."[33]

How Much Has Carbon Dioxide Increased Already?

The level of carbon dioxide in the air has been rising since the Industrial Revolution (around 1750) due to the burning of fossil fuels and the burning of forests. Scientists estimate that the concentration of carbon dioxide in the air before 1850 was less than 290 ppm (parts per million).[34] By 1958, the concentration had risen to about 315 ppm. Today, the concentration is more than 370 ppm, the highest level for at least 420,000 years—and still rising.[35]

Who Is the Biggest Culprit?

Guess which country produces more greenhouse gases than any other? The United States. We produce 27 percent of the world's carbon dioxide although we have only 6 percent of the world's population. The main reasons for this are our vast numbers of big cars, trucks, and gas-guzzling machinery and our massive consumption of meat. We use the words "vast" and "massive" because our use of gasoline per person and our consumption of meat per person are greater than any other country's.

How Much Have Temperatures Already Increased?

Since 1900, the average surface temperature of the Earth has increased by about 1.1 degrees Fahrenheit.[36] Places with cold climates have had much more dramatic increases. In just the last thirty years, the average temperature in Alaska has risen by seven degrees.[37]

But What's the Effect of Just a Few Degrees?

- Mountain glaciers all over the world are receding.[38]
- A growing number of studies show animals and plants are changing their range and behavior in response to shifts in climate.[39]
- The Arctic ice pack has lost about 40 percent of its thickness during the past four decades.[40]

- Sea levels have risen three times faster during the past 100 years than for any time in the previous 3,000 years.[41]
- Ocean currents have changed in temperature and direction, causing decreases in marine animal populations.[42]
- We have more extreme weather events. The 2004 hurricane season was the first since 1886 to see four hurricanes strike a single state (Florida), where 20 percent of all homes were damaged.[43]

How Much Will Temperatures Go up in the Next Century?

According to a 2001 report by the U.S. Global Climate Change Research Program, average temperatures in the United States are likely to increase three to ten degrees Fahrenheit by the year 2100.[44]

How Will That Extra Heat Affect Us?

If current trends continue, sea levels will continue to rise as glaciers and polar ice keep melting. Flooding of coastal areas will have devastating effects on wildlife and beaches as well as coastal towns and cities worldwide. Some computer models predict that New York, Miami, and Los Angeles could all be flooded by the year 2100.

Warming is likely to alter patterns of global rainfall and farming. The grain belts of the central United States and central Asia may become drier and unable to support the crops that are grown there now. Forests in semidry areas could become deserts.

Warming by even three to four degrees Fahrenheit would probably be devastating to many species found in high mountains. Some scientists predict that 60 percent of mammal species on mountain peaks in the western United States could be lost because they would be unable to migrate to colder areas. Songbirds on the East Coast are already losing habitat due to global warming.

Some penguin populations are shrinking now as seas warm and food webs change. Some nature reserves will be too changed to support threatened species whose survival depends upon them. Tropical diseases and other heat-related illnesses, such as malaria, will spread into areas that are free from them right now.

Student Voice: Alan, Age 18

Obviously, no one wakes up with a desire to be an obese contributor to the greenhouse effect, while also causing intolerable cruelty to animals and destruction of the environment. People make these choices out of ignorance and the lack of knowledge of solutions.

WHAT SHOULD WE DO?

As a Nation ...

Most scientists have already called for drastic cuts in the use of fossil fuels in order to slow temperature increases. The majority of scientists and world leaders have called for immediate steps to slow the warming trend, in order to prevent catastrophic global change.

More than 165 countries have agreed to a tough international global-warming treaty that requires most industrialized nations to limit or cut carbon dioxide emissions. The United States is one of the few that have refused to sign the treaty. Why? Many believe that our leaders resist signing because reducing carbon dioxide emissions would be too expensive for our industries and would reduce profits and hurt our economy.

But many scientists—and many citizens as well—feel that this is a price we must pay in order to protect future generations and our wildlife from a worldwide calamity. Sometimes short-term benefits must be sacrificed for long-term solutions.

As Families and Individuals ...

Fortunately, we are not helpless. We can take action to slow global warming. According to the Union of Concerned Scientists, "Global warming results primarily from human activities that release heat-trapping gases and particles into the air. The most important causes include the burning of fossil fuels such as coal, gas, and oil, and deforestation. To reduce the emission of heat-trapping gases like carbon dioxide, methane, and nitrous oxides, we can curb our consumption of fossil fuels, use technologies that reduce the amount of emissions wherever possible, and protect the world's forests."[45]

Two practical things that your family can do to help are to drive smaller cars that use less gas and to eat less meat, especially less beef. Eating less meat reduces our use of fossil fuels, reduces the release of methane from cows' rears and nitrous oxide from fertilizers, and reduces the burning of tropical forests to create pastures for cattle.

On a broader scale, we can write to the president and to our representatives in Congress to urge our government to join with other industrialized nations in limiting carbon dioxide emissions.

Wildlife Are Becoming Extinct

In the year 1900, we had fewer than 2 billion people on the planet. In 2000, we started the new century with more than 6 billion. Our numbers are increasing by more than 200,000 people every single day. At this rate of increase, the current world population will increase by 50 percent in the next fifty years.

Because the human population is growing so fast and changing the environment so drastically, we are causing other species to go extinct at a rapid rate, and that rate is accelerating. We lose one or more entire species of animal or plant life every twenty minutes—that's about 27,000 species each year.* This rate of extinction has not occurred in 65 million years.[47] If it seems unbelievably high, consider that it includes plants, invertebrates, and microscopic organisms, as well as vertebrates such as ourselves.

Eleven percent of the animal species in the United States are threatened or endangered. These include the grizzly bear, gray wolf, whooping crane, California condor, Florida panther, Pine Barrens tree frog, ivory-billed woodpecker, red-cockaded woodpecker, Utah prairie dog, and West Virginia spring salamander.

Across the planet, extinction rates are high because impoverished people in developing nations cut forests and hunt wildlife in an effort to keep their families alive, because multinational corporations cut tropical forests to maximize profits, and because citizens of industrialized nations burn fossil fuels and demand meat at every meal. A 2000 joint study by the World Conservation Union and Conservation International and a 1999 study by the World Wildlife Fund found that 34 percent of the world's fish species, 25 percent of amphibians, 24 percent of mammals, 20

*Estimates of extinction rates vary from 1,000 to 75,000 species per year (three to 200 species per day). The wide range of estimates is a result of the differing assumptions about the Earth's total number of species, the proportion of these species found in tropical forests (50 to 80 percent), and the rate of the clearing of tropical forests (0.5 to 2 percent per year). The estimates of Earth's total number of species vary from 5 to 100 million, with a best estimate of 12 to 14 million species.[48]

A NEW REPORT ABOUT GLOBAL
WARMING, FROM *WORLD NEWS
TONIGHT WITH PETER JENNINGS*[46]
ABC-TV
November 8, 2004
Peter Jennings: Global warming is the gradual
increase in the temperature of the Earth's
lower atmosphere as a result of the increase in
manmade gases since the Industrial Revolution. There was a sobering report today about
the effect of global warming on the Arctic.
As far away as it may seem to some, what
happens up there has an effect on the rest of
us everywhere else. An international team of
scientists warns of devastating consequences.
ABC's Bill Blakemore has more.

Camera switches to Bill Blakemore: This
polar bear has nowhere to go. [Shows bear on
small floating piece of ice.] Way too much
open water. And ships now find passages
where it should be frozen over. Scientists
from eight countries on the edge of the Arctic now agree the Arctic is melting far faster
than they thought.

Camera switches to Fred Krupp of Environmental Defense: This report is a wake-up
call to the planet that we need to do something about global warming now because the
impacts are already upon us.

Bill Blakemore: The study finds that since
1970, almost 400,000 square miles are gone,
a meltback of more than 8 percent. Arctic
temperatures on average are up 4 to 5 percent.

Camera switches to Robert Correll, Arctic
Climate Impact Assessment: Things are going
very rapidly and changing the landscape.

Bill Blakemore: And this severe climate
change is accelerating.

Fred Krupp: For wildlife in the Arctic this
report spells disaster.

Bill Blakemore: Already polar bears are
starving as the ice they hunt on vanishes,
along with the seals they eat. Millions of

birds are affected as spring comes too early
and the fish they eat gone ... to seek cooler
water.

Robert Correll: The United States will be
much warmer because this air conditioner is
not working anywhere near as well in the Arctic as it did in the past.

Bill Blakemore: Another report today
showed much U.S. wildlife ranging from the
red fox to butterflies trying to move north
seeking cooler weather but often finding its
way blocked by superhighways and suburbs.

Today's Arctic report warns that all the
ice melting will raise sea levels throughout the
world, up to three feet this century, wiping
out thousands of human and animal habitats
on coastlines.

Robert Correll: You want to know what's
going on twenty-five, thirty years from now
on the rest of the planet, keep your eye on the
Arctic.

Bill Blakemore: The report says cutting
back emissions from burning fossil fuels
should eventually stop the warming but will
take many decades, so life on this planet has
no choice but to try to adjust.

percent of reptiles, 14 percent of plants, and 12 percent of bird species are threatened with permanent extinction.[49]

In 1999, Peter Raven, president of the International Botanical Congress, reported, "We are predicting the extinction of about two-thirds of all mammal, butterfly, and plant species by the end of the twenty-first century."[50]

WHAT IS A "MASS EXTINCTION"?

A mass extinction is defined as a catastrophic, widespread, or global event in which large groups of existing species (perhaps 25 to 75 percent) are wiped out. Most of the mass extinctions that occurred prehistorically— before humans evolved—resulted from global climate changes that killed many species and left behind those able to adapt to the new conditions.

A collared peccary, a common rain forest animal of Central America.

Deforestation, as in these tropical mountains, is a leading cause of extinctions worldwide.

According to a 1998 survey, 70 percent of biologists believe we are in the midst of a new mass extinction.[51] Although the Earth experienced other mass extinctions before humans evolved, biologists point out two important differences between the current mass extinction and those of the past:

- This mass extinction is taking place in a very short period of time, during a few decades, rather than over thousands or millions of years.[52]
- We are eliminating or fouling many environments, such as tropical forests, coral reefs, and wetlands, that in the past fostered the evolution of new species during the 5 to 10 million years after a mass extinction.[53]

No One *Wants* to Cause Extinctions. What Are We Doing Wrong?

Why is the increase in human numbers so devastating to other species? As we take up more space and use more resources, we destroy habitats. Animals depend on particular habitats for their survival. For example, many North American songbirds escape winter's food shortage by flying to tropical forests where seeds and insects are abundant year-round; tadpoles develop only in healthy ponds and streams. When these places vanish, the animals that depend on them die out. Today, songbirds, frogs, and many other species are threatened as tropical rain forests and North American wetlands are destroyed.

The destruction of habitats by humans is responsible for about 75 percent of extinctions.[54] Another major cause is unregulated hunting and fishing. The introduction of non-native species such as honeysuckle, aquatic plants, kudzu, and starlings is another leading cause of extinctions.

HOW ARE EXTINCTIONS RELATED TO MEAT CONSUMPTION?

The production of meat requires much more land than the production of an equally nourishing quantity of plant protein. So, given that most Americans eat meat two or three times a day, we must devote a tremendous amount of our land to either grazing livestock or raising grain or hay to feed livestock. About 40 percent of all land area in the United States is used for grazing livestock that we will eat. And two-thirds of all the grain we grow goes to feed livestock.

Does it have to be this way? Consider this: although we, in the United States, feed 66 percent of our grain to livestock, the rest of the world feeds only 3 percent of their grain to livestock. If we weren't eating so much meat, think of all the agricultural land that could be restored to its natural state as forests, prairies, and wetlands.

Is Our Meat Binge Making Us Healthy and Happy?

About 65 percent of Americans are overweight or obese.[55] We also have high rates of heart disease, high blood pressure, colon cancer, and various other ailments related to a high fat and high meat diet. We're not healthier.[56]

But are we happier? No. Although our consumption of resources has doubled since 1957, the proportion of Americans who report they are "very happy" has remained the same.

Student Voice: Alan, Age 18

The adoption of a vegetarian diet would vastly improve the outlook on the future for both humankind and wildlife. Our gross addiction to the meat industry has terrible effects on the environment, all of which can be prevented. Cows are one of the greatest sources of methane, which is one of the main pollutants in our atmosphere. The majority of grain grown in the United States is used to feed our cows, when instead the land could be used to grow soybeans, or be allowed to revert to native habitats.

"Even the Smallest Person Can Change the Course of the Future."

Those were Galadriel's words of encouragement to Frodo, and she was right. The problems facing the world seem enormous sometimes, but one step at a time, one person at a time, we can change things.

Raising livestock doesn't have to be destructive, if done on a smaller scale. Only a few decades ago, manure naturally fertilized crops and enriched the soil. Livestock consumed crop waste and kitchen waste. Animals and people maintained a balance. It's only since the production of meat has become so industrial in scale that it has begun to damage the Earth so severely.

Why has the meat industry come to this? In our system of production, farmers have to compete against each other. And the way to win is to produce more and spend less. If any farmer adopts a money-saving method, such as a new growth supplement or a way of fitting more animals into less space, then all the competing farmers must do the same or be left behind. In this competitive system, farmers can't afford to consider issues like the environment or they'll go out of business. That is, unless either the government or consumers force them all to make the same adjustments.

The average American eats 250 pounds of meat a year. It's not possible for everyone on the planet to have that much meat. And yet, in the world's most powerful country, some of us feel entitled to eat as much as we like.

There's a different way though. We can, as individuals, make diet choices for a sustainable future. We can then join together with others to make these choices as communities. If we persist, and continue to tell others about the choices we're making, we can, like Frodo, change the course of the future. It happens all the time.

© Reprinted with permission of King Features Syndicate.

Chapter Three

Visiting Factory Farms:
Likable Farmers Trapped in a Bad System

I am in favor of animal rights as well as human rights. That is the way of a whole human being.

—*Abraham Lincoln*

What Is a Factory Farm?

Today, the vast majority of animals that wind up on our dinner tables come from industrial-sized farms. One of these farms may house as many as a million animals. We visited an egg farm with more than a million chickens and three other farms with tens of thousands of animals.

On factory farms and in feedlots for beef cattle, animals live very short lives in very crowded conditions. The animals we visited on factory farms were all housed in huge metal confinement buildings reeking of feces and ammonia. Many of the animals were so crowded that they were unable to carry out even their most basic instincts, unable to stretch or move about. Others were alone in tiny, barren stalls, devoid of any kind of stimulation, unable to even turn around. You can read more about these farms in detail later in this section.

FACTORY FARMS ARE NEW ON THE SCENE

Huge farms are a fairly recent development. Before 1950, smaller family farms were the norm. Farm animals were kept alive longer then, and they spent much of their time in outdoor pastures. Because they lived longer and farmers had fewer of them, the animals were raised with greater respect for their comfort as well as their long-term physical needs. It wasn't practical to keep cows or pigs or chickens in extremely crowded conditions because crowded animals couldn't graze adequately, were too hard to care for, and were too prone to illness.

An Industry Turned on Its Ear in Fifty Short Years

After World War II, things changed. A number of factors played a part in the shift toward keeping huge concentrations of animals in small spaces. Chemical fertilizers and high-speed pumps for irrigation made it possible to grow vast amounts of cheap corn, which could then be fed to livestock. With improved transportation and cheap fuel, corn could be moved easily over long distances. Instead of grazing at pasture, animals on a diet of corn and other grains could be fed from troughs and kept crowded together in pens. The use of feedlots to fatten cattle year-round greatly expanded.

With the invention of automated feeders and plucking machines, feed companies began buying out poultry farmers and raising chickens in enormous sheds. The new debeaking machines kept crowded chickens from pecking and eating each other. After the mass production of poultry was ironed out, the pork industry followed the model. Before long, hogs too were being raised in huge, crowded buildings with automated feeders, foul air, and feces underfoot.

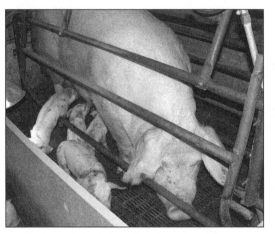

Each sow is locked in place in a tiny stall.

Antibiotics Played a Part

Antibiotics played a part in the development of factory farms as well. Animals in very crowded conditions, in constant contact with piled-up feces, and breathing ammonia all day every day are more likely to get sick than animals spread out in pastures. Cattle eating a diet of corn often develop stomach and liver ailments. Bacterial and viral diseases can spread easily in crowded animals. On the factory farms

we visited, we saw pigs and chickens smeared with feces; we walked among chickens standing on floors covered with eighteen months' worth of feces. Many farming professionals believe that daily doses of antibiotics help keep some diseases at bay in crowded animals, although European countries that have outlawed preventive antibiotics would disagree.

When we first started working on this book, we knew that animals on factory farms lead lives of misery and that factory farms create a whole new world of environmental

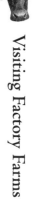

problems. Someone had to be responsible for these abuses, and we thought the guilty parties must be the farmers who own industrial-sized livestock farms.

That perspective has changed.

CORPORATIONS HAVE TAKEN OVER LIVESTOCK FARMING

It's hard to blame the farmers, many of whom would prefer to farm the way their parents did. Farmers had little part in transforming the meat industry to its present state. The guilty parties are the giant corporations that have taken over meatpacking and the American public that demands two or three meals a day centered on meat or eggs. Almost all the factory farmers we talked to inherited their farms from their families and inherited a way of life that was enjoyable. For most of them, that way of life has all but disappeared.

A factory farm with dozens of hog buildings. The cylinders hold feed for automated feeders.

The vast majority of poultry and hogs now live completely indoors in huge climate-controlled metal buildings. Many of these modern animal buildings now have computerized sensors and feeders that regulate everything, so that only one or two people can manage 100,000 animals.

It might seem that a farmer with 100,000 animals would make a lot of money. But that is often—or usually—not the case.

Contract Farming

The name of the game these days is contract farming. In the poultry and pork industries, corporations such as Tyson and Smithfield own almost all of the animals. A corporation like Tyson hires farmers, under contract, to raise chickens or hogs for them—using the corporation's methods of production. The farmers are paid by Tyson for their work, according to their contracts.

Who owns the farm and the buildings? Farmers are not rich people, but to qualify for a contract with Tyson or another big corporation, a farmer has to provide the modern confinement buildings for the animals. So farmers borrow money from a bank, from $200,000 to $1 million, to build their climate-controlled sheds. When anyone borrows that much money, he must offer the bank something of equal value that the bank can take if the loan is not repaid, called collateral. Farmers offer the banks their homes and their land as collateral for their loans.

What happens if Tyson decides to end a farmer's contract? A corporation can end a contract at any time with only thirty days' notice. If that happens, the farmer is left with the expensive sheds. With no income to make the loan payments on his sheds, he can lose his home and his land to the bank.

Farmers bear the risk for environmental damage as well. If a waste lagoon spills and someone downstream files a lawsuit, the farmer is liable for the damages.

One reason North Carolina has so many hogs and chickens and is such a popular state for meatpacking companies is that the state has few laws to protect farmers from exploitive contracts.

Who's Getting Rich?

Who's getting rich under this system? Not the farmers. Certainly not the workers in the meatpacking plants, many of whom are immigrants from Latin America. These workers, who may be here illegally and may not speak English, are willing to take dangerous, low-paying jobs with few complaints. More than any other industry, meatpacking has attracted a growing Latino population to the Southeast. In the egg factory we visited, described later in this chapter, every single worker on the egg-processing line was Latin American.

The folks who are banking the profits from this arrangement are the executives of Tyson, Smithfield, Perdue, IBP, ConAgra, and the other megacorporations that own the meatpacking plants and that contract with farmers to raise the animals.

Some people have compared this system to feudalism, an abusive and exploitive economic system prevalent during the Middle Ages. Or to sharecropping, an equally abusive system common in the South after the Civil War. In these two systems, impoverished families farmed the land but were forced to turn over all crops and profits to the few rich people who were in control.

What if a livestock farmer wants to opt out of this system and make a living as an independent farmer, owning his own animals? That is very hard to do. . . .

It's All about Efficiency

The huge meatpacking corporations compete with one another for deals with major stores, such as Wal-Mart. Wal-Mart wants to buy the cheapest meat products available to sell to their customers. Meatpackers compete for Wal-Mart's business by trying to be as efficient as possible, which means cramming as many animals as possible into sheds that are as automated as possible in order to save on expenses. That's why factory farms operate the

way they do. Animal comfort is irrelevant in a corporate-driven, competitive market focused on shaving pennies from animal-care costs.

In order to compete with huge corporations for grocery stores' business, an independent farmer would have to operate the same way: with huge numbers of animals in automated sheds. A farmer can't afford to own all those animals. Even if he could, he can't take the risk. If a disease or a fire breaks out in a shed of 30,000 animals, an independent farmer could go bankrupt. If that happens to a farmer under contract, the corporation absorbs at least some of the loss.

An independent farmer would also have a very hard time finding a facility to slaughter and package his animals because the big corporations, such as Tyson and Smithfield, own almost all the meatpacking plants and distribution centers. An independent farmer who is not under contract is usually locked out of large processing plants.

Of course, underlying all of this is the American public's demand for massive amounts of meat. All of the huge meat corporations are consumer-driven. They could not exist if the public were not gobbling down their products. This puts the responsibility for factory farms squarely in our own laps.

There is one quick way to put a stop to this whole sad system, and that is to quit buying meat. At least we can choose to buy less meat, or choose instead to buy pastured meat from small suppliers.

VERTICAL INTEGRATORS

The huge meat corporations in this system of contract farming call themselves vertical integrators. Since they own all the animals and pay farmers under contract to raise the animals, they may hire different farmers to manage different parts of the animals' life cycle. Then handlers and drivers who work for the corporation move the animals by truck from one farm to the next. The corporation "integrates" the care of several participants.

Hogs are often raised on three different farms. One handles pregnant and nursing sows, a stage called farrowing. Another farm might raise young pigs, called feeder pigs, for the three months or so after weaning. And a third farm might take care of finishing, or raising the feeder pigs up to their slaughter weight at age twenty-five weeks. A few hog farms keep pigs through all stages—from farrowing to finishing. The hog farm we visited was a farrowing-to-finishing operation, but these are unusual.

A Tyson broiler shed holding tens of thousands of young chickens.

in cardboard boxes. All the sheds on a given broiler farm are stocked in one day so all the birds are the same age. In fact, all the birds on a given route of several farms are the same age.

Tyson has thirty-four of these complexes in the United States, each one with about 200 broiler farms. When we drove around within the Tyson complex nearest to our home, we passed a Tyson farm every couple of miles. Each one has a Tyson sign stuck in the ground by the driveway.

The main objective of the vertical integrators is profit, so everything is organized to maximize efficiency.

On a factory farm rows of dark, crowded indoor pens hold young feeder pigs. Feces litter the aisles.

An Integrator's Chicken Complex
A chicken farm that raises birds for meat is called a broiler farm. Most broiler farms operate as part of a complex of broiler farms, all within a fifty-mile radius of a central feed mill, hatchery, and a processor for killing and packaging the broilers.

When a broiler shed is ready for new chicks, truckers that work for the vertical integrator, often Tyson, deliver the chicks from the central hatchery to the farmer's broiler sheds

Beef, Egg, and Milk Producers
Although the great majority of hog and chicken farmers work under contract with a vertical integrator, this is not the case for farmers who raise beef or dairy cows or for farmers who produce eggs. Dairy farmers and egg producers are usually independent farmers, although often they too have huge factorylike farms. One dairy may have as many as 4,000 cows, and the egg factory we visited had more than a million hens.

Beef cattle are raised by independent ranchers for six to seven months, then they often leave the ranch for a feedlot owned by a big corporation. More than 80 percent of beef cattle in the United States are slaughtered and

47

marketed by one of four big corporations. Many of the farmers we talked to said that, more and more, the cattle industry is moving toward contract arrangements like the hog and chicken industries have now.

WE VISITED FOUR FACTORY FARMS AND FOUR SMALL FARMS

We were fortunate to be able to visit four factory farms in researching this book. The names of these four farmers, who showed us around their establishments and answered our questions, have been changed. Don and his brother, Wade, Gary Davis, Frank McAuley, and Wesley are not their real names. They all requested that their real names not be used.

We also visited four small family farms where livestock are raised in much the same way they were 100 years ago. The real names of those farmers are used with their permission. You'll meet them in chapters four and five.

We are indebted to all of the farmers who were willing to take the time and energy to show us their farms and explain their operations. All of them were kind and generous people. All of them were hard workers who were dedicated to doing the best job possible with the type of farm they had.

Small Farmers Have Different Priorities

All four small farms seemed to meet the needs of the animals—social needs, behavioral needs, and physical needs. They had room to stretch, lie down, run, groom, scratch, play, and interact with others. The animals had mud to roll around in and hay to nest with. They all seemed quite contented and were fun to watch.

The small farmers we interviewed all seemed to have animal comfort, human health, and environmental safety as high priorities. They are willing to pay the extra costs to achieve these goals. They're able to make a living by selling their products to families in their local communities rather than to grocery stores. In every case, the local communities of the small farmers seem willing to pay more for products that are grown with humane, safe, and environmentally sound methods by farmers who are their neighbors.

The Factory Farms Were a Different Universe

The factory farms were a completely different story. Which of the animals' needs were met on these farms? The animals all had enough water. Those that were being raised for meat were fed amply, but animals kept for breeding or egg-laying were fed less than they would choose to eat. Temperatures were managed for the animals' comfort.

Beyond that, the animals' needs were not met in the conditions within the sheds. They did not have fresh air to breathe, but rather had to breathe ammonia, hydrogen sulfide, and fecal dust around the clock. Many didn't have room to stretch their limbs, much less exercise. Many of the animals didn't have room to lie down comfortably, to take a step, or to turn around. They didn't have nesting materials or the opportunity to interact normally with others of their species. Many of them had nothing whatsoever to do in order to fill the long hours of every day and night except to alternate sitting and standing. For some, even that wasn't an option.

WORKERS AT FACTORY FARMS AND SLAUGHTERHOUSES

Factory hog farms are not great places to work. With ammonia fumes and fecal dust in the air, 70 percent of all workers in pork facilities suffer from some sort of respiratory illness or irritation. A 2004 paper from the School of Public Health at Johns Hopkins University reports that workers at factory hog farms are exposed to something that's even more frightening than ammonia and fecal

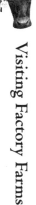

dust: researchers have found airborne bacteria at hog farms that are resistant to multiple antibiotics. The bacteria are resistant because they come from the feces of pigs that are fed low doses of antibiotics daily. So when workers at hog farms breathe the air inside the buildings, they may be inhaling bacteria that can't be controlled by antibiotics.[1]

As unpleasant as factory hog farms may be, facilities that slaughter animals and package the meat have far worse working conditions. Many or most of the workers at these plants are young and Latino, about half of them women. Immigrants who speak little English and lack education have few choices, and they wind up taking low-paying, dangerous jobs that no one else wants. According to *Fast Food Nation* by Eric Schlosser, meatpacking is now the most dangerous job in the United States. The injury rate for these workers is three times higher than in a typical factory.[2]

After animals are killed at a meatpacking plant, they are hauled along on an overhead conveyor belt, dangling by one foot. They are skinned, gutted, and cut into pieces by unskilled workers wielding power saws and heavy knives, rushing to keep up with the steady flow of animals. Someone slows down, a hand slips, a worker gets distracted, or a knife is dropped, and someone is injured or killed.

More miserable than the cutting jobs are the clean-up jobs. These pay even less and are often taken by illegal immigrants who have the fewest choices of all for employment. The clean-up crews come in after everyone else leaves and spray everything with a mixture of hot chlorine and water shot from a high-pressure hose. Schlosser toured a meatpacking plant and describes it in fascinating detail in his book *Fast Food Nation*, which was the source for some of these facts.[3] Michael Pollan offers another detailed account in his article "Power Steer."[4]

SENSITIVE CREATURES OR MINDLESS PRODUCTION UNITS?

There are two completely different mind-sets when considering factory farms. If you look at the animals as sentient creatures, which we, the authors, do, then the whole picture of the factory farms is absurd and unbelievably cruel.

But if you look at them as mindless production units, then the system makes perfect sense. Many of the agricultural professionals we spoke with, in government and at our state agricultural university, seem to choose the second perspective. Many of the factory farmers seemed to, but we think for some of them, maybe all of them, it was just a veneer. Sometimes people adopt a certain attitude in order to cope with a stressful situation, especially one they have no control over.

All of the factory farmers we spoke with during our visits took pride in some aspects of their operation. All of them seemed to be conscientious about keeping animals in accordance with industry standards and government regulations.

Some of What We Learned Is Disturbing

While writing this book, we have shared much of what we have seen with friends and family—many of whom have been shocked, many of whom have not wanted to hear the details. That's understandable—it's hard for us to know the details too. We believe most Americans are simply not aware of the misery of animals on industrial-sized farms. How can anyone object to something they're not aware of?

Throughout the rest of this section, you will read accounts of our visits to four factory farms. You will also read summaries of what we have learned about factory farming from interviews and a variety of other sources.

Later, in chapter four, you can read about our visits to the smaller, more humane farms.

The contrast may surprise you.

HOGS ON FACTORY FARMS

*Pigs may not be as cuddly as kittens or puppies,
but they suffer just as much.*

—Actor James Cromwell, who played the role of
Arthur Hoggett in Babe

A happy and muddy pastured piglet
on a small family farm.

Student Voice:
Dana, 17

The first time that I really learned about factory farms was when I went to the lecture Bobby Kennedy gave here last year. It was about the impacts of the pig farms on the North Carolina coast; it was pretty bad. A lot of people's properties are being degraded because the farms are so nasty.

Actually, it must have been before that, because I haven't eaten pork for a few years. Pigs are above my food-intelligence threshold—basically, if it's as smart as a dog, or smarter, then I'm not going to eat it, even if it is served to me, because that would make me uncomfortable. And pigs are up there, so I'm not going to eat them. That's my single hard rule.

The owners of this small farm allow their sows
to build nests outdoors for giving birth.

Wallowing and Rooting—The Nature of Pigs

We had the chance to interact with quite a few pigs on our farm tours.

Pigs are very playful, at least young pigs. On a farm, most pigs are young because they are slaughtered at six months of age. Only hogs kept for breeding are allowed to reach their full size.

On the small farms, the pigs were kept in pastures. When we approached the pig pastures on these farms, the youngest pigs ran to greet us. They were as eager for attention as puppies in a pet shop. They wanted to be pat-

ted and have their bellies rubbed, and they chased each other in play.

On these small family farms, the older pigs at pasture had little interest in us. They were too busy lying in mud, rooting in the soil, grazing, exploring, sniffing, or interacting with their peers.

We were told that a wild pig that has the freedom to do so will wander up to thirty miles a day looking for food. At night, wild pigs will make a group nest of leaves and branches. Their instinct is to urinate and defecate far away from the group nest.

The pastured pigs we saw on small farms had ample room to explore, exercise, socialize, and keep themselves sanitary. On one farm where the pigs had access to a wooded area, each pregnant sow made a nest of twigs and leaves to deliver and nurse her babies in private.

The life of a pig on a factory farm is another story.

Life on the Factory Farm

Today in the United States, about 80 percent of pigs are raised in confinement.[5] This is a term used by the industry to describe the standard housing on factory pork farms. It was one thing to read about this practice, but it was altogether something else to see it with our own eyes.

Young hogs in rows of crowded, dirty pens in automated confinement buildings.

Confinement means that the animals are kept in small pens or tiny stalls indoors in dimly lit rooms that are usually without windows. There are hundreds of pigs in each room. The waste is hosed out from under the slatted floors at most twice a week, so you can imagine the fumes in each room.

We Were Not Allowed to See Who Was Screaming

Pregnant pigs are kept alone in tiny "gestation crates." The crate is only inches wider than the sow's body, so small she can't turn around and can't take more than one or two steps forward or backward. The pig is completely boxed in. Pigs are at least as smart as dogs, but in these conditions, they have no relief at all from boredom. Gnawing at the bars of the stall is one of the few actions available in this stark and bare environment.

We were not allowed to see the pregnant sows on the factory farm we visited, but we could hear a cacophony of screaming coming from their building. One farmer told me that pregnant sows sometimes thrash against the walls of their tiny stalls in an effort to get out, especially in the beginning. Maybe that's what the screaming was about.

We Were Allowed to See the Mothers, Pinned Down

Although we were not allowed to see the pregnant sows on the factory hog farm we visited, we were allowed to see the mother pigs with nursing young. A nursing sow has a different cage that is a bit wider in order to allow room for the piglets. The standard cage has a metal grill that fits over the mother to prevent her from rolling over and crushing her piglets. She can lie down, but she is unable to rest her legs normally, having to rest the top two legs across a horizontal bar instead. The grill prevents her from moving to either side, forward, or backward. Of course, wild animals do not crush their own young, but pigs have been bred to gain so much weight that they have lost some control over their own body mass.

We had read that this metal grill—sometimes called an iron maiden, after the medieval torture device of the same name—often prevents the sow from standing. However, the grills we saw were designed to flex upward so that, with some effort, a sow could sit or stand if she pressed the grill with her back. But she could not take a full step in any direction.

The metal grill clamped over each mother pig, day and night, keeps her from taking a single step.

Sows are kept in either the gestation crate or the nursing stall for at least ten months of the year—all of the time that they are either pregnant or nursing. The confinement farmer we interviewed said that the sows are allowed one week between the time their babies are removed and weaned and the time the sows are bred to become pregnant again. Since they have an average of 2.6 litters per year, that means there are less than two weeks out of every year when they are neither pregnant nor nursing.

Not Everyone Is Fattened

In addition to the discomfort of having to lie still all day every day in semidarkness and alone, the sows may also be hungry. Breeding pigs on factory farms are often fed only 60 percent of what is given to the pigs being fattened for slaughter—because they are regarded as machines, and decisions are based on profits, not comfort. The farmers save money on feed if the breeders are underfed. But it doesn't pay to underfeed the pigs that are headed for packaging as bacon, ham, and pork because their value increases with added weight.

THE PROFESSOR SAID ...

I called a professor of animal science at a nearby state university to ask him about the stalls for sows. This professor specializes in agriculture related to raising hogs. I wanted his expert opinion, as an academic who studies these things.

"Some people feel the small stalls for sows are not humane. What do you think?" I asked him.

"Well, the size is the issue. They have room to get up and lie down. They can have their own space and not be harmed. The question that comes up is whether their welfare is inhibited by not being able to turn around. I don't know. The sizes are all very appropriate. Pigs can be cruel. They can fight with each other," he replied.

"One thing I've read about is the sensory deprivation of being in the stall all the time with nothing to do. But I don't know how intelligent pigs are," I continued.

"Oh, they are intelligent. They can learn things. They have learned responses. They have family instincts, they take care of their babies," said the professor.

"So I wonder if the stalls are big enough," I repeated.

"I don't know," he said.

I think the professor probably does know. Why he doesn't want to say, I'm not sure. As far as pigs fighting, Sara Kate and I saw lots of pigs housed together in pastures or pens, interacting freely with each other. We didn't see any fighting.

At any rate, tiny stalls are not the only solution if fighting is a problem. Other options are bigger single stalls, or spacious group enclosures.

—Sally

"LIKE SHE HAD GOOD SENSE"

I called an agricultural extension agent, the man in charge of hogs and dairy cows for a North Carolina county. I asked him for his opinion of a sow's living conditions on a typical industrial-sized hog farm.

He replied, "In Europe, there is more concern about animal welfare. They believe it's an animal's natural instinct to roll around in bedding. Sure, a sow will grab straw if she sees it and act like she's gonna make a nest, like she had good sense. But that doesn't mean anything. As long as she's warm and has water and feed, she's just as happy as can be."

We encountered the same insistence on the animals' satisfaction in a wide range of industry professionals, from hog farmers to agricultural professors. It seems to be a way of coping with an unpleasant reality. Recognizing and acknowledging the animals' actual plight would require a long and difficult process of change; it's much easier to go with the status quo.

—Sally

It Stinks So Much It Burns

Everybody knows dogs have a great sense of smell—they can tell who's been around just by sniffing the floor and the furniture. Well, pigs are the same way. Most mammals with long snouts are very sensitive to odors; their long nasal passages pick up scents very efficiently. Pigs sniff for food in the ground with their snout and use the flat end of it to root out their discoveries. Because of their keen sense of smell, trained pigs are used to sniff out truffles, a valuable fungus that grows underground and is regarded as a delicacy by gourmet cooks.

So imagine what the stench inside of a pig factory smells like to a pig—acres of pig feces stewing under the cages! After Sara Kate and I visited the factory hog farm that we describe below, our clothes, hair, and shoes stank so much that we still reeked hours later.

If you've ever sniffed a bottle of ammonia, you know that a good whiff will make you jerk your head back in pain. It burns the sensitive skin inside the nose. Ammonia was used as a traditional "smelling salt" in decades past, something to hold under the nose of a person who had fainted or passed out. The pain of inhaling the ammonia would revive them.

The ammonia and fecal particles in the air of a factory hog farm constantly burn the lungs of the pigs. About 70 percent of pigs have pneumonia at the time of slaughter.[6]

Tails Chopped

The pigs we visited on small farms had normal tails. But the pigs on the factory farm had little stumps—their tails had been clipped. That is standard practice because pigs like to bite anything that catches their attention, in the same way puppies do. Crowded, bored, and unhappy piglets will particularly go after each other's tails. If a bitten tail bleeds, it attracts even more biting, which can end in death. So factory farmers cut off the tails of all their pigs that are not breeders, leaving only a half-inch stump. In Europe, it is illegal to cut pigs' tails without anesthesia. But the United States lags behind Europe in most matters of animal welfare, and there is no law here about anesthesia, so none is used. The recommended tool is either pliers or a blunt instrument whose crushing action tends to stop the bleeding.

THE FIVE BASIC FREEDOMS

In 1964, Ruth Harrison published a groundbreaking book about the treatment of animals in meat production, titled *Animal Machines*. The following year, a committee of experts was appointed by the British Minister of Agriculture to discuss the matter of animal confinement. The Brambell Committee included

TESTICLES TOO

Tails are one thing. But male pigs on factory farms are also castrated without anesthesia.

I called a professor in the food science department at a local state university, a person who specializes in meat science, to ask about castration.

"Are pigs routinely castrated?" I asked him. "I read that they are, but that doesn't make sense, since they are slaughtered before they're mature, before they could mate."

"In this country, a high percentage of pigs are castrated," replied the professor.

"Why?" I asked.

"It's a production issue," he responded.

Puzzled, I asked, "What do you mean, a production issue?"

"It has to do with efficiency," he said.

Ah. "You mean they grow faster if they're castrated?" I asked.

"Yep," he replied.

"Is anesthesia used?" I said.

The professor paused, "You'll have to ask my colleague about that."

Following his suggestion, I did call his colleague in the animal science department, who confirmed that pigs are routinely castrated.

"How old are they when they're castrated?" I asked the colleague.

"Less than one day old," he replied.

"I've read that in Europe anesthetic is used for castration, but not here. Do you think that's a problem?"

He answered, "In Europe, they do it at an older age. Pigs can't feel anything at one day old."

I've heard that argument before. But how do we know that? Has someone documented that somehow? We used to think newborn humans couldn't feel pain, but in the last ten years, research has shown that in fact they do.[7] Pigs are also mammals and have nervous systems very similar to our own. I tend to think that if newborn humans feel pain, then newborn pigs do as well.

I called the food science professor again a couple of months later for permission to quote him on the connection between weight gain and castration. I explained what I had heard him say during our earlier conversation.

"No, I didn't say that," he replied. "I said it was a management issue."

"Oh. Okay. Well, what does 'a management issue' mean?"

"Castrated males tend to be less aggressive and less likely to fight. Then there's the 'boar taint' issue as well, from male hormones in the meat. Pork from males that are intact at the time of harvest tends to have a taste and odor that most consumers find offensive."

"So castrating has nothing to do with weight gain," I asked again, to be sure.

"No."

Confused about his contradiction, I e-mailed a friend in animal science at Iowa State University, a person who is interested in issues of sustainability and animal welfare. Iowa is another state with a huge hog population and a large research community interested in hogs. My friend sent me a research article showing that intact boars actually gain 3 percent more daily and eat 9 percent less feed than castrated males![8] So I asked him, "If intact males gain *more* weight, which would be a good thing for producers, then why are they all castrated?" My friend said, "In my opinion, pigs in the U.S. might be castrated more out of habit than legitimate necessity. From the minor digging I have done, I have not been able to support the claim that intact males lead to boar taint, however there is intense concern over that issue from packers and academics." He continued, "Last fall, I was speaking with an Australian researcher who laughed at the idea of castrating market pigs. Apparently Australians do not, although it must be noted that typical slaughter weights in Australia are closer to 220 pounds rather than the 275 pounds that are typical in the United States, so their hormone levels may be lower. Intact young bulls [cattle] from Iowa State have entered the commercial slaughter steer market with no apparent problems, suggesting that the meat quality concerns relating to the slaughter and consumption of intact males may be overstated."

In a later e-mail, he pointed out that boar taint varies with the age and breed of the animal and is less detectable with certain meat-processing techniques. Consumer acceptance of the taste also varies widely. Like corn-fed beef, which Americans have learned to love, pork from intact males might be something that, with familiarity, could become quite acceptable.

So. *Why* are male pigs routinely castrated in the United States? It doesn't seem to be weight gain. Boar taint, maybe. Management issues, maybe. Habit? That may be a bigger piece of the puzzle. Seems like a lot of painful slicing of testicles for the sake of a lot of maybes.

—Sally

experts in agriculture, livestock science, veterinary medicine, and zoology. They published an official report on their findings. In their report, they concluded that all animals should have, as a minimum, the "five basic freedoms." The committee wrote that a confined animal should have enough room to turn around, to get up, to lie down, to groom itself, and to stretch its limbs.[9] These freedoms are not much, but consider your own life without them. It's hard to imagine that anyone could argue with these minimal recommendations. But yet, pregnant and nursing sows, hens that lay eggs for consumption, and veal calves are denied these basic freedoms.

We've seen devices designed to prevent a human from having these freedoms. They're in the Museum of Torture, in the Tower of London.

Do Pigs Deserve a Different Standard?

If a dog or a horse were kept in a space so small that it could not turn around, were forced to breathe ammonia twenty-four hours a day, and were fed only 60 percent of the food it would choose to eat, then the owner would be arrested for cruelty. Why is it, then, that animals whose bodies are destined for the dinner table are subjected to these conditions? The double standard just doesn't make sense.

It must be because the public is unaware and because there are not yet laws to forbid it. Factory farms keep animals this way because it is cheaper to do so. Providing spacious enclosures with fresh hay, soil, and room for exercise would increase a farmer's costs so much that he could not compete for grocery stores' business. That is, unless legislation forced everyone to do the same. But the legislation will come only when the public demands it.

Animals as Machines

If conditions are so uncomfortable for animals on factory farms, how do farmers and their families live with the situation? The industry has developed a language of detachment. Animals are regarded as products or machines.

"The main thing we look at is the bottom line. We just have to be more efficient. It's as humane as ... I am just totally impressed with processing!" said a hog farmer we interviewed on a farm that has 40,000 pigs.

"The breeding sow should be thought of and treated as a valuable piece of machinery whose function is to pump out baby pigs like a sausage machine," said a corporate manager with Wall's Meat Company, quoted in *Animal Liberation.*[10]

The U.S. Department of Agriculture,

also quoted in *Animal Liberation*, put it this way: "If a sow is considered a pig manufacturing unit, then improved management at farrowing and on through weaning will result in more pigs weaned per sow per year."[11]

I ASKED DR. TEMPLE GRANDIN …

I called Dr. Temple Grandin, a compassionate livestock scientist at Colorado State University. She has single-handedly made great improvements in the standard way livestock are handled, especially in slaughterhouses, and has been profiled on National Public Radio and in numerous articles for her innovative solutions.

I asked her, "Why are pigs kept in such tiny stalls on conventional pork farms, so small they can't turn around?"

She summed it up quickly. "Efficiency," she said. "It saves money."[12]

And that's the bottom line.

—Sally

We all love animals. Why do we call some "pets" and others "dinner"?

—k. d. lang

Visiting a 120,000-Acre Hog Farm

THE INTERVIEW

We were told more than once that we wouldn't be able to find a factory hog farmer willing to talk to us, but we did. We looked on the Web site of the North Carolina Pork Council and found a farm with 40,000 hogs not too far away. North Carolina is a state with more pigs than people—we knew there had to be a farm that would work as a day trip. We called to ask if we could come by. To our amazement, the owner we spoke to said okay, as long as we weren't from PETA (People for the Ethical Treatment of Animals).

On the day of our meeting with Don, one of the farm's owners, we drove for some time out into the country, past endless fields of cotton, soybeans, and corn. Many of these, we later realized, were owned by Don and his extended family as part of their 120,000-acre farm. We finally recognized our destination by the cluster of brick and metal farm buildings next to a ranch-style home. A little nervous, we pulled into the gravel parking lot, wound around a parked truck, and pulled up next to a silo. As we waited in our car for Don to arrive, his brother, Wade, walked by and made us jump by calling out, "We usually shoot people with those bumper stickers!" Ha, ha! He was smiling. Sara Kate and I just smiled back and waved, unable to think of an appropriate reply.

Don arrived soon, apologetic for being a bit late. He had taken a load of soybeans from the farm to another town to be ground into meal. Now he was hauling them back in a tractor-trailer as soybean meal for the pigs. He escorted us into the covered garage, where his fifteen-year-old son and his young nephew were helping someone work on a farm tractor. We trooped uncertainly up an old staircase to the office above the garage—a barren and dimly lit space with two or three metal desks, a couple of metal chairs, and filing cabinets. It was a bare-bones kind of place, lacking any adornment, with dark paneling on the walls, a linoleum floor—a space that, perhaps, is used only by the men of the family. It reminded me of the basement bedroom my three brothers used to share, the kind of surroundings you'd have to tune out in order to feel really comfortable.

Don walked over to his desk chair. In the window behind him, the sky was gray and bleak. He rearranged some of the papers on his desk, sat down, and folded his arms over his chest. If the light was on, it was too dim to make much difference.

Right away he began to tell us why times are hard on the farm. They have chickens as well as hogs and 2,500 acres of corn to feed the hogs. There was a "market crunch" two years ago; they had to cut production from 50,000 hogs per year to 40,000. They are making less money per bushel of soybeans than they were twenty years ago. He saved the newspaper from the day his son was born fifteen years ago. From that newspaper, he can tell that they were getting $9.80 for a bushel of soybeans back then. Today, they're getting $4.53 a bushel.

"Twenty years ago, before we had the shop, I remember sitting under the cedar tree that was in this spot while my dad and my uncle tried to decide: should we sell the soybeans now for $13, or should we wait for $14? And today, they're $4.53."

As the price they get for their farm products has dropped drastically over the last twenty years, the prices for farm machinery have gone up.

"We have five combines now. One combine costs $230,000—the cost went up this year by $42,000. Costs for machinery are up 280 percent in the last few years."

We were amazed by the sheer price of large-scale farming. As Don explained, "It costs $180,000 to $200,000 for a chicken house, just to build the structure, nothing else. We have twenty chicken houses that hold 3 million chickens over the course of a year. Our power bill just for the chicken farm is $3,000 a month."

We began to get an inkling of just how much is on the line in an enterprise like this one.

"We're one of the largest landowners in the county. We could start building houses. As much land as we have, we could make a lot of money. But our families stay in it for the lifestyle. My son has been driving a combine since he was eleven."

We were interested to hear about the family aspect of the farm. This wasn't exactly the hard and cold factory we'd envisioned; but then again, there were no goats and chickens scampering about as there had been at the smaller farms we'd visited. Nonetheless, as our interview progressed, we both began to feel ourselves softening toward Don. He seemed to relax as well: he uncrossed his arms and leaned back in his chair. When it was clear we were there to listen, not to attack, the talk began to flow more freely.

What About the Environment?
We read on the North Carolina Pork Council's Web site that the council has recognized the farm for some of their environmental practices. So we asked Don about that.

"We've had to implement a lot of changes," he explained. "We don't use a disc for plowing, so the soil is not disturbed. We just cut right where we're going to plant. And a lot of chemicals are more environmentally friendly nowadays. Our cotton has BT [*Bacillus thuringiensis*] genes, a natural insecticide. Our soybeans are Roundup ready. We can just spray it over the top, which is the safest way."

He was referring here to crops that have been bred to be immune to the herbicide Roundup, so the chemical can be sprayed over the whole field, rather than just on weeds. Some would question whether this is the "safest way."

Don described an experiment that he says was carried out recently at the state university to see if the pesticide Roundup shows up in meat after it has been sprayed on soybeans that the animals eat. He says the experimenters put Roundup into the drinking water of some turkeys. According to Don, they kept increasing the concentration until the "water" was straight Roundup. Still, he says, it didn't hurt the turkeys or show up in their meat. This proves that the chemical is safe, he said.

I raised my eyebrows, but offered no comment.

"College kids come from NC State, they have never farmed and don't know what they're talking about. They say, 'You must be doing something wrong and I'm gonna find it.'" Don was starting to get animated.

"I am a certified pesticide applicator and certified fertilizer applicator," he stressed. "The guys who work for lawn services are not. The boss is, but the guys who do the spraying are not. They spray extravagant amounts of herbicide on lawns and cause much more pollution than a hog farm does."

He's right, they do pollute, but more than a hog farm? Hmm …

Why So Many Hogs in North Carolina?

Although I know it's a complicated question, I asked Don why there are so many hog farms on the coastal plain of North Carolina when it's an area so prone to flooding from hurricanes.

He said that because jobs here have been hard to find, a processing plant can move in and find workers easily—workers willing to accept low wages. And because the area has been relatively unpopulated, land has been inexpensive as well. Plus, he added, up north it costs so much to heat the buildings.

Don didn't mention that North Carolina is attractive to meatpacking companies for legal reasons too. The state has few laws to protect contract workers such as Don from exploitive contracts with meatpacking companies. And until the late 1990s, the state had hardly any enforced laws protecting the environment from livestock waste.

All hog farmers in North Carolina have problems with too much drought and too much rain, he acknowledged. He said that, in 1996, a lot of the hog lagoons in the area flooded into nearby rivers. Including his.

"But we can't help that. We can't do anything about the rain."

He's right that 1996 was a bad flood year. But what about 1999? In that year, back-to-back hurricanes Dennis and Floyd flushed thousands of waste lagoons and drowned hogs into North Carolina's coastal rivers, devastating wildlife, the environment, and the local fishing and seafood industries.

How Has PETA Affected Your Business?

We began to talk about struggles within the meat industry and his experiences with opposition. Don told us that fast-food restaurants are a huge market for meat suppliers. PETA tells fast-food restaurants what conditions their meat suppliers must adopt for their animals. For example, PETA dictates how many egg-laying chickens are allowed per square feet of cage and the amount of lighting in a chicken house. They also require "no drugs and no sick chickens," he said. If suppliers don't comply, then PETA boycotts and pickets the restaurants served by that supplier. They keep it up until the restaurant drops that supplier. So fear of PETA is a big motivator for meat suppliers to comply with PETA's rules, said Don.

Don is right that no detectable drugs are allowed in chicken meat, although chickens are routinely given antibiotics until seven to ten days before slaughter.

Don's farm has had to make adjustments as a result of PETA's rules. But he believes PETA has been good for the industry.

"It keeps people on their toes. PETA has had a major impact. Our chickens get just one vaccine, for bronchitis. We don't use any steroids in our chickens or our hogs. We've even had unexpected benefits. Our chickens have gotten bigger. They used to be six-and-one-half pounds at eight weeks, in a tighter space. Now they are eight pounds at eight weeks."

"Because they have more room?" I asked.

"Yes," said Don. We sat in silence for a moment.

Then Don continued, "Most PETA people are vegetarians." He shook his head.

"I'd hate to know I had nothing to eat but vegetables."

We decided to leave that comment alone.

Would You Rather Be Independent?

Taking a different tack, I asked, "How are things different from fifty years ago?"

"The basic concept is the same— till the soil, plant a seed, nurture it, … " Don began.

"No, I mean in relation to corporations," I butted in.

Don began to talk about how dealing with corporations has affected his farm. "We have a deal now with Tyson. All our chickens go to Tyson for the same price, regardless of whether the market is good or bad. It allows us to stay in business. Our hogs go to Green-wood Packing. They make Gwaltney and Jimmy Dean."

We wondered, is that a good thing for his business, being committed to particular corporations? Sara Kate asked Don if, given the choice, he would rather return to being an independent farm.

"Well, yeah," he conceded. "A few years ago we tried with six other families to make it as independents and the corporations ran us off." Don said his farm, in a partnership with several other farmers, also tried to buy their own pork-processing plant. "We got a nasty letter from a big producer telling us they'd never let us make it." And that was the end of that.

In order to survive, Don said bluntly, "the main thing we look at is the bottom line. We just have to be more efficient. There are no independent poultry farmers in the county anymore, they all work with integrators. Eight years ago was the last independent. There are only two hog farmers in this county that don't work with integrators."

An integrator, as you may have read

earlier in this section (page 46), is a corporation, such as Tyson, that contracts with different farmers to raise livestock through different life stages. A chicken farmer may have breeders that lay fertile eggs, for example, or may raise broiler chickens for cooking, but usually not both. The corporation that owns the chickens, such as Tyson, moves the birds from one place to another.

Farms such as Don's used to be able to pick who to sell their hogs to, but now they have only one buyer—essentially, it's a monopoly. This affects the customer too, he was quick to point out. "There's less variety in the meat—you get more of a cookie-cutter product. All the meat companies want Wal-Mart's business, so Tyson is gonna give Wal-Mart the cheapest split-breast cut. That has been a big advantage for a big corporation, a disadvantage for small businesses."

As our interview drew to a close, I was surprised to feel a degree of understanding for this man. In spite of his decision to raise hogs and chickens using what I consider cruel confinement practices, he is very likable. He is a soft-spoken and polite man who loves his family, takes pride in his heritage, tries to keep his business afloat in a challenging market, and worries about animal activists. We couldn't help but feel sympathy for his struggles. He works long hours in an industry that grows increasingly difficult. I got the feeling that he often wonders himself if the payoff is worth the effort.

As we ended our interview, however, Don offered one last comment that kept any overly sympathetic feelings in check. As his final defense of the industry, he said emphatically, "It's as humane as … I am totally impressed with processing!"

Well, then.

SEEING 40,000 HOGS IN CONFINEMENT

We pulled into the farm's parking lot at 2:31 P.M. on the Sunday after Thanksgiving, a minute late. Don had agreed on the phone to actually show us the hogs during this second visit, and we were psyched. We'd been told by others that we'd never get into a hog-confinement facility. Yet here he was, waiting, in jeans and clogs, a flannel shirt. I'd forgotten his thick shock of steel-gray hair—maybe he'd worn a cap when we'd met with him before. He was hustling around, moving back and forth from his huge pickup truck to the farm garage. Clearing off the truck's seats for us, I guess.

He looked better outdoors than in our earlier interview in his dimly lit office, when he'd kept his arms folded over his chest, wary. He was more handsome than I remembered, a soft vulnerability in his expression. There was something comforting about his presence, bustling around the truck, although I couldn't say exactly what. Maybe it's that he seemed as uncertain as I felt. He looked like a dad worried about a son, or a husband needing a hug, or a farmer, maybe. He is a dad and a farmer, I know that much. I remember him proudly pointing out his teenage son working on the combine the day we'd come before. "He keeps a walkie-talkie with him when he's out on the combine," he'd said of his son, "in case something goes wrong."

On this second visit, Sara Kate and I could still hardly believe our good luck. Don opened the door to the backseat of his big new truck and Sara Kate climbed in. I asked if he wanted me to get in the front or the back. "Up front," he said, "unless you're afraid of me." I stepped up into the front seat and thanked him again for letting us come. He backed the truck up and then sped off down the country road toward one of several hog-production sites on the 120,000-acre farm he shares with his dad, uncle, and brother, Wade.

On the day I first met both Don and Wade, I could feel the yin and the yang of the two—Don being the gentle one.

As we sped along, I tried to make friendly conversation, commenting on how beautiful the land was. I didn't mention that there was nary a tree left; it was almost all farm fields. I asked him if every day on the farm was the same or every day different.

He said every day brings something unexpected. For example, if you wanted to plow or plant or harvest in one particular field, it might rain there overnight and be too wet, so you'd have to move all the machines to another field that hadn't been rained on.

The truck was really flying—I thought about my seat belt. I thought that if I hadn't wanted to see the hog buildings so badly, I might've asked him to slow down or let me out. It seemed that fast.

After ten minutes of racing past farm fields, we pulled into a drive with a locked gate. He got out and looked for the key behind several fence posts, said he couldn't find it.

Oh, okay. So he's not really going to let us in, this is just an act—because he can't say no.

But then he found it.

We drove down the long drive, with winter-wheat fields on either side, just beginning to sprout. A long irrigating pipe was in one field, resting on multiple pairs of wheels. He pointed out the motor for each pair of wheels—the pipe can move under its own power! But how could it get over all the little hills? I didn't ask.

Huge flocks of starlings and cowbirds were eating the unsprouted wheat seeds in the fields. He said the geese do much more damage, pulling up whole plants over an entire area. There's nothing you can do but try to scare them away.

Like a distant town on the prairie, a series of long, low buildings began to take

Each mother pig is held in place around the clock by a grate of metal bars.

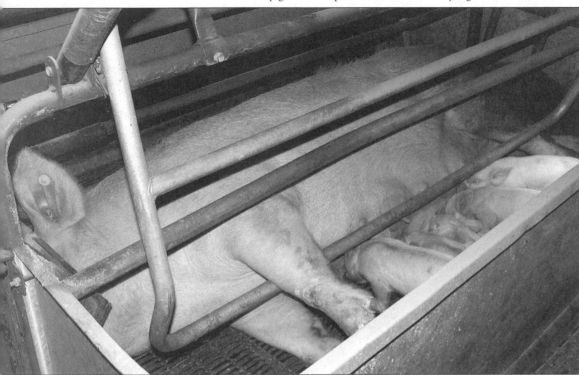

shape at the far end of the road. There were too many buildings to count, perfectly parallel, situated on scoured, sterile, and plantless grounds—as if someone vigorously raked the entire area every day.

As we pulled to a stop, I thought of a concentration camp. The buildings were all metal, without windows. There was a small room–sized office apart from the series of hog buildings. Don went in to look for a key and some boots for us. While he was gone, Sara Kate wondered if she should slide over to the other window to take a photo of the buildings. I told her to do it quick, but it was too late. "Here he comes," I cautioned her, and she slid back.

He opened the truck door and said the new shipment of boots hadn't come in yet. We told him we didn't care about boots.

We got out and Don led us straightaway in between two of the buildings and onto a sidewalk of wooden slats with wooden handrails. As we approached the door of one of the buildings, we came to a dead piglet, about a foot long, lying on the slatted sidewalk. Sara Kate and I both badly wanted to take a picture of it. But we had decided in the car on the way to the farm that we wouldn't say a word about pictures until we were actually inside one of the confinement buildings, actually seeing the hogs. None of us mentioned the pink carcass on the slats. We all just stepped over it.

Don opened the door and we entered a long corridor that ran the length of the building, along one edge. On one side of the corridor were a series of doors. Each door opened into a separate room of pigs. Don opened the nearest door and we all stood in the doorway, looking into the barely lit room, inhaling the thick scent of feces and ammonia that saturated the air. Sara Kate and I jostled each other for a better view.

The room was the size of a small house, I guess, maybe 1,500 square feet. There were no floor-to-ceiling walls, but rather a series of compartments separated by low metal barriers. In each compartment, roughly four by six feet, lay a mother pig, a sow, with a number of piglets. A sow is about five feet long. Over each reclining sow was a grate of parallel bars that kept her from moving sideways or rolling over. It also kept her from resting her legs normally. While lying, she was forced to rest her two higher legs on one of the bars.

I said to Don, "Is it okay if we take some photos?"

The bars make a form-fitting cage over each mother pig. Note clipped tails of piglets.

"I suppose it's okay," he replied.

So we took a few steps down the walkway that ran the length of the room, a row of sows on either side. There must have been about fifty sows in the room. Each had a litter of piglets, up to ten or twelve each. The floors of the cages were made of metal mesh in order to allow urine and feces to drop through

In spite of the slatted floors, each compartment has feces piled up against the rear wall.

to a space below. But in many of the cages, feces were piled up at the back of the cage, behind mama's rump. Some of the piglets were smeared with feces. I could see where someone might feel daily antibiotics were needed.

Don said that about twice a week, a worker hoses off the area under the cages, washing the feces and urine into a lagoon. From the lagoon, the waste is sprayed directly onto their crop fields as fertilizer. So for three to four days, the urine and feces build up under and around the sows. I remembered reading that 70 percent of hogs have pneumonia at slaughter due to the constant irritating fumes. I could understand that now.

Because of the feces on the floor, we didn't get far down the walkway. But the closest sows struggled to get up as we drew near with our cameras. The bars over each sow were hinged somehow so that the center ones raised up when pressed from below, allowing her to sit or stand with the bars still enshrouding her. She still could not take a step to either side or step forward or backward. But she could sit or stand, which was an improvement over the device I had been expecting. On some hog farms, the mother is pinned down so that she can neither roll over nor stand.

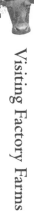

We paused to look at one sitting sow who had a yellow rope tied in a circle running through her mouth and around her snout. What was it for? Don said he didn't know.

I don't know why the sows sat up for us, what they wanted. Or feared. Even extracting their resting legs from the side bars was an effort. Were they hungry? I'd read that nursing sows are given only 60 percent of what they can eat. They're not due for slaughter, so no need to fatten them. And heavier bodies are more likely to crush piglets. The sows beyond us didn't bother to stir. Don said that later in the day someone would check on the automatic food and water dispensers to make sure they were functioning. And to pull out any dead piglets, I guess.

But except for us, there were no other humans present at the facility at all. I wondered to myself, what if one of the pigs was sick? What if one of them went berserk? I thought about my friends who worry whether their dogs are depressed, and how pigs are at least as smart as dogs. What if one of the pigs needed to get out, needed to run, needed some fresh air? What if one was in pain, was bleeding, had a virus? I wondered if to Don these would be ridiculous questions. Although he seemed like someone's nice daddy, he had grown up seeing these hogs as production units in a factory. A factory whose bottom line, he said, is efficiency.

I felt baffled as we looked at the sows and their piglets. As a society, we find it unacceptable to keep zoo animals or pets in untended cages with piled-up feces and caustic fumes, in quarters that make it impossible to assume even a normal resting posture, much less grooming or stretching. Maybe I'm wrong, but it seems to me that for these pigs, existence is probably an inescapable living hell. The only good thing is that, for most of them, life is short—about six months long. The breeding sows, on the other hand, are

kept for about twelve years, Don said, until their litter size begins to decline. Then they are sold at auction.

As we left the sows' room, Don told us that this particular site on the farm is mostly made up of buildings for nursing sows or young, weaned pigs. But at least one of the buildings is for pregnant sows. I wanted to see that one. I know that pregnant sows are kept in stalls only inches wider than their body, like a Big Mac in its cardboard box. We walked past the pregnant sows' building and we could hear a cacophony of screaming from inside. But he wouldn't let us go in.

Instead, he took us to look at the young, weaned pigs, which are being raised for slaughter. They are grouped by age and gender. We stopped in to look at several age groups. The rooms had long rows of pens, similar to those we'd seen before, except there were no sows. Each pen, about four by six, held around fifteen young pigs. The corridor down the center of each room was littered with feces, some fresh, some caked. The youngsters seemed eager to see us, moving toward the front of their pens as we went by. Don assured us that they were not hungry, as profit depends on weight at slaughter.

A room of pens holding young, weaned pigs.

"They're just like puppies," said Don. "They'll jump all over you if you go in there."

But the flashes from our cameras frightened them and they backed away from us. Without windows and with minimal lighting, they're not accustomed to light.

We asked about the timeline. Piglets are weaned at three weeks of age. Then they are moved to the "nursery" building, where they stay for twelve to sixteen weeks. Their next and last move on the farm is to one of the "finishing" buildings, where they are fattened to a market weight of 250 to 280 pounds by the time they reach twenty-five weeks of age. Then it's off to the slaughterhouse. Many hog farms these days handle only one of these life stages—either birth (farrowing), or the nursery, or finishing—but Don's farm houses them all.

Young hogs in a pen in one of the finishing buildings.

"What kind of cycle are the sows on?" we asked.

After a sow's piglets are weaned at three weeks, she is allowed seven days off, then she is impregnated again. She spends the 114 days of her pregnancy in a metal "gestation crate" in a building that's just for pregnant sows, with rows and rows of such crates. A sow's complete cycle of pregnancy, nursing, and rest is 142 days. That works out to 2.6 litters per year.

The small farms we visited operate on a two-litters-per-year cycle, allowing each sow 137 more days each year of either nursing or reproductive rest.

As we approached the last room we were to visit, Don hesitated. We had to climb up onto a wooden platform to get into the building.

He said, "Well, there's blood up here. I don't know if you want to see that or step in it." He said someone had bought a hog and wanted it slaughtered before he took it away.

I asked how it was done, and he said with a captive bolt stunner, a gun that shoots a seven-inch steel cylinder into the animal's brain.

Don was right, there was a lot of blood, but it was dried. We just stepped around it.

I asked him what happened when the pigs were finished and ready for slaughter. Since they're grouped by age, one whole room is moved out at once. He said they get movable plastic walls and make a corridor right from the room into a truck. Then the pigs are herded onto the truck and are driven to a slaughterhouse, or processing plant, where they walk in as pigs and come out as wrapped cuts of meat.

We had to go so Sara Kate could catch a train back to school. As we climbed into the truck, I thanked Don again for letting us come. I thanked him for sharing with us earlier what he had said about the challenges of farming, how the prices for their products keep going down, while expenses go up. He said that in his county, in the last ten years, the amount of agricultural land has decreased because of farmers selling land to home developers. But in spite of this, the amount of agricultural production has increased due to increases in efficiency. For hogs, that means less space per hog, less time between litters, less food for sows, more automation, fewer minutes spent checking on them.

Don asked about the book we were working on, and we all laughed that neither farming nor writing pays very much. But I thought about the hefty new pickup truck we were riding in. We drove by Don's house and he pointed it out. A two-story brick, nice, new. A big house, by my standards. In the fields beyond it were the long, low chicken buildings, very similar to the pig buildings.

"See, I live near the chickens; the smell isn't that bad," he offered, as if that proved it.

He told us that the land his house is on has increased in value in the last ten years to more than $2 million, that the farm itself is worth much more. He told us too about the beach house, the mountain house, and the lake house he shares with his brother, dad, and uncle, the co-owners of the farm.

Tens of thousands of Tyson broilers are raised in each warehouselike building.

But wait ... he'd spent most of the first interview telling us how tough it is to keep the farm profitable. Okay, maybe all this is balanced by a tremendous debt. But still,

if they're able to live as if they're rich, what's the difference?

I looked over at Don as he talked and noticed for the first time the fine lines on his cheeks. Working outside will do that, or troubles, or just middle age.

"How do you feel about us using your name or the name of the farm in the book?" I asked.

"Well, I'd rather you didn't," he said.

"That's fine, we don't need to," I told him.

We rode in silence for a minute or two. I could smell the hogs on my clothes, the ammonia scent of urine and feces. I thought about Sara Kate stinking on the train.

"I want a copy of the book," he said.

"Sure," I replied, not offering to send him one, hoping he would forget by the time it came out.

He pulled into the driveway and parked next to our car. We gathered our stuff and stepped down from the pickup. We traded e-mail addresses with Don and thanked him again.

Part of me wanted to cut the crap and lay it all out, show him pictures of the happy pigs on the small farms, ask him how he really feels deep down about his pigs' comfort. I wanted to know what he would say.

But we didn't have time, and I wasn't sure about asking. We had already gotten far more from him that I had ever hoped. He has his perspective, and he's already explained it. His bottom line, he said, is efficiency.

Chickens Packed Tight

What does the clucking of 20,000 chickens sound like? Most modern-day chicken farmers could tell you.

Unfortunately, the carefree yard chicken of children's books and movies, scratching in the dirt and pecking for seeds with its flock, is a rare find in America today.

REFLECTIONS ON A HOG FARM

Our visit to the huge hog farm brought up a lot of conflicting feelings in me. On one hand, I was even more stunned by the sheer vastness of it than I had expected to be. Mile upon mile of land—before we were even within sight of the farm headquarters—all belonged to the same person. It just didn't make sense. How can one person effectively oversee such an immense expanse of land? With so much to care for, it would be impossible to manage it responsibly.

But on the other hand, our interview with Don unearthed far more common ground between us than I'd anticipated. Before we spoke, I was so nervous I could barely pry myself out of the car. What if he yelled at us, denounced our crazy hippie ways? What if things got really ugly? When he was late meeting us, I became convinced this was a terrible idea. "Let's just leave," I said urgently. "Quick, before they see us!" But fortunately, Mom wisely ignored me. As it turned out, in the end I was glad we stayed. I realized that although we were coming from two very different perspectives, there were some things we both understood.

For one thing, before our visit, I'd imagined a farm of that size as an evil giant gleefully stomping out quaint family farms right and left. And, as Don told us, it's true that the average farm size is only 172 acres, a mere thousandth of their sprawling monolith. But what I didn't know is that even the biggest farms, like his, aren't the winners in this situation. In fact, they're being victimized by an even larger beast. Just a handful of integrators—nationwide corporations such as Tyson and Perdue—tightly control even the largest and most powerful farm operations, like Don's.

After visiting Don's farm, I realized that owners of factory farms are not evil. They aren't operating these systems for the fun of being cruel. But neither are they blameless, for they have the option of making different choices. Still, to a large extent, they are pawns in a larger game.

As Don expressed, most of his business is a desperate struggle to cut a profit and stay afloat. The best way he knows to do this is the way everyone around him does it, the way nearly all modern agricultural advice tells him to do it. I can hardly fault him for not thinking outside of the box.

Perhaps I was being too soft, but although I was sickened by the torn landscape and the long, low sheds, I couldn't be mad at Don. I would make different decisions if I were in his situation, but I can't fault him too much for being a businessman or for making the decisions that are expected of him. Not everyone has the drive or the gumption to step beyond that.

The real bad guy here is the system itself. And we, the customers, are the ones who control that. Now, more than ever, I see that we live in a capitalist system, where money is paramount. Farmers produce what is profitable. But we, the customers, determine what that is, based on what we are willing to spend money on. As long as people keep buying cheap, mass-produced food, factory farms like Don's will continue to be the most profitable. Change will come when we demand it, when farmers can earn a profit by producing a quality-made, ethical product. That is when it will happen, and not before.

—Sara Kate

More than 11,000 adult chickens are packed into each breeder shed.

Chickens these days are raised in metal warehouselike buildings longer than a football field. Some are sold as meat, some lay eggs for the breakfast table, and some lay eggs to make more chickens.

Chickens we eat are called broilers. They live on the floor of long metal buildings on a covering of sawdust that mixes with their feces. Each building, called a shed or a house, holds 20,000 to 30,000 birds. These windowless sheds are lined up side by side, one after another, holding sometimes hundreds of thousands of birds on one farm.

More than 5 billion broiler chickens are slaughtered for food in the United States every year.[13]

Chickens that make fertile eggs for hatching are called breeders. About 10 percent of the birds in a breeder shed are roosters, that mate with the hens. These chickens live on the floor of huge warehouselike buildings, just like broilers do, except roosting boxes are provided for the egg laying. A moving belt under the roosting boxes carries the eggs to a room at the end of the building, where they are collected and stored. Every three days, a batch of eggs is sent to a hatchery. When the

chicks hatch, they'll be delivered to a broiler shed to be raised as fresh chicken meat.

Hens that lay infertile eggs for people to eat also live in long metal sheds with almost no windows. But they don't live on the floor. They live in long rows of cages, called battery cages. The rows of cages are stacked one atop another, like a high-rise apartment building.

The inside of the egg factory we visited was a lot like the inside of a supermarket, with row after row of long aisles. As you walk down an aisle in a grocery, you pass floor-to-ceiling shelves of groceries. Walking down an aisle in an egg factory, you pass floor-to-ceiling rows of caged hens.

These hens are called layers. Their eggs are called table eggs, to distinguish them from fertile eggs meant for hatching.

An escaped hen inside an egg factory for a major grocery store chain.

Chickens with different roles are usually kept on different farms. A farm may have broilers, breeders, or layers, but usually not all three.

Corporate Chickens

Most broiler and breeder chickens in the United States are owned by eight big corporations, which are called vertical integrators. These include companies you might have heard of, such as Tyson, Perdue, and Pilgrim's Pride. Tyson is the biggest chicken producer in the world.

A vertical integrator such as Tyson owns the chickens and pays different farmers to breed them and to raise them for slaughter. The farmers own the sheds though, and the land that the sheds are on. The vertical integrator provides the feed for the chickens. The chicken farmers we talked to did not even know what was in their chickens' feed.

As you may have read in chapter two, most broiler farms are part of a complex of broiler farms, all within a fifty-mile radius of a central feed mill, hatchery, and a meatpacking plant, where the broilers are slaughtered, cut up, and packaged. When a broiler shed is ready for new chicks, workers hired by the vertical integrator—Tyson, for example—will deliver the chicks from the hatchery to the broiler shed in cardboard boxes—a hundred chicks per box. All the sheds on a given broiler farm will be filled with chicks in one day, so all the birds are the same age. In fact, all the birds on a given route of several farms are the same age.

As with most livestock raised for food in the United States, the main objective of the vertical integrators is profit. Everything is organized to reduce the cost of labor and materials.

The Chickens That Lay Our Breakfast Eggs

In general, the companies that provide eggs for people to eat are not the same companies that provide chicken meat. Tyson, the biggest broiler company, does not do table eggs. There are exceptions, such as Pilgrim's Pride, which produces both table eggs and fresh chicken meat.

But in general, table eggs are produced by companies that have only one location, only one factory. The owner of the company works at that site. The company does not have contracts with off-site farmers. So in that way, egg producers are structured very differently from broiler-chicken companies such as Tyson and pork companies such as Smithfield, which contract with farmers to raise their animals.

We visited a breeder farm, a broiler farm, and a layer farm. All chickens on industrial-sized farms are crowded. But if chickens had a competition to see who was the most miserable, I believe those that lay table eggs would win. They are the only chickens that live in cages, and the cages are not very pleasant.

In the following three sections, we describe our visits to these three different chicken farms. Read for yourself and see what you think.

DROPPING IN ON 38,000 BREEDER CHICKENS

I left Gary Davis a message to ask if we could visit his chicken farm. He called back the same day. He was polite, but hesitant. What did we want? How did we get his name? He has to be careful about "biosecurity." A germ could wipe out both sheds of breeders, a year's investment. Had we been around any birds, any birds at all? I explained who referred him to us and assured him we hadn't been around any birds.

Gary has two different kinds of chicken sheds. He contracts with Tyson to raise broilers and to house breeders that provide fertile eggs for a nearby Tyson hatchery. The broilers, he said, had all reached market age a week ago and been crated up and trucked to the processor. There they would be slaughtered and packaged as fresh chicken breasts, legs, and thighs to be sold in grocery stores. But we could see the breeder sheds, he supposed. How about Sunday at 2:00?

Sunday was a typical Carolina December day—cold, gray, and drizzly. But there was a little break in the clouds. Maybe the sun would show itself later.

We drove for an hour out into the country and finally found the road, a dead-end rural lane where Gary's dad raised broilers before him. Unlike the pork farmers we had visited, Gary lives in a modest home that looks like it's been there for a while. As we eased down the gravel road past his house, three long metal sheds came into view when the road petered out—the breeder sheds.

An automated chicken shed.

Each is a metal building 42 by 500 feet, more than one and a half times the length of a football field. They looked very much like the metal sheds that housed the hogs we had visited, and again I thought of a concentration camp.

We pulled up to the first shed and stopped. Gary was waiting. He was younger than I had thought, friendly looking, wearing jeans and a sweatshirt.

"Now *how* did you get my name?" he asked again.

We reminded him, and chatted about our mutual acquaintance for a minute or two. Then our attention turned to the sheds. These breeder sheds are new, he explained. The old ones were several miles away, and the constant driving was hard. The broiler sheds are still at the old location. He seemed proud of the new sheds: they have all the latest in chicken technology. While his chickens belong to Tyson, the sheds are his.

As the biggest chicken producer in the world, Tyson owns the majority of chickens in the United States. They have contracts with the farmers who breed, hatch, and raise their chickens. Driving down the rural back roads of this area, every big chicken shed has a "Tyson" sign out front.

The Control Room

Gary had already told us on the phone that we couldn't go into the chickens' part of the sheds because of biosecurity concerns. We could only go in the control room, which has big windows facing the chickens. When inspectors come from Tyson, they have to wear full-body biosecurity suits to go in with the birds. Gary and his three helpers can regularly go in without suits to pull out the dead hens and to check the automatic food and water dispensers.

"Because we know where we've been," he explained. They haven't been around other birds that could be sick.

Gary held the door for us to enter the control room of the shed. The room was mostly bare and immaculate. It had concrete floors and glass windows providing a view of the full length of the shed. The windows revealed a sea of white chickens with red combs and wattles—thousands of chickens disappearing into the distance.

"These are special chickens," Gary said.

"They are bred to make eggs that will grow into the tastiest possible fresh meat. They have everything they need."

Sara Kate and I peered through the windows of the control room, mesmerized. The chickens were elbow to elbow, like French fries crammed in a paper holster. The closest ones were right up against the glass, and they were fascinated with the activity in the control room, craning their necks and turning their heads to see us. Dozens of light-brown eyes followed our every move, their stares disrupted by their jostling neighbors. Red combs and wattles jiggled as each one jockeyed for position. I was surprised that they seemed so curious. I thought chickens were supposed to be dumb.

Thousands of breeder chickens in a single shed.

Some Hens Have Blowouts

These breeder sheds, Gary told us, each hold 11,500 hens and 1,200 roosters, minus the three to five hens that die every day. The hens, Gary said, have "blowouts" during their peak egg-laying months. A blowout is when a hen drops dead from the stress of laying so many eggs. The chickens arrive at twenty-one weeks of age, start laying at twenty-three weeks, and stay for another forty weeks. Each hen lays on average 170 eggs during that time. If four hens a day drop dead, then blowout takes about 10 percent of the hens.

Gary said he wanted to "clear up one thing that people talk about—what happens to the dead chickens. They are incinerated."

What happens to the surviving chickens after they've spent forty weeks in the shed and are laying fewer and fewer eggs? A company from Georgia comes in and catches them all. The birds are trucked off to the next stage, a chicken-canning factory. They're too old and tough to be marketed as fresh meat, so their flesh is sold in those little cans that look like tuna cans.

Broilers Are Even More Crowded in Order to Keep Them Still

Although the breeder chickens we were watching seemed jammed together, they are not nearly as crowded as the broiler sheds, Gary said. Each broiler shed, he explained, holds 30,000 chickens—more than twice the number of breeder chickens—in the same-sized shed.

I was astonished; I thought I'd heard him wrong. I looked again through the window. Each bird was up against another bird on every side. How could you fit more?

Gary explained, "You don't want the broilers running around. It makes them lose weight."

Broilers, after all, are sold by the pound, so weight is money.

Gary said you need the breeders, the ones we were watching, to be more "comfortable" so they'll breed. And the breeders are bigger. The hens weigh around nine pounds and the roosters twelve, so they need more room. But the more-crowded broilers are slaughtered at about six pounds. Still, these breeders were hardly "running around." Most of the ones we could see were so tightly packed they could barely move. Some could not even find the air space to extend their necks.

As we peered through the windows at the ocean of chickens, Gary explained some of the automated mechanisms inside the shed. Above the chickens, there were three long pipes that ran the length of the shed. One was a food dispenser, in the center. Two were water dispensers, on either side of the food pipe. Each of the two water pipes had little dishes suspended every foot or two. The dishes attached to the food pipe were bigger. Water is available all day, but the food is lowered only once a day, at 4:30 in the morning, for a brief period. They eat 3,500 pounds of food at a time. "We don't have any idea what's in the food. It's a mix that Tyson makes up," Gary said.

Hungry All the Time

These breeders are the same genetic stock as broilers—since they are the parents of the broilers. Broilers are bred to be very hungry and to eat continuously, so that they will gain as much weight as possible, especially in the breast, the most expensive cut of meat. Broilers have food available all the time. They gain so much weight in the breast that many of them are unable to walk by the time they are slaughtered at six or seven weeks of age.

Yet the breeders are kept alive for more than a year, long enough to grow to maturity. Why don't they have weight problems that cripple them? Because they are fed only once a day. Some people speculate that breeders are probably hungry most of the time, since their genes are telling them to eat, eat, eat.

Antibiotics, but Not Hormones

The breeder chickens are not given hormones. "Everybody thinks they are," Gary commented, "but they're not."

They do get antibiotics daily in their drinking water as a general preventive.

"Sometimes they get mouth lesions, because of the stress," Gary told us.

The mouth sores are treated with something that looks like iodine, added to the drinking water.

Gary's chickens get shots against various kinds of chicken diseases before they're placed in the breeder sheds at twenty-one weeks of age. How do you give shots to more than 12,000 chickens at once? They are hung by their feet on a carousel.

Gary said that a yard chicken at a small farm or a country home comes across so many diseases outside that it builds up a natural immunity. But the breeder chickens sealed inside the shed—they never go out and only clean people come in—are not exposed to anything. And so, Gary said, they have no natural immunity. Any little thing could wipe out the whole 12,700 in a shed.

She Packs 9,000 Eggs a Day by Hand

In addition to the food and water pipes, there were also two rows of roosting boxes running the length of the shed extending farther than we could see. They were elevated off the floor, and the hens coming and going from the roosting boxes did have room to flap their wings and stretch a bit.

The hens are trained to lay their eggs in the roosting boxes. To train them, Gary walks through the shed and shoos the new hens into the boxes, shooing the roosters toward the floor area between the two rows of roosting boxes. Each hen lays on average one egg per day. A narrow belt runs under the roosting boxes and carries the eggs into the control room. The boxes are closed at night so the hens won't poop on the belt. Any stain on an egg will cause an infection in the egg and keep it from hatching. The belt can be turned on and off, like the wide belt at a store's cash register that moves the items toward the cashier.

Gary's wife stands at one of the tables in the control room for six hours every day and takes eggs off the belt—that's 9,000 eggs

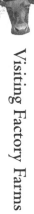

in each shed. She has three employees to help. They place the eggs into molded trays that are then stacked and stored in a small room off the side of the control room. These eggs are all fertile. Every three days, the eggs are trucked to a Tyson hatchery, where they will hatch into baby chicks.

When they are one day old, they are moved from the hatchery to a farmer who has broiler sheds and a Tyson contract. They grow for seven to eight weeks in the broiler sheds, until they weigh about six pounds. Then they are slaughtered and packaged as fresh Tyson chicken for grocery stores.

Who's the Culprit?

Some of Gary's hens, though, lay their eggs on the floor instead of in the roosting boxes. Gary said hens are creatures of habit. Once a hen has started laying on the floor, you can't train her not to. But who did it? In a seething mass of 11,500 hens, it's hard to find the culprits. He, or someone, has to walk through the shed every day and pick the stray eggs off the floor. These eggs are stained or cracked and no good.

The floors in Gary's breeder sheds are made of rounded plastic slats that are much easier on the chickens' legs and feet than the old type of flooring. Gary showed us a sample slat. He's proud of the new development.

The Combs Are Trimmed

Gary said his roosters have their combs trimmed when they're just one day old. Otherwise, the combs would be so long and dangly that they'd get caught in something. The blood would make the other chickens peck the injury relentlessly.

The roosters also have their "claws" trimmed, Gary said, or else they would scratch the hens when they mate and the hens would get infections. (According to a number of agricultural documents, it's actually the toes and not the claws that are trimmed.)

A Haze of Fecal and Feather Dust

There was a haze in the air that kept us from seeing the far end of the shed. What was it?

Gary said, "Dust."

"Yes, dust, but what kind of dust?"

Poultry journals say it's feather particles, fecal particles, ammonia particles, and microorganisms. Gary told us that the feces lie where they fall, under the slatted floor, for a whole year between cleanings. So it would make sense that some of the haze was fecal dust.

What Do You Do with a Year's Worth of Stinky Poop?

Gary says people complain about chickens stinking, but when they're in a closed up shed, they don't really stink all that much.

On the annual poop-cleaning day, though, look out. "That's when it really stinks," said Gary. "When these chickens go to market, we'll have to tear this house completely apart and clean it out. We use formaldehyde, it kills everything."

"What do you do with the chicken feces after the yearly cleaning?" we asked.

"We spray the litter on our fields. We have to keep soil samples. It tells you how many pounds of litter you can put out per acre so you're not creating runoff. If your land starts getting too much phosphorus or nitrates or potash, you cut back on your litter output." Soil testing is mandatory now in North Carolina, but only for some nutrients, not all.

Farmers spray the feces onto their fields because it's the only thing they can do with it legally, other than keep it in a waste lagoon or in covered-up piles. When a lagoon is full, the only way to empty it is by spraying it on fields. Runoff and evaporation from both sprayed fields and lagoons can pollute air and water with fecal bacteria, ammonia, and an overload of nitrates and phosphates. The nutrient overload can be dangerous to people as well as to ecosystems.

The Neighbors Just Don't Understand

Gary says greenhorns move out to the country thinking it's going to be all "wildflowers and honeysuckle." They move in next door, and then they're offended by the smell, even though Gary and his family and the chickens have been here all along. What did the neighbors think they were moving next to?

"One of the neighbors called the environmental people and complained about us using pesticides. We don't even use pesticides. There are no bugs in here."

The neighbors just don't understand modern chicken farming. They don't understand the modern advances, the closed sheds, the control room, or the technology.

"They think you're out here getting dirty, but this is what we do. This is what chicken farming is today. You don't have anyone running around feeding chickens out of a bucket. I don't ever have to touch the chickens, other than ... well, never."

We asked Gary if he ever eats these eggs. He doesn't. His family buys eggs at the grocery. He says these "taste too eggy," the taste is too strong. A store-bought egg has a milder, more pleasant taste, in his opinion.

Time to Go ...

Sara Kate and I apologized for staying so long and thanked Gary for telling us so much. We both shook his hand. But as we started to go, he suddenly became more talkative. He wanted to show us the egg-storage room, to explain how the humidity and temperature have to be precisely controlled. He wanted us to see the control panel for the chickens' environment. It was an electronic box on the wall, providing digital readouts of temperatures in various places in the shed, as well as humidity and air pressure.

The sheds don't need heating, he explained, with all those chicken bodies. But they do need ventilation in summer. Cooling is provided by an evaporation system in the walls near the control room, and there are big fans at the other end to pull the cooled air down the length of the shed. In the summer, he said, the haze disappears because of the air current generated by the fans. You can see the chickens' feathers ruffling in the steady breeze.

Would You Rather
Be Independent of Tyson?

I asked him if he'd prefer to operate without Tyson, as an independent. No, he said. He wouldn't be able to stay in business without Tyson. They pay him the same, regardless of the market.

"These facilities are very expensive. You couldn't build one unless you were guaranteed a return. We had to sign—well, we wanted to sign—a seven-year contract with Tyson. The chicken market could hit rock bottom and I'd still get the same return on my chickens. Basically, if you're a good grower, you'll do all right. If you have a problem, they'll put you on an intensive management program and be down here every day telling you what to do."

Tyson pays him per egg, although he wouldn't say how much.

But *is* he guaranteed a return? According to the Raleigh *News and Observer*, Tyson can cancel any North Carolina farmer's contract with only thirty days' notice. In that case, he would be stuck with the payments for the expensive buildings with no income whatsoever. This is one reason North Carolina is so popular with meatpacking companies such as Tyson: the state provides little legal protection for contract farmers.

We walked outside to leave and Gary followed, asking about this book. He was hoping to get a copy. "My children might want to see it," he said.

He takes pride in his state-of-the-art technology, and I can see his point of view. He runs a shipshape operation. Gary seems like a capable and conscientious factory manager, if you look at the chickens as production units, or food units, as most people do. He's up at the crack of dawn and works seven days a week. Tyson must regard Gary as one of its very best providers.

Confused Again

We thanked Gary again and got into the car. As we made our way out the long gravel drive, I looked back through the cold drizzle at Gary, standing by his pickup, his sweatshirt getting wet. I felt the same confusion I did after leaving Don's hog farm. I liked Gary and felt grateful for his willingness to talk to us. He had nothing to gain by being so open with us.

Part of me wanted to reward his generosity by sharing and affirming his perspective: that his sheds represent the cutting edge of chicken technology and that he's helping to feed a hungry nation.

Part of me thought about the debt he has shouldered to support a rich corporation that many people feel exploits its farmers and its meatpackers. Gary grew up in a business that has morphed into something altogether different from what it was when his family started out, a change he has little control over.

Another part of me thought about the 38,000 breeder chickens, sealed inside the three long metal sheds with the latest digital readouts.

Who is the most powerless player in this scenario? Who suffers the most? Who, most of all, needs some kind of advocate? I don't know. But for now, I lean to the chickens.

VISITING A TYSON BROILER FARM: 72,000 CHICKS ARRIVE IN CARDBOARD BOXES

We arrived at Frank McAuley's chicken farm a few minutes early and parked near the chicken buildings. Although it was New Year's Day, the sun was hot, and I opened the door to let some cool air in while we waited. A stink wafted in, and I was glad I hadn't worn our coat so I wouldn't have to wash it again. This was our third visit to a factory farm, and I'd learned how the smell permeates everything.

After a couple of minutes, Frank and his eleven-year-old son pulled up in a pickup truck. He had the same stocky shape as the other factory farmers we'd interviewed, solid and compact, on the short side. He also had the same warm and gentle southern manners, welcoming us to his farm and introducing his young "assistant." He had no reason to give us an hour, nothing to gain. But he hadn't hesitated at all when I'd asked to visit.

Frank had told me on the phone that he's up at daybreak every morning and works until "dark-thirty" every evening, so Sara Kate and I didn't waste much time before jumping to my list of questions.

Frank has three warehouselike buildings for raising broiler chickens, chickens destined for the dinner table. These buildings are typically called sheds or houses. As most chicken farmers do, Frank works under a contract with a meatpacking corporation, in this case Tyson. A Tyson contract farmer like Frank has the costly sheds constructed at his own expense, but Tyson owns all the birds and provides all their food and medication. Each of Frank's three sheds holds 24,000 chickens, which add up to 72,000 chickens on the farm at any one time. Some of Tyson's farmers have more sheds than Frank, some with 100,000 broilers at one time.

Frank receives the 72,000 chicks to fill all three houses on one day, sent from a Tyson hatchery when they're one day old. They arrive in cardboard boxes on a tractor-trailer truck, packed a hundred chicks to the box. They haven't had anything to eat or drink at all when they arrive, having just hatched the day

before. At that age, they weigh only a few ounces, the size of a child's fist.

"When they get here, they're pretty eager for food and water," Frank said.

The boxes are carted into the sheds and the chicks are turned loose on the sawdust-covered floor. Each shed has long food and water pipes running the length of the building, with dispensers at regular intervals.

At one week of age, the broilers had room to move around in the shed.

The chicks stay in Frank's sheds for forty-nine to fifty-six days, until they weigh five-and-one-half to six-and-one-half pounds. Then Tyson workers come to pack the entire flock into crates and take them to a Tyson meatpacking plant, or processor, where they are slaughtered and packaged for the grocery store. After a week or two of vacant sheds, a new flock of chicks arrives in cardboard boxes, and the cycle starts again. Frank goes through five or six cycles each year, for a grand annual total of around 400,000 chickens.

They Go Down in their Legs

Broiler chickens are bred to eat a lot and gain weight fast. Frank said that they weigh sixty-five times more when they leave his sheds than when they arrived. At that rate of growth, a seven-pound human newborn would weigh 455 pounds at eight weeks of age! All baby birds gain weight faster than humans, but even for a bird, that's a very fast rate of growth.

Frank's broiler chickens are hybrids that are bred not only to gain weight fast, but especially to develop heavy breast muscles fast, because the breast is the most expensive cut of chicken meat.

Frank explained that you've got to get the genetics and the feed just right with these hybrids. The breasts can get too big. If that happens, "they'll go down in their legs," said Frank. The extra weight damages their legs and they can't walk. He has to keep the feed adjusted so that doesn't happen.

As we walked toward the chicken sheds for an inside look, I noticed that the three long buildings are clean and well tended on the outside. Each one is 42 by 400 feet, about the length of one and a third football fields. The buildings are perfectly parallel, which seems odd somehow out here in the country where most things are kind of ramshackle and casual. The grounds around them are clipped to a T and immaculate. It looks like a place where someone works every day until dark-thirty.

Later, when the broilers are older, chickens cover the shed from wall to wall.

I Felt Claustrophobic

Frank's son opened the door to the building, pushing a mass of chickens out of the way as we stepped in. The floor was a sea of chickens receding into the hazy distance. The interior was dimly lit, warm, humid, and stinky, almost overwhelming. My glasses fogged and I had to take them off. The air was so thick with white particles of feces and feathers that I was hesitant to take a deep breath.

Approaching slaughter weight, the broilers are crowded.

The floor of the shed was cushiony soft, like walking on thick moss. I wondered what it was. Frank explained that the litter on the floor was a mixture of pine sawdust and feces over a soil floor. He said the litter is scooped out only once every eighteen months, and it was about time for that to happen. So we were walking on eighteen months' worth of poop from more than 100,000 chickens that had lived in that shed during that time. I felt claustrophobic for a few moments, unable to either see clearly or breathe normally. But Frank and his son seemed comfortable, so after a minute or two, I got my glasses squared away and adjusted to the fetid air.

Frank astonished me by saying that he has to walk the entire length of each shed five times every day to check for dead birds. Because the birds are densely packed, it takes five routes per shed to be able to see almost every bird. I understood now what I'd read about the high rates of respiratory ailments in poultry farmers.

Warmed and Fed by Automation

Frank showed us the temperature sensors dangling from the ceiling. The temperature is controlled by a computer in each shed with a control panel mounted on the wall. Each building has ten propane burners suspended six feet or so above the floor. The computer fires up the burners, called brooders, every so often to warm the air.

He showed us the horizontal water pipes about a foot above the floor. Two of them ran the entire length of the shed. Little cuplike water holders sprouted from the water pipes about every twelve inches. Some of the cups were empty and a few chickens were pecking at the tiny drip mechanisms that filled them. But no one seemed to be dropping dead from thirst, so I supposed that was okay.

Heads are crammed around the automatic food dispensers.

The two food pipes, also running the length of the building, had bigger dispensers, each about the size of a dinner plate. All the available space around the dispensers was packed with white heads. A couple of heads were crammed down onto the plate, unable to move in the crush. While Frank was showing us around, the automatic feeder came on and gold pellets poured out of the food pipes into each dispenser. The chickens showed a new burst of attention to the feeders, even though there was food in them before.

Frank said that the food is prepared by Tyson, but other than corn, he doesn't know what's in it. It does contain antibiotics, he acknowledged, until seven to ten days before slaughter. At that time, the chickens are switched to a non-medicated feed so the meat will not have detectable levels of antibiotics.

Raw, red bottoms attract pecks from the other chickens.

Each Chicken Has the Space of One Sheet of Paper

Since each shed is 42 by 400 feet and holds 24,000 chickens, each chicken has 0.7 square feet of floor space. That is the size of one sheet of standard computer paper plus one inch. But the space for each chicken actually works out to a bit less than that, because you have to subtract the space occupied by the food and water pipes running the length of

the building just above the floor, along with the dispensers. I don't know exactly how much floor room they end up with.

In the beginning, when the chicks are tiny, they have ample room to move around. Toward the end of their stay, they get crowded. Very crowded. The crowding reduces costs of course. Heated space is expensive, automated food and water dispensers are expensive. Frank said that the propane bill for the heaters in just one year can be $5,000 per shed. So the more chickens you can cram into the expensive heated and automated space, the more profit you can make.

But the crowding has another purpose: it keeps the chickens from moving around. Immobile chickens will gain more weight than active chickens. Since all fresh meat is priced by weight, heavier cuts of chicken make more money for Tyson in the grocery store.

Because there are too many chickens for them to establish a pecking order, aggression is common. Many of the chickens had raw bottoms, I don't know why. Maybe from sitting on eighteen months' worth of feces, if they ever sit. But the bare, red skin seemed to attract the attention of the other chickens. Chickens will peck at anything that draws their attention. And pecked skin just continues to get redder and more raw.

One Spring Flock Was Wild

I asked Frank if pecking is ever a problem in broiler sheds since there are too many birds for them to establish a pecking order. Normally a flock of chickens establish a dominance hierarchy so that everyone knows who's strongest and the weak can stay out of the way. But chickens can't remember more than eighty or ninety individual birds, so it doesn't work in a big shed.

But Frank said that pecking is not usually a big problem, although it was one year. When spring changes to summer, the chickens usually get restless. One spring flock was so wild they pecked all the feathers off each other until none had any feathers left.

"What about piling?" I asked. When chickens are frightened by a loud noise, sometimes they pile up in a corner, smothering the ones on the bottom.

"Oh packing up, you mean," he said. He said that hardly ever happens. But once, one of the lines holding a food pipe broke loose, and the pipe hit the floor. The chickens all ran to one wall in a panic and packed up along the seam where the wall meets the floor. Real quick, Frank ran the length of the wall while leaning over with one arm extended, scooping up chickens and tossing them back into the middle of the floor. He didn't lose a single one.

A Model Tyson Farmer

I was led to call Frank by a farming friend who told us Frank was a "model Tyson farmer."

Said the friend, "If I was going to eat Tyson chicken, I'd eat Frank's." Frank does his best to care for his chickens in a conscientious and responsible way. He is proud of the quality of care they receive.

"These chickens have better living conditions than some people," said Frank, and he means it.

Maybe so, but my mind has to wander around the globe and through history to find people who would make that a true statement.

I don't blame Frank for the crowding. He has lived on a farm all his life. He's middle-aged now, so he has seen the industry transformed. For poultry and hog farmers with big operations, working under contract for a company such as Tyson is about the only option. And when you're under contract, you have to use the corporation's methods.

If a farmer tried to operate independently, he would not be able to produce meat cheaply enough to compete for supermarkets' business. An independent farmer would also have a hard time finding a meatpacking plant to slaughter and package his animals—these plants are all owned by the same corporations that hand out the contracts, such as Tyson, Smithfield, and ConAgra.

The fault lies with the corporate grip on the industry; with a system that values efficiency and profit above all else; and with the government's failure to protect animals, the environment, and the farmers. Government regulations could level the playing field so that all producers had to provide more spacious and humane conditions for farmed animals. As it is now, any farmer who does so is at a financial disadvantage.

Crowding keeps broilers from moving much, enhancing their weight gain.

The World's Largest Is No "Mr. Nice Guy"

Tyson is the number-one chicken producer in the world, slaughtering 35 million broilers each and every week. It's an aggressive company, looking to grow even more. Some of Frank's friends used to raise chickens for Holly Farms. When Tyson bought out Holly Farms several decades ago, Tyson stopped the profit-sharing bonuses that Holly Farms used to hand out to its farmers.

"You don't get to be the world's biggest by being Mr. Nice Guy," said Frank.

A Bonus for Spending Less on Chicken Care

Instead of bonuses, Tyson gives financial rewards to farmers who have below-average expenses per chicken. For example, farmers who use less of the feed provided by Tyson are rewarded. Farmers with above-average expenses per chicken are docked or fined. Because of that policy, Frank put in a new cooling system for the hot Southeast summers. It uses evaporative cooling and tunnel fans. With the new cooling system, "we get bigger chickens using less feed," says Frank, which qualifies him for the Tyson reward. The less of Tyson's materials used per chicken, the bigger the reward.

"Naturally, It's Going to Smell"

Chicken and hog farms are notorious for stinking up neighborhoods. Frank acknowledged that scooping up the litter in the broiler sheds every eighteen months does create a powerful stench. Spreading the litter on his fields does too.

"When you're spraying litter, naturally it's going to smell for a few days," Frank admitted.

But, he said, he has never had a complaint from a neighbor in his decades of farming on this land. Frank also pointed out that he is careful not to pollute with the chicken litter. He said he is "a steward of the land."

"How so?" I asked.

He doesn't spray litter within 100 feet of streams or property lines, which is a government regulation.

He tests the soil for nutrients before spraying the litter to gage how much he can spray. If a farmer applies more nitrogen than his particular grasses or crops can use, then the extra nitrogen is washed out of the soil into streams and rivers, where it causes pollution problems.

In Frank's opinion, sprayed litter is better than chemical fertilizers because it lasts longer and it's "natural."

"People want to get back to nature. I don't know how you can get more natural," he said.

As further evidence of his stewardship, Frank explained that he has plans to put fences along his streams to keep his cattle from trampling the streambeds and to keep manure out of the streams. The fences will be fifty feet from the stream. The soil will filter the cows' waste as it runs downhill to the stream, he said.

On Duty Every Day, Including Holidays

Frank said he likes the lifestyle, although he has to work every day, whether it's Thanksgiving, Christmas, or Easter. Every day he has to do the walk-through of each shed to check for dead birds, which takes quite a while. When there is a problem with the automated pipes and temperature controls, the computer pages him and he has to go sort that out.

Don't Grumble about the Farmer with Your Mouth Full

After we'd covered just about everything, we left the shed and walked back toward my car. I stopped to thank Frank and his son for letting us come and showing us around.

"Is there any last thing you'd like to say to our readers?" I asked him.

He thought for minute. "Yeah," he said. "Don't grumble about the farmer with your mouth full."

Well, I couldn't argue with that. I expect that summed it up for me as well.

VISITING AN EGG FACTORY WITH MORE THAN A MILLION CAGED HENS

We knew that 98 percent of egg-laying hens in the United States live in cages, and we'd seen photos of them on the Internet, but we wanted to see and photograph the cages for ourselves. So we called an egg factory that produces eggs for a major North Carolina grocery store chain. A member of the management, Wesley, invited us to visit on the condition that we not mention him or his company by their real names. Sara Kate and I agreed.

Wesley said his company has around 1.2 million laying hens at any one time. They used to have even more hens than that, but they now keep only five birds in each cage rather than seven. That change is a result of pressure from fast-food companies, who have in turn been pressured by the animal-rights activist group PETA. PETA has pushed hard for laying hens to have more room in their cages.

When we pulled into the parking lot, we could see that the egg factory really had no connection with the word "farm." The only thing farmlike about it was its rural location.

On the front of the building were several loading docks for tractor-trailer trucks and an office door. We went into the office, which was divided into a waiting room, much like a dentist's waiting room, and a separate space for a secretary. A hallway led to other offices.

The secretary paged Wesley, our host. He appeared, wearing a business shirt and tie. Wesley is a businessman, not a farmer. He asked what we wanted to see and we told him: the hens.

We headed out the back door of the waiting room, which opened directly into the egg room. The egg room was the size of a gymnasium, more or less. It was filled with automated machines for washing eggs, loading eggs into molded crates, and moving the eggs from the crates into Styrofoam cartons by the dozen. Around twenty workers were involved with the automated machines. Some of them picked up the Styrofoam cartons from the moving belts and stacked them onto trolleys to be wheeled into a room-sized cooler that opened onto the loading docks. All twenty of the workers in the egg room were young Latin American men.

Table eggs are washed by machine before going into cartons.

DESPERATE IMMIGRANTS TAKE DANGEROUS JOBS

A high proportion of meatpacking workers are immigrants from Latin America. The meatpacking industry has three times the injury rate of any other factory work. Latin American immigrants sometimes have a hard time finding work because they often have little education and speak little or no English, so they wind up taking low-paying, dangerous jobs that no one else wants. The meat industry is happy to have them. Many immigrants are here illegally, so they don't complain about injuries or low wages. Losing a job could force them to return to their country of origin, where they would make even lower wages.

The Air Was Thick with White Particles

We took a quick look at the egg machinery, then passed through the rear door of the egg room into the first of the chicken buildings. At this factory, there are twelve gigantic buildings for the laying hens. Each building is at least as big as a huge supermarket or warehouse, but longer.

As we entered, I was instantly struck

with the foulness of the air. This was my fourth visit to a factory farm, but this was by far the worst air. It reeked of ammonia, which I expected. But worse, the air was thick with white particles, like the finest snow. The smell was worse than the broiler sheds. A layer of white dust covered everything, and it soon covered me and my camera. I knew the dust was a mixture of fecal dust and feather particles and asked Wesley if this was so.

But he said, "No, it's just dust."

As we walked, we left footprints behind like tracks in a dusting of snow or volcanic ash.

As we walked across the front of the first building, we were able to see down each of the many aisles of hens, as though we were walking across the front of a grocery. The aisles were so long and the air so thick, we couldn't begin to see the other end.

Like a Rusted Shipwreck

The laying hens live in long rows of cages made completely of wire. They are called battery cages, battery meaning a series. The rows of cages are stacked four deep, one on top of another. So walking down an aisle was rather like walking down a grocery store aisle, except that the end wasn't visible. And instead of

The end of an aisle. Cages are stacked so feces fall onto the hens below.

cereal boxes and cans on the shelves, there were cages of hens.

The outside of the buildings and the egg machinery in the egg room had looked clean and new, so I was surprised that the hens' cages and the racks holding them looked ancient. They looked corroded, like a rusted shipwreck underwater, with stuff all over them, like some kind of growth. Was the ammonia and hydrogen sulfide in the air causing the metal to corrode? I then realized that at least some of the glop on the cages and corroded racks was feces, with feather particles stuck to it.

Each cage was eighteen by twenty inches and held five hens inside. Each hen had seventy-two square inches, about three-fourths the size of a standard piece of typing paper. Many cages had only four hens. These were cages where an occupant had died and been removed. The cages are all stocked at once,

At the end of each long aisle, belts carry the eggs to the floor. White dust covers everything.

81

and when a hen dies, she is not replaced. I asked Wesley how long the hens stay and he didn't know, but he guessed about two years.

"Longer Fasts Give Superior Results"
I started a walk down one of the aisles in the first building, and Wesley said we should go to the next building. The hens in this building, he said, were undergoing a procedure to make them lay eggs for a longer period, and they were a bit under the weather. Ah.

"A forced molt?" I asked him.

He conceded.

When laying hens stop producing enough eggs, the managers correct the situation with a forced or induced molt. The hens are deprived of food for several days, which forces them to molt or shed their feathers and to stop laying eggs altogether. But the aftereffect is to "rejuvenate the reproductive cycle of the bird." Those that survive the shock tend to lay more eggs for another six months. It saves money for the egg producers because they don't have to replace the hens as often. This practice is discussed in the guidelines from the United Egg Producers (UEP), the professional organization of egg producers in the United States. You can see these guidelines at the UEP Web site, at www.animalcarecertified .com/docs/UEPanimal_welfare_guidelines.pdf.

The United Egg Producers document states, "A fast of 4 to 5 days will usually cause a flock to cease egg production. Longer fasts will usually give superior results, but extreme care must be taken to monitor body weight loss and mortality daily during the fast. ... Feed should be returned when body weights reach no less than 70 percent of the starting weights."[14]

Although this process has been illegal in Great Britain since 1987, it's still legal here in the United States.

What about human health concerns? According to the UEP, "Insufficient research

The top two rows of laying hens at the beginning of an aisle.

has been conducted to develop a conclusive decision on the impact molting may contribute to food safety risks."[15]

The hens in the first building were quiet and still. I asked Wesley how long it had been since they'd been fed. He said he didn't know.

"Ventilation Is Critically Important"
We moved on to the second building. The birds were more animated here. I got out my camera and took a few steps down the aisle, aware of the junk I was breathing, wondering how the birds could stand breathing it day in and day out. Many of the flash photos I took of the length of the aisle look like shots taken during a snowstorm, with white circles in the air—the reflection of the flash off the particles.

The UEP has an official seal of approval they bestow on egg factories that meet their guidelines 100 percent. The egg cartons produced by Wesley's factory sport that seal of approval. Yet the guidelines say, "Poultry houses should be designed to provide a continuous flow of fresh air for every bird. Sufficient ventilation to minimize levels of carbon monoxide, ammonia, hydrogen sulfide, and dust is critically important."[16] There were huge fans installed in the outdoor walls at the end of the each building, but the fans were not on. If they had been on, the air might have been even worse because the settled particles might have become airborne.

Bare Skin and Stripped Feather Shafts
I paused in the aisle to peer into some cages. The hens were more bedraggled than the breeders and broilers we'd seen at other poultry farms. Broilers only live for six to seven weeks before slaughter, so they don't have time for much wear and tear on the feathers.

All of these caged hens had bald areas of red skin, especially the rump and sometimes the breast and neck. Many of the wing and tail feathers were stripped, with only the central shaft remaining.

The bald, red areas on the chest and rump were from friction. Caged hens rub their breast against the wire floor of the cage in an effort to dust bathe, an instinctive activity carried out by most kinds of birds. Birds rub their chests in dust to gather dust into the feathers because the dust kills feather mites—

A more spacious cage, due to the death and removal of one of the hens. All the hens have bald spots and stripped feathers.

although of course there is no dust in battery cages, only wire. As the hens try to bathe, the friction against the wire rubs their feathers off and chafes their skin.

The bare spots on the hens' rumps were from trying to incubate eggs that are no longer present. Again, friction against the wire rubs the feathers off.

The Eggs Travel by Themselves
In years past, on family farms, a hen might lay about 100 eggs per year, but today's laying hens have been bred to lay more. When egg production drops off, forced molting causes it to pick up again. Today's factory hens lay on average one egg per day.

When an egg is laid in a battery cage, it rolls down the sloping wire floor of the cage to a moving belt that runs along in front of each row of cages. At the end of an aisle, the belts descend to a much wider horizontal belt that carries the eggs through the multiple chicken buildings, all the way to the egg room with the automating washing and packing machines. The eggs we saw travel all the way from the hen to the egg room untouched by human hands. This makes a huge difference in labor costs, since more than a million eggs are laid every day at this factory.

Beak Trimming Recommended at Any Age ...for an Outbreak of Cannibalism
I asked Wesley if these birds have their beaks trimmed, which is a standard practice for caged hens. In cages, more aggressive birds may peck continually at weaker birds that are unable to get out of the way. Trimming can reduce the damage caused by pecking. Wesley said he didn't know, but I could see that many of the birds had an upper bill that was much shorter than the lower bill, a sign of previous trimming.

Some egg producers cut both the top and bottom of the bill, or have in the past at least. But since chickens do have tongues in the lower half of the bill, cutting only the top is a bit more considerate.

Beak trimming is performed with a very hot blade. The burning is supposed to somewhat seal off the cut blood vessels.

The United Egg Producers' guidelines provide "Recommendations for a Single-Trim Program" and "Recommendations for a Second-Trim Program."[17]

The first instruction for the single-trim program states, "The beaks of chicks should be trimmed at ten days of age or younger with a precision automated cam activated beak trimmer with a heated blade." Later instructions for the trim program warn that "recently beak trimmed chicks may have difficulty activating watering devices." They also may need extra vitamin K to aid in clotting; that is, to stop the bleeding.

Although a one- or two-trim program is recommended, the UEP document asserts, "Therapeutic beak trimming is recommended at any age if an outbreak of cannibalism occurs."

Who Does the Trimming?

I wondered who does the beak trimming, so I asked Wesley. He said the woman who used to do it did not use a machine, she just eyeballed it. But that was a while back.

The UEP document suggests it be carried out only by "properly trained personnel monitored regularly for quality control." That could be reassuring. Except that the UEP training videos are in English, yet all the workers I saw were Latin Americans. If they had a good mastery of English or had been in this country long, they probably wouldn't be working in an egg factory.

In the Deep Pits under the Cages, I Saw Mounds of Gray Waste

In the industry guidelines, the UEP document I read before our visit said, "Cage configuration should be such that manure from birds in upper cage levels does not drop directly on birds in lower cage levels." So I was surprised to see that in this particular factory, the cages were arranged vertically so that feces from the top birds could rain right down into all the cages below.

Could and did. Many of the hens had brown smears on their backs. The openings in the top and floor of each cage were big enough to allow a fifty cent piece to pass through, so feces fell through easily. Of course it did; there was nowhere else for it to go. It couldn't pile up on top of the cages, or they would quickly be completely covered.

So after the feces was through raining on the hens, where did it wind up?

Under each row of back-to-back battery cages was a long pit, probably ten feet deep. In each pit was a mountain range of gray piled-up feces running the length of the row. The mountain range of poop was at least six feet high in each pit. I asked Wesley how often the poop was cleared out. He said that the waste is removed only when the hens are removed, somewhere between one and two years, depending on when egg production slacks off for the group as a whole.

Okay, so that makes sense. No wonder the air quality in the room was less than ideal.

"When They're Done, We Can Hardly Give Them Away"

We asked Wesley what it's like on the day the hens are taken away. Contract workers come in and push carts up and down the aisles. Given the air in the room and the settled particles that must be stirred up by the carts, I'm guessing the contract workers are probably immigrants who can't find better work and can't make waves.

The UEP guidelines caution that, for the hens, "there is a high risk of bone fractures occurring when they are handled prior to slaughter. Catching appears to be the primary source of injury prior to arrival at the slaughter plant." It seems that constantly producing

eggs with calcium in the shells robs the hens' bones of calcium and weakens them.

To lower the risk of injury when pulling hens from the cages, the UEP recommends grabbing the hens only two at a time, grabbing both legs rather than one, and keeping the hens upright. A hen's breast should be supported "as she is lifted over the food trough." The "catching crew" must be "skillful" and "supervised." The crew should "use the lowest light level possible" while "dropping of hens should be minimized." Sounds like a fun few days in the layer buildings.

It's interesting that the UEP guidelines that tell us how things *should* be done cast so much light on how they *might* be done in the real world of underpaid and hurried workers who may not even understand the language of the training video.

"What happens to the hens after they leave?" we asked Wesley. The hens looked too scrawny to be sold for meat. Wesley confirmed this.

"We can hardly give them away," said Wesley. The contract workers who carry them away dispose of them. He declined to say how.

Our Host

It was interesting to me that our host seemed to have no idea that we might find anything in the egg factory objectionable. Not the particles in the air, not the mounds of feces, not the smell, not the tattered, chafed hens, not the crusty hardware holding up the cages. This surprised me more than anything else we saw, although given the other factory farmers we had already met, it shouldn't have. Being young, male, and a member of the dominant culture in this country, he has other job options. He probably wouldn't be working at the egg factory if he saw it the way we did.

But like the other factory farmers we met, he grew up in the business. As a kid he said he "kept pens with all kinds of chickens."

WHY ARE THE ANIMALS WE EAT EXEMPT FROM ANIMAL PROTECTION LAWS?

The Animal Welfare Act of 1970 and its revisions require that cages for animals be big enough to allow normal movements and social behaviors. Chickens have the same basic needs of all sentient animals. Those needs include the ability to move, to stretch, to rest comfortably, to clean themselves, and to interact.

For chickens, normal behaviors include nesting, dust-bathing, foraging for food, preening of feathers, brooding of eggs and chicks, and interacting with the flock to establish a pecking order, or dominance ranking, so that weaker birds can avoid conflict by staying out of the way.

Yet layers are denied all these instinctive needs. They spend their lives trapped in cramped cages, unable to perform even the most basic self-caring behaviors.

The Animal Welfare Act applies to animals in homes, zoos, pet stores, research labs, and circuses. But animals raised for food are excluded. Why? Because the meat industry has more money, power, and political influence than any of these other animal industries. All too often in this country, money and power can influence legislation through lobbyists and campaign donations.

He grew up with that mindset so aptly summarized by an agricultural professor I spoke with: "To us, it's just meat on the hoof." Farm animals are just meat with legs. Or in this case, egg machines with legs.

Why Is the Egg Factory So Big?

I asked Wesley, "Since this egg factory is not owned by a giant corporation like Tyson or Smithfield, why has it grown so big?"

Wesley said that they can make more money by using automated technology that allows them to keep a million hens. By having automated feeding and watering systems and having belts to move the eggs to the egg room, they can operate with very few employees.

There was no one in the chicken buildings we visited. Only the rustling and clucking of hundreds of thousands of hens.

Beef Cattle, Feedlots, and Slaughter

If slaughterhouses had glass walls, everyone would be a vegetarian.

—Paul McCartney

Calves that are destined to become regular beef have a relatively easy time of it, at least in the beginning. Many beef calves get to spend their first six months at pasture—with mom and nursing! The cattle ranches where they live are probably the least-changed part of the meat industry, although thirty years ago, the calves stayed at pasture for a full two years. These ranches are often owned by families or individuals.

Although beef cattle spend their first six to seven months in relative freedom, the time is not entirely carefree. Those that are headed for a feedlot are branded and castrated during the first six months, neither with anesthesia. During branding, a red-hot iron is pressed hard against the calf's bare skin for a full five seconds. Not so pleasant! When a calf is castrated, he is pinned down, then his scrotum is sliced open with a knife. The testicles are grabbed, one in each hand, and pulled out until the sperm cord breaks free. If it won't break, it's cut. Many European countries require anesthesia for this extremely painful

procedure, but the U.S. government does not. And so in America no painkillers are used.

After six months of roaming the range with mom, the young cow is weaned from its mother. This is an upsetting time: the mother cow moos loudly and sulks, while the calf may get sick. But if he's going to survive on a feedlot, the youngster must learn to eat an entirely new diet of corn and perhaps alfalfa hay. Cows' digestive systems are designed for grasses after weaning. The corn diet is so unnatural to the young cow and so distressing to his digestive system that it's likely to cause ulcers or liver problems. The diet might kill him if not for the hefty daily dose of antibiotics mixed in with the feed—although some would argue that the medicines have little benefit.

Beef cattle are allowed to spend their first half-year at pasture.

HASTA LA VISTA, BABY

Around the time the young cows are trained to their new diet, they are shipped off to a feedlot to be fattened for slaughter. They are usually sent by truck because there are no government regulations on how often they must be fed and watered on trucks. Train travel, on the other hand, is regulated, so it's more expensive.

A feedlot can be a massive operation, with as many as 100,000 young cows. Most are steers or castrated males since females are used for breeding. When the animals arrive at the feedlot, they are grouped in pens. Even though there may be 900 animals in a one-acre pen, each animal has enough space to walk around. He can also interact with other cows. It's better than a cage, but not exactly paradise. Grass cannot survive the trampling, so the ground is a muck of urine and manure. The air is filled with the stink of ammonia and feces. The animals become caked with manure, and some of the manure finds its way into the feeding troughs. With usually dirt roads between the pens and open sewage on the ground, the feedlot is like a crowded city before the days of bathrooms, back when chamber pots were emptied onto the streets.

The young cows spend six to eight months gaining lots of weight at the feedlot. They are fed three times a day, still mostly corn. The unhealthy corn diet causes their muscles, which will be sold as beef, to become marbled with fat—which the American public prefers. Corn also gives the meat a particular taste that Americans have come to like.

But the feed contains other added ingredients that will raise your eyebrows, such as "protein supplements." These protein supplements can be chicken feathers, chicken feces, and ground-up animals in pellet form—the remains of pigs, horses, and chickens. Not long ago, cows at feedlots were fed protein pellets made from dead cows, sheep, cats, and dogs, until those sources were outlawed in 1997. Cows were eating cows, until an outbreak of mad cow disease in Great Britain. It was discovered that cows get the mad cow virus by eating other cows that were infected. And when people eat an infected cow, they get sick too. The virus causes swelling of the brain and, sooner or later, death.

Oddly, cattle blood is still allowed in the protein pellets fed to cows.

Slaughter

When feedlot steers are about fourteen months old, they are considered finished. They are then sent by the truckload to a big slaughterhouse or meatpacking plant. They walk into the building as living cows; they come out as refrigerated pieces wrapped in plastic. What happens inside to bring this about? If you're thinking that the steers are peacefully "put to sleep" with gas or an injection, well, that would be nice. But that's not how it happens.

The arriving cattle are herded off the truck into a holding pen. After a few hours, they are hustled into a passageway that narrows down into a single-file chute. As they amble along the chute, they come to a ramp that leads into the building. Indoors now and still moving through the narrow chute, each steer passes over a bar that he straddles as he keeps walking. The floor begins to slant downward, but the bar doesn't. It turns into a conveyor belt and now the steer is being carried along on the belt, his feet off the ground. Because the cows are smeared with manure from the feedlot and from the holding pen, the conveyor belt is smeared with feces too.

On a catwalk that crosses over the belt stands a worker holding a stun gun. When a steer passes underneath him, he leans over and puts the stun gun to the animal's forehead. It fires a steel bolt about seven inches long and the width of a thick pencil into the cow's head. This process is called captive bolt stunning. If the first shot doesn't knock the animal unconscious, then a second shot is fired. But the animals are moving along at a rate of about one every ten seconds, so there isn't much time. Sometimes, the cow is not knocked out.

After the shot, a chain is wrapped around one of the steer's back feet and he is hoisted into the air by one foot, to get him away from the feces on the belt and the floor. The chain is attached to a trolley that carries him along into the "bleeding" area, where his

Sara Kate and a young beef cow
on a small family farm.

WE VISITED FOUR SMALL FARMS WHERE THE COWS ARE PASTURED AND GRASS FED UNTIL SLAUGHTER

There is a strong and growing movement in the United States in support of pastured beef, or grass-fed beef. The meat of a grass-fed cow has a lower fat content than corn-fed beef and less marbling. It also tastes different. Although people in the cattle industry say that Americans prefer the fatty, smooth taste of corn-fed beef, many people we met in our investigations said they prefer the taste of grass-fed beef. They said the taste varies, depending on what kind of grass the cow has eaten.

At any rate, there is no question that grass-fed cows are happier and vastly healthier than corn-fed cows. Grass-fed meat and milk is also healthier for the consumer. You can read more about grass-fed cows in chapter four of this book.

On one small family farm we visited, we were invited to walk out into the pasture and mingle with the cows as they ate from a few

bales of hay stacked in the pasture. I was surprised that the cows were friendly. A couple of them followed us around and seemed to want their heads scratched, nudging our hands with their heads, like a dog will when he wants a rub. When we stopped walking, they stood next to us. When we moved, they moved with us. A couple of them were downright pretty, with heads of curly white hair. I could see myself getting attached to a cow like that. I reflected that the cows had no idea what lucky lives they led—if only they knew. Although their luck was not infinite ...

The wife of the family, which includes a house full of children, told us that their cows are bottle-fed as calves, explaining their friendliness. She said the whole family cries when one of the cows goes off to be slaughtered by someone else and comes back home wrapped in packets for the freezer. I can understand why.

—Sally

throat is cut to drain out all the blood. If he is still awake here—that is, if he is trying to raise his head or moaning—then he is shot again by a second stunner. As the animal moves along hanging by one foot, he is skinned, and then his rectum is tied shut to keep the feces inside. Next he is eviscerated—his internal organs are removed. This is done very carefully in order to keep feces off of his muscles, which will be sold as beef.

Student Voice:
Anna, Age 17

I first became a vegetarian to challenge myself, and also because I was opposed to eating dead animals, in addition to health reasons. My sister told me about a video she had watched in biology about how the fat from meat lingers in your blood vessels. Two years ago, after reading *Fast Food Nation*, my reasoning changed to a strong opposition of the abuses of the animals and the slaughterhouse workers. Plus, I have never liked the concept of having animals killed—usually inhumanely.

WHAT'S IN THAT DANGLING MEAT?

At a large processing plant where the dangling carcasses move along the processing line at a rapid clip, it is not possible to get rid of all the manure that came in on the animals' coats. Even though the bodies are suspended above the dirty floor as they move briskly from one worker to the next, the manure gets on the workers' gloves, on the knives, and on the saws. When the cow pieces leave the slaughterhouse for the grocery store, there will be some small amount of manure mixed in with the beef. That can't be helped. So they try to disinfect the manure to kill the dangerous germs in it.

I CALLED DR. TEMPLE GRANDIN TO ASK HER MORE ABOUT SLAUGHTER

One scientist, a remarkable woman named Dr. Temple Grandin, has been largely responsible for redesigning the slaughter process for cattle to reduce the amount of stress and the amount of pain experienced by the animals. She has published more than 300 papers in professional journals on the management of livestock. Before she became involved, a large proportion of cows were not being killed or knocked unconscious by the first shot. A large number were even surviving long enough to be skinned alive.

I read in my research for this book that 95 percent of cows going through a slaughter conveyor belt must be killed or knocked unconscious on the first shot in order for the processing plant to pass government inspections. I called Dr. Grandin at Colorado State University to ask her if this means that 5 percent, or one in twenty, can legally pass through alive to the hanging, bleeding, and skinning phase. If cows are being stunned at a rate of one every ten seconds, then a 5 percent failure rate would mean that an animal gets by the stunner still awake every four minutes.

She insisted that this no longer happens, or only very rarely. And then the second stunner positioned farther down the line gets them.

She went on to say that the huge failure rate used to be due to the stun guns themselves. Because they were not properly serviced and maintained on a daily basis, the guns often malfunctioned, allowing cows to pass through the stunning stage still conscious. If they are truly dead or properly stunned, their tongues hang out and their head lolls as they are carried along by one foot. On the other hand, if they try to lift their heads, then that's bad. They're still conscious.[18]

I don't know many people like her who

89

could make an entire career of carefully and relentlessly examining such a disturbing process. The workers in slaughterhouses are mostly unskilled immigrants who have few other choices. But a professional with Dr. Grandin's credentials could have chosen to turn her attention elsewhere. Although the slaughter of animals is still a distressing situation, she has done more than any other individual within the system to prevent unnecessary suffering. Her work has also included redesigning the chutes that lead the cows onto the conveyor belt so that they can't see ahead and won't feel as much fear.

If you go to her Web site, you can see diagrams of her design and layout for cattle slaughterhouses. It's www.grandin.com.

—Sally

Dangerous Bacteria

E. coli is a species of bacteria that has many varieties, most of which are harmless to humans. It is abundant in the human digestive system. But one strain can be deadly to humans, causing bloody diarrhea and kidney failure. This strain, E. coli O157, lives in the bowels of half of the beef cattle in the United States. A small number of these microscopic bacteria can kill a person—some say as few as ten bacterial cells.

When carcasses are contaminated with manure, they are often contaminated with this dangerous E. coli O157. To kill the deadly bacteria in the slaughterhouse, the carcasses pass through a hot steam area. Then they are sprayed with a disinfectant. In some processing plants, the carcasses are also irradiated. The radiation kills bacteria, although there is some debate about bad effects of the radiation. Some people object to eating irradiated meat.

Outbreaks from Hamburgers

In the past, there have been occasional outbreaks of E. coli O157 poisoning where several people in one town will become extremely ill and a few may die. Since children eat more than half the hamburgers sold in the United States, the victims are often children. The poisoning is usually traced to a single hamburger restaurant that has a batch of meat with E. coli in it.

It used to be that dangerous E. coli from cows could not survive in the human digestive tract because of the pH, or acidity, of our stomachs. But the corn diet increases the acidity of cows' stomachs so that it is more similar to ours. So the cows' dangerous E. coli have adapted to a more acidic stomach and now can survive in our stomachs too. In addition, increased acidity in a cow's stomach makes the E. coli grow faster.

A POSSIBLE SOLUTION

There is a solution. According to a study by Dr. James Russell at Cornell University, feeding cows hay instead of corn for five days before slaughter will reduce the acidity in their stomachs and get rid of the acid-loving and dangerous E. coli O157. Any remaining E. coli would not be able to survive in our acid stomachs and so would not be a danger to us.[19] Is this happening in the feedlots? We're not sure.

Of course, if cows were not fed corn in the first place, but were fed hay or allowed to graze, then we wouldn't have any problem at all with the nasty E. coli O157. So, remind us, why is it that cows are fed corn? Oh yes, corn-fed beef is cheaper to produce and has more fat in it.

Antibiotics in the Meat

At most feedlots, daily doses of antibiotics are mixed with every meal to prevent bloating and to reduce the chance of liver infection from the unnatural corn diet. As you just read, the corn diet makes the cow's stomach more acidic than it would normally be. The acid eats away at the stomach wall and bacteria such as E. coli pass through the stomach wall into the blood, which allows the bacteria to infect the liver. Even with the antibiotics, 13 percent of cows from feedlots have infected livers when they are killed.

Seventy Percent of All Antibiotics Used in the United States Are Given to Farm Animals!

Feeding antibiotics to each cow in a feedlot is a big problem for us as well as for the cows. As your doctor will tell you, when a population of bacteria is continuously exposed to a low dose of antibiotics, the weaker bacteria are killed, but there are always a few that are more resistant than others. If these resistant bacteria survive the antibiotic and then reproduce, the resulting population of bacteria are *all* resistant. When that happens, the bacteria are no longer affected by the antibiotic.

That's why the American Medical Association urges doctors not to prescribe antibiotics unnecessarily, especially in situations where they are not really needed. But the overuse of antibiotics by doctors is a drop in the bucket compared to overuse by the meat industry. The Union of Concerned Scientists estimates that 70 percent of all the antibiotics used in the United States are given to healthy farm animals for reasons that are hardly essential: to promote weight gain or as a preventive measure.[20] And increasingly, they are becoming less effective against diseases. Some strains of tuberculosis, for example, have become resistant to major antibiotics. In the last year, professional basketball player Grant Hill was in danger of losing his life because of a staph infection. Staph, or *Staphylococcus*, are a type of bacteria, and some strains of staph are now resistant to common antibiotics. Outbreaks of resistant staph bacteria in hospitals are a serious problem nationwide.

The most distressing thing about resistant bacteria is that cattle would not need these medicines if they were cared for differently. If they were not fed so much corn, or any corn at all, and if they were not kept in crowded and dirty feedlot conditions, then they would not need daily doses of preventive antibiotics.

Hormones in the Meat Too

In most feedlots, a hormone pellet is implanted behind an ear of each cow. It steadily releases estrogen into the steer's body and causes him to gain forty to fifty more pounds than he would otherwise. Since we pay for meat by the pound, this means more money for the steer's owner. Almost all beef in the United States has estrogen in the meat from these hormone pellets.

Estrogen is also a hormone found in humans. It causes different kinds of effects in girls and boys. Many scientists believe that hormones in beef are at least partly responsible for American girls entering puberty at an earlier age. Some medical researchers believe that estrogen in beef may also cause lower sperm counts in American men, making them less able to father a child.

Excess estrogen also causes problems for wildlife. Since everything an animal eats shows up in its feces, the manure that piles up in feedlots has lots of estrogen in it. This washes into streams, where it causes abnormalities in fish and frogs, among other problems.

Ranchers, who usually care about their cattles' well-being to some extent, don't necessarily approve of hormone implants. But if everyone else is doing it, then they feel they have to in order to stay competitive.

"A Dairy Cow Is a Milk Factory"

We tried to get an interview at two huge dairies with more than 1,000 cows but were turned down. Much of the information in this chapter came from talking to a dairy farm agent with a county agricultural extension office in North Carolina. He spoke freely with us on the condition that his real name not be used. We will call him Bill. We also talked to several professors in the agricultural departments of animal science and food science at state universities, most of whom did not want their names to be used.

We were able to interview the owner of a smaller dairy, one with eighty-two milk cows, who has switched from confinement to pasturing. That interview and a description of his dairy follows on pages 112–114. He was happy for us to use his name.

We also talked to three other farmers who have small numbers of cows.

> ## Student Voice: Malcolm, Age 19
>
> My dad calls himself a "vegetarian of convenience." My stepmom is vegetarian and they don't have meat in the house, but whenever Dad's out and it's convenient, he has meat.
>
> I told myself when I was going to school that I was going to work on becoming vegan, on giving up cheese and dairy and eggs, but it's quite hard. I'm addicted to cheese, I have to say. But I'm picking mostly from the vegan section in the caf because the impact of dairy and egg production is a lot the same as meat production as far as suffering and working conditions.

GRASSY HILLSIDES REPLACED BY CONCRETE FLOORS AND ODD RATIONS

Although a mural at our local grocery store shows cows ambling over grassy hillsides, between 85 and 95 percent of dairy cows are now kept in factorylike confinement. A high proportion of them spend the bulk of their day standing on concrete.

Rather than a natural diet of grass, most dairy cows are fed some combination of grains, fermented silage, and "concentrate." The grain is often cracked corn. Silage is any whole forage crop, such as alfalfa, millet, wheat, or oats, that has been chopped and placed in an airtight container and allowed to ferment. Silage includes the whole plant, leaves and all. The fermentation preserves it. Dairy folks call the silage ingredients "green chop." In the Northwest, alfalfa hay is a common green chop for silage. In the Midwest, corn is a common green chop in mixed silage.

The concentrate that is fed to dairy cows is a high-energy mixture of agricultural by-products such as corn gluten, brewer's grain, and soybean hulls. In the South, popular ingredients are cottonseed, cottonseed meal, and cottonseed hulls. The mixture changes week to week, depending on what ingredients are cheapest.

"If the Super Bowl was last week, so a lot of beer was sold, then brewer's grain is going to be cheap this week. So brewer's grain will be a component of the concentrate this week," explained Bill, the county agricultural agent we interviewed.

According to one farmer we talked to, a dairy cow's feed can include ground-up chicken feathers and chicken litter, which are high in protein. An agricultural professor told us that this mixture is legal only for immature cows, not lactating cows. Chicken litter is the mixture of sawdust and feces that are scraped off the floor of a broiler chicken shed every eighteen months with a Bobcat loader. We were told ground-up dogs and horses can no longer be included in dairy feed, at least not legally.

Cows that make a lot of milk are given more concentrate than skimpy producers. "The harder you work, the more concentrate you earn," said Bill, the county agent.

A typical dairy cow makes about 15,000 pounds of milk per year. A cow producing 12,000 to 13,000 pounds won't get much concentrate. But a good producer will get about twenty pounds of concentrate per day.

Dairy cows waiting to be milked.

THREE YEARS AND SHE'S SPENT

A dairy cow that eats fresh grass at pasture and has pregnancies at reasonable intervals can produce milk for ten to twelve years. But a cow in a confinement dairy produces milk for only about three years before her body is worn out and she is "culled from the herd."

The exhausting cycle for a typical dairy cow begins when her first calf is born. Like all mammals, a cow begins to make milk only after she has given birth, which occurs for the first time when she is about two years old. The calf is allowed to nurse for twenty-four hours in order to get the first milk, called colostrum, which is full of antibodies to protect it from infection. When the calf is one day old, it is removed permanently from its mother. A milking machine takes the calf's place and mama is milked twice a day from

there on out. Her milk production increases for about ten weeks after giving birth, then begins to decrease.

Two or three months after giving birth, she is impregnated again through artificial insemination. The milking continues during most of her nine-month pregnancy, up until two months before the birth. The second calf is born, nurses for one day, is removed, and the cycle continues.

The continual pregnancies keep the milk flowing in maximum amounts, although they place a huge strain on the mother's body. The concrete floor is hard on a cow's feet and legs, and the weight of pregnancy makes it more so.

Dairies vary widely in their layout, much more so than chicken sheds or hog facilities. Some dairies provide an exercise period each day during which cows can leave the concrete or at least leave their stalls. Others don't.

When a dairy cow's milk production drops too low or she has chronic health issues or fails to become pregnant, she is slaughtered for low-grade meat production. In a typical confinement dairy, this happens to about 30 percent of the herd each year.

WHAT HAPPENS TO THE CALVES?

Dairies usually sell the bull calves and often keep the heifers, or females, as replacement cows. Or the female calves may be sold to farms that raise them for a year and a half to two years and then sell them back to dairies. Male calves are likely to be sold to veal producers. Veal is the flesh of calves slaughtered at four months of age. Veal calves are raised under conditions that keep their muscles very pale and tender—you can read more about that on page 95. Bill told us that veal is not very popular in North Carolina, that there is more of a market for it in the Northeast. But our local grocery stores carry veal. Someone is buying it here.

HORMONE INJECTIONS WIND UP IN THE MILK

Dairy farmers do not have a big profit margin; they are generally not wealthy folks. Most of them feel a lot of pressure to increase milk production per cow in order to help them pay expenses and earn a living. For this reason, when milk production begins to decline between pregnancies, many dairy cows are injected every two to three weeks with bovine growth hormone, or BGH. BGH stimulates the cow to produce more milk. It is sometimes called BST, for bovine somatotropin. Bill, the county agent, told us that BGH is perfectly legal, that it is allowed in milk sold to consumers "because it is a naturally occurring substance in the cow"—although the levels of BGH in a cow getting injections is not natural.

"A DAIRY COW IS A MILK FACTORY. WE DON'T KEEP THEM BECAUSE THEY HAVE BEAUTIFUL EYES."

Some consumers are not happy about drinking BGH, regardless of whether cows produce some of it naturally. And some people are concerned about the strain BGH injections put on a cow's body when she is already making enough milk to feed a small herd of calves.

I called a professor in the animal science department at a local state university. Animal science is not zoology, but rather the study of agricultural animals and farming issues. I asked him if BGH injections shorten the life of a dairy cow because of the added strain of producing ever more milk.

He replied, "Maybe. But I need to explain something to you here. There is not much quality of life in a dairy cow. It doesn't live to a ripe old age. The argument that BGH shortens the life of the cow doesn't hold water. A dairy cow is a milk factory to the industry. That's what it is. That's why we keep them. We don't keep them because they have beautiful eyes." He chuckled deeply.

"Oh. Okay," I said.

He continued, taking an odd turn, "Now dairy cows are around longer than beef cows, so long that the farmer gets to know them. Some of them can be eight or ten years old. Farmers get attached to them."

"I see," I said.

"But it's just meat on the hoof as far as we're concerned," he said, laughing again.

I'd heard that laugh before. It was the same laugh I'd heard from fellow lab instructors when we were teaching human anatomy using cadavers. The same laugh I heard from my friends during the gruesome movies in drivers' ed. Sometimes people laugh to keep from feeling the reality of the situation. A laugh, a joke, can be an effective barrier. I understood his need to laugh. But if he's laughing, who's looking out for the cows' interests? He's an academic, a professor, not a dairy farmer or food-company executive.

I called him back a few months later, after I'd written up his comments, to make sure he was okay about being quoted. I explained who I was and summed up the gist of his remarks.

"I'm not sure exactly what I said, but that sounds like it might be slightly off the mark," he replied. "Most owners of dairy cows are anxious to provide for the comfort of the cow … because it improves productivity. When production drops off, the cow is culled and sold for meat. This is not an emotional or ethical decision. The issue is not the quality or length of life of the dairy cow but production and the productive period."

Okay, same answer, but in professional lingo. When I pressed about using his name, he decided the material was too "inflammatory."

SEE?

YOUR VOICE MAKES A DIFFERENCE

I asked Bill, the county agent, about BGH too. He said its use has decreased lately. I'd heard that too from a farmer, who said BGH use is down because of production problems. But Bill had another explanation.

"Everything is consumer driven," said Bill. "Even though the majority don't care what's in the milk, the minority that does care makes a lot of noise. They drive the industry. That's what happened to the growth hormone."

If you ever wonder if your voice makes a difference, remember that comment from a government agricultural agent.

PULLED FROM THE MILK STRING FOR ANTIBIOTICS

We asked several people—farmers, Bill the county agent, agricultural professors—about the routine use of antibiotics in dairy cows. Bill said antibiotics are too expensive to be used routinely in dairy cows, at least "not to amount to anything." Everyone we asked said that if the government can detect antibiotics in milk, the milk will be thrown out. If a cow is given large amounts of antibiotics for, say, an infection in her milk glands (called mastitis), then "she'll be pulled out of the milk string" for thirty days. Well, that's good to hear.

Veal: The Flesh of Young Calves

I tremble for my species when I think that God is just.

—*Thomas Jefferson*

My perspective of veganism was most affected by learning that the veal calf is a by-product of dairying, and that in essence there is a slice of veal in every glass of what I had thought was an innocuous white liquid—milk.

—*Rynn Berry*

If you've ever read the *Little House on the Prairie* books, you've got to have a fondness for cows. In one of the most touching scenes, Laura teaches the family's young calf to drink milk. She dips her fingers in a bucket of milk and puts them in the calf's mouth. She does it again, bringing her hand and the calf's nose close to the bucket this time. She does this again and again until—whoosh! The calf's nose is in the bucket and it is drinking! They are both splashed with milk and the whole family is delighted.

What would Laura say if she could see how American calves are raised today? Starting in 1962, less than a decade after Laura's death, the meat industry began implementing its most cruel technique yet: veal confinement.

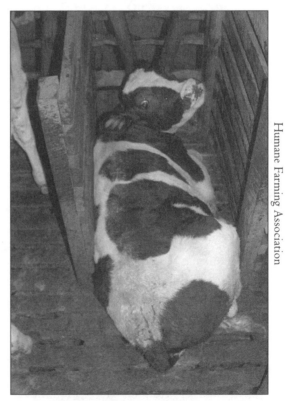

A veal calf spends its entire life in a tiny stall, chained at the neck.

IS VEAL SOMEHOW BETTER THAN OTHER BEEF?

Veal calves are the babies of dairy cows, removed from their mothers when they are only one day old. Each calf is placed alone in a tiny, dark stall only twenty-two inches wide and fifty-four inches long, the same width and just a bit longer than a standard bathtub. Chained at the neck, a calf in such a stall can't even turn around.

In this tiny space, calves cannot stretch their legs out in order to sleep or cool off. They can't groom themselves, although the calves are hot, shedding, and often covered with parasites.

WHY ARE THEY CONFINED LIKE THAT?

Meat is really muscle tissue, as you probably know. When all calves are born, their muscles are very tender, soft, and pale because they've never been used. But as soon as they begin to run around and eat grass, the muscles become tougher and redder, like an uncooked beef-steak. The goal of veal farmers is to keep the calves' muscles pale and tender until they are fifteen weeks old. Then they are slaughtered and their muscles are sold by the pound as veal.

The saddest thing of all about the veal industry is that it's pointless. Veal has no more nutritional value than other beef, it's just more tender and lighter in color. Because of this, it's more expensive than other beef and is served in fancy restaurants.

The life of a veal calf is so sad that many cattle ranchers object to it.

NOTHING BUT MILK?

A veal calf is fed nothing but milk. No water is given, so the calf must drink milk when it's thirsty, which forces more weight gain. More weight when slaughtered means more money for the owner. No hay or other bedding is provided, because the calf might eat it, which

again could affect its muscle color and texture. The floor of the stall is wooden slats.

SOMETHING TO SUCK, PLEASE!

Like all baby mammals, a calf has a strong urge to suck. But a veal calf's stall is completely barren, with nothing to suck or chew, nothing to do at all outside of the two brief feeding periods each day.

THE GOVERNMENT DOESN'T CARE BUT THE AMERICAN PUBLIC DOES

Such is the life of a veal calf in the United States. But, in contrast to the rest of the meat industry, this is not as prevalent as it once was. Although neither the U.S. government nor the American meat industry has done anything to reduce the suffering of veal calves, the American people have. Since 1987, growing awareness of this abuse and misery has reduced the demand for veal in this country by 62 percent. This just goes to show that change is possible. We can do it! Consumers have the power, truly.

It Doesn't Have to Be This Way

Never doubt that a small group of thoughtful, committed citizens can change the world. Indeed, it's the only thing that ever has.

—Margaret Mead

It doesn't have to be this way. In fact, it has only very recently *become* this way. A mere twenty years ago, beef cattle spent two entire years outdoors before they were shipped off. Thirty years ago, barely more than half of pigs were kept in confinement. Fifty years ago, most livestock was raised on small family-run farms instead of giant factory farms. And today, there is a thriving resistance to factory farming. Many farming families are finding a

**Student Voice:
Meg, Age 13**

I decided to be a vegetarian in the sixth grade. We were learning about endangered species in science. I was thinking about a way I could be kinder to animals in nature, and then I learned about the meat industry, the way they take care of animals before they're processed. They don't care about how they feel or how comfortable they are. It's just really not good at all.

way to raise animals humanely and still make a living by selling directly to their local communities. The small farmers we've interviewed call their way of doing things pasture-based agriculture or community-supported agriculture. In our state of North Carolina, there's an organization that supports small, humane, environmentally responsible farms called the Carolina Farm Stewardship Association. This year, for the first time, their annual conference was sold out, a testament to their growing numbers and support. We have profiled several of these farmers in this book. Chapter four describes in detail how these small livestock farms are different from the industrial-sized farms that are controlled by corporations.

Many countries have more humane standards of animal welfare than our government does. Although Great Britain's meat industry is not too different from our own, they have made some improvements over ours. For example, anesthesia is required during castration, while here it is not. Britain has also outlawed veal-confinement pens and their poultry are given more space than American birds are. Switzerland, the Netherlands, and Sweden have all banned tiny, cramped, and stacked cages for poultry, and this hasn't affected the price of the product much. The European Parliament has recommended many drastic changes to all branches of the meat industry, granting farmed animals a more bearable existence.

Here in the United States, the public is becoming more aware. Numerous organizations, including the Humane Society, have worked hard to publicize the cruel treatment of veal calves. As a result, more people are aware of the fate of veal calves than of any other animal in the meat industry, and veal consumption has declined in recent years. That, hopefully, is a sign of things to come.

Change is possible—here, in Europe, in confinement sheds, and in feedlots. But right now, the reality is that animals raised on huge farms are suffering, no matter where they are. To take the power from these abusive industries, we, as consumers, must take their profits away. The easiest way to do that is to not buy their products. Eating vegetarian and boycotting animal products is the firmest way you can refuse to endorse this system, and it's the first step you can take toward promoting change.

Our task will be to free ourselves ... by widening our circle of compassion to embrace all living creatures and the whole of nature and its beauty.

—*Albert Einstein*

GROUP PSYCHOLOGY
It's hard to get my head around the situation that has developed with factory farming. How have we gotten to such a sad state of affairs? For years, I couldn't stand to read about it. It was too painful to think about animals suffering and to feel so powerless to stop it. But it seems that the tide is starting to turn. More and more people are speaking up, consumer groups are making demands, fast-food companies are changing their policies, little by little. Little changes can gain momentum.

There is something very numbing about group psychology. There is a paralyzing effect in the thought "If no one else is complaining, why should I?" If no one else is complaining, it can't really be that bad.

I can make more sense of the current state of affairs with animal rights when I remember how Americans have accepted injustices in the past—injustices that now seem unfathomable. In the past, many Americans believed that women should not vote. In the past, slavery seemed acceptable to many Americans. In the not-too-distant past, many Americans accepted schools that were segregated by law. Less than a hundred years ago, many Europeans believed that Hitler was a sensible man.

In other words, we have seen many, many times in history when popular opinion and public policy have proved to be all wrong. This is going to be one of those times. On down the road, people will look back at the way animals were treated by the corporate meat industry back in the early twenty-first century, and they will be aghast.

If more people knew today what really goes on in animal factories, big changes would begin right away. But the big operators in the meat, dairy, and egg industries do their best to create an image of happy animals. Wall murals over supermarket meat counters show blissful animals strolling through nature. Cartons of eggs and milk show contented animals grazing under trees, or even cartoon animals dancing.

Like all the shameful stages we've been through in our history, the end begins with awareness. Awareness leads to action. And when the clamoring is loud enough, changes occur. The sooner we speak what's on our minds, the sooner it will happen.

—Sally

I want the animal rights movement to get more organized and political, like other movements, to have their representatives vote on issues. So far, the animal rights movement just hasn't been able to do that. And also, you know, groups like PETA are not concerned with how the public views them. Part of that is good, but I kind of wish they had a little more sensibility as far as trying to mainstream the issues. It seems like PETA has a really bad reputation, so that needs to change. If I ever got into a position of power within the animal rights movement, I would definitely break with tradition.

Animal rights are my principle concern, but a very close second is the environment, and also the impact on communities, human rights, and workers. Most of the workers in slaughterhouses and on factory farms are immigrants. Many of them are illegal, they are paid very low wages, and they do some of the most dangerous jobs in the United States.

It's said that every factory farm puts ten family farmers out of business, and all the profits go to stockholders in these big corporations in the multinational market. It takes all the money away from the community and leaves the community with industry that provides horrible jobs and not very much in terms of wages. It takes everything out and leaves the community all the costs, like in terms of pollution.

What needs to happen in regard to factory farming in the short term is that all the groups concerned about factory farming from any of those perspectives [animal rights, environmental concerns, and workers' rights] need to unify and become a force, put aside their differences. Unfortunately, the animal rights movement tends to have the hardest time doing that because they tend to be absolutists: you have to be vegan, you have to not wear leather, you have to do all these things or you're not on the animals' side. That seems to be a common feeling.

The books I've been reading in one of my classes this year have been pointing to a much larger need for a sustainability revolution that would keep the basic infrastructure of the economic system in place but with a different focus. Rather than perpetual growth, the revolution would have the goal of meeting human needs and generating natural systems. And also with that, I would hope that it would improve humane treatment of animals and end factory farming.

Chapter Four

A Kinder and Cleaner Choice for Animal Products:
Livestock Raised in Pastures

The Benefits of Pasturing

If you like animals, it's fun to see farm animals doing the things they like to do: piglets running through the grass, small flocks of clucking hens rambling around, a cow lying under a tree chewing her cud. On small farms across the country, animals do still live this way. They represent a tiny fraction of the livestock in the United States, but at least these farms still exist.

In the United States, there is a growing movement of meat eaters who object to factory farming but who support the eating of contented animals raised in pastures. The meat of animals raised this way is called grass-fed or pastured or pasture-based meat. These terms apply only to animals that spend their whole lives in pastures, so it excludes beef cattle that head off to feedlots and a diet of corn at six months of age. Farmers who raise pastured animals often call themselves grass farmers because they put a lot of effort into raising nutritious varieties of lush grasses for their animals to eat. Supporters of pastured meat point out that it's better than factory-farmed meat in just about every way. And they're right.

In this chapter, you can read about three small livestock farms we visited that sell their pastured meat, eggs, and milk to their local communities.

IF YOU WANT TO EAT MEAT, THERE'S A BETTER WAY TO DO IT

Meat from pastured or grass-fed animals is better for the environment, better for you, and better for the animals. The pasture-based farms we visited are all small operations, without the problems of huge numbers of animals; the problems of factory farms don't exist when animals are raised in modest numbers in spacious pastures. Manure can stay where it falls, fertilizing the soil in the pastures. If animals are eating grasses and clover, then chemical fertilizers are not needed to grow corn and other grains. Pasture-based animals are generally not given hormones.

All of the grass farmers we interviewed sell their meat products locally, directly to families. Since they are not competing with Tyson and other corporations that sell meat to supermarkets, they don't have to be as concerned with pinching pennies to edge out competitors. Instead, they are supported by people in their communities who value animal comfort, healthy meat, and a healthy environment—enough to pay what it costs to provide it.

If you are interested in eating meat, you may be able to find a grass farmer selling locally in your area. Go to www.eatwild.com for listings of providers across the country. Or ask at local farmers' markets and health food stores.

Organic animal products are another option. Organic products, including meat, are grown without hormones, antibiotics, or pesticides.

ONE ENVIRONMENTAL PROBLEM REMAINS, NO MATTER HOW YOU SLICE IT

There is one environmental issue that remains with eating livestock, no matter how the animal was raised: producing meat uses more land than growing plants, period. This is true whether the animals are eating grass in lush pastures or corn from troughs. In terms of pollution, pastures are better than crops doused with pesticides and chemical fertilizers.

Pastured piglets.

But in terms of the space required to support a soaring human population, livestock are still an inefficient use of land. Producing meat still uses ten times more land than a comparable amount of plant food would.

Raising animals at pasture has benefits, but it is still an inefficient use of land.

Still, all things considered, pasture-based farming is much more environmentally friendly than factory farming and feedlots are.

WE GET WHAT WE ASK FOR

When we, the consumers, decide that we object to the methods used by factory farms and we object to the consequences of factory farms, then maybe small farms can become the norm once more.

In order for that to happen, we will all have to eat less meat. We eat so much meat now that the demand could not be met by small farms alone. By eating meat two or three times a day, by making meat, eggs, and cheese the main dish of every meal, we are asking for factory farms. Can Americans change? We think so.

My parents raised my brother and me vegetarian, but they definitely never forced their views on us. I chose to stay vegetarian for sure because I'm disgusted by mainstream meat, especially by hormones. It's really unhealthy! It makes me think of the saying, "You are what you eat." Well, this is the only body you're going to get, so it's really important to make food and lifestyle choices to take care of your body. And unfortunately, the FDA doesn't really have our best interests at heart.

I was in Mexico last year with this girl who was a really serious vegetarian. She hated the whole hierarchy thing and thought it was basically wrong to survive by consuming another animal. She thought the whole world should be vegetarian, that it was disgusting and wrong to eat meat.

I don't think so, though. I feel like it's okay if people want to eat animals. It's just that the meat industry nowadays is out of control. There's such a difference, though, between mainstream meat and eating pastured animals. If people want to hunt or raise their own animals or eat animals from small local farms, that might even be better than eating vegetarian food that's not organic or local or anything.

ARE ANIMAL PRODUCTS FROM PASTURED ANIMALS BETTER FOR MY HEALTH?

One health benefit of eating grass-fed beef is that it has about one-third the fat of corn-fed beef.[1] If you eat the American average of

sixty-six pounds of beef per year, that can add up to a hefty advantage. The saturated fat in beef increases the risk of heart attack, various cancers, and other ailments. (See chapter eight for more information on nutrition.) Fat also has a lot of calories. A six-ounce serving of grass-fed beef has 100 fewer calories than the same amount of corn-fed beef.[2]

Supporters of grass-fed beef point out that it is higher in certain good nutrients than corn-fed beef, such as omega-3 fatty acids, vitamin E, and conjugated linoleic acid, or CLA. This is true, but there are easier ways to get these nutrients than from eating grass-fed beef. The easiest sources of omega-3 fatty acids are walnuts and flaxseeds—both vegetarian—or some fishes. A quarter cup of walnuts per day will give you a bit more than the recommended amount of this important nutrient. In our house, some of us get omega-3 fatty acids by mixing ground flaxseeds in a bowl of hot cereal or sprinkling the ground seeds over salads just before eating. We grind the flaxseeds in the coffee grinder just before using them. Exposure to air reduces the nutrient level, so it's important to grind them at the last minute.

Young animals in pastures have a chance to play and interact normally.

GRASS-FED MEAT
IS LIKELY TO BE ORGANIC

In terms of grass-fed benefits, pastured meat is also likely to be organic, even if it isn't certified so. Animals who spend their lives at pasture are usually not given hormones or routine daily doses of antibiotics. If pastured cattle eat grasses their entire lives, then they probably don't eat pesticides.

Pastured poultry and pigs are more likely to have their diets supplemented with grain that may be grown with pesticides. Many grass farmers value buying grain locally more than buying grain that was grown organically. Organically grown grain may be hard to come by locally. And they may be right that buying locally is a bigger benefit to the environment and to human health than having organic grain shipped in from hundreds of miles away.

JO AND JOEL,
PASSIONATE ADVOCATES

Grass farmers who raise pastured animals can be quite adamant about how healthy the meat is compared to meat from grain-fed, confined animals. Two of the most vocal advocates for pasturing livestock are Jo Robinson and Joel Salatin, both of whom have several books and Web sites on the subject. Robinson's most recent book is *Pasture Perfect*.[3] On her Web site, www.eatwild.com, she covers nutritional aspects and every other aspect of pastured livestock in well-documented detail.[4] Salatin's most recent book is *Holy Cows and Hog Heaven*.[5] He is regarded as an authority on the subject of grass farming and alternative agriculture by most of the grass farmers we visited.

Pastured Meat versus Organic Meat—Which Is Better for the Environment?

How many times have you seen "All Natural" on a package in the grocery store? It would be interesting to keep a tally on a routine shopping trip. But, as common as it is, "natural" on a food package is all baloney. It's not a regulated term. It can mean anything or nothing.

On the other hand, "organic" on a food label has a specific meaning that is regulated and enforced by the federal government. For vegetables, organic means that the plant was grown without pesticides and chemical fertilizers. For meat, organic means that the animal's

Pigs love mud, a happy aspect of pastured life. Those on factory farms never see it.

feed was grown without pesticides and that the animal was free of antibiotics and hormones, at least at the time of slaughter. One feedlot operator told us that cows to be sold as organic beef can have hormone implants several weeks before slaughter, as long as the hormones are not detectable in the cow's body at the time of slaughter.

Not to be a killjoy for anyone's enjoyment of organic meat, but it's not a fix for all that ails the meat industry. Animals to be marketed as organic meat can still be raised in conventional confinement facilities—in feedlots, in stalls barely bigger than their bodies, and jammed wing-to-wing on factory floors.

Cows providing organic beef are usually still fed an unnatural diet of grain that can cause stomach ulcers, liver disease, bloating, and so on. Although no pesticides can be used, the grain or corn can still be grown using chemical fertilizers. The most common chemical fertilizer, nitrogen, is produced using large amounts of oil and natural gas. As these are fossil fuels, their use generates air pollution. And as you learned in chapter two, chemical fertilizers cause both water and air pollution when applied to fields.

The waste from organic livestock can still be collected in unlined lagoons that leak, stink, and overflow during storms.

Organic meat can be and often is trucked across the country to markets, or even flown in from other countries. Trucks and planes burn fossil fuels that pollute the air and contribute to that Godzilla of all environmental problems, global warming.

THE BUTCHERS SAID …
We talked to a couple of butchers at North Carolina health food stores that sell organic meat. If they are conscientious enough to buy organic meat, we thought they might buy it locally as well. Asked where their organic beef comes from, they replied "Texas" and "Uruguay." Their organic chicken came from Pennsylvania. Their organic pork, from Canada. Their tilapia fish, from Latin America. We asked if they considered buying meat locally to reduce the pollution from fossil fuels in transportation. After all, the Union of Concerned Scientists ranks transportation as the number-one most environmentally harmful consumer activity.[6] The grocers replied that this wasn't possible because there are no local

organic grain providers, and organic meat must be fed organic grain, if they are fed grain at all, which they are.

TRUCKING ORGANIC MEAT ACROSS THE COUNTRY OFFSETS ENVIRONMENTAL BENEFITS
The butchers' responses were frustrating because one of the big benefits of organic food is to the environment. When food is grown without pesticides, that's a tremendous boon to wildlife, especially to songbirds, many of which are declining in numbers due to loss of habitat and pollution. Raising livestock without hormones and antibiotics is also helpful to the environment, as both of these substances wind up in manure and hence in our groundwater, rivers, and lakes.

But these benefits are offset by the fossil fuel pollution from truck exhaust when organic meat is shipped across the country. So, all in all, does buying organic meat really benefit the environment? That might depend on where its alternative would come from.

At any rate, organic meat certainly has benefits to human health over conventional meat since it is free of pesticides, hormones, and antibiotics. But what about health concerns related to the saturated fat in meat? Organic has no effect on that. Most organic beef is still corn-fed, and it is just as high in saturated fat as nonorganic meat. Chapter six details health concerns related to a diet high in saturated fat. Cows that provide organic beef can still cause *E. coli* poisoning and can still harbor mad cow disease viruses.

So how does organic meat stack up against grass-fed meat?

THE SIERRA CLUB ENDORSES GRASS-FED MEAT OVER ORGANIC MEAT
Grass-fed meat, even if it's not certified organic, may be a more responsible food choice than certified-organic meat. The Sierra

Club, one of the biggest environmental organizations in the country, promotes grass-fed beef over organic.[7]

Farmers who raise pastured livestock usually take great care of the land and they take pride in their pastures. On the first pasture-based farm we visited, the manager was actually more interested in showing us his lush pastures and the four kinds of grasses and clovers he nurtures there than in showing us his cows! He took loving pride in his pastures and explained the careful rotation of his animals from field to field to prevent damage to the plants and soil. He is a careful steward of the farm environment, using manure as compost and keeping livestock away from streams. Although none of his meat or produce is legally certified as organic, he does not use pesticides, hormones, or antibiotics. His animals are not kept in confinement. He also feels strongly about buying his supplies and selling his products locally. By staying local, he avoids the use of fossil fuels and he helps to develop a strong sense of community with his customers and suppliers. He believes that when people feel connected to their community, they are more likely to take care of the environment in the community, as well as each other.

Visiting Pasture Farms

CONTENTED PIGS AND COWS ON A COLLEGE FARM

Sara Kate and I visited two small farms in the mountains of North Carolina that are, we hope, a sign of things to come. Although they are models for the future, they are also reminders of the good ol' days—before factory farms took over livestock production in the 1950s. Both farms sell meat and eggs, but the animals are treated with kindness and respect, in spite of the extra costs of doing so. These small farms also use methods that are good for the

environment and for human health. It was exciting to see them both making a go of it.

The first was Warren Wilson College Farm. The farm is managed by two full-time professionals, but the rest of the staff are students at the college who work fifteen hours a week. Many of the students who work on the farm are majoring in sustainable agriculture or preveterinary studies. Nestled on the college's 1,160 acres in the Blue Ridge Mountains, the farm produces corn, alfalfa, and grains in addition to raising cows, pigs, and chickens. No pesticides are used on the plants and no growth hormones or routine antibiotics are given to the animals. The cows and pigs spend their lives in wholesome outdoor environments—lush pastures for the cows, open fields and mud wallows for the pigs.

Chase Hubbard of Warren Wilson College Farm.

Our guide for the farm tour was Chase Hubbard, the farm's assistant manager, who believes passionately in what he does. He is a fierce advocate for pasture-based agriculture and for selling the farm's products to the local community rather than shipping long distances. He seems committed to the physical and mental comfort of the farm's animals,

106

which was obvious in the general layout of the farm. He also took pride in showing us some of the farm's innovative approaches to environmental and financial goals. And most important, he shares these ideals with the students. He's teaching them how to meet the community's demand for animal products while nurturing the environment and respecting the animals' needs. Before I met Chase, I didn't know that was possible.

So just what does a happy farm look like? After all of our visits to factory farms, it seemed that we might have stumbled onto Old MacDonald's Farm, with a few modern twists.

Sex Machine and Niels Bohr

The first stop on our farm tour was an introduction to the farm's two huge, fully grown boars. They were jokingly named Sex Machine and Niels Bohr by the students (as you might guess). I was astonished at their size—they both looked as big as cows to me, although not as tall. Sex and Niels were in outdoor pens that were roofed but open at the sides, with a great view of the pig pastures below and the lovely Blue Ridge Mountains beyond.

I was surprised not only at the hogs' great length and girth, but also at their massive snouts. Mammals with a strong sense of smell have long snouts, and pigs are excellent sniffers. The broad, flat end of a pig's snout is good for rooting, or digging up bits of food they smell in the soil.

WINDOWS TO THE SOUL

What surprised me most about Sex and Niels were their eyes, which looked quite human. Pig eyes have the same shape as human eyes, much more so than dogs, cats, cows, or horses. I've never seen eyes like that on an animal, except maybe on chimps. It was a bit weird, as if there was a person inside that head. Seeing their eyes helped me believe what I've read about pigs' intelligence; that pigs are just as

smart as dogs, if not smarter. They are said to be among the very smartest of mammals. Yeah, their big snoots look funny, but their eyes are haunting.

Pig Heaven

The two pig pastures below Sex and Niels were just as interesting as the enormous hogs. The left pasture, for the fifteen teenage pigs, was a scene of blissful slopping and wallowing in a very big mud puddle. Ahh, luxury! Every pig was covered in mud from head to hoof, and they were diggin' it. Those who weren't in the mud hole were sniffing at each other, rooting in the soil for morsels, or taking a turn at the feed trough, a circular gizmo with multiple openings around the outer edge. Each opening was covered with a pig-operated flap to keep birds and mice out. Near the food trough was a wooden structure to provide shelter from bad weather.

If a pig had wanted to run laps around the three-quarter-acre pasture, he could have. It was much bigger than a gym floor. But the mud, the food, the other pigs, and the lovely October day seemed entertainment enough for the pigsters. Said Chase, "They get to do what pigs do, which is lie around in the mud, feed, and root. This is the environment that pigs really like."

Teenage pigs enjoy a snack in their spacious enclosure at Warren Wilson College Farm.

Puppy Style

The adjoining space was the farrowing pasture, where baby pigs are born and raised with their moms. It had about a dozen metal farrowing huts arranged in a large circle around a food dispenser with multiple flaps. Each mama pig had her own hut, where she gave birth and nursed her babies. Around twenty young pigs roamed about the pasture, which had a sizable mud hole just like the one next door. From time to time, one little pig would chase another, puppy style. As we stood at the gate to take pictures, most of the little pigs scampered up to check us out. Pretty cute. It was easy to see why piglets are stars in works such as *Babe* and *Charlotte's Web*.

Chase was enthusiastic about pasture farrowing: it's both economical and environmentally sound. The huts cost only $250 apiece, which is peanuts compared to the cost of a confinement building, the conventional home for mama pigs. With a building, the farmer has not only construction costs, but also the costs of heating and cleaning. The huts require neither heating nor cleaning. There is no need to move the pigs' waste to a lagoon. Instead, the little critters of the pasture (dung beetles, worms, fungi, and so on) break down the manure where it falls and mix it with the soil. The usual stench, air pollution, and water pollution that go along with hog lagoons are not a factor. Yea!

Lined Up Like Vienna Sausages

Although most of the sows on the farm with babies stay in the farrowing pasture, some that have just given birth stay indoors temporarily. Our next stop was this modified confinement shed. It was a long cinder-block building with a series of sizable stalls along one side of a long corridor. Each stall had the floor space of a small bedroom, maybe ten feet by eight feet, with its own small door in the back wall opening into an outside enclosure of equal space.

As Chase explained, the sows are naturally clean creatures, and they prefer to go outside to use the bathroom.

Only three of the stalls were occupied. One mama strolled over to give us a casual sniff, but another was outraged at our presence. She threw a major tantrum in protest, squealing, huffing, leaning stiff-legged into the bars that separated us, and glaring at us angrily. After a couple of minutes of her ruckus, I was astonished to see a beard of foam drooling from her mouth. Just as I was thinking we should give way and leave her in peace, she suddenly backed off and regained her composure. She then flopped back down on the floor and sacked out, allowing the delighted piglets access to her ample bosom. The piglets scrambled wildly, nudging each other out of the way for a nipple until they were all lined up like twelve little Vienna sausages with one or two nestled on top of their siblings. It was a picture of serene domestic tranquility.

Snuggly piglets at Warren Wilson College Farm.

No to the Iron Maiden

In a conventional hog-confinement facility, nursing sows are pinned down by a metal grate that is sometimes called an iron maiden, ironically

A heat lamp lures the piglets away from their mother's heavy bulk.

named after a gruesome human torture device from the Middle Ages. Farmers use the device to keep mother sows from rolling onto their piglets and squashing them. But the grate restricts the sow's movements almost completely, and so supporters of animal rights object to it. How does this small farm handle that issue? We thought their solution was a clever one. One corner of each stall was blocked off with a pair of horizontal bars, keeping mom out but letting the little ones in. Behind the bars, in the corner, a heat lamp was suspended over the floor to attract the piglets. So, when not nursing or romping, the piglets snooze in the corner under the heat lamp, while their hefty mother is free to roll around as she likes.

Grass? You Bet She Likes It!
We visited the cows as well, although they were all grazing far out in large pastures, so we didn't get as close. This farm has no crowded, stinky feedlot. Rather, the cows graze on grasses and clover up until the very end. They are regularly moved from one pasture to another to give the plants three to four weeks

of cow-free recovery. This prevents overgrazing and erosion. It also benefits the cows because it allows them to dine solely on the leafy green tops of the plants, rather than damaging the plants by cropping them down to the ground. More nutrition means more weight gain, a benefit for the farmer as well.

The Feed and Waste Shed
Chase showed us an experimental setup in one of the cow pastures, funded by a recent grant they received. It's a large concrete slab covered with a solid roof, similar to a covered picnic shelter at a city park. In the center of the slab are bales of hay. The cows come onto the slab of their own accord in order to nibble the hay. As a result, manure collects on the slab, where it is very easy to collect to use for compost and fertilizer. This saves time and effort for the farmer. The feed and waste shed seemed quite popular with the munching cows, which looked as pleased and contented as any folks at a park picnic.

Even Happy Cows Wind up as Meat
What happens to the pigs and the cattle when they're grown, when they've reached the desired weight and age? They leave the farm in a truck for a local slaughterhouse, where they wind up as sides of beef or cuts of pork. Although the slaughter process is probably about the same as for animals raised in factory buildings or fattened at feedlots, at least the animals on this small farm spend their lives up to that point in relative comfort, in the care of people who value their comfort. Unlike the factory farm, where we were told that efficiency is the bottom line, priorities here are different. Efficiency is not the bottom line.

Well then, what is the bottom line here? Is it balance? That word came up a time or two. The staff at Warren Wilson College Farm seem to seek a balance between the rights of the animals to live without pain and suffering and the right of local people to eat meat. I saw no suffering on the farm. Rather, I saw animals as comfortable as family pets. They have short lives—less than two years for the cattle, less than a year for most of the pigs. That's short compared to a pet's life in the United States, but compared to a deer or a wolf or a songbird at your birdfeeder, two years is generous. The life expectancy of wild animals is surprisingly brief, their lives usually cut short by hunger, disease, predation, or highways.

Picky Eating

Balance came up again when Chase talked about diets that rule out whole groups of food. He is concerned that some teenage vegetarians may not be careful about their nutrition. He feels a diet that includes a little bit of everything is safer, more likely to be balanced and healthy.

"Extremes don't do much to promote balance," said Chase. "When I was a student, I ate a macrobiotic diet for a couple of years. I still like traditional Japanese food, but here I am living and eating in the southern Appalachians these days. Eating in season and eating local are more important to me now."

Clean piglets at Warren Wilson College Farm have room to romp.

What Is the Real Bottom Line at Warren Wilson?

Balance is important here, but sustainability may be even more important. That concept underlies every choice they make here with the livestock, with pasture management, and with their crops. Just as the first goal of a physician is "Do no harm to the patient," perhaps this small farm's first goal is "Do no harm to the environment, to human health, or to the future of the farm." For these farmers, that means no pesticides, no herbicides, no hormones, and no antibiotics except for sick animals whose meat is then not marketed. The farm staffers reduce the need for chemical fertilizers by rotating crops and by spreading the fields with manure.

The Most Important Message

When we asked Chase for his most important message to people trying to make responsible diet choices, he was quite passionate about one issue that we hadn't expected: buying local.

"Raising food and eating it in our own communities, developing relationships with farmers, shopping at local farmers' markets—the benefits of staying local can outweigh organic labels." He pointed out that moving food across the country burns a lot of fossil fuels and generates a lot of air pollution. The average supermarket item is shipped 1,500 miles![8] I thought about the food-delivery trucks I see backed up to my local supermarket's loading dock, cranking out diesel exhaust.

"Community-supported agriculture is important for families too," Chase continued. "It's important to know where your food comes from. I think we all make more responsible choices when we can see how our food is grown."

We saw a number of bumper stickers near the farm bearing Chase's simple message, "Local Food." Chase and the bumper stickers make a valid point. If you look at scientists' ranking of Americans' habits that are most damaging to the environment, transportation is first.[9] Meat consumption is second. Global warming as a result of vehicle emissions is perhaps the scariest environmental problem of all, one that will have truly profound and irreversible effects all over the planet.

I made up my mind to ask my local grocers to seek out more local products and to label where all their produce is from, and to make the effort to do more of my shopping at farmers' markets—my town has several. I want to make buying local a new priority when I choose food.

VISITING HICKORY NUT GAP FARM

Just a few miles away from the Warren Wilson farm is Hickory Nut Gap Farm. It's operated by Jamie and Amy Ager, who learned sustainable agriculture as students at Warren Wilson College. In addition to managing extensive apple orchards, they raise turkeys, chickens, cows, pigs, and sheep on the 600 acres that have been owned by Jamie's family for four generations.

Sara Kate chats with Amy Ager and her son Cyrus at Hickory Nut Gap Farm.

We visited Amy at the family's apple stand, where she spends October afternoons with their young son, Cyrus, selling at least ten varieties of apples grown on their farm, along with jams, preserves, and other homemade foods. Although each apple bin was four feet deep, holding hundreds or thousands of apples altogether, she often sells out on weekends.

Amy held her grinning baby and chatted with us as we looked through the bins to select some apples. As we browsed, she told us about the farm. All of her animals are raised in pastures, she explained. The cows and sheep are strictly grass-fed in open fields with no hormones and no antibiotics. She mentioned the problems of people eating hormones in meat, that some children develop signs of puberty too early, such as enlarged breasts on seven-year-olds. She takes pride, she said, in raising animals without hormone implants.

Humane treatment of animals is important as well, Amy stressed. She loves that her chickens run to meet her when she tends to them and that all of their animals are comfortable and content. There's a world of difference between the open spaces and sunshine her animals experience and the crowding, misery, and ammonia fumes on the factory farms we visited.

Like Chase at Warren Wilson, Amy and her husband work hard to develop working relationships within their community. They buy the grain for their pigs and poultry at a local feed mill.

"It's better economically to partner with local providers," said Amy. Local partnerships can evolve together, making adjustments to fit the changing needs of each partner. Amy's cousin-in-law is working on a grant to start organic grain production in North Carolina. "That would be ideal," said Amy.

The Agers' marketing efforts are all aimed at the local community. They sell all of their meat and eggs straight from the farm under the business name Spring House Natural Meats. Two days a week, they sell to local people at nearby farmers' markets. To educate local people and develop new relationships, they take turns with other farms hosting an annual Harvest Festival. It's a chance for hundreds of folks from the area to spend the day on a working farm. The festival is complete with food, crafts, live music, and games for the children. It's important to Amy and Jamie to promote their way of life as well as their business. Farms in western North Carolina have been disappearing for decades, with land being snatched up for development, providing more houses and more services for newcomers. The Agers have been trying to preserve farmland and turn more of it back into active farm production. They know that the support of the community is essential to the survival of their farm and others. Even though their meat prices are higher than supermarket prices, local people who know how the Agers raise their animals and who understand their broader goals are eager to support their business.

After we talked to Amy, she invited us to wander around and take a closer look at some of the animals, so we did. We walked past some cows at pasture grazing. We passed a herd of sheep in another pasture trotting briskly toward an unknown destination, or maybe away from us.

A flock of very young turkeys, however, seemed more open to a visit, so we stopped to take a closer look. At this particular site, the center of activity was a large open tent that covered a grain feeder and a water dispenser. Many of the youngsters were inside the tent pecking at the grain. But most were busy exploring the grassy field outside the tent, looking for seeds and insects, scooting through the long grass. We tried to cajole them into standing still for a photo, but none were willing. Young turkeys are surprisingly active and surprisingly fast. I thought sadly about the vast majority of young turkeys in this country who are so crowded they can barely move. Although the Agers' turkeys will be eaten eventually, at least they lead carefree lives before that time.

Is meat grown under these circumstances available in every community? Not yet, but the day is not far off. Said Amy, "I respect vegetarians. It's a wonderful way to live. But if you want to eat meat, it's better to eat healthy and happy meat."

Amen to that.

THE HAPPY COW CREAMERY

We were intrigued to learn of a different kind of dairy farm in South Carolina, one owned by Tom Trantham and his family. Tom has been in the farming business for thirty-seven years. For the first twenty years, he had a conventional confinement dairy, where the cows were kept indoors eating grain and fermented

Dairyman Tom Trantham, owner of 12 Aprils Farm and the popular Happy Cow Creamery.

silage grown the usual way, with chemical fertilizers and pesticides. Then in 1988, he made a major switch and turned his cows out to pasture. You might say it was the cows that first proposed it and Tom wound up believing they were right.

Tom says he was on the brink of financial disaster with his confinement dairy, waiting for a loan and seriously worried about ever getting the farm finances squared away. One April evening as he despaired over his bankbooks, the cows broke out and went for a romp in an overgrown field on the farm. After grazing for a good while, the cows were rounded up and brought back in. In the next few days, Tom was surprised to notice a jump in their milk production. One thing led to another, and, after a bit, Tom figured out that, sure enough, the cows made more milk when they were allowed to graze.

Tom is an astute businessman and he recognized a good opportunity. Why spend so much money on silage and feed when pasture worked better? Not only did his grazing cows make more milk, but grazing cows are also healthier and happier cows. Concrete is hard on a cow's feet and legs. And what can be more natural for a cow than eating grasses?

After his discovery, Tom turned his attention to growing the best forage, the best grasses he could grow. He has tried to simulate the lush growth of April all year-round, hence the name of his farm, 12 Aprils. He has twenty-nine pastures and he rotates his cows through all twenty-nine every month. With only one day in each pasture per month, the cows eat only the top half of the plants, where most of the protein is. He figured this out from watching the cows closely and believes that this particular kind of grazing boosts milk production. By the time the cows rotate back around through any given pasture, the plants have fully regrown.

Tom's cows are able to forage outdoors for the bulk of every day, which they no doubt prefer to confinement. The pastures include shade trees, a necessity for the hot South Carolina summers.

"They'll graze for fifty-four minutes, then go lie under a tree, chew their cud, and make milk," says Tom.

His cows have an easier reproductive schedule too, with a birth every fourteen or fifteen months, rather than the dairy standard of every twelve to thirteen months.

Not only has Tom made a happier herd and gotten his farm on solid footing financially, he has made a number of other changes in his dairy. He no longer uses any chemicals or fertilizers to grow grasses or grains for the cows. Instead, he uses organic matter to add nutrients to the soil. He has turned his silo into a bottling plant and bottles his milk right there on the farm, the same day and just a few feet away from where the cow parted with it. He turned part of his barn into a store, called the Happy Cow Creamery.

"A happy cow is a productive cow," Tom explained.

Tom's wife, Linda, rang up customers at the cash register as Sara Kate and I looked around the store. The glass-fronted cooler holds jugs of Happy Cow Creamery whole milk, buttermilk, and chocolate milk. The store sells vegetables and other farm products as well. Business is booming, and the family may open a second store soon. Tom and Linda are happy that their son, Tom III, has returned to work with them on the farm too.

"Our whole dream was the family farm to pass on from generation to generation," says Tom. That dream is a firm reality now.

Tom believes strongly not only in his methods but in his product. His whole milk has none of the fat removed, with a fat content as high as 4.5 percent. Buy a jug of whole milk at the Happy Cow Creamery, and the fat will rise to the top unless you shake it. Just like in the old days. That's because Tom's milk is not homogenized.

To homogenize milk for supermarkets, conventional bottlers shoot the milk through a filter that breaks up the fat cells into small fat particles that stay suspended in the milk rather than rise to the top.

Tom likes the high fat content of his milk because fat-soluble vitamins A and D naturally reside in the fat. And whole milk has a rich, creamy, delicious taste.

He didn't mention, though, that milk fat is a saturated fat, as is all animal fat. The United States Department of Agriculture advises limiting the amount of saturated fat in our diets to less than 10 percent of our total calories. Many nutritionists recommend much less than that. When fat is removed from milk, the vitamins are generally added back from other sources.

Tom says that one of the main problems with conventional milk production is "the emphasis on more milk" at all costs. "Not product quality, not water quality, not soil quality—just produce more milk." Many dairy farms inject cows with growth hormones to boost milk production, but Tom doesn't. On the 12 Aprils Farm, the emphasis is on fresh and hormone-free milk, healthy and happy cows, and environmentally sound practices.

After our interview, Tom headed off to a chore that needed his attention and invited us to have a look in his milking barn. It was a warm January afternoon and the cows were wandering up from the pasture to the barn of their own accord. They stood in line peacefully, waiting their turn for the afternoon milking. One by one they walked up a ramp and entered a long aisle in the barn. Along one side of the aisle was a series of milking stations. Each station offered a bucket of feed and a cluster of metal cylinders to slide over the cow's teats as she ate. There were only a

few stations and eighty-two cows, so there was a lot of waiting, like a line of women in a public restroom.

As a cow moseyed into a station, a herdsman, David, fitted the cylinders over her teats and the pumping began. The milk passed through the metal cylinders into hoses that took it to a collecting tank in the milk room. When the pumping stopped, David removed the cylinders and squeezed a few teats to make sure the milk really was all gone, and then lifted a cup of antiseptic to bathe each teat and prevent infection. All done, the cow ambled off to make room for the next heifer in line. The cows didn't seem to mind our watching.

After ambling in from the pasture on their own, Tom's cows line up for milking.

The whole milk we bought at the Happy Cow Creamery did taste good. I enjoyed it for a few days and was sorry when it was gone. But I appreciate the Tranthams' farm more for the way they treat their cows and for their chemical-free farming methods, which are kind to wildlife and to all of us who share the planet.

Chapter Five

Organic, Local, and Seasonal

Behind the Scenes at Food Markets

Is all organically grown food certified as organic? The answer is no. We interviewed several farmers who grow their vegetables without pesticides, yet do not bother to have it legally certified as organic. Why not? There were a number of reasons. For one, the certification is expensive. It requires an annual fee of $500 to $1,000, a hefty sum for a small business. Two, to qualify for certification, a farmer must keep careful and time-consuming records to verify that his produce meets all the requirements for certification. Aside from the time required for record-keeping, some farmers find it a nuisance to submit their books and records for inspection. Third, the organic farmers we talked to all have small farms and would not benefit from having the certification. They are selling to their local community, to people who know them and their practices. They are already selling the products they grow for good prices. Because their consumers know that they can visit the farms and see how things are being done, the customers trust the farmers' assurance that no chemicals are used.

A GROWING DEMAND

Nationally, slightly more than 1 percent of our food is certified organic. It's a small percentage, but growing. Each year, the number of organic products sold is 15 to 20 percent higher than it was the year before.[1] We can see this locally. Ten years ago, only health food stores in our area carried produce that was certified organic. But now our supermarket chains carry organic produce too.

The biggest growth in organics is not in meat or fresh produce but in packaged food, such as frozen meals, baby food, baked goods, cereals, and dairy products. The increase is great news because Americans buy far more packaged food than they do fresh ingredients.

THE PRODUCE MANAGER SURPRISED US

At our local Harris Teeter supermarket, maybe one-tenth of the fresh produce is labeled organic. During the first week in November, which is still mild here in North Carolina, we asked the produce manager if *any* of the produce for sale was grown locally. Spring and fall crops, such as greens, carrots, broccoli, and lettuce, still thrive here in November in our garden and on small farms in the area. In fact, many of these cool-weather plants will grow through the winter. But the Harris Teeter produce manager said, "No, we don't have anything local, not this time of year. Most of our produce now is from Texas and Arizona." That's more than 1,000 miles away.

A week later in the same store, we asked a produce worker about the bell peppers, which were a steep $2.99 apiece. He checked the stickers and reported matter-of-factly that the red bell peppers were from Israel, the yellow ones from Holland, and the green ones from Florida. "Why from Israel and Holland?" we asked. "I don't know about Israel," he said, "but Holland grows great bell peppers." We asked again if any of the rest of the fresh produce was locally grown. "No," he replied. "This time of year, a lot of it is from South America." That makes Texas seem close.

The most interesting thing in both of these conversations was that the workers believed we would be pleased to have Harris Teeter going so far to get the very best produce in spite of the high price—the very opposite of our real reaction. Working in the retail business, their job is to provide what the consumer seeks, so we can't fault them for that. The responsibility lies with those of us who value locally grown food to let our voices be heard. All producers have told us the same thing: they want to sell whatever people want to buy.

We're glad Harris Teeter is carrying at least some organic produce. But carrying produce that is organic *and* local would be so much better. Seasonal and locally grown food is more likely to be truly fresh, so it's better for our health. Buying locally grown and seasonal food is also easy on the environment since there is no pollution from transportation that uses fossil fuels and also no energy or materials used for freezing or packaging.

Student Voice:
Dana, Age 17

I try to keep a little garden out back to try and avoid all these California vegetables that are shipped out here in giant trucks and stuff. I do tomatoes, peppers, lettuce, squash—you know, random things. But the lettuce died because of the groundhog out there that I just can't seem to get rid of ...

FOCUSING ON LOCAL AND SEASONAL PRODUCE

We interviewed the cafeteria manager at a school and asked about her priorities in purchasing food. She gave remarkably well-informed and sensible answers, given the reputation that school lunches have. She doesn't buy organic because her budget can't afford it, but she does buy fresh produce that's in season and local. It's cheaper, she says, and she was hired to save money. During October, for example, she had her chef make pumpkin soup and several other pumpkin dishes because October is harvest time for pumpkin. She said the pumpkin was a big hit, and cheap. It's inspiring to see that in at least one instance, buying local and seasonal products is still feasible for an operation as large as a school.

Local farmers' markets are a good way to buy seasonal and locally grown produce, which may or may not be organically grown. In North Carolina, where we average about six inches of snow a year, one farmers' market near home is open five days a week year-round.

INTERVIEW WITH A SUPERMARKET MANAGER

After talking to the produce manager and a produce worker at our local Harris Teeter, we cornered the store manager, hoping to resolve our questions about the factors that guide their product selection. Do they care about buying local foods? Their promotional signs, such as "Fresh Market," suggest that they do. Do they care about environmental concerns? What about humane treatment of livestock?

Us: As far as product selection, is your store guided at all by environmental concerns or animal welfare concerns?

Manager: No, all decisions about what we carry are made at the corporate level. We can decide how much of a product we need in order to keep it in stock, but we have no say in product selection.

Us: Well, in general, do the people at the corporate level consider environmental issues or humane issues when deciding which products to carry?

Manager: No. It's all customer driven. It's all supply and demand. We really want to please the customer. Sometimes we'll order a big box of something because someone wants it, sell one item from the box, then throw it away. Like lemon zest or some root in the produce section. We wind up throwing most of it away.

Us: Some people feel that buying local is a high priority because local produce is fresher and because less fossil fuel is used to get it here, so there's less pollution. Is buying local a high priority for your store?

Manager: Yes, we do try to buy local when we can.

Us: We can't tell what's local.

Manager: You can tell if you look on the little stickers on the produce. Everyone wants to see that local sticker.

Us: It would be nice if there were big signs that are easy to read saying what is local.

Manager: We do have signs over the apples saying they are local.

Us: I'm wondering about the red bell peppers from Israel and the yellow bell peppers from Holland. Is it not possible to get them from a closer source?

Manager: No, that's the best place this time of year, in December. Because their growing season is the opposite of ours.

Us: Let me ask you about meat. You all carry veal, right? Some people object to the way veal calves are raised. Would Harris Teeter consider not carrying veal because of concerns about animal welfare?

Manager: No. If there is a demand for it, we'll carry it.

Us: Unless a bunch of people put up a big stink about it.

Manager: No, the only way we would stop carrying it is if people stopped buying it. We are completely customer driven.

Us: What about organic? Is the amount of organic products you carry based solely on the demand for them?

Manager: Yes.

Us: What if something were available locally but you could get it cheaper from farther away? Which would you do?

Manager: I don't know. Probably get it locally.

What else could we say? He made it very clear that customer demand is the company's top priority. It's sobering to realize that supermarkets aren't going to make our ethical choices for us. That would be much easier, but in a way this is more empowering. It means we have the responsibility to demand principled products ourselves. We can't wait for someone else to make the leap for us.

—Sally

117

Small farmers and gardeners bring their fresh produce and sell it themselves, or hire someone to sell it for them. The fruits and vegetables are displayed on tables, and each seller sets his or her own prices. Maybe a quarter of the produce is organic, although most is not certified organic. As one farmer said, "If people want to know how I grow my vegetables, if I use pesticides, they can come out and take a look, night or day. Just don't wake me up."

Some of the produce at our farmers' markets is much cheaper than at the grocery, as well as being safer, fresher, and tastier. Said one seller, "The food at the grocery, you don't know where it's been. It's been handled and in and out of trucks. What else was in those trucks? We have beautiful big red tomatoes here. Those hard, pink tomatoes at the grocery, they were picked green and gassed to make them pink. They're just awful."

We couldn't argue with that. Instead, we bought some of her fresh greens, snap beans, and apples and headed home to make a tasty supper.

Visiting New Town Farms

We were looking for a local organic farmer to interview and kept hearing about Sammy and Melinda Koenigsberg and their New Town Farms. Sammy and Melinda started the farmers' market in the town of Matthews, North Carolina, about ten years ago as a place to sell their own organic produce. They sounded like experts, so we called and asked to visit.

We drove up the narrow driveway to the farm, over a creek and through a dense stand of trees, then into a clearing. We passed an outdoor pen of clean, white turkeys and a three-acre field of vegetables, which, even in late November, was still full of healthy-looking plants. We parked next to the handsome house they share with their eight homeschooled children, overlooking a scenic pond.

I wanted to dash back home and get my suitcase. What a beautiful place to raise a family.

Sammy strolled up from the chicken house and pen, a clean and spacious affair with door flung wide so that his laying hens could come and go as they pleased. A couple of pretty brown hens strolled about the driveway as Sammy welcomed us to the farm.

The three of us walked down to the pond and sat on a picnic bench where their only employee was washing carrots. We admired the carrots, hinting perhaps. Sammy handed us each a plump one, plucked from the ground just minutes earlier.

"Our produce is really fresh," Sammy said. "And it's the same price you'd pay at a supermarket, only theirs may be a week old." It was a crisp carrot, no debate about that. Sweet and crunchy.

Just how fresh is Sammy's produce when he sells it? We asked Sammy to explain

A couple of roaming yard hens welcomed us to New Town Farms.

how his business works. One-third of his produce goes to families who pay an annual fee. The yearly sign-up is February 1 and it's first-come, first-served. Those who make it will get a box of produce every week year-round. The veggies in the boxes are whatever happens to be in season. In November, that means broccoli, cauliflower, Brussels sprouts, collards, and carrots. He harvests for families every Tuesday and delivers the boxes to a local health food store in Charlotte—the same one where Sara Kate works—where the customers pick up their boxes the very same day. So Tuesday night, his customers are eating vegetables that were living that very morning.

On Thursdays, Sammy and his family harvest for local restaurants. That produce too is delivered the same day. Restaurants have more of a say in what they want.

The final third of Sammy's business is Friday's harvest, which he and his kids sell on Saturday morning at the Matthews Farmers' Market. They always sell out within two hours.

We asked him, "How are your vegetables different from those in a grocery store?"

I know his veggies are all grown organically, but he didn't start there. He started with the soil. I was surprised at the warmth of his comments about his soil, as if it were a pet project, which I guess it is.

"First of all, we focus on building the soil instead of using it as a medium to transfer chemical fertilizers to plants. We look at soil as something alive, something we need to understand and work with rather than imposing our own system on top of it. To do that, we feed the soil with compost and by cover-cropping with alfalfa and clover—they're grown to be turned under and mixed with the soil, rather than harvested. Clover is nitrogen fixing. Alfalfa has long roots that go down and mine things, or pull nutrients into the top layers. We don't douse the soil with chemical fertilizers and pesticides. There are more than a

million living organisms in each pinch of soil. We're making the soil the best possible environment by having the soil in balance. As a result, the vegetables taste better and have more nutrients in them.

"I like to compare it to a chair made in a shop that makes only one or two chairs instead of in a factory. It's made with more care, more thought about it. That future vegetable is your body. Whatever we're doing to the soil, we're also doing to our bodies.

"Supermarket vegetables travel an average of 1,500 miles to get to us. Usually, they are a week old, sometimes older than that. How much diesel fuel is on them, how many different workers have handled them?

Sammy and Melinda's children help manage New Town Farm's produce and poultry.

"We care for the soil and care for the plant. Our vegetables are fresh, harvested daily, carried to the consumer the day they are harvested."

Wow. I felt a new appreciation for fresh and unpolluted vegetables. Really fresh vegetables. What if everybody took such care in the things we turn out? Wouldn't the world be a comfy, safe place?

We left the picnic table and walked down the rows between the vegetables. In shades of green and purple, each plant looked as carefully tended as a favorite houseplant.

So what about the chickens and turkeys? During the summer, Sammy has 500 chickens that are sold as broilers. His customers buy five to ten birds at a time. The chickens live in movable pens outdoors. Every day each pen is shifted onto a new patch of grass so the chickens have fresh plants to nibble and unsoiled ground to walk on. Sammy's chickens don't get antibiotics or copper supplements to speed growth. They are fed a diet of corn, soybeans, kelp, acidophilus, and fish meal. Sammy slaughters them himself. Where? He pointed to a small wooden table next to a tree. He uses a killing cone, which looks like a traffic cone open at the tip. The chicken goes into the cone headfirst so his neck hangs out. The bird can't flap and seems to be relaxed, Sammy said. A single vein in the neck is cut with a sharp knife. But Sammy leaves the windpipe intact so the chicken bleeds to death rather calmly. Then it goes into the scalding and plucking machine.

Our visit happened to be the week before Thanksgiving. The thirty-five turkeys, Sammy said, would all be slaughtered the following Monday for Thanksgiving dinners, using the same method as for the broiler chickens. They would be delivered on Monday as well to the customers who had already bought them. We walked over to look at them. They were curious, coming up to the edge of the pen as though we had treats, making their gobbling noise and looking around. Their red wattles jiggled as they lurched about.

"Most chickens and turkeys get antibiotics," Sammy pointed out. "They live in excrement, in a building that smells like a bucket of ammonia, with no greens and no fresh air."

But not these birds. Both the pen and the turkeys were immaculate, as though they'd all just had nice hot showers.

I couldn't imagine a more pristine farm. Is this why Sammy has more demand for his products than he can supply? Is it because the food is grown without pesticides, chemical fertilizers, or antibiotics? Because his customers value fresh food grown locally? Or is it something more personal about Sammy and his home-schooled family, his passion for living soil?

"What motivates your customers?" I asked him.

"Where it's all at is relationships," he answered. "People getting to know where their food is coming from. You can walk around my farm and see what I'm doing. I reconnect people to where their food comes from and the processes that bring it about. The aisles of plenty at supermarkets have hidden things behind them, pesticides and other chemicals. Local is the answer to this mess. Know and trust your farmer, have that relationship.

"When we started this," he continued, "I was an architect. I never thought I'd be a farmer. But I was sick for two years and didn't know what I had. I started looking at what I was eating, where our food comes from, and then started doing this.

"I think there's a movement, people are trying. In some areas, there are a lot of small organic farmers practicing community-supported agriculture. By starting the farmers' market, we've tried to make it easier for others to follow."

It seems that Sammy and Melinda have succeeded in creating a sustainable and responsible model that's well worth following. Their way of farming promotes the health of their customers, protects the environment, connects members of the community, and preserves a rural way of life. Any customer who wants to can visit their farm and see for themselves how the food is grown. And while the poultry do wind up on the dinner table, they live in clean, airy quarters until the very end. If all farms were like the Koenigsbergs' farm, how different our world would be.

Get Local

Vegetarian. Organic. Local. Seasonal. So many priorities to consider. Sometimes buying a simple ear of corn seems overwhelming. But these considerations don't always conflict, as I realized on our trip to two small farms in the North Carolina mountains. (See pages 106–112 for accounts of these visits.)

Idyllic as they were, our visits stirred up some confusing turmoil in me. Before we went, I firmly believed that the most pressing ethical food concern was unquestionably vegetarianism. After all, that's why we were writing this book. A few months before, my housemates and I had hosted a school cookout featuring ethical foods. I'd been reluctant to serve meat options at all—could eating meat *ever* be ethical?—but finally conceded when we agreed to buy organic hot dogs and turkey burgers. After all, if it was organic, it had to be a responsibly made product, right?

After our day in the mountains, however, I realized that I could be missing the point entirely. In my vegetarian-versus-organic debate, I'd been completely overlooking an issue that might be more important than either of those two: buying local.

Chase, the assistant manager of Warren Wilson College Farm, was quite passionate about this issue. When we asked, "What's your most important message to people who read our book?" I thought surely he'd say something about sustainability, or perhaps pesticides, or meat consumption.

But to my surprise, he said thought-fully, "I'd say local. I would rather eat sweet corn grown here with fertilizer than corn grown organically 200 miles away, in terms of sustainability. You burn so much fossil fuel to get the corn here, it doesn't make any sense."

He brings up an important point, one I heard reiterated later that day by Amy of Hickory Nut Gap Farm. As she explained, they feed their animals locally milled, nonorganic soybean meal. They'd like to buy organic, she said, but it just doesn't make sense to buy chemical-free feed in Pennsylvania and then generate a lot of pollution by shipping it down here. From an environmental standpoint, I realized, buying local may be more effective than buying organic.

But what about the issue of vegetarianism? I was startled by a rhetorical question from one of Chase's colleagues, who wondered, "Are you really helping the environment if you avoid eating cows and pigs raised locally with sustainable farming practices, but instead buy vegetarian products that are shipped here from across the country?"

Whoah! It was an uncomfortable question because I didn't know the answer. On one hand, I do think that the small meat producers we spoke to are overlooking at least one issue related to meat production. Raising meat is simply less land efficient than raising vegetables, even on a humane farm. Right now, these producers have the land to do it. In a future world that's more crowded, that may not be the case.

But vegetarian or not, organic or not, Amy of Hickory Nut Gap Farm explained that buying local benefits much more than just the environment. Most important, she said, there's the issue of community. By buying their animal feed locally, they develop a relationship with their feed provider. He knows their farm and their family and helps them out when they need a favor. In turn, they supply him with fresh and healthy food products that he can feel good about.

Chase made an almost identical point. "Raising food and eating it in our own communities, developing relationships with farmers, shopping at local farmers' markets—the benefits of staying local can outweigh organic labels. … Community-supported agriculture is important for families. It's important to know where your food comes from. I think we all make more responsible choices when we can see how our food is grown."

I think he's right. If you're buying food from producers fifteen states away, they have no responsibility to you. It doesn't matter to them if their product is substandard because they'll never see you eat it or know if it makes you ill. On the other hand, if one of Amy's customers has a problem with her apples, Amy will hear about it. If Chase's customers have a question about the way the meat is raised, they can come and discover the answers for themselves. If we're pursuing a responsible and ethical food industry, we need to develop relationships between producers and consumers.

But it's not just that. The more I think about it, the more I see that buying local is crucial in endless other ways. Local food is also fresher because it doesn't have to be stored, packaged, and shipped. And for the same reason, it's cheaper—yet farmers earn more money. If you don't have to pay a factory for packaging a product, or a trucker for hauling it, or a supermarket for selling it, food costs less and more of the price goes straight to the farmer. This in turn stimulates the local economy—if Amy's making more money on her farm, she has more money to spend at her neighbors' shops.

These are a lot of issues to deal with—and pretty complicated ones at that. But in the end, I figure that prioritizing vegetarian versus organic versus local food is not the most important issue. What's key is to realize that these are all important concerns and they all must be acknowledged in order to develop a healthy and sustainable food industry.

Tracking down local food can be tricky though. While a food package will tell you if the contents are vegetarian or certified organic, it's not likely to tell where the food was grown. If you resolved to eat only local food, you'd probably starve in your own supermarket. As we've mentioned elsewhere in this book, the average bite of food travels 1,500 miles from farm to fork.[2] And as the process of globalization continues, this will grow more extreme.

The more global our world becomes, the less we depend on the people around us. One way to rebuild that connection is to know where our food comes from, so that's what I have resolved to do. My personal goal is to continue eating vegetarian, to buy organic when possible, and to try much harder to find local options. When I'm at the grocery store, I now look at stickers on produce and the fine print on boxes and cartons. Did you know, for example, that grapes come from Chile? Apples, on the other hand, are grown right here in my county. I'll be happy with an apple, thanks. And when I can, I buy these items directly from the people who grow them. For instance, cabbage at the farmers' market costs only $.39 a pound, and those pennies go straight into the pocket of the woman who grew it. At the grocery store, an ordinary cabbage costs $.79 a pound and an organic one $.99 a pound, yet the farmer gets only $.08 out of that dollar.

I'm looking forward to doing more of my shopping at farmers' markets and getting to know more of the farmers close to home. I also plan to ask the produce manager at my nearby supermarket to carry more local foods. These are choices I can feel good about. I think getting local is a big piece of the picture in working toward a more wholesome future for food consumers, producers, and the whole world economy.

—Sara Kate

Chapter Six

Vegetarian Nutrition

Stay Healthier without Meat—Research Proves It

If you've decided to go vegetarian, you've probably had at least one worried relative or well-intentioned friend tell you that you're going to waste away. A young friend of ours who had never eaten meat in her life surprised many people when she moved to Montana. On one of her first days there, as she vigorously chopped and hauled wood, one man kept staring at her. "What is it?" she finally asked him. "Why are you staring at me?" He shook his head, puzzled. "I didn't expect you to be so … healthy!" he exclaimed. He had never met a vegetarian before. He thought she'd be thin and sickly.

Unfortunately, this stereotype of vegetarians is all too common. But it's not true at all. Every day more research is proving that the vegetarian diet is perfectly healthy—it's actually healthier than eating a lot of meat. As a result, public opinion of vegetarianism is gradually changing, and veggie meals are popping up all over the place.

Although the government lags behind, many independent organizations are now encouraging us to eat less meat: the American

Heart Association, the National Academy of Sciences, the American Academy of Pediatrics, and the American Dietetic Association, to name a few.

They base this recommendation on studies here in the United States and all around the world that show the same thing: eating less meat, or no meat, is healthier. A study of Uruguayan women, for instance, found that a diet heavy in red meat led to a higher risk of breast cancer, an increase of anywhere from 230 percent to a whopping 770 percent.[1] Other studies have drawn similar conclusions in the United States, Italy, and Japan. In fact, diets high in animal products have been proven to lead to a higher risk of colon, prostate, ovarian, endometrial, and lung cancer as well. Yikes!

These diseases probably seem like old people stuff. It's true that you don't hear of many teenagers kicking the bucket from colon cancer. But many of these conditions start early—the first signs of heart disease can appear before your first birthday! And sadly, American kids have the most clogged arteries of any children in the world. So fend off that heart attack now, and get a load of this.

Student Voice:
Alan, Age 18

When you are eating healthy foods, you are doing your body a favor. It's like pulling a trick play in football when the defense isn't looking. A vegetarian diet is the single best way to make you feel better every day.

HEART DISEASE

Did you know that heart disease is the number-one killer in the United States? The main problem is plaque—no, not the stuff on your teeth. This plaque comes from eating too much cholesterol and saturated fat. It accumulates inside your arteries, clogging them up and preventing the blood from chugging through. When plaque clogs an artery that carries blood to the heart muscle itself, it can cause a heart attack.

Since plants have no cholesterol and very little saturated fat, it's not surprising that by cutting your consumption of animal products in half, you reduce your risk of a heart attack by 45 percent. By following a vegan diet, you reduce your risk by a whopping 90 percent.

As those facts suggest, not only can a vegetarian diet prevent you from getting sick in the first place, but it can actually turn a preexisting condition around. In a landmark study, a low-fat, low-cholesterol vegetarian diet lowered heart patients' cholesterol levels as effectively as drug treatments. Inflammation and plaque actually began to shrink due to the shift in diet alone.[2] Clearly, eating veggie is pretty powerful.

HIGH BLOOD PRESSURE

Also known as hypertension, high blood pressure affects more than 50 million Americans over the age of six. That's right—six, not sixty. When plaque lines your arteries, it leaves less space for your blood to pass through. The harder your heart has to work to squeeze blood through these narrowed blood vessels, the higher your blood pressure is. So, just as with heart disease, eating less cholesterol and saturated fat helps vegetarians keep their blood pressure low.

CANCER

Again, poor diet is the biggest cause of cancer. Smoking causes about 30 percent of cancer cases, but eating poorly causes up to twice that much. Fortunately, with just about every kind of cancer, vegetarians have an advantage. Vegetarian men, for example, are almost four times less likely to get prostate cancer than men who eat animal products every day. And of those who get cancer, vegetarians are more likely to survive than are meat eaters. This is because vegetarians eat less damaging fats and toxins and more cancer-fighting substances, such as fiber, beta-carotene, and antioxidants.

OBESITY

We're a blubbery nation and our chubby ways are spreading throughout the world. It's hard not to eat so much when food is as cheap and abundant as it is in our country. But vegetarians are consistently more trim than meat eaters, which is probably due to eating more fiber and less fat. Extra weight makes it hard to exercise, which we need for a healthy heart, strong muscles, and emotional well-being.

Obesity is associated with a variety of diseases, one of which is diabetes. An additional danger of being overweight is that many cancer-causing toxins are stored in body fat, so the more fat you have, the more these toxins build up in your body. High levels of chemical toxins can cause liver ailments and a host of problems.

OSTEOPOROSIS

The fact that vegetarians and even vegans are less likely to get osteoporosis flummoxes most meat eaters—after all, vegans aren't drinking enough milk, right? But recent research reveals an interesting twist: eating a high-protein meat-based diet is dangerous to your bones. Most Americans eat more protein than they really need. When you eat too much protein, it makes your body acidic, so your bones release calcium to neutralize the acidity. The upshot is this: if you eat too much protein, then you will have trouble getting enough calcium, no matter how much of it you consume. Fortunately, vegetarian diets are inherently more moderate in protein, making it easier for your body to retain the calcium you eat. Lucky yet again.

CONSTIPATION AND BOWEL HEALTH

Bowels: a delicate subject, but one that is intimately linked to diet. Most people move their bowels every day, or at least every other day, with no problems. Yet for some people, it's not so easy. Sluggish bowels can be a major pain in the ... well, let's just say it can be an unpleasant situation. Some people stay constipated for years, struggling every day to get their bowels in action. Most of the products you see in commercials about constipation—Metamucil, Citrucel, Fibercon, and so forth—are just fiber, they're not really medicine. But they work because a diet high in fiber gets the bowels in gear.

What causes constipation? Imagine your digestive system as a very long tube that starts at your mouth, makes a lot of twists and turns, and ends with your rectum. The walls of this long tube are muscular. Muscle contractions that you can't feel are pushing the food from your mouth all the way through the esophagus, stomach, small and large intestines,

Student Voice: Brooke, Age 18

I started veganism just after my sixteenth birthday. At that time, I hadn't eaten any red meat for two years or poultry for almost a year, so I didn't plunge into the diet. But since veganism would limit my sources of food even more, I read a book about it to learn about how to become a healthy vegan.

I disagree with the food industry's treatment of animals, but my main reason for continuing as a vegan is my health. I feel healthier, both physically and mentally, than when I was eating animal products, especially meat. I feel less lethargic and get sick less often and my concentration has improved. And I'm glad to know my diet has decreased my chances of suffering from strokes and heart attacks.

to the end, where the unusable remains of your food move on out as poop.

Fiber in the food we eat stimulates the muscular walls of the tube to contract and causes the food to move through more quickly. Drinking lots of water helps things move along quickly too because it keeps the material in your intestines soft. If you eat lots of fat, meat, and cheese, these materials tend to slow down and collect in the twists and turns of your intestines. Meat, cheese, and other fiberless foods don't stimulate muscle contractions very much. When food is in the intestines, the intestinal walls absorb water from the food. Food or waste that stays in the intestines too long loses a lot of water and can get very hard. Then it *really* doesn't move very well. The result is constipation. To the rescue: rough, fibrous foods, such as fruits, vegetables, and whole wheat bread, stimulate the muscles of your digestive tract and scrape everything on out. Exercise also seems to stimulate these muscles, maybe by increasing blood flow to the abdominal area.

Generally, people who eat a diet high in fruits, vegetables, and whole grains, who drink a lot of water, and who don't eat much meat have no need for fiber additives. They get all the fiber they need from their food.

The next time somebody brings up your vegetarianism over a meal, make sure you bring this up. It's bound to get the conversation going!

FOOD CONTAMINATION

"It was terrible," our friend Janie said, her eyes wide. "I had to sleep in the bathroom by the toilet all night long because I couldn't stop puking. I threw up the chicken and just kept going and going until there was nothing left. When I wasn't barfing, I fell asleep with my face on the toilet seat."

As this story proves, food poisoning is no joke. But fortunately for you, most of the really icky risks of contamination are found in meat and other animal products. Mad cow disease, for example, is one of the most feared forms of food contamination. Victims of this disease get it from eating infected beef. *Salmonella* poisoning comes from eating meat, poultry, milk, or eggs contaminated with *Salmonella* bacteria. Gross! *E. coli* bacteria is also found in contaminated beef. Another bacteria called *Listeria* typically contaminates raw meat and unpasteurized milk and occasionally deli meats and hot dogs, which are infected after packaging. Pork products sometimes contain a parasite that causes a disease called toxoplasmosis, which is also found sporadically in beef.

TOXIC CHEMICALS

To increase efficiency and remain competitive, the meat industry these days uses various chemicals to raise the animals that will wind up on our dinner tables. Meat has about fourteen times more pesticides than typical plant foods do. And dairy products have about five and one-half times as much as plant foods.[3] This means that more than 95 percent of toxic chemical residues in the American diet come from animal sources. Chemicals collect in fatty tissues, which animals have a lot of, so when animals eat pesticide-covered plants, these chemicals build up in their bodies in high concentrations. If you eat a steak marbled with fat or drink a glass of whole milk, you're consuming a fatty cocktail of chemicals as well.

Nicci (left) and Sara Kate chop veggies for supper.

VEGETARIANS ARE HEALTHIER

Vegetarians as a group are healthier in just about every way than people who eat a diet high in meat. In fact, vegetarians go to the hospital 22 percent less than meat eaters. So the next time someone tells you you're going to die from lack of meat, just shake your head and say, "If only you knew. ... "

Most People Eat Meat—
How Come They're Not All Sick?

A lot of adults who eat a diet high in meat *are* sick, it's just that the illnesses associated with meat are not necessarily obvious to the casual observer. Many of these illnesses, such as heart disease and high blood pressure, take years to develop. The dangers of diet are a matter of probability and risk. We all know people who ride bicycles and motorcycles without helmets who are perfectly healthy. Today. But their risk of injury is much greater than that of people who wear helmets. Likewise, your risk of future illness is greater if you eat a diet high in meat.

If Meat Is So Unhealthy,
Why Do Americans Eat So Much of It?

You may be wondering, if meat is not particularly healthy for us, then why do Americans eat so much of it? And why do many Americans believe that meat is essential for health? The answer to that question is not a simple one, but it is an interesting question that will be addressed as you read on. Essentially, the answer is that we became accustomed to eating meat before scientific discoveries revealed the health risks associated with eating a diet that is high in animal fat and low in fiber. Also, a century ago, animals destined for the dinner table were not pumped full of hormones and other dangerous chemicals. There is also the fact that at that time, cows and pigs and chickens were more likely to live on family farms where they were treated humanely and had relatively happy lives. At that point, we also had ample room on the planet to grow food for all of the human population. Many concerns about meat eating are relatively recent developments.

But Now That We Know These
Problems Exist, Why Do So Many
of Us Keep Eating Meat?

During the last few decades, we have developed a huge meat and dairy industry, and the people who make a living in the industry want it to remain profitable. It's in their personal best interest to promote the consumption of meat and to conceal bad news about it. Not that they are bad people, that's just the nature of business, and it's what they need to do to make money.

There is also the matter of social inertia. Inertia is a law of physics which states that things will continue on in the same direction and at the same speed until something causes them to change. Our meat-eating habits, as a nation, will continue on due to inertia until something causes them to stop. Our pattern will continue until we, as a nation, become aware of new health, environmental, and humane concerns and make a decision to change. It's bound to happen; it has to happen. You can be a forerunner, a trendsetter for the future, or you can wait until the change becomes inevitable.

How Do I Get Enough Protein, Iron, and Vitamins without Meat?

Without a doubt, within your first week as a vegetarian, someone asked you, "But how will you get enough protein?!" To which you sassily replied, "What a question! Don't you know that most Americans actually eat more protein than they need? Plant proteins are nutritional staples in most countries around the world, where people are healthier than American meat eaters."

Okay, so maybe you didn't say that, but you could have. The truth is, while a lot of uninformed people think that a vegetarian diet is dangerously unhealthy, with a little knowledge you can easily get all the nutrients that you need, and then some.

But to know what you need, you have to know what's out there. So let's start at the beginning. The basic building blocks of food are carbohydrates, proteins, fats, vitamins, minerals, and water. You need all of these, in varying amounts. That's right, even carbohydrates, even fats—despite what dieters tell us.

So what does that mean? What are you supposed to eat? And how much of it?

CARBOHYDRATES

Carbohydrates are getting a bad rap these days with all these no-carb diets. But ironically, avoiding carbohydrates is one of the worst things you can do to your body! Low-carbohydrate diets mean eating more protein and more fat, which is a bad idea, for reasons we'll talk about in a minute. Ignore the diet commercials. Carbohydrates are *really* important.

So What Is a Carbohydrate?

Think of carbohydrates as little bundles of sunlight.

Do you realize that the energy that shines down on the Earth as sunlight is the very same energy that makes you alive? The amazing thing is how that energy gets from the atmosphere into our bodies. The process starts as the sun radiates out energy in the form of light and heat, which travels outward into space. A tiny fraction of that energy hits the Earth, making the planet warm and bright enough for us to live on.

When sunlight shines on a plant, the plant's leaves capture that energy through a chemical process called photosynthesis and store it in the form of carbohydrates. Then, when an animal eats the plant, digestion breaks down those carbohydrate storage units and the energy is released for the animal's body to use. That's why eating a bowl of cereal in the

Student Voice:
Jessie, Age 18

I became vegetarian a year and a half ago. When I first began to give up meat, I had a vague idea of why eating meat was harmful to the environment and how horribly animals in factory farms were treated. For me, there was not a defining moment where I transformed into a vegetarian, it was more of a gradual metamorphosis. The more open I became to listening to my vegan older brother and others, and also doing my own research, the more it made complete sense to make the switch. Now it seems ridiculous to switch back.

People often ask me, "What can you eat as a vegetarian?" But finding alternatives hasn't been hard. The truth is, other countries don't eat as much meat to begin with, and so looking to other cultures is a great place to start. The key is being open to new things. The American diet can be very meat oriented, but there's so much out there to choose from.

I always find it amusing when people scoff at all the different ways tofu is eaten, when chicken dominates so many of their own dishes. Many of my friends have tried vegetarianism because it's a fad. While it can tarnish the integrity of the movement by having "vegetarians" who still eat chicken and pork, I still believe any bit helps.

morning gives you the energy to go to class or your job and work really hard. (Theoretically, anyway!)

But some foods give you more energy than others. Did you know that calories are a measure of energy? The more calories a food has, the more energy it provides your body. This depends on the proportion of those basic building blocks that make up food— specifically carbohydrates, proteins, and fats. (Vitamins, minerals, and water have no calories and therefore provide no energy.) Fats provide nine calories for every gram that you eat and carbohydrates and proteins both provide four. But because it's hard for our bodies to digest complex carbohydrates, such as fiber and cellulose, scientists figure they actually provide more like two calories per gram.

Nonetheless, our bodies are meant to get energy from carbohydrates. Despite their low-calorie yield, carbohydrates are nature's most efficient way of passing energy from one living thing to another. Digesting protein is hard on your liver and kidneys and eating a lot of fat leads to all kinds of diseases, from obesity to heart disease. If you don't eat enough carbohydrates, you may feel sluggish or tired.

But all carbohydrates are not created equal. Basically, "carbo" means carbon, and "hydrate" means water. That's because a carbohydrate is a little unit of carbon attached to water. A simple carbohydrate is just one of those units, or maybe two linked together. Simple carbohydrates are sugars, such as sucrose, which is white table sugar, or lactose, the sugar that's found in milk and other dairy products.

On the other hand, a complex carbohydrate is lots and lots of those little units linked together in a long chain. The fiber found in a bran muffin and the starches in potatoes are examples of complex carbohydrates, as are most of the carbohydrates in whole grains, beans, vegetables, and fruits. Complex carbohydrates are really good for you.

Eating lots of them reduces the likelihood of just about every disease that's common in the United States these days.

A high-fiber diet can help reduce cholesterol and fat, not to mention the risk of heart disease, cancer, diabetes, obesity, and gastrointestinal diseases, just to name a few possibilities. And here's the good news for you: vegetarian diets are naturally richer in fiber because there's no fiber in meat, none at all. You have to get carbohydrates from veggies and plant foods, which we vegetarians, of course, eat a lot of.

How Much of My Food Should Be Carbohydrates?

A healthy diet should consist of between 55 and 75 percent carbohydrates, according to international health organizations. Why? Well, populations that eat lots of animal products— and therefore lots of animal fats and protein—have high rates of heart disease, cancer, diabetes, obesity, and other chronic diseases. But populations that eat plant-based diets, which are high in carbohydrates, have fewer health problems. Also, eating plant-based foods means you're consuming more antioxidants, micronutrients, and phytochemicals— tiny compounds that keep you healthy.

What Foods Have Lots of Carbohydrates?

Your carbohydrates should come from a lot of different foods; a varied diet is always healthier. Good sources of fiber include veggies, fruits, beans, whole grains, and nuts, not to mention cereals and whole wheat bread. Check out that box of raisin bran—there are eight grams of fiber in just one cup. Whoa!

Starch comes from grains, such as oats, barley, and wheat, which can take the form of bread, noodles, cereal, and so on. Starch is also found in some veggies, such as potatoes and corn.

PROTEINS

Vegetarians get ragged on about protein more than any other nutrient. It's true, meat is high in protein, but so are lots of other foods. And, you guessed it, plant proteins are healthier than animal proteins.

What Is Protein?

You may know that amino acids are the building blocks of proteins. Amino acids come with weird names, such as tryptophan (that's the one in turkey that makes you sleepy) and phenylalanine. Despite the fancy names, amino acids are just the building blocks of proteins. There are twenty different kinds of them, nine of which your body can't produce. We need to get these nine, called the essential amino acids, from eating foods with protein. Animal products, as well as soy, have what's called complete protein—protein with all nine of the essential amino acids. Both cows' milk and soy milk have complete protein. All plant products besides soy have incomplete protein—protein with only some of the essential amino acids. But this is not a problem. Eating a variety of plant foods generally provides all of the essential amino acids. For example, a combination of legumes (beans or peas) and grains (wheat, rice, or corn) provides complete protein. Black beans on rice with salsa—bingo! You've got all nine essential amino acids.

People used to think you had to eat the complementary foods, for example, beans plus grains, at the same time in order for your body to assemble all the essential amino acids into proteins, but we now know that's not true. Your body can store them for a while. So if you eat a whole wheat bagel for breakfast and lentil soup for supper, your body will be able to assemble proteins just fine.

And get this: only 20 percent of your protein needs to be complete anyway. The adult requirement for the essential amino acids is covered by just eleven grams of complete protein a day.

Protein is used by your body to make and repair muscles and other tissues. Hormones, antibodies, and enzymes are also built from proteins. But all in all, our bodies are made of only about 15 percent protein.

How Much Protein Do I Need?

This might surprise you, but only 10 to 15 percent of your calories should come from protein. (Compare that to 55 to 75 percent for carbohydrates.) You can figure out how many grams a day that means for you by following this formula:

_____ pounds ÷ 2.2 = _____ kilograms
your weight, in pounds   your weight in kilograms

_____ kilograms x 0.8 = _____ grams
your weight in kilograms   grams of protein you
                                  need per day

A person weighing 125 pounds needs about forty-five grams of protein a day. At 150 pounds, you would need fifty-five grams of protein a day. This varies with level of exercise.

What Foods Have Lots of Protein?

Fortunately for you, between 10 and 40 percent of the calories in most plant foods come from protein, which is a lot more than the 10 to 15 percent that you need per day, so getting enough protein is really no problem. Corn, for example, has 15 percent of its calories from protein, and corn isn't even a particularly protein-rich food.

Clearly, all the worry about vegetarians getting enough protein has no basis in reality. Did you know that a cup of raisin bran has six grams of protein? Or that a cup of soy milk has seven? When you need forty-five grams a day, knocking out thirteen grams with breakfast gives you a good start. If you're looking for more protein in your diet, keep an eye out for beans, nuts, and even grain products that we usually think of as carbohydrates, such as whole wheat bread.

Here are some tasty sources of protein, and the number of grams of protein in each:

- ¼ cup soy nuts (roasted soybeans): 19 grams
- I cup cooked lentils, beans, or peas: 15 to 17 grams
- I soy protein bar: 14 grams
- 4 ounces firm tofu: 13 grams
- I veggie burger: 10 to 12 grams
- I soy "hot dog": 11 grams
- ¼ cup peanuts: 10 grams
- ¼ cup tempeh (a soy product for cooking): 10 grams
- I cup soy milk: 7 to 10 grams, depending on the brand
- 2 ounces dry whole wheat pasta: 9 grams
- 2 tablespoons peanut butter: 8 grams
- I cup cows' milk: 8 grams
- I cup yogurt: 8 grams
- ¼ cup almonds, cashews, or walnuts: 7 to 8 grams
- I soy "sausage" link: 6 grams
- I cup cooked brown rice: 5 grams
- I cup cooked oatmeal: 5 grams
- 2 biscuits shredded wheat: 5 grams
- I soy "chicken nugget": 3 grams
- ½ cup ice cream: 3 grams
- ½ avocado: 3 grams
- ½ cup cooked broccoli: 2 grams

FATS

When you go in the grocery store, you can't escape the low-fat and fat-free messages on food packages. And the messages are right: too much fat is dangerous to your health. A cinnamon bun sporting fifty-seven grams of fat, for instance, is obviously not a wise choice. But not all fats are bad. In fact, some fats are just as important as protein and carbohydrates. It doesn't take much of them, but without them, your body wouldn't be able to function, so it's important to become a savvy consumer of fats.

Student Voice:
Heidi, Age 20

I'm really interested in nutrition; I want to be a nutritionist. I've studied nutrition for a number of years now, and over and over again I am fascinated that there are all these foods that can do things that we just don't know about. When I study nutrition in graduate school, I don't want to go to a traditional nutrition program that will tell me to teach people about the food pyramid and serving sizes because I really don't think that's what it's about. I think it's about listening to your body.

I have hypoglycemia, so I can see clearly how the food that I eat affects me. Like in the mornings, I can't eat a bagel for breakfast or I'll fall asleep in class. I have to have protein. If I don't have protein and fat and it's just carbohydrates, I go to sleep, because my body burns that up so fast. So that's part of how I got interested in it. Realizing that connection between the food I eat and how I feel makes me think twice about what else I eat, because there's just such a connection between how you eat and how you feel.

Learn which fats you need and which ones you don't, and where to find each of them.

What Is Fat?

You know what fat is. It's greasy stuff, stuff that makes you lick your fingers. It's butter, it's oil, it's the soggy cardboard pizza box, the creamy inside of an avocado. Fat's special trick—besides making food taste rich and heavy—is that it doesn't dissolve in water. That's why salad dressing separates into oil and vinegar. It's also why fat can line the insides of your blood vessels without getting washed away.

But don't get too alarmed just yet. There are three kinds of fats you need to know about: saturated fat, monounsaturated fat, and polyunsaturated fat. And there's also one crazy thing called a trans-fatty acid, but we'll get to that in a minute. First of all …

Saturated Fat

Three fats walked into a bar. One was a puddle of liquid, one was kind of squishy, and one was a stick of butter. Which one was the saturated fat? Answer: the stick of butter. Generally, saturated fat is solid at room temperature, liquid when warmer. This is because it's saturated with hydrogen. Being saturated means that in its chemical structure, every empty space is packed with a hydrogen atom. You wouldn't think that would matter much, but being stuffed full of hydrogen like that is what makes it stiff and solid and is also what makes it bad for you. Think of the fat that people trim off the sides of steaks and pork chops. Think of lard, margarine, and ice cream. Because we don't eat much coconut or palm oil, animal products are generally where you find the most saturated fat in American diets.

As you can probably predict, saturated fat is the one you don't want. Eating too much saturated fat increases the level of cholesterol in your body, which is dangerous to your health. Although a little bit of saturated fat is okay—up to 10 percent of your daily calorie intake—too much leads to heart disease, cancer, and, well, fatness. These are rampant medical problems here in the United States. On page 134 you can read about how cholesterol almost killed former president Bill Clinton.

Monounsaturated Fat

Monounsaturated fat, on the other hand, is the healthiest fat. In fact, it actually makes you healthier. It's called monounsaturated because it's missing just one of the hydrogen atoms that saturated fat has (mono means one). This makes it liquid at room temperature. When chilled in the fridge, some monounsaturated oils, such as olive oil, become a mushy solid.

Monounsaturated fat protects against chronic diseases, such as heart disease and cancer. It helps to raise your levels of good cholesterol, called high-density lipoprotein (HDL), lower your bad cholesterol, called low-density lipoprotein (LDL), and stabilize your blood sugar. Some scientists believe that it even allows your blood to flow better and reduces blood pressure. It's in avocados, nuts other than walnuts, and olive, canola, and peanut oils. But even with good fats such as these, no more than 30 percent of your daily calories should come from fat.

Polyunsaturated Fat

Polyunsaturated fat is missing more than one hydrogen atom (poly means many), which means it stays a liquid unless the temperature drops well below freezing. The effects of polyunsaturated oils on health are debatable: they are definitely better than saturated fat, but no one seems to agree on just how good they are. The oils from corn, soybeans, safflowers, and sunflowers are mainly polyunsaturated oils.

Essential Fatty Acids

Essential fatty acids, or EFAs, are a type of polyunsaturated fatty acids. There are two main kinds, commonly known as omega-3 and omega-6 fatty acids. Although they are important for our reproductive, cardiovascular, immune, and nervous systems, our bodies cannot make them, so we have to get them from the food we eat. Omega-6 is found in many places, but omega-3 is only found in a few. The best sources are walnuts, flax, hemp, pumpkin seeds, soybeans, olive oil, wheat germ, and salmon, if you eat fish. Just five walnut halves a day—eighteen grams—is enough to meet your omega-3 needs. Likewise, one tablespoon of flaxseed oil also delivers enough EFAs for one day. Some cereals and soy milks are also fortified with EFAs.

Trans-Fatty Acids

This is the Frankenstein, the monster of the fat world. Trans-fats are totally unnatural, a freak produced in the laboratory. They're created during food processing when an unsaturated oil—one that's missing some hydrogen atoms—has hydrogen forced into the empty spaces. This process is called hydrogenation and it turns the liquid fat into a solid. Food manufacturers like to do this for a couple of reasons. One reason is that hydrogenated fats boil at a higher temperature, which is better for deep-frying food. (Better because the food is crisper and absorbs less oil during cooking.) The second reason is that solid fats don't spoil as fast as nonhydrogenated fats do. This means that Twinkies and potato chips can sit on the shelf for a lot longer without getting too old to eat. I mean, can you imagine a bag of Ruffles going bad the way a loaf of bread does? Well, they don't, and that's because they're hydrogenated.

Useful as this is, it's terrible news for your body. Trans-fatty acids are two to four times as bad for you as saturated fat. Keep an eye out for them in all processed foods, as well as margarine. Most margarines, while lower in saturated fat than butter, replace it with trans-fats. But there are a few brands that are safe. Check the nutritional facts.

That's a lot of numbers and confusing chemistry stuff to remember when you're in the grocery store staring at packages and trying to figure out what to put in the cart. Don't

stress about the percentages and big words too much. In general, you can bet that any food that's part of a plant, even if it has a lot of fat, such as olives, is probably good for you. And any highly packaged food or high-fat animal product probably isn't. The healthiest fats or oils are olive, flaxseed, canola, and soybean. The worst are cottonseed and palm oil.

WHAT IS CHOLESTEROL? AND WHAT IS A HEART ATTACK?

Cholesterol has a very bad reputation. People associate it with heart disease, and rightly so.

No matter what we eat, everybody has some cholesterol—our bodies make it. We need some cholesterol. It is a building block of vitamin D, various hormones, and the bile salts that break down fats in the intestine. It has its good points.

Some of the foods we eat are high in cholesterol or in saturated fats, both of which can increase the level of cholesterol in our bodies. Egg yolks and organ meats have a lot of cholesterol, but those aren't the only dangers. Labels are deceiving. A food label that says "No Cholesterol" can be technically correct but purposely misleading. For example, many kinds of margarine are labeled "No Cholesterol." The food producer wants you to think that eating this product will not increase the level of cholesterol in your blood. However, the truth is that any food with saturated fat can increase the amount of cholesterol in your body. Saturated fats may be called "hydrogenated oil" or "partially hydrogenated oil" on a label.

When we have too much cholesterol, our bodies are not able to get rid of it very well. We can't break it down and very little is excreted in our urine. The extra cholesterol is deposited on the inside of our blood vessels and this causes circulation problems. These deposits are called plaque. When plaque clogs up the blood vessels that carry blood to the

CLINTON HAD
QUADRUPLE BYPASS SURGERY

Former president Bill Clinton had quadruple heart bypass surgery on September 6, 2004. His doctors said that several major blood vessels were so clogged that only 10 percent of normal blood flow could get through. They said their surgery prevented a potentially massive and fatal heart attack.

During bypass surgery, a vessel cut from elsewhere in the body is sewn in to detour blood flow around the clogged blockages. A quadruple bypass means he had four detours sewn into the vessels around his heart. These vessels that supply blood to the heart muscle itself are especially crucial. If they are blocked, then heart muscle dies. This is known as a heart attack and is often fatal.

After surgery, Clinton had to change his diet. No more fast-food burgers. His doctors put him on a diet very low in saturated fat.

Any foods fried in animal fat or in hydrogenated or partially hydrogenated vegetable oils are high in saturated fat. In the language of fats, hydrogenated is another word for saturated. So margarines, salad dressings, and baked goods made with hydrogenated or partially hydrogenated vegetable oils are high in saturated fat. They can raise your cholesterol level.

This is not to say you should never eat anything made with saturated fat. Heredity plays a big part in determining your blood cholesterol level. Some people can eat moderate amounts of saturated fat and still keep their blood cholesterol low. Others must be very careful about their diet in order to keep their cholesterol in the healthy range. For some, even diet is not enough. Many adults take medication to reduce their cholesterol.

**Student Voice:
Anastasia, Age 19**

My mom's all about health—she hates hydrogenated oils! When we were little, we couldn't have any food with hydrogenated oils in the house. It is *painful* for her to hear about us eating food she wouldn't choose for us! It's funny, at home I eat so much brown rice and vegetables, it's like "Oh, jeez, not this … " because that's what she eats all the time. But now that I'm in college, I'm like, "Oh, man, what I wouldn't do for some brown rice and veggies!"

I feel lucky to have been raised vegetarian. It might be harder if I knew what I was missing, if I really loved and missed a hamburger.

muscles of the heart, it can cause the muscles of the heart to stop or almost stop working. This is what we call a heart attack.

What Foods Are High in Saturated Fat?

Any fat in an animal product is saturated fat that can raise cholesterol. Some meats, especially beef and pork, are high in fat. Meats with visible fat, such as bacon, have more fat than lean meats do.

Dairy products made from whole milk are high in saturated fat. The word "whole" means that much of the original fat in the milk still remains. Skim milk has had almost all the milk fat removed. Milk labeled as 1 percent is only 1 percent milk fat. Likewise, milk labeled as 2 percent is 2 percent milk fat. These are both lower in milk fat than whole milk. Most cheese is made from whole milk, unless the wrapper says that it's made from skim.

The following chart describes different kinds of fats, or oils. The healthiest oils to cook with or use for salads are olive oil or canola oil.

Type of Fat	Main Source	State at Room Temperature	Effect on Cholesterol Levels
Monounsaturated	Avocados, almonds, cashews, peanuts, peanut oil, olives, olive oil, canola oil	Liquid	Lowers LDL, raises HDL*
Polyunsaturated	Corn oil, soybean oil, safflower oil, fish	Liquid	Lowers LDL, raises HDL
Saturated	Butter, cheese, milk, ice cream, red meat, chocolate, coconuts, coconut oil	Solid	Raises LDL and HDL
Trans	Most margarine, vegetable shortening, partially hydrogenated vegetable oil, chips, fast food, prepackaged baked goods	Solid or semisolid	Raises LDL

*LDL is bad cholesterol, which you want to be low, and HDL is good cholesterol, which you want to be high.

MICRONUTRIENTS: VITAMINS AND MINERALS

Vitamins and minerals are two of the six basic building blocks of food, but unlike carbohydrates, proteins, and fats, they do not provide energy. They fulfill roles that are different but equally important, as we'll discuss in a minute.

The list of minerals that the body is known to need is constantly increasing. Some of these, such as iron and calcium, are familiar. Others, such as selenium and magnesium, aren't as well known. Many of these are only needed in tiny amounts, hence they are called trace minerals.

While minerals are inorganic, vitamins are organic compounds (meaning carbon based). The number of vitamins is firmly established at thirteen. These are split into two categories, water soluble and fat soluble. The fat-soluble vitamins, A, D, E, and K, can be absorbed and stored by the fat in your body—so if you eat a carrot on Tuesday, you can use the vitamin A on Saturday afternoon. Water-soluble vitamins, on the other hand, can't be stored in your body, so you need to eat them every day. These include all the B vitamins and vitamin C.

So that's all fine and dandy, but what do all those letters *mean*? What do vitamins and minerals do, and where can you find them?

Iron and Vitamin C

Iron is one of the nutrients that vegetarians worry about the most. It is important because your body uses it to make hemoglobin, the part of your blood that carries oxygen. Our bodies know how to recycle iron pretty efficiently, but still, we lose a little bit every so often, so we need to replenish it through our diet. As you know, blood is iron rich; therefore, girls and women in particular need to consume lots of iron to compensate for blood loss during menstruation. But it's important for guys too. Women over age eleven need fifteen milligrams a day. Guys under age eighteen need twelve milligrams a day, but only ten milligrams after that.

It's a common belief that getting enough iron on a vegetarian diet is hard to do. It is true that there's a lot of iron in red meat, but that doesn't mean you can't get any without it. In fact, vegetarians are no more likely to suffer from iron deficiency than are meat eaters.

There are two kinds of iron: one is found in animals, one is found in plants. It's harder for your body to absorb the kind of iron found in plants, but eating vitamin C at the same time makes it a lot easier. Vitamin C is found in citrus fruits, bell peppers, and leafy green vegetables such as spinach. Iron comes from all kinds of places, from chickpeas to spinach to fortified cereals and milks. There are lots of ways to combine iron-rich and vitamin C–rich foods. For example, bean chili with tomato sauce or breakfast cereal plus a class of orange juice are logical ways to combine the two.

Vitamin C is also important on its own. It keeps your skin stretchy and healthy and helps hold together blood vessels, scar tissue, bones, and teeth.

Here are some examples of iron-rich foods:

- 1 cup cooked lentils: 7 milligrams
- 2 tablespoons blackstrap molasses: 6 milligrams
- 1 cup kidney, pinto, or garbanzo beans: 5 milligrams
- 4 ounces seitan (wheat protein): 4 milligrams
- 1 cup cooked Swiss chard: 4 milligrams
- 1 cup cooked black beans: 4 milligrams
- 1 cup cooked spinach: 3 milligrams
- 1 baked potato with skin: 3 milligrams
- 2 tablespoons sesame seeds: 3 milligrams
- 5 medium figs: 2 milligrams
- ½ cup tempeh: 1 milligram
- 5 dried apricots: 2 milligrams
- ½ cup raisins: 2 milligrams
- 4 ounces tofu: 1 to 10 milligrams, depending on the brand

Here are some examples of vitamin C–rich foods:

- 1 cup cranberry juice: 100 milligrams
- 1 cup orange juice: 97 milligrams
- ½ chopped red pepper: 95 milligrams
- ½ medium papaya: 94 milligrams
- 1 cup strawberries: 85 milligrams
- 1 cup grapefruit juice: 83 milligrams
- 1 orange: 80 milligrams
- 1 kiwi: 75 milligrams
- 1 cup chopped cantaloupe: 68 milligrams
- ½ cup chopped green pepper: 64 milligrams
- 1 cup cooked kale: 54 milligrams
- ½ cup cooked broccoli: 49 milligrams
- 4 Brussels sprouts: 48 milligrams
- 1 cup raw cabbage: 34 milligrams
- ½ cup cooked cauliflower: 34 milligrams
- 1 cup raspberries: 31 milligrams
- 1 baked sweet potato: 28 milligrams
- 1 baked potato with skin: 26 milligrams
- 1 tomato: 22 milligrams
- 2 tablespoons fresh parsley: 19 milligrams
- 2 tablespoons fresh lemon juice: 14 milligrams

One farmer says to me, "You cannot live on vegetable food solely, for it furnishes nothing to make the bones with"; and so he religiously devotes a part of his day to supplying himself with the raw material of bones; walking all the while he talks behind his oxen, which, with vegetable-made bones, jerk him and his lumbering plow along in spite of every obstacle.

—Henry David Thoreau

Calcium

Many of us grew up hearing our mothers insist every day, "Don't get up until you finish your milk!" And if we didn't hear it from Mom, we got it loud and clear from celebrities in the popular "Got milk?" ads: drink your milk for healthy bones.

Yeah, calcium's important, and it's true, milk is a good way to get it. But no one ever seems to mention the fact that it's not the *only* way. The truth is, soy milk, leafy green vegetables, dried fruit, and nuts are just a few of the many sources of calcium. In fact, some soy milks are so well fortified that they have even more calcium than cows' milk.

However you consume it, calcium makes your skeleton strong. It helps prevent broken bones and makes you less likely to develop osteoporosis later in life. It's especially important to consume a lot of calcium when you're young, because that's when bone mass is forming. It's a lot easier to add calcium to bones during your youth than it is after you've finished growing.

In one way, vegetarians have an advantage with calcium. Experts have noticed that in other countries, people consume a lot less calcium than Americans do, and yet their bones are stronger and healthier. How can that be? The explanation is that eating lots of protein makes it hard for your body to retain calcium. So Americans, who eat more meat than people in most other countries, need extra calcium to balance out all that animal protein. Vegetarians, however, don't have this problem.

In another way, though, vegetarians have a disadvantage: calcium is harder to absorb from plant sources than from animal products. So whether you eat spare ribs or asparagus spears, you need to be aware of your calcium intake.

But where can you find it? As we all know, dairy products, such as milk and yogurt, have a lot of calcium, but so do fortified soy milk and rice milk, as well as kale, broccoli, navy beans, and lots of greens. These days, calcium-fortified orange juice and tofu are available too. If you're worried about getting enough, you can take a calcium supplement. Many doctors suggest two Tums taken twice a day (that's four in all) as an easy and cheap calcium supplement. The size of the Tums doesn't matter because your body can't absorb more than 600 milligrams of calcium at one time. Better safe than sorry.

Vitamin D

Known by its friends as calciferol, vitamin D is necessary for bone formation and for retention of calcium and phosphorus. These three nutrients work together: vitamin D absorbs calcium into the bloodstream and phosphorus helps add the calcium to your bones and teeth. So if you're worried about calcium, make sure you're getting enough of these helpers too. Phosphorus is plentiful in lots of foods, from beans and dairy products to chocolate and peanut butter. Yum! Meanwhile, there are far fewer dietary sources of vitamin D, such as egg yolk and fortified milks and cereals, but the neat thing is that your body can also produce it from sunshine. That's right—a little sun now and then will help you have strong bones. It's one of nature's little secrets. And while you're outside, try a little walking or jogging—weight-bearing exercise also helps strengthen bones.

Vitamin B12

The last of the supposed big worries for vegetarians is B12. Unlike iron and calcium, this one actually is a bit of a concern because it's only found in animal products. Some people use this as an argument against veganism—if it were a healthy diet, wouldn't you be able to get all the nutrients you need? The answer is a surprising one: a long time ago, you could. There are bacteria that produce B12, and once upon a time, these bacteria mildly contaminated our fruits and vegetables, making it easy for humans to get all the B12 they needed from plant sources. But in this highly sanitized era of antibacterial soap, there is a lot less bacteria in our food and, consequently, very little B12.

Nonetheless, if you eat cheese, milk, or eggs, you shouldn't have a problem. One cup of fortified soy milk has 0.75 micrograms. A slice of cheddar cheese—40 grams—contains 0.5 micrograms. A boiled egg contains 0.7 micrograms. But even if you don't eat dairy, you can get B12 easily. Fortified cereals, such as raisin bran, have about 0.4 micrograms per cup. You can also take supplements.

You need about 1.5 micrograms of B12 a day. That is a very tiny but necessary amount. To put it in perspective, one gram of B12—the weight of a couple kernels of popcorn—would be enough to last you 1,826 years. But even though the amount required daily is microscopic, it's essential for maintaining the central nervous system.

The Other B Vitamins

There are eight B vitamins in all, but it seems like the only one you ever hear about is B12. It's just because the other ones are easier to find, so no one worries about them as much. Nonetheless, they're important. The less famous B cousins include thiamin (B1), riboflavin (B2), niacin (B3), pyridoxine (B6), and folic acid. They all work in different ways to keep your body functioning and healthy and can be easily found in whole-grain foods, veggies, beans, nuts, and fortified milks and cereals.

Vitamin A

Vegetarians and meat eaters alike need vitamin A, which is also called retinol. Vitamin A contributes to your skin, bones, teeth, and, most important, vision. There are two ways to get it in your diet. One is in its ready-made form, from animal products such as milk, cheese, and egg yolks. But your body can also manufacture

it when you eat foods containing a substance called carotene. Carotene comes mostly from foods that are orange, such as carrots, squash, and sweet potatoes, as well as foods that are green, such as spinach and broccoli.

Zinc

As with calcium, vegetarians have an advantage with zinc. The less protein you eat, the less zinc you need, and it's kind of hard to find. Fortunately, chickpeas, kidney beans, and lentils are all good sources of zinc. If you cook them in something acidic, such as tomato sauce or lemon juice, the zinc is easier for your body to absorb. Yay for beans!

AHH!
HOW DO I REMEMBER ALL THIS?

Take a deep breath. After reading this section, your brain is probably overflowing with numbers, weird combinations of foods, and images of malnourished refugees, but there's no need to stress. You don't need to memorize all this information and recite it before every bite you take. Basically, with a few rules of thumb you'll be fine.

- Eat a varied diet. If you eat a lot of different things, even if one of them isn't particularly nutrient-rich, the others will help balance it out. This will keep you from getting too little or too much of any one nutrient.
- Eat colorful food. It may sound strange, but it's true: brightly colored foods are often the healthiest. (Food coloring doesn't count!) Orange sweet potatoes, green spinach, red peppers, yellow bananas, blueberries, and purple eggplant are all better for you than white rice or pasta.
- Eat ethnic. A lot of cultures around the world are mostly vegetarian. As a result, they have a lot more variety in traditional vegetarian fare than the American diet does. Try going to a Mexican, Indian, or Greek restaurant instead of Chili's or Applebee's—you'll be amazed by

Vitamins	Sources	Function	Not Enough?	Too Much?	Notes
Vitamin A	Green and yellow veggies, fruits, and whole milk	Keeps skin, mucous membranes, bones, teeth, and night vision healthy	Causes blindness, night blindness, and stunted growth	Only from taking animal form in pills. Causes headache, nausea, diarrhea	Wards against cancer. Vegetarians get plenty without supplements.
Vitamin D	Egg yolk, sunlight, and fortified milk	Regulates use of calcium and phosphorus	Causes bone deformation and stunted growth	Causes calcium deposits in kidneys and blood vessels	Get outside—sunlight produces vitamin D in our skin.
Vitamin E	Vegetable oils, nuts, and grains	Acts as an antioxidant	This is very rare—causes fragile blood cells	Causes excess bleeding or blood clots	The more polyunsaturated fat you eat, the more vitamin E you need.
Vitamin K	Spinach, leafy greens, and cauliflower	Enhances blood clotting	Causes easy bruising and blood doesn't clot		Half the vitamin K you need is produced by bacteria in your intestines.
Vitamin B1 (thiamin)	Whole grains, beans, and yeast	Converts fats, carbohydrates, and protein to energy	Causes beriberi, weight loss, depression, and crankiness		Deficiency is much more common due to common use of refined grains.
Vitamin B2 (riboflavin)	Legumes, green vegetables, yeast, and milk	Metabolizes fats, carbohydrates, and protein	Causes irritated eyes, scaly skin, and a purple tongue		It's easily destroyed by exposure to light.
Vitamin B3 (niacin)	Legumes, grains, green vegetables, milk, and coffee	Converts fats, carbohydrates, and protein to energy	Causes crankiness, insomnia, diarrhea, dementia, and skin irritation	Causes hot, prickly skin, nausea, and diarrhea	It's not broken down by heat, but is leached out when cooked in water.
Vitamin B6 (pyridoxine)	Beans, grains, carrots, bananas, and eggs	Metabolizes protein and forms nerve tissue and blood cells	Causes anemia, dizziness, and confusion	Causes neurological damage	Most Americans need more, due to eating too much protein.
Vitamin C	Citrus fruit, melons, berries, tomatoes, green vegetables, and potatoes	Acts as an antioxidant, transports hydrogen, forms collagen, and heals wounds	Causes scurvy, bleeding gums, and joint pain	Causes urinary stones	All animals except fruit bats, guinea pigs, humans and other primates produce their own.

the number of choices you have. And a lot of them are things you can cook at home.

- Avoid junk food. Sure, eat that candy bar if the craving strikes and don't feel bad for downing a potato chip or two. But in general, if you're filling up on junk, there's no room for all the healthy foods that you need to keep you going.

- Eat fruits and vegetables for snacks. An apple's just as easy to grab as a handful of candy, and far better for you.

- Don't overdo the dairy products. As you cut meat out of your diet, don't replace it with cheese and eggs. While dairy products are okay in moderation, they do have lots of fat,

Minerals	Sources	Function	Not Enough?	Too Much?	Notes
Calcium	Milk, yogurt, soy milk, broccoli, and leafy greens such as kale	Keeps bones, teeth, blood, and muscles healthy	Causes rickets and stunted growth	Causes calcium deposits and urinary stones	It is complemented by magnesium.
Chromium	Grains and brewer's yeast	Controls blood sugar	The body can't break down sugar well.		Refined sugar and flour make it hard to find.
Copper	Nuts, beans, grains, and water	Keeps blood, protein fibers, and skin pigment healthy	Very rare	Causes neurological problems, liver damage, vomiting	Calcium decreases absorption; zinc increases need.
Iodine	Salt and sea vegetables	Boosts energy and metabolism, keeps thyroid hormone and cell growth healthy		Causes goiters and birth defects	It's added to table salt and many processed foods.
Iron	Beans, molasses, grains, dried fruit, potatoes, egg yolk, and cocoa	Assists blood cell formation and oxygen transport	Causes anemia and weakness	Causes iron deposits and constipation	Black tea and meat inhibit absorption; vitamin C helps it.
Magnesium	Nuts, beans, grains, leafy greens, and milk	Keeps bones, teeth, nerves, muscles, and bowels healthy	Causes stunted growth, weakness, and seizures	Causes diarrhea	It is complemented by calcium.
Manganese	Nuts, grains, beans, tea, fruits, and nonleafy veggies	Aids the use of sugar and enzyme activation	Very rare	Causes problems with nervous system	It is found in almost all plants, making it easy to get enough.
Molybdenum	Whole grains and beans, depending on soil	Assists formation of enzymes		Causes gout and the loss of copper	It's needed to form uric acid, a component of urine.
Phosphorus	Milk, cheese, soy milk, nuts, cereals, and legumes	Keeps bones and teeth healthy and is used in energy-releasing reactions	Causes weakness, rickets, and neurological problems		Most Americans get plenty.
Potassium	Fruits, root vegetables, and leafy greens	Acts as an electrolyte within cells	Causes weakness	Causes weakness and heart difficulties	The toxicity from pills is dangerous.
Selenium	Plant proteins, depending on soil	Acts as an antioxidant	Causes heart damage and muscle pain	Causes hair and nail loss and difficulty breathing	It lowers the risk of cancer.
Sodium	Salt	Acts as an electrolyte in body fluids	Causes weakness, cramps, confusion, low blood pressure, and loss of appetite	Causes high blood pressure and heart failure	Processed foods have extremely high amounts of sodium.
Zinc	Nuts, wheat germ, eggs, and cereal	Enhances growth, wound healing, sexual maturation, protein synthesis, immunity, and the ability to taste	Causes rash, stunted growth, delayed puberty, and an abnormal sense of taste and smell	Interferes with absorption of magnesium and affects cholesterol usage	Most zinc poisoning results from drinking fruit drinks in steel containers.

and many have chemicals in them as well. Plus, they lack the fiber and many of the nutrients of plant foods.

The beef industry has contributed to more American deaths than all the wars of this century, all natural disasters, and all automobile accidents combined. If beef is your idea of "real food for real people" you'd better live real close to a real good hospital.

—Neal Barnard, M.D.

Wait, Aren't We Supposed to Eat Meat?

Imagine: you're crouched in the swaying grasses on the edge of a meadow. Under your taut skin, you can feel your empty tummy rumbling in your gut. Before you, nosing around in the brush, is your prey: a plump, juicy rabbit. You tense your leg muscles, push your toes down into the dirt, and flex your fingers and hands. You can feel the sweat beading on your forehead, feel your heart thumping. Ready? Okay, one, two, three ... go! Now your feet are pounding through the grass. You're racing forward, diving, sailing through the air. Arms stretched toward your prey—but oh, no! The rabbit saw you coming and—zoom!—in a flash it dove into its hole. No supper for you tonight.

Oh, so that *isn't* how you do your grocery shopping? Well, why not?

I guess it's no wonder that many of our ancestors didn't eat much meat. We're not exactly fearsome predators. Of course, many of our predecessors did eat meat, but modern humans evolved over millions of years with a wide variety of dietary habits. In fact, that's one of the reasons we've made it this far: humans are remarkably adaptable, surviving on all kinds of diets in all kinds of climates.

WHAT CAN TEETH TELL US?

The teeth of fossil animals can tell anthropologists a lot about their diets: herbivores and carnivores have different kinds of teeth. But scientists are not as clear about the clues found in the structure of our own teeth. On one hand, we have canines, the pointy, puncturing teeth that carnivores use to snap spinal columns and tear flesh. But many herbivores, or plant eaters, have canines too. Gorillas, for example, have canine teeth, but they eat a strictly vegetarian diet. Chimps, our very closest relatives, also sport canines, and they eat mostly leaves and fruit.

More conclusive evidence is found behind the canines, in the shape of our premolars and molars. In herbivores, these teeth are flat with opposing surfaces that are used for grinding and crushing grains and plants. In carnivores, the premolars and molars have more points and interdigitate for cutting and tearing. Our own premolars and molars are more like those of herbivores, suggesting that our ancestral diet was mostly plants.

There is some debate among anthropologists about when our own species, *Homo sapiens*, first began to eat meat. But there is strong evidence that organized hunting began only recently in our evolution—in the last 60,000 years of our 200,000-year history as *Homo sapiens*.

Even though we've been eating some meat for tens of thousands of years, human intestines and digestive enzymes are still more like those of plant eaters than of meat eaters. In general, human bodies are not very efficient meat-eating machines. We do have canine teeth, but they are not the sharp daggers of carnivores, such as cats. We lack strong, deadly jaws. Where are our fierce claws? Could we run fast enough to ambush any animal other than a turtle?

FROM WHALE BLUBBER TO CACTUS FRUIT

In spite of these physical setbacks, humans are pretty brainy and we've figured out a trick or two over the years. The earliest humans scavenged for already-dead meat and learned to set traps and use tools to enhance their physical limitations. Particularly in colder climates, hunting became necessary in order to survive the long, cold months when plant food was scarce. Some groups, such as the Alaskan Inuits, have thrived on very high quantities of fish and meat for thousands of years. However, at the same time, their relatives thousands of miles to the south have subsisted for just as long on corn and beans, which grow well in a desert climate with few prey animals. In fertile areas that lent themselves to agriculture, many groups never incorporated more than occasional meat into their way of life.

TRADITIONAL FOODS AROUND THE WORLD COMBINE THE RIGHT PROTEINS

Many of these ancient diets persist in the modern day. In fact, two-thirds of the world population currently follows a vegetarian or nearly vegetarian diet. In most places, this isn't considered unusual, although it may seem incomprehensible here in the land of "The Beef People." In many parts of the world, people eat the same diet that their ancestors have followed for thousands of years, in which meat traditionally plays a secondary role. This may seem strange when you're used to the American model meal: a main dish of meat is the star, complemented by a couple of humble side dishes. Other cultures, meanwhile, form the most important part of the meal from grains, vegetables, and beans, while meat is occasionally used as a humble flavoring or side dish.

Think about the traditional food from different cultures around the world. Consider Latin America, for example. What comes to mind when you think of Mexican food? Corn tortillas and beans, right? Or in the Middle East, it's pita bread and hummus. In India, chapattis and lentils. In Asia, rice and soy. Do you notice a trend? All these diets are ancient ways of combining proteins to provide all the essential amino acids. Long before humans knew that protein even existed, cultures all over the world had independently figured out that these food combinations made them healthy and strong.

Both vegetarianism and eating meat are part of our cultural and biological history as a species. In nature, animals are eaten by other animals—this is a necessary part of natural ecosystems. For humans, eating a completely vegetarian diet or supplementing it with small amounts of lean, healthily raised meat can both be wholesome choices. In our modern American culture, though, eating meat has gotten way out of control. A 1,420-calorie Monster Burger is just not the same as a trim rabbit leg.

Reprinted with permission of Mike Keefe.

In light of how our planet is changing these days, some people choose a vegetarian diet because our planet can't support 6 billion meat eaters. They believe that the quantity and quality of meat from modern factory farms is seriously unhealthy and unsustainable, for our bodies, our communities, and our environment. Eating some meat is okay, particularly pasture-fed meat. But perhaps no meat is even better.

THE USDA IS A TRUSTWORTHY SOURCE, RIGHT?

Dietary advice changes. Up until January of 2005, the federal government was recommending that we eat two or three servings of meat a day.

That advice was coming from the United States Department of Agriculture, or the USDA, the agency in charge of providing the public with nutritional guidance. Oddly, their other job is to protect agricultural producers, including the meat, egg, and dairy industries. This results in a questionable conflict of duties that gets a little shady when you look at it closely. Historically, many people involved in creating dietary guidelines for the USDA have had strong ties to the meat, dairy, egg, sugar, and processed food industries. When you consider this, it's not surprising that vegetables are underrepresented.

The Old Food Guide Pyramid Was Revised to Satisfy Meat and Dairy Producers

Starting in the 1950s, the USDA advised Americans about the four basic food groups: meat, milk and dairy, breads and cereals, and fruits and vegetables. According to the USDA, if we ate from all four groups every day, especially the first two, we would be healthy. Dairy and meat farmers were pleased with this: the more of their products that Americans consumed, the more money they made. It was very convenient for them that the government recommended their products.

Americans faithfully stuck to these rules for the next several decades, but by the 1970s, nutritional science was changing. Medical research was revealing the negative effects of eating red meat, and scientists were advising

against it. So why did kids in the 1980s and 1990s learn the rules of nutrition from the same outdated posters as their parents?

As a new generation of American children blithely drank free milk and colored pictures of chicken drumsticks, turmoil seethed at the USDA. Conflict was brewing between those who were researching health and those who were serving farmers and food companies. From 1980 until 1991, food scientists at the USDA worked to develop a Food Guide Pyramid that would reflect current research on healthy eating. They placed grains across the broad base of the pyramid, as the food group we should seek out most. Fruits and vegetables took up a lot of space on the next level, with meats and dairy as minor players near the top, and sweets and fats taking up very little space at the pointed tip. This Food Guide Pyramid was released to the public in April of 1991.

The National Cattleman's Association and the National Milk Producers' Federation were not pleased. Their products were not recommended in big enough quantities by this pyramid. If the USDA reduced demand and they had to cut back on production, they would lose a lot of money. When the first edition of the pyramid came out in 1991, these groups demanded that the USDA withdraw it—and so it was withdrawn. The USDA changed it to suit these organizations, and an altered pyramid debuted in April 1992. The revised guidelines and pyramid suggested *at least* two to three servings of meat and dairy each day and recommended larger meat servings, five to seven ounces instead of four to six ounces. The cattlemen and dairymen were satisfied.

In the spring of 2005, the USDA released a brand-new pyramid. It can be seen at www.mypyramid.gov.[4] The USDA says that the purpose of the new pyramid is "strictly motivational." That's sounds about right, because the picture of the pyramid itself provides no information whatsoever. If you click on its vertical stripes on the Web site, then a couple of vague phrases come up for each food group, such as "Eat more dark-green veggies" or "Eat a variety of fruit." Although these two particular recommendations are good, the messages overall are disappointing. In addition to being vague, the pyramid and Web site still cater to the dairy and meat industries, although not quite as much as the old one. Click on the pyramid stripe for dairy and read, "MILK. Go low-fat or fat-free. If you don't or can't consume milk, choose lactose-free products or other calcium sources." Click on the meat stripe and up pops this message: "Meat & Beans. Choose low-fat or lean meats and poultry. Vary your choices—with more fish, beans, peas, nuts, and seeds." These guidelines continue to endorse dairy and meat, although I know of no evidence to support such a recommendation over other sources of calcium and protein. With this new pyramid, the USDA has again avoided taking a stand that could antagonize meat and dairy producers.

ALWAYS CONSIDER THE SOURCE

It pays to look at meat and dairy promotion, at any food promotion, with a skeptical eye. What messages do we get about eating animal products? Think about those "Got milk?" ads, for example. They say they're promoting milk because it's full of calcium and it's good for you. Well, why aren't they promoting soy milk too, then? It has just as much calcium as cows' milk, if not more. The reason is that this campaign, purportedly for our health, has an ulterior motive. The National Milk Mustache campaign, as it's called, is funded by America's dairy milk processors. The more cows' milk we consume, the more money they make. It's the same deal with those The Power of Cheese commercials. They're funny, sure, but I stop laughing when I realize they're

funded by the American Dairy Association. Those ads aren't about our health, they're about profit.

Meat eating is deeply ingrained in our culture. A lot of people believe in it just because it's the way things have always been, at least as far as they know.

It's rather scary to realize that the advice we get—even from the government—doesn't necessarily represent reality. The 1992 Food Guide Pyramid was more of an advertisement than a health recommendation, since it was created to serve the health of the meat and dairy industries over that of the American public. The 2005 USDA "My Pyramid" is not much better.

Harvard University School of Public Health offers an alternate "Healthy Eating Pyramid" on their Web site, www.hsph .harvard.edu/nutritionsource/pyramids.html.[5] A variety of vegetarian food guide pyramids are available on the Internet. You can find one at www.utexas.edu/depts/he/ntr/NTR311 pyramidpage5.htm. [6]

NEW AND IMPROVED DIETARY GUIDELINES FROM THE USDA

The USDA has been criticized soundly in the last few years over its food pyramid failings. An eye-opening 2002 book by a prominent food scientist, Dr. Marion Nestle, revealed to the public the sordid details behind the recalling of the 1991 Food Guide Pyramid. That book, *Food Politics: How the Food Industry Influences Nutrition and Health,*[7] is a great read if you're curious about how money and business interests affect our ideas about food. Dr. Nestle was one of the experts interviewed by Morgan Spurlock in the movie *Super-Size Me.*

Although the 2005 "My Pyramid" is disappointing, the USDA's new written guidelines, released in January of 2005, are an improvement over the old ones. In their list of Food Groups to Encourage, there is no mention of meat or fish. The full seventy-one-page document of guidelines can be seen at www.healthierus.gov/dietaryguidelines/ or www.health.gov/dietaryguidelines/.

Following are the key recommendations from the new Dietary Guidelines for Americans 2005 from the USDA and the U.S. Department of Health and Human Services.

Key Recommendations[8]

• Consume a sufficient amount of fruits and vegetables while staying within energy needs. Two cups of fruit and 2 ½ cups of vegetables per day are recommended for a reference 2,000-calorie intake, with higher or lower amounts depending on the calorie level.

• Choose a variety of fruits and vegetables each day. In particular, select from all five vegetable subgroups (dark green, orange, legumes, starchy vegetables, and other vegetables) several times a week.

• Consume 3 or more ounce-equivalents of whole-grain products per day, with the rest of the recommended grains coming from enriched or whole-grain products. In general, at least half the grains should come from whole grains.

• Consume 3 cups per day of fat-free or low-fat milk or equivalent milk products.

No meat. Wow!

NOT GOOD ENOUGH

Although these guidelines are a definite step in the right direction, several details suggest that the dairy and packaged-food industries still have had some influence over the final product. For example, soy milk, despite its popularity, is completely omitted as an option in the dairy category. Soy milk is increasingly common, and dairy products have no advantage over soy. Also questionable is the recommendation that at least half the grains should come from whole grains. Research indicates that whole grains are far more healthful than

refined grains, period. Why not recommend that all grains be whole grains? The huge processed-food companies may have had a part in that decision.

School Cafeterias

WHY DO SCHOOL CAFETERIAS SERVE SUCH UNHEALTHY LUNCHES?

In kindergarten, I bought my lunch only one time all year. For some reason, I remember that it was a hot dog. Thrilled as I was by the rare pleasure of being allowed to eat such junk food, I was too scared of talking to the lunch ladies to do it again. But I got braver over the summer, and the next year I began buying my lunch regularly: chicken nuggets, squares of pizza, red Jell-O with fruit cocktail wads stuck in it. In second grade, I even lost a tooth on a particularly chewy corn dog.

At the time, I loved it all—except maybe that corn dog. I hated it when I had to bring weird, healthy lunches from home. My young life was consumed with one goal: to jettison the carrot sticks my mother sent to school with me and somehow, *somehow*, get my hands on Kay Goodman's Handi-Snacks. Remember those little crackers with tubs of fake, spreadable cheese and a red plastic stick? Mmm, just what a growing kid needs.

—Sara Kate

SCHOOLS GET DONATIONS OF SURPLUS FOOD

More than 27 million children in the United States eat school cafeteria lunches every day.[9] You've probably had quite a few yourself. You probably know that schools offer lots of foods that are loaded with saturated fat, such as pizza, French fries, Tater Tots, chicken nuggets, hamburgers, hotdogs, corn dogs, and so on. Almost three-fourths of school lunch items exceed the U.S. dietary guidelines for fat. Why is that?

Schools have the option of participating in the National School Lunches Program. Schools that participate receive cash and donated food from the USDA. In return, they agree to serve lunches that meet USDA nutrition requirements. In theory, anyway.

Where do the donations come from? They are surplus food that the USDA buys from farmers, food that the farmers can't sell for a profit. The government spends more than $5 billion on surplus food for schools each year. Wow! That sounds good. We might hope that the money is spent on the kinds of foods that nutritionists say are healthiest, such as fruits, vegetables, and whole-grain foods. That would make sense.

The Physicians Committee for Responsible Medicine visited ten school districts that are part of the National School Lunches Program in order to report how well they are meeting the USDA nutritional requirements. One school district received a B. The majority received a D or an F. A copy of the full report is available at www.pcrm.org.

What's the problem? Well, let's have a look at the surplus foods the USDA is buying from farmers. In 1991, 90 percent of the surplus foods bought by the government for school lunches were butter, cheese, whole milk, beef, pork, and eggs. Ninety percent! Compare that to the modest 25 to 45 percent of your daily calories that are supposed to come from protein and fat.

Here's one more thing to ponder. In October of 2002, 27 million pounds of meat were found contaminated with the dangerous bacteria *Listeria*. This tainted meet, from more than 100,000 turkeys, had found its way into the school lunch program and had to be hastily recalled.[10] Since then, the USDA has

Student Voice: Alan, Age 18

All school cafeterias have real issues with the food they provide. When I entered my college dining hall, I was planning to eat vegetarian. They had a small section for vegetarians, almost always consisting of a pasta dish. It has now been a full semester, and I can recall only three tofu dishes all year. Even people with the strongest vegetarian constitution cannot endure pasta two times a day, seven days a week.

I think it's time for the vegetarian diet to enter the mainstream. I don't want to be served the same dish every day, shoveling spaghetti into my mouth, my only amusement being watching the rapid consumption of junk food around me. The cafeteria should be a fun place to go, with healthy solutions, so that you can leave feeling energetic and lively, instead of engorged and greasy.

allowed irradiated meat to be served in school lunches—the process of irradiation kills bacteria but creates chemical by-products whose potency is not certain.

Why Can't They Donate Soy Products or Veggies?

But why can't the USDA do the same thing with, say, the soybean industry? Or what about vegetable farmers? Surely they need help too.

Well, it almost happened. In 1996, when Bill Clinton was president, the USDA

**Student Voice:
Elise, Age 21**

I've been a vegetarian since my freshman year in college, although I occasionally eat seafood. I'm not a vegan because I couldn't survive in my house and be a vegan.

I decided to become a vegetarian because I found a beetle in my meatloaf at college. I was so disgusted by this. There were vegetarian options at school and I'd been eating a lot of the vegetarian options anyway because they were nicer than that … slop.

I got completely blown away by that six-legged creature and I thought, what else have I been eating that I didn't know about? I don't like ingesting small creatures, which I think I was doing unwittingly for some time.

And, you know, I'm diabetic, so I'm susceptible to heart disease and I have borderline high cholesterol, so…a vegetarian diet is better for that.

But the beetle, that really grossed me out. That was really the precipitating factor.

was about to pass a regulation making it really cheap and easy for school cafeterias to serve soy protein. Tofu for all! But before the regulation passed, the beef and livestock industries made it clear that if soy got that kind of support, they would withdraw their donations to Clinton's reelection campaign. Beef is a big industry in this country, and they had a lot of money to give. So what happened? The regulation was cancelled. No soy. As a USDA aide said bluntly, "Unless [the cattlemen] approve this, we can't."

Money is very powerful.

INTERVIEW WITH A SCHOOL CAFETERIA MANAGER

We interviewed the school cafeteria manager at a private K–12 school in the Triangle area of North Carolina, where Sara Kate and her brother are in college. Ruth agreed to talk to us on the condition that her last name and the name of her school not be used.

This dining hall has a cafeteria line where students can choose from a selection of hot meats, vegetables, and fast-food items, such as pizza, chicken nuggets, and French fries. The dining hall also provides a variety of à la carte items, including a soup and salad bar, fruit, bagels, yogurt, juice, chips, ice cream, and refrigerated sandwiches. A microwave oven is available for heating sandwiches.

We met Ruth at 1:00, as the lunch crowd was dwindling. She showed us to her desk in a corner of the kitchen, which at this time of day was quiet. Her desk was situated to provide her a view of both the kitchen and dining area.

She began by telling us her background, which includes extensive experience as a chef and a restaurant manager.

What Is Your Biggest Challenge?

We asked what her biggest challenge is in providing inexpensive and nutritious food to K–12 students. She said the biggest hurdle is accommodating the variety of different diets— for athletes, for kids with allergies, kids with wheat intolerance and dairy intolerance, dieters, vegans, and kids with eating disorders. While football players want to gain or maintain weight, wrestlers are often trying to lose weight in order to make a certain weight class.

Ruth is deluged with complaints and requests from parents, so many that she can't read them all.

Typical complaints from parents include:

"Why can't you serve pizza every day?"

"My child wants chicken nuggets every day, why aren't they always available?"

"My child is vegan, why don't you have more choices for vegans?"

The parents who complain most are the parents whose kids have the worst eating habits.

Ruth refuses to serve pizza, French fries, and chicken nuggets every day, even though some students and parents clamor for them, especially the middle schoolers.

Five Bags of French Fries for Lunch, plus Ice Cream

Middle schoolers have the worst diets of all the age groups she serves. A typical lunch for a middle schooler is pepperoni pizza, French fries, potato chips, and soda. Kids who are overweight often make the poorest choices, such as five bags of French fries for lunch, with a soda. Or French fries, then ice cream.

Upper-school students make better choices, especially the cross-country runners and the track team.

The younger children are more interested in trying new things than either the middle schoolers or the upper schoolers are.

What Are Your Personal Priorities?

"What is most important to you as a food service provider?" we asked her.

She explained that her first goal is to get the students to eat nutritious and healthy foods. "I don't serve any frozen foods," she answered. "I save money for the school by buying fresh, local, and seasonal produce." She explained that seasonal vegetables are available close by and can be bought cheaply from farmers' markets or other local providers. Because local and seasonal produce doesn't

have to be boxed and shipped and refrigerated, it costs less. It's also more nutritious because it's fresher.

Wow. We didn't expect that from a school cafeteria manager.

"The key is education," she continued, "particularly educating the parent to educate the students at home."

A Child's Choices Start at Home

"Your child's choices start at home," Ruth said emphatically. "You need to educate them about why they don't need French fries.

"We feed a lot of visiting parents too. And the kids are carbon copies of their parents. If the parents have good eating habits, their kids do too. If the parents make poor choices, their kids do too.

"I educated my children by giving them a wide variety of foods starting as soon as they could eat finger foods. Encourage them to try a variety, but not by saying 'because I said so' or 'because it's good for you.' Instead, let them help in the kitchen. Help them to develop a sense of accomplishment. Being able to say 'I did it myself' creates good self-esteem. As soon as my kids were old enough to sit on the counter, I let them toss the salad or cut the meat. It's a way of spending quality time together. I have given both of my children their own cooking utensils and measuring cups to help them feel in charge in the kitchen, to help them become educated and capable food consumers."

A Lucky School

We were excited to find someone with such healthy goals in charge of a dining hall. Being employed by a private school, Ruth is not dependent on the federal government for food handouts, so she doesn't have to serve as many high-fat foods as a public school might.

But even Ruth is driven to some degree by what the students and parents want, and

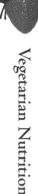

she has to be, since the parents are paying. It reminds us once again that consumers are in the driver's seat. What we demand, we get. When we demand healthy, environmentally sound, and humane choices across the board, we'll get them.

Student Voices: Heidi and Peter, Ages 20 and 29

Peter: As a society we don't support healthiness in our food. Our medical mindset is reactive instead of preventive, which ties into diet because if you ate well, you wouldn't be as sick. Most of the food we eat is processed with salt and sugar and fat and chemicals, which are all addictive and make us lose touch with what our body is telling us we need. We're just overwhelmed with, "I really want a Big Mac." And then you eat it, and you're like, "Why did I eat that?" Heidi: Yeah, like the other night, we had a pizza. And then we had an orange. And we were like, "You know what? This orange is so much better!" It was so much more wholesome than the pizza. Even though the pizza is really good, you eat the orange and it's just *better*, for some reason. Peter: And yet, for some reason you'll pick the pizza over the orange. But when you eat them both side by side, the orange is better than any cake or anything you could ever buy. Heidi: I went to Japan with the Guilford group and we would go out to eat and have the most lavish meals: sashimi and sushi and tempura and soup and rice—huge

meals! I would walk out of a restaurant after eating a lot of really good, nourishing food and I would feel great. And I notice a lot of times *here*, I'll walk out of a restaurant after eating a bunch of carbohydrates and fried food and I just feel like crap! I feel like I ate too much, I feel full, I feel tired. I can't go out to a restaurant here and not leave feeling overly stuffed. Whereas in Japan, I just felt nourished.

What Is the Difference between Vegan, Vegetarian, Macrobiotic, and So On?

So, you're vegetarian and you don't eat eggs, but your brother's a vegetarian and he eats fish. And your best friend, she doesn't even drink milk, but your neighbor calls herself vegetarian, even though you saw her eat chicken the other day. What's going on?

The truth is, being a vegetarian can mean lots of different things. Everyone has a different definition of what they do and don't want to eat. Fortunately, if you want to be more specific, there are a number of useful terms. Let's break it down.

VEGETARIAN

This is a general term. About 5 percent of the current U.S. population considers themselves to be vegetarian, although a number of varying dietary habits fall into this category. Usually this term refers to someone who doesn't eat any kind of meat, including beef, pork, chicken, turkey, and seafood. However, there are many people who don't quite match this description, but still use this label. These include ...

Pollo-Vegetarian

This is someone who follows a mostly vegetarian diet but is known to eat the occasional McChicken sandwich or nibble at some turkey jerky. In reality, birds are meat, so this isn't really a form of vegetarianism, but lots of people who call themselves vegetarians do indulge in a bit of chicken every so often.

Pesco-Vegetarian

Again, this is someone who follows a mostly vegetarian diet but who does eat a little meat—in this case, seafood. For some reason, lots of people don't seem to count aquatic creatures as animals. This is often for health reasons: fish is a healthier choice than pork or beef, for instance. Other people choose to eat fish because it doesn't affect land use as much as raising livestock does. However, overharvesting and polluting our seas and lakes is a significant environmental concern. Nonetheless, this is a popular diet, although, like pollo-vegetarianism, it's not technically vegetarian.

Lacto-Ovo-Vegetarian

This person eats no meat, including seafood, but does eat dairy products and eggs. Most lacto-ovo-vegetarians follow this basic rule: if you have to kill the animal to get the product, then don't eat it. Therefore, milk is okay, but gelatin, which is made from horse hooves, is not.

Lacto-Vegetarian

This person eats no meat or eggs but does eat dairy products. Dairy products include cows' milk and any food you can make from cows' milk, such as ice cream, yogurt, cheese, cottage cheese, sour cream, butter, and so on. Other animal products, such as goat cheese, are also included.

Ovo-Vegetarian

A person on this diet eats no meat and no dairy products but does eat eggs. This isn't too common. (The lives of hens that provide table eggs are at least as miserable as chickens raised for meat, and eggs are no healthier in our diets

than meat, so it's little wonder there are few ovo-vegetarians.)

Vegan

About I percent of the U.S. population follows a vegan (pronounced "VEE-gun") diet. This excludes all meat, eggs, and dairy products, and usually any other food produced by animals, such as honey. A strict vegan also avoids products that may seem innocent, such as refined sugar (white table sugar), because animal bones are used to process it. Many vegans also refuse to use nonedible animal products, such as leather, silk, wool, feathers, and so on. This can get really complicated. For example, did you know that camera film isn't vegan? Gelatin is used to manufacture it. Or that some lotions contain lanolin, which comes from wool? Strict vegans have to be very well informed.

Macrobiotic

A follower of the macrobiotic diet is mainly vegetarian, but this diet sometimes includes seafood. All other meat products are excluded, as well as eggs and dairy products. Basically, this diet focuses on eating local and seasonal foods that balance each other in harmonic ways. Some people follow this diet as a philosophy of life and others follow it for health reasons.

Fruitarian

A fruitarian is a person who eats only fruits and vegetables, often including beans, nuts, and grains, usually raw. It is important that these things are taken from the plant without killing it.

Raw or Living Food Diet

A person who follows this diet eats only raw foods. The concern is that heating foods above 116°F destroys important enzymes that help with digestion. This person also believes that cooking diminishes the vitamin and mineral content of the food.

Hurray for all types of vegetarians! All of these choices can be healthy—some more than others—but it is important to be well informed about the health benefits and risks of any diet that you choose to follow. Although people often feel strongly that their choice is the best and may be critical of others, the reality is that cutting your meat consumption in any way is a positive step. Reducing the amount of meat in your diet benefits your health, promotes animal well-being, and helps the planet support the growing human population.

Student Voice: Dana, Age 17

Ethical food choices in general interest me because I've never really been able to pin mine down. I can't tell somebody I'm a vegetarian or a vegan because I'm not. So if somebody asks why I get the veggie dog instead of the hot dog, then I have to go on this five-minute explanation. I don't do "strict vegetarian" because I don't really see anything wrong with eating animals; it's mostly just the way they're raised. How an animal is treated while it's alive is a whole lot more important than whether you eat it after it's dead.

Right now, I'm pretty much an acting vegan, I suppose, because I don't want to spend the money on products from ethical farms because it's really expensive. And someone suggested that I go and shoot squirrels in my backyard and eat those, but I was like, "No!"

I've always been interested in nature things and always thought about environmental things more than most people, ever since I was little, mostly just because I like nature so much—you know, walking in the woods and all that. So at first, it was completely an environmental issue for me, not animal welfare or anything, because it's so much more sustainable and efficient not to eat things from animals. That was the only reason. And then, I'm in an environmental ethics class this semester, and so reading the books got me thinking more about the animal rights, animal welfare side of it. And that fit with the environmental issues pretty well.

So I don't have a completely logical system for what I do or what I don't, I just do what won't make me feel guilty.

What If I Just Eat Less Meat—Does That Help?

Yes. Avoiding meat doesn't have to be all or nothing. If you eat one slice of pepperoni pizza, it's not going to cancel out the veggie stir-fry you had the night before.

As you've learned in reading this book, there are four main reasons to be vegetarian: your health, the environment, animal welfare, and global population issues. All of these are affected by every meal you eat. If you choose a peanut butter and jelly sandwich over a ham sandwich just one time, that helps. And the more you do it, the more it helps.

Consider just the amount of water you can save by cutting back on meat. Over half the amount of water used in the United States goes toward irrigating land to grow food for livestock. Producing a single pound of meat takes from 2,500 to 8,500 gallons of water. Producing one day's food for a typical meat-eating American requires about 4,000 gallons of water. But only 1,200 gallons are required to grow one day's food for a lacto-ovo-vegetarian. And only 300 gallons are needed to produce the food consumed in one day by a vegetarian.[11] So if you have been eating meat, eggs, and dairy products at every meal and you switch to just one meal a day without animal products, then you are saving hundreds of gallons of water per day.

For another example, what about grain? A cow must eat sixteen pounds of grain to produce just one pound of beef.[12] If that grain were fed directly to people instead of a cow, it would make mountains of food, as compared to just a couple of hamburgers. Skipping one burger can make a difference.

If you're still not convinced, consider chickens. The average American eats fifty-three pounds of chicken a year, which comes to about one pound of chicken each week. A grown chicken provides about five pounds of meat after it is killed and packaged. So, for every five weeks that you don't eat chicken, one less bird dies on your behalf.

As you can see, taking even a tiny step makes a difference. Every time one person buys a burger, he is creating a market for beef. Spending $3 on a burger is basically a personal $3 contribution to the meat industry. It's a message to beef farmers and sellers telling them that it is profitable to raise cows and that you support their efforts. On the other hand, every time you buy a salad or the veggie burger at Burger King, you're sending a very different message to the management. You're proving that people are willing to choose veggie products and that it's profitable to provide nonmeat alternatives. Your choices make a difference, each and every time.

Organic and Certified Organic: What's the Difference?

Although they are not the same thing, organic and vegetarian food often overlap. As you'll read in other parts of this book, animals on factory farms eat a variety of chemicals, such as hormones, antibiotics, and pesticides. These toxins are stored in the fatty tissues of the animals' bodies, so when humans eat these animal products, we're consuming the toxins as well. Pesticides and fertilizers are also sometimes used on the plant products we eat, but the concentration is not nearly as high as in animal products.

You can avoid eating toxic chemicals by choosing organic foods. Even mainstream grocery stores nowadays often carry organic fruits, vegetables, and grains. Many chain groceries now carry organic meat, eggs, and cows' milk too.

If you ask shoppers why they choose organic foods, most will probably say for their health. They may not realize that buying organic foods also protects wildlife and the environment. When pesticides are sprayed on crops, these chemicals wind up being eaten by local wildlife, sometimes with devastating effects. The pesticides also wind up in streams and rivers. Likewise, chemicals in the feed of livestock pass into their manure and, eventually, from there the chemicals move into our water.

The USDA has created four categories of organic foods. It's important to know what they all mean, because the titles can be deceiving.

USDA FOOD CATEGORIES

100 Percent Organic
Every ingredient in this product must be certified organic, as well as all the facilities that handle the product before it comes to you. According to the USDA Web site:[13]

Organic food is produced by farmers who

emphasize the use of renewable resources and the conservation of soil and water to enhance environmental quality for future generations. Organic meat, poultry, eggs, and dairy products come from animals that are given no antibiotics or growth hormones. Organic food is produced without using most conventional pesticides; petroleum-based fertilizers or sewage sludge-based fertilizers; bio-engineering; or ionizing radiation.

Organic
At least 95 percent of the ingredients in this product must be certified organic.

Made with Organic Ingredients
At least 70 percent of the ingredients in this product must be certified organic.[14]

Free-Range[15]
The meaning of this term depends on the product. For poultry to be called free-range, the USDA requires that the birds have some access to open air every day—but it could be as little as five minutes. For eggs and beef, the term is not regulated at all and has no standard definition.

All-Natural, Hormone-Free, and Cage-Free
These labels can mean anything or nothing. They are not regulated by the USDA, so producers can use them as they wish. But even in products that are less than 70 percent organic, individual ingredients can legally be labeled organic.

If you can't buy organic, there are still ways to minimize your pesticide exposure. Washing and peeling fruits and vegetables helps, but only to a certain extent. However, you can drastically reduce your pesticide intake just by eating carefully. Some foods contain higher concentrations than others. If you can't buy organic all the time, compromise on products that are less likely to be contaminated. The least contaminated fruits and vegetables include bananas, kiwi, mangos, payaya, avocados, asparagus, broccoli, cauliflower, sweet corn, and onions. On the other hand, the most heavily contaminated products are strawberries, red raspberries, apples, cherries, peaches, nectarines, pears, grapes, bell peppers, celery, spinach, and potatoes.

BUT ORGANIC PRODUCTS ARE SO EXPENSIVE
Organic products can be pricey for several reasons. For one, if a farmer avoids the use of chemical fertilizers and pesticides, his total harvest may be less than a crop that's artificially jacked up on chemicals. Because he's producing less, he has to charge more per item to stay in business.

Second, organic certification isn't cheap. Often small farmers can't afford the heavy annual fees. As a result, many farmers who work without chemicals are not certified, although their product may truly be organic. If you have the opportunity to shop locally, at a farmers' market or local co-op, talk to the people you buy from! Ask how their products are grown and what other local options exist. This is a great way to buy responsibly produced food that's also cheaper than in supermarkets.

It's usually better to buy food that is produced locally rather than food that comes from far away. Not only can you find out more about where your food comes from, but it's probably better for the environment as well.

Using Guides to Plan
Do all food pyramids include meat? Heck no. Several vegetarian food guide pyramids have been published that exclude meat altogether, replacing it with beans, nuts, tofu, and other plant-based protein. Most of these vegetarian pyramids are very similar to one another. The

recommendations below are from a vegetarian pyramid on the Web site www.utexas.edu/depts/he/ntr/NTR311pyramidpage5.htm[17] and another one in the book *Being Vegetarian for Dummies.*[18]

Whenever I see a list of recommended servings from any food guide pyramid, I can't help but notice that if you really eat all of this, it can add up to twenty-two servings of food a day. But take note of the serving sizes. A half-cup of cooked pasta, for example, is not very much. Most people would eat more than that in one sitting. A dinner portion of pasta in a restaurant is usually eight ounces—that's half a box of noodles! So a lot of the time, it's easier to meet these goals than you think.

For help in reading labels, remember that one ounce equals twenty-eight grams and eight fluid ounces equals one cup.

GRAINS

Vegetarian food pyramids recommend six to eleven servings of bread, cereal, whole grains, and pasta a day. Examples include:

- 1 slice of whole-grain bread
- ½ cup of cooked whole wheat pasta
- ½ cup of cooked brown rice
- half a bagel
- 1 cup (about one ounce) of a ready-to-eat toasted oat cereal (such as Cheerios)
- ½ cup of heavier ready-to-eat cereals
- ½ cup (40 grams) of cooked cereal

Always choose whole grains; they have more fiber and more nutrients. Good examples include familiar foods such as brown rice, oats, barley, and whole-grain breads and cereals, as well as more exotic choices such as quinoa, millet, and wheat berries.

VEGETABLES

Almost all sources agree you need at least three to five servings of vegetables a day.

Student Voice: Heidi, Age 20

I don't eat even close to how I'd like to, mainly out of the last-minute rushes to get breakfast in. And money is huge—I have a really big problem with the fact that organic food is so much more expensive. We do buy a lot of organic vegetables and stuff, but I rarely can afford things like organic milk, which I would like a lot because of the stuff they put in milk.

This summer we started a really large organic garden at our house and it was really exciting because the land we were using had never had any pesticides or herbicides or anything on it, so it was completely organic. We had this dream that we'd be able to live off our garden, or at least get most of our fruits and vegetables that way. But it was my first time gardening in North Carolina, so I didn't know about the weather and stuff. It worked out pretty well, though, except that the amount of work involved eventually took over and we weren't able to keep up with it as much as we would have liked. But vegetables are something that I definitely feel are important in somebody's diet.

Examples include:

- 1 cup of raw spinach or lettuce
- a big handful of baby carrots, cucumber slices, or pepper strips
- ¾ cup of vegetable juice

Include some raw vegetables every day; cooking usually destroys some nutrients. Colorful vegetables provide a wide variety of vitamins, and green veggies are full of folate and often calcium.

TOP TEN REASONS TO BUY ORGANIC

The best reasons to buy organic are more numerous than you might think![16]

1. **Protect Future Generations**
   The average kid consumes four times the amount of pesticides that an adult does.

2. **Prevent Soil Erosion**
   Three billion tons of topsoil erode from American croplands every year—mostly due to conventional farming practices. Organic farming protects the soil.

3. **Protect Water Quality**
   Sediment caused by soil erosion is one of the biggest water pollutants, not to mention the pesticides that contaminate more than 50 percent of our country's drinking water.

4. **Save Energy**
   Modern farming techniques use vast amounts of petroleum and fossil fuels instead of sustainable, labor-intensive organic practices.

5. **Keep Chemicals off Your Plate**
   The EPA considers 90 percent of all fungicides, 60 percent of herbicides, and 30 percent of insecticides to be cancer-causing in humans.

6. **Protect Farm Workers**
   Farm workers have high cancer rates due to exposure to toxic pesticides and other chemicals. They are also vastly underpaid for their dangerous and exhausting work.

7. **Help Small Farmers**
   Most organic farms are family operations of less than 100 acres, as compared to the giant factory farms, often more than 100 times that size, that produce conventional products.

8. **Support a True Economy**
   Non-organic products are cheap because they don't include the real costs of the product: the costs of pesticide regulation and testing, hazardous waste disposal and cleanup, environmental destruction, and billions of dollars of our tax money that the federal government uses to subsidize farmers.

9. **Promote Biodiversity**
   Conventional farming techniques exhaust the soil and waste the land, requiring more and more chemical aids to produce the same output. These toxins are destroying our natural environment and wildlife.

10. **Taste Better Flavor**
    Organic products are grown from healthy soil, and as a result are more nourishing to our bodies. And more delicious!

BABY BLUES BY RICK KIRKMAN & JERRY SCOTT

© Reprinted with permission of King Features Syndicate.

FRUIT
You also need at least two to four servings of fruit a day. Examples include:
- 1 good-sized fruit, such as an apple, orange, or banana
- ½ cup fresh berries or grapes
- ½ cup 100 percent fruit juice
- ¼ cup dried fruit

Fresh fruit is better than fruit juice because it has more fiber. Eat a wide variety of fruits, not just apples. Occasionally treat yourself to kiwi, mango, or papaya—these fruits have the least levels of toxic pesticide residue and are chock-full of vitamin C.

DAIRY PRODUCTS
The USDA's new Dietary Guidelines for Americans 2005 recommend "three cups of fat-free or low-fat milk or equivalent milk products per day" in order to get enough calcium and protein. However, as you now know, there are plenty of plant sources for these nutrients that are healthier choices. Some plant-based alternatives that are equal in calcium to a cup of cows' milk include:
- 1 cup of soy milk or rice milk
- 1 one-inch cube of soy or vegan cheese
- 5 cups spinach

Include a calcium-rich food with every meal. It doesn't have to be something from this list, though. Many foods provide calcium, including calcium-set tofu, fortified orange juice, almonds, greens, and many beans (soy, navy, great northern, and black turtle) also provide plenty of calcium.

BEANS, NUTS, AND OTHER HIGH-PROTEIN SOURCES
On the USDA pyramid, this group includes meat, but you have a lot of other choices. You only need two to three servings a day. Examples include:
- ½ cup tofu, tempeh, or TVP (see Soy Products in chapter eight)
- ½ cup cooked beans
- 1 soy hotdog
- 1 veggie burger
- 1 tablespoon of peanut butter
- 1 egg
- ¼ cup almonds

If you like nuts, they are a great resource because they provide vitamin E as well as many minerals. Switch up your protein sources; soy hot dogs are good once in a while, but not every day.

NOW LET'S PUT IT TO WORK
So how can you organize all these servings and vitamins and new foods into something you actually want to eat? It's easier than you think. Let's walk through a sample day.

Breakfast:
- A cup of raisin bran: 2 servings of grains
- A cup of soy or dairy milk on your cereal: 1 serving of dairy
- A cup of orange juice on the side: 2 servings of fruit

Snack:
- Half a whole wheat bagel with honey: 1 serving of grains

Lunch:
- A peanut butter and banana sandwich on two slices of whole wheat bread: 1 serving from bean group, 1 serving of fruit, 2 servings of grains
- A glass of soy or dairy milk: 1 serving of dairy

- Veggies cut into strips with a salsa dip: 1 serving of veggies
- An apple: 1 serving of fruit

Snack:
- Snack mix of nuts and raisins: 1 serving from the bean/nut group

Supper:
- A baked potato, served with chili (made of navy and kidney beans, bulgur wheat, tomato sauce, and chopped peppers, onions, and carrots): 2 servings of grains, 1 serving from bean group, 1 serving of veggies
- Steamed spinach: 1 serving of veggies

Dessert:
- Chocolate-flavored soy or dairy yogurt: 1 serving of dairy
- Fresh strawberries: 1 serving of fruit

Total:
- 7 servings of grains
- 3 servings of veggies
- 5 servings of fruit
- 3 servings of dairy
- 3 servings from bean group

Voilá! Now that wasn't so hard, was it?

Because you can't eat the same thing every day, here are some basic meal patterns you can mix and match:

Breakfast
- Hot whole-grain cereal, such as oatmeal, topped with fruit and nuts
- Granola or other ready-to-eat cold cereal with fruit and milk
- Breakfast sandwich, such as eggs or beans on toast, plus fruit on the side

Lunch
- Sandwich with raw veggies and fruit
- Hummus or cheese on crackers, with a salad

Dinner
- Casserole, plus vegetable side dish
- Stir-fried vegetables and beans or tofu, served over a cooked grain
- Soup and salad with bread, tortilla, or a muffin
- Several small dishes to make a variety plate: vegetables, beans, and a fruit salad

Chapter Seven

How to Handle Fast-Food Friends
and Turkey-Loving Relatives

No Steak for Me— Negotiating a New Vegetarian Diet with Your Family

POTATO GRANNY

When our vegetarian friend Carra goes to visit her grandparents, she knows what she'll have to eat: a potato. No matter how long she stays, her grandmother just can't think of a single vegetarian dish besides a baked potato. So, dutifully, Carra eats potatoes: potatoes with butter, potatoes with broccoli, potatoes with cheddar cheese, potatoes with sour cream, potatoes with potatoes. Needless to say, she's glad when it's time to go home again!

HOW TO ASK YOUR FAMILY FOR WHAT YOU NEED

So what's the best way of talking to your family about a new vegetarian diet? Here are some tips to help them feel cooperative:

• Before you talk to your parents, think about the situation from their point of view. What will this change mean for them? If you can sympathize with their feelings, they will probably be more sympathetic to yours.

• Set aside time to talk to your family. Let them know you want to sit down and have a relaxed conversation about something that's important. They'll be more receptive if they're not rushed.

• When you sit down, explain to them your reasons for avoiding meat. Instead of making demands, tell them what you want to do and why. Make it clear to them that this is a personal decision for your own well-being and that it's not just a passing phase. Talk about it calmly and maturely, even if they seem distressed or confused. If your family understands your reasons, they will be more likely to respect you as an individual with needs of your own. Who knows, they may be interested in getting healthier or in helping out the planet as well.

• Assure them that you are interested in good nutrition and will make the effort to get all the nutrients you need for good health.

• Be willing to begin with small changes and go slowly. Most changes are easier for everyone if they are gradual.

Student Voice: William, Age 18

My mom cooks a lot of meat and vegetables. When she cooks meat, she'll make me something else, like a grilled portobello. About half the time she makes meals that are all veggie. She thought my interest in a vegetarian diet would pass pretty quickly, but it hasn't. She wants me to take vitamins, which I do when I remember to.

Student Voice: Catie, Age 18

I went through some hard years when I really felt that animals were the only ones I could turn to, so I started to not eat meat. I didn't like meat. I started to get this feeling that I just couldn't eat it, like I was actually eating the animal itself. That's all I could think about. I would taste the blood, and I just couldn't eat it. And so I didn't.

I was twelve when this started, but I've always loved animals. My cat got hit by a car when I was in third grade and then I had two other cats who got hit by cars and died when I was in fifth grade. I really needed my animals—I felt like they couldn't criticize. I had a love for all animals. And so I felt like I just couldn't eat them, I couldn't force it into my mouth. It made me so angry. I couldn't do it. I would have tears streaming down my cheeks when my parents would make me eat it.

• Decide how your family can most easily handle this change. Is it easier for everyone to eat vegetarian or for you to eat a separate dish? Be willing to compromise and meet them in the middle. Instead of expecting your family to fix you your own separate meal, offer to help find recipes and help with the cooking.

• Take charge of some meal planning. There are several steps to making this easy. Sit down with the current family cook and do some brainstorming.

• Make a list of the foods that your family currently eats that are vegetarian. These might include things such as:
  - Beans and rice
  - Grilled cheese sandwiches
  - Lentil soup
  - Macaroni and cheese
  - Pasta with tomato sauce or pesto sauce
  - Salads
  - Vegetable soup

• Now make a list of foods that are easy to serve with or without meat. Rather than cook two separate meals, it's much simpler to make one dish that can be served with meat on the side for family members who insist on it. Examples include:
  - Breakfast for supper—pancakes with eggs or bacon on the side
  - Baked potatoes with a variety of toppings
  - Homemade veggie pizzas, one with pepperoni slices
  - Spaghetti with tomato sauce with optional meat, tofu, or beans to add in
  - Tacos filled with an option of refried beans or ground meat
  - Vegetable stir-fry with optional meat on the side
  - Vegetarian chili with ground meat on the side

- Now try to think of completely new vegetarian dishes. This might include dishes such as:
  - Hummus and pita bread
  - Lentil loaf instead of meat loaf
  - Marinated tofu
  - Quesadillas
  - Tabouli
  - Using meat substitutes in favorite meat dishes (See page 184 for examples of soy products.)
  - Veggie burgers or tofu hotdogs

Look through recipes, such as the ones in this book (see pages 189–226), or search the Internet for ideas. For starters, try these Web sites: www.vegsource.com, www.vrg.org, and www.veg.org. With a little effort, you can come up with a variety of easy dishes that everyone can eat. Share some of the nutritional information with your family; it will help in planning nutritious meals for everyone.

IF YOU SUBTRACT, DON'T FORGET TO ADD

There is one thing that's important to remember: as a vegetarian: you can't just knock out meat and not replace it with anything. At some meals, it's okay to eat the same dish as everyone else minus the meat, but at least some of the time, remember to replace the missing meat with beans, tofu, nuts, or whole grains so you'll get all the nutrients you need.

FRIENDS AND FAMILY NEED STROKES TOO

In addition to finding foods you're happy to eat, living comfortably as a vegetarian requires some extra sensitivity to meat eaters around you.

- Support your family's efforts. If your dad bravely attempts a new vegetarian Indian dish he read about in the newspaper and it comes out tasting like pond scum, don't scorn him. Eat what you can (and make a PB and J later).

**Student Voice:
Meagan, Age 13**

When I quit eating meat, my mom was a little anxious and confused at first. But as time went on, she agreed with it. I think it was just seeing that I was really serious and how I talked about it—being kinder to nature and the animals around us. And then she was fine with it. My mom just wants to make sure I get the nutrition I need.

**Student Voice:
Heidi, Age 20**

One thing with kids—we have four nieces and nephews in one family. Their parents feed them Swiss cake rolls and honey buns. So I want to feed them good food, but I don't have the time when I'm with them. Not only that, but they don't *want* good food; they want to be satisfied immediately. So I end up just giving them crap. And it's a bad feeling, but it's a cycle because packaged foods like that are convenient and they're cheap. You can go into a store and spend $10 on a ton of junk food—so much food! But you can't go in with $10 and get stuff for a really good meal for a family of six. That's what they are, a family of six, so they have to do what's cheap and easy, what they can afford.

Tell him you appreciate the effort. If you make fun of your family's attempts to accommodate you, they'll probably stop trying.
- Don't be a vege-evangelist. Pushing and preaching about vegetarianism will not win

anybody over; it will probably just make the people you love angry and defensive. If you want people to see it your way, be patient. Set a good example. Cook tasty-looking veggie dishes and make it clear how good vegetarian eating can be. Offer other people bites if they want, but don't launch into a lecture unless they ask. Even then, just talk about the benefits of being vegetarian—don't attack meat eaters. They have the right to do as they wish, just as you do.

I've found without question that the best way to lead others to a more plant-based diet is by example—to lead with your fork, not your mouth.

—Bernie Wilke, artist

Eating Veggie with Meat-Eating Friends—Honesty and Flexibility Are Key

So once you've talked it out with your family, being vegetarian is fairly easy in your own home. If the people you live with are willing to work with you, you pretty much have control over what you eat: you know what has meat in it and what doesn't and no one's going to be offended when you skip the beef brisket.

But going out is another story. It can be a very uncomfortable situation to be served a meat dish that you just can't eat, whether it's at a friend's house or in a restaurant.

EATING AT OTHER PEOPLE'S HOUSES

As a vegetarian, sooner or later you will be served something that you don't want to eat and you'll be forced to choose between feeling rude or eating something you find noxious.

To avoid this unhappy choice, the simple solution is to *let people know your preferences* as soon as possible. In all situations, this is the best plan. Hosts want their guests to enjoy themselves. Your host will feel far worse seeing

TRICKS OF THE TRADE

People don't like to have decisions forced upon them, especially decisions about what to eat. Knowing this, I didn't want to pressure my friend Josh who really loves meat, although I knew he'd like vegetarian food if he just gave it a chance. Then one day, the perfect opportunity arose.

I was sitting on a couch in our college dorm flipping through TV channels and snacking on some spicy imitation buffalo wings. He flopped down beside me and casually swiped one off my plate. "Mmm, this is good," he said. I nodded. We sat in silence for a minute, chewing. "Hey, wait!" he exclaimed suddenly. "Why are *you* eating *chicken*?!"

I burst out laughing. "It's not chicken. It's soy!" I said with a devious smile.

His mouth hung open. "Are you serious?" he said. "Wow, I had no idea. It's hardly any different." He sat in thought for a moment. "I never would have eaten it if I had known," he said, shaking his head. "But you're right. It wasn't half bad."

And as he headed for the door, he grabbed another one and took a bite.

Victory!

—Sara Kate

you nibbling on rolls the whole evening than she will if you give her enough warning so that she can be prepared.

Situation one: You get an invitation in advance to a party or a dinner out.

Solution: When you RSVP, mention that you're a vegetarian. Be specific about what you do and don't eat. Offer to bring a dish with you. For example, "I'd love to come to dinner on Saturday. One thing, though—did you know that I'm a vegetarian? Yeah, I don't eat meat or seafood anymore. I don't want to inconvenience you though—could I bring a salad or something?" If the person refuses your offer to bring something, forget about it—you've done your duty. They've got it under control.

Situation two: You're at your friend's house and she invites you to stay and eat supper.

Solution: If you know what they're serving and it seems adaptable to your vegetar-

THOUGHTS FROM ELAINE, A PARENT OF THREE VEGETARIANS

As the mother of three vegetarians/vegans, I'm personally very inspired by both the commitment and sacrifice the choice has meant for them and by the heart that's gone into each of their decisions.

It's a quieter, more focused "protest" than the bra-burnings and sit-ins that so many of us of the 1960s participated in, but the zeal, the commitment, and the idealism are the same. For many of the members of this newer generation, adopting a vegetarian or vegan diet seems to be a statement and a very personal step forward in an effort to aid the welfare of the world.

I adopted a modified vegetarian diet eighteen years ago, mostly out of respect for the sanctity of life and as a reaction to inhumane farming methods. But I've learned so much more about the ultimate impact on our environment through my three children.

In a world where the problems that face us seem so enormous, I'm very heartened by the numbers of young people stepping forward in this very personal, committed way. In a world that offers this newer generation so much in the way of cynicism and doomsaying, I see them opting for the empowerment that comes from the discipline, sacrifice, and global awareness that this choice offers.

ian diet, accept conditionally. "Thanks. I'd love to stay, but the thing is, I'm a vegetarian. Would it be all right if I had my spaghetti without the meat sauce?"

If the meal doesn't seem vegetarian friendly or you don't know what they're serving, decline, but explain yourself. "That's so nice of you, but I can't—you see, I'm a vegetarian. It makes things complicated." Chances are they'll probably protest and find a way to make it work for you, in which case you can graciously accept.

Situation three: You're eating at someone's house and you've told them you don't eat meat, but for some reason, they serve you meat anyway.

Solution: Being a vegetarian is common enough these days that no one should react to your meatlessness as though it's a bizarre state of affairs. If someone forgets or overlooks your stated preferences and serves you a plate with meat on it, no need to panic. One option is to eat the other foods and leave the meat alone. If the other foods are not going to be enough, there's nothing wrong with reminding the host that you don't eat meat and asking for a sandwich.

EATING IN RESTAURANTS

Eating in restaurants is significantly easier than in people's homes because there's no chance of the social discomfort of rejecting someone's home-cooked food. And fortunately, in the past few years, vegetarian dining has been on the rise. Most American cities have vegetarian or ethnic restaurants with lots of meatless dishes.

The number of ethnic restaurants is on the rise, and they often have more vegetarian options than traditional mom-and-pop diners. Middle Eastern, Japanese, Indian, Thai, Chinese, Mexican, Vietnamese, and Greek restaurants all offer lots of delicious and different vegetarian choices. Cooks are willing to tone down spices and exotic flavors to please even

163

AN UNFORTUNATE EVENT

Sometimes other people just don't get it. You tell them you don't eat meat and they act like they didn't hear you. This can lead to a very awkward situation, as I found out one day in Mexico.

The day started off innocently enough as I went to eat lunch at the house of my work partner, where I had eaten delicious vegetarian meals several times before.

Luisa greeted me at the door with a friendly kiss and ushered me inside to the table, where I sat down as she bustled into the kitchen to get the food. She returned a moment later bearing a large, steaming bowl of *birria*, a common local dish made of shredded, barbecuelike meat.

She placed the dish in front of me and sat down, beaming. "I was going to make you some cauliflower-and-potato pancakes," she said, "but then I thought, no! Sarita wants good food! So I made this instead."

I stared. "Luisa ... " I said uncertainly, "does this dish have meat in it?" Obviously it did—there were bones sticking out of the bowl—but I didn't know what else to say.

"Oh, no, it doesn't!" Luisa shook her head.

"No?" I repeated incredulously. "This doesn't have any meat in it?"

Luisa looked at me like I just might be crazy. "No!" she said. "It's mole!"

It was definitely not mole. Mole is a spicy reddish brown sauce.

"Well? Go on!" Luisa encouraged me, nudging the stack of steaming tortillas and the bowls of rice, lime, and salt closer to me.

I didn't have the nerve to refuse. Gingerly, I lifted a spoonful of broth to my lips and swallowed it, giving a watery smile. "It's ... good," I said. Meanwhile, inside I began to pray. "Dear God," I said, "please just don't let me barf inside this kind woman's house. I don't care what happens as long as I just don't throw up in her house."

At that moment, the baby began to cry and Luisa whisked her away to change her diaper. That house was inhabited by close to twenty people; I had never before been alone in it for even an instant, but there I was, alone with my *birria*. I took it as a sign.

Without a moment to lose, I grabbed the stack of tortillas and began spooning greasy wads of meat into the tortillas. I frantically wrapped them in paper napkins, squashed them all together, and dropped the sodden wad into my backpack just as Luisa reentered the room.

"Oh, you've already eaten so much! You like it!" she said happily. "I'll serve up everybody else's." And she began scurrying back and forth between the kitchen and the table, bringing out bowls to serve to the rest of the family.

This was no time for politeness. While Luisa busied herself in the kitchen, I began frantically spooning my remaining meat into the bowl next to mine. When she returned, all that remained were a few bones lying in the bottom of my bowl and a little broth.

I nibbled on a tortilla and insisted that I was far too full to push the bone marrow out of the bones and make a taco out of it. No, really, I couldn't possibly.

Fortunately, a dainty appetite is an acceptable feminine virtue, so Luisa cleared my bowl away and I was saved. Aside from the mysterious greasy stains on my book bag and notebooks, no one ever knew.

—Sara Kate

the most timid palate. And in the meantime, you'll probably learn a lot about interesting combinations of foods that you can re-create in your own kitchen.

If your family or group of friends insists on going somewhere more traditional, you'll still be fine. Even steak houses have salad bars and baked potatoes. Be careful of fast-food restaurants, though. Foods that appear to be vegetarian may not be. For example, French fries may be cooked in lard. However, some fast-food restaurants have begun offering vegetarian choices. Some fast-food salads are meatless, Burger King now has veggie burgers, and Wendy's serves baked potatoes with toppings. These restaurants realized that groups with one or two vegetarians in their midst weren't coming to eat because there was no vegetarian option, so they added these items to win back business from veggies and meat eaters alike. Smart move!

EATING AT POTLUCKS AND COOKOUTS

The easiest of all the eating-out options, potlucks and cookouts put you in control. This is a great way to introduce other people to vegetarian foods and at the same time make sure you have something to eat. For a potluck or cookout, choose a food that you like a lot, that's popular with your friends or family, and that's not hard to eat with your hands or with your plate in your lap. Good suggestions include:

- Any finger food
- Bean dip with toasted tortillas or crackers
- Black bean-and-corn salad
- Carrot-raisin salad
- Hummus with pita bread or veggies to dip
- Tabouli

And so, sally forth into the world without fear. You are fully equipped to be a tasteful and polite ambassador for vegetarianism, setting a good example and spreading yummy food wherever you go.

You Can't Be Serious!— Defending Your Diet

What made you decide to become vegetarian? Was it a friend who had already switched over? Was it an article you read in a magazine? Or did you think of it on your own?

Whatever it was, it probably *wasn't* someone wrenching a pork chop out of your hand and telling you you're a murderer. Tempting as that may sound right now, believe me, it's not the way to go about convincing people.

I became a vegetarian while on a trip with my best friend. We'd both been toying with the idea for a while, and, all of a sudden, I noticed that she wasn't ordering meat in restaurants anymore. She didn't say a word to me about it, but it only took one meal before I switched over too. We were in an Applebee's. She ordered the veggie plate—it was something involving steamed cauliflower, I remember—

Just about every restaurant has at least something without meat on the menu. In fact, in my entire life, I remember only one restaurant with no vegetarian option—and I still managed to eat. It was in rural Wyoming, deep in the heart of cattle country. The menu boasted sumptuous platters of sixteen or thirty-two ribs—I wasn't even sure what that meant. When I explained myself, the waitress seemed somewhat mystified, as if I were perhaps from some foreign country and had just told her that I couldn't eat anything that started with the letter "B." Nonetheless, she was willing to help me—the way you might humor a slightly but benignly insane person. Together we put together a vegetable plate for me: mashed potatoes, green beans, stewed apples, and lima beans. Easy enough, and a far sight cheaper than the ribs!

—Sara Kate

and I suddenly became hideously embarrassed by the grilled chicken salad I was eating. I never ate another bite of meat after that. And yet, if she'd lectured and pressed me, I probably would have kept eating meat with a vengeance, just to spite her.

Even when you're feeling fervent about your vegetarian ways, gentle persuasion is the way to go. Lecturing people or making them feel guilty will probably just make them angry. The best way to get people interested is to make it clear that you are enjoying yourself, that vegetarianism is a pleasure, not a chore. If they have questions, be pleasant and informative. For example, "Soy's a bean, you numbskull!" is not a constructive response.

If you decide you'd like to have a supportive group of meatless friends, it's not that hard to do it. At school, you can try to round up similarly minded people and start a club or group. I hate it when people tell you to do that in books—it sounds like way too much work, and who will be interested anyway? But you might be surprised. At our public high school, populated by your average cross section of the teenage population, a friend of mine founded a veggie-minded group that is still flourishing now, six years later. At college, my friends and I kicked off a brand-new vegetarian co-op last year. You find vegetarians in the strangest places. Try hanging up some fliers or putting a message in your school's newsletter or newspaper and see what happens.

If you're trying to get people interested at a meeting or club fair, food samples always draw a crowd. Vegan brownies or fried falafel will have people crowding around and asking for more, believe you me!

—Sara Kate

SARA KATE'S STUDENT HOUSEFUL OF VEGGIE-CRUSADERS

"*Veggie* dogs?" The football coach ran his hands through his sweaty hair, squinting in the hot afternoon sun. "What, it's made of, like … tofu?"

We were getting used to this question. Erica nodded patiently. "It's a soy-based meat alternative," she explained. "Eight grams of protein and it's all organic." She paused hopefully. "Are you sure you don't want to try one? With a bun and some mustard and onions, I bet you won't even notice the difference."

The coach chuckled. "Betcha I will. But aw, what the heck, they're free! Sure, gimme one. … I'll give it a shot."

Matt and I high-fived. This was our hundredth—or two hundredth, or five hundredth, really we'd lost count—tofu dog of the day. We were hosting a free Ethical Foods Cookout at our school's homecoming football game, featuring veggie products, organic meat options, sprouted-wheat buns, and lots of information about the food industry. The fans strolling about the stands seemed surprisingly willing to read about eating organic and buying local—as long as they were tucking away the burgers and dogs as fast as we could cook them.

This was our house's first major event of the year. As a group of thirteen concerned students, that autumn we'd founded Guilford College's first-ever Food Ethics House—an on-campus household dedicated entirely to exploring ethical issues related to food.

The idea had blossomed the year before as our frustration with the school's cafeteria mounted. The college—like many universities across the country—has dining services provided by a company that is notorious for poor treatment of workers and unethically produced food. We were sick of paying thousands of dollars a year to eat food that we were morally opposed to and sick of the school refusing to listen to our complaints and suggestions. If you can't beat 'em, then get out, we decided, and resolved to set an example by forming a radically different kind of household.

And amazingly, for once all went according to plan. When we moved into the house in August, we began buying our produce through a co-op of local organic farmers. For $20 a week, we received two giant boxes of fresh produce, harvested right there in Guilford County on Tuesday and sizzling in our kitchen on Wednesday. This system supports the local economy and eliminates the transportation and packing waste that results from the grocery store. We cooked communally several nights a week, sharing cooking and cleaning duties, and less of our food went to waste through leftovers and repackaging. We composted our organic waste and used this to fertilize the school's organic fair-share garden, which we took turns tending with other students.

We also "Dumpster dived"—a practice that gets most people's attention, especially our parents'! It's not as crazy as it seems though. Ever notice that lots of bakeries, for example, offer bread "baked fresh daily"? Ever wondered what happens to the bread that doesn't get sold by the end of the day? It won't be fresh enough to sell the next day, yet it's still perfectly good. The answer is that it gets thrown away—along with mountains of other perfectly edible restaurant, store, and bakery food that no longer meets their standards at the end of the day. Dumpster diving is a way of saving and making use of that food. No diving is actually required—though quite a bit of it does literally come out of Dumpsters (only if it's safely packaged!). Other stores are willing to cooperate and set the food aside for us to pick up before it hits the Dumpster.

With only a couple of collections a week, we recovered far more food than we could eat. The excess went to Food Not Bombs, a sort of roving anarchist soup kitchen. This organization, although it has no leader, has local chapters in most cities across the country. Volunteers drive around to local restaurants, bakeries, and stores that have agreed to set aside the food that is no longer for sale. Using church kitchens, parks, and other collective spaces, this food is then cooked into free vegetarian meals and served to the homeless or anyone else who shows up to eat. Volunteers and patrons eat together, building community, relaxing, and, best of all, making use of food that would otherwise become garbage.

I always came home from Food Not Bombs feeling energized and enthusiastic—I usually wound up talking to someone I otherwise would never have spoken to, often having a really meaningful conversation. I was often impressed and amazed—and the food was *always* delicious.

More difficult were overtures on campus. Our house took turns with other campus houses in hosting vegetarian potlucks—community meals where everyone brought one dish, and, presto!, we had an instant smorgasbord. The goal of our potlucks was to promote discussion of ethical food issues and consciousness of food-related choices. But there was one problem: talking about these issues with our friends, the people who had opted to attend such an event, was preaching to the choir. The people we really wanted to reach out to weren't choosing to come.

And that's how we found ourselves at the homecoming cookout. Armed with $500 from the student union, informational signs and handouts, and thirty bottles of ketchup, we were out to spread the word. Other groups around us were sending up clouds of greasy smoke from their "real" hamburgers and dogs, but a steady stream of interested folks kept us reloading our veggie grill with healthier options.

I can't say we changed anybody's life that day, but we did get some people thinking. For sure, a lot of people tried veggie dogs and veggie burgers for the first time—and liked them. And certainly, a lot of people read our signs and asked us questions: "So why are *you* vegetarian? Does this stuff really matter? Why? What can I do?"

We respect our peers' choice to eat the way they do, but projects like this one do make us feel excited and empowered. It's one thing to make a change in your own eating habits; it's something else entirely to stir up your community and the other people around you and pass on whatever spark made you change your ways in the first place.

None of us are perfect little messengers all the time. Sometimes we feel like reaching out, other days it takes all our energy just to do the tasks on tap for the day. But it's exciting to try to make contact, even if the effort is just occasional. And it's even more exciting when someone seems to be listening.

So what about you? Is there anyone in your life you can talk to about the issues you're learning about? Are your friends or family interested in getting involved? Or even if it involves no one else but you and your own plate, what positive choices can you make today?

Chapter Eight

Cooking to Save the Planet

Learning to Cook Vegetarian

You can cook. Don't let anyone tell you otherwise. Cooking is something you can learn to do quite easily—first master the basics and then, with growing confidence, add your own flair.

The most important thing to know is that vegetarian cooking is not boring. Many new vegetarians are at a loss—without meat, what are you supposed to cook? After all, traditional American meals are centered on meat. When you holler out, "What's for dinner?" the answer comes back in the form of the meat—"Pork chops!" or "Hamburgers!" or "Fried chicken!" When you take away the meat dish, what's left?

The answer is, a lot more room for creativity! Without focusing all your attention on that main meat dish, you can explore a wide variety of spices, flavors, and styles of food. You aren't restricted to one main dish and a couple of sides. You can make soups and stews, casseroles and goulashes, spreads and sandwiches. You can try recipes from cultures around the world—many of which are, after all, primarily vegetarian.

Vegetarian food can be just as mouth-watering as meat dishes, even to meat eaters. If you're ready to wow your friends and family, let's get down to some cooking basics.

TIPS FOR GETTING STARTED

Cooking's easy . . . if you've got the time.

—Joe Kneidel

Read First

If you're reading this, good job! Before using a recipe from this book or any other, take the time to check out the beginning sections. For example, if you're about to embark on a bean recipe, take a look at the intro to beans. You'll probably pick up some important tips that aren't repeated at the beginning of every recipe.

Double Check

Before you start, read through the entire recipe and make sure you have all the ingredients. Often, we actually assemble all the ingredients on the counter before we begin just to make sure no one ate them for a midnight snack or lent them to the neighbors. Also, make sure that you have enough time for the dish to

169

bake, marinate, or do whatever it needs to do—and preheat the oven if you need to.

Experiment

As you first start cooking, you'll probably feel more comfortable following the recipe exactly. But recipes, *especially* the ones in this book, are just guides. Taste what you're making and if you don't like it, trust your instincts. Playing with spices and flavor combinations is how you'll learn what works and what doesn't. Make notes about what you try so you'll remember next time. If you feel cautious, take out a small portion and try adjusting the flavors in it—and if you like the results, apply your change to the whole dish.

Go Little by Little

Taking liberties is great, but be cautious. If an amount isn't specified—particularly of something potent such as salt or hot sauce—remember that it's a lot easier to add a little bit more than it is to frantically spoon it back out. Add a little, taste, add a little more, taste again.

Substitute

Consult the lists of substitutes and variations if the recipe doesn't suit your needs. Most recipes can be made vegan, for instance, by using soy milk and an egg substitute. Wheat allergies can be accommodated with other grains. Seitan or beans can replace soy products. Don't write off a recipe just because of one ingredient.

Don't Try to Replace Meat

Vegetarian meals are different. If you're trying to eat meaty meals without the meat, you'll probably be disappointed. Do try foods that have meatlike textures, such as tofu, seitan, or eggplant, but accept that they will be different.

SUBSTITUTIONS FOR VEGAN COOKING

Any recipe in this book can be made vegan. Even if you're not vegan, you may want to use these substitutions anyway. They generally make the recipes healthier and particularly lower in fat and concentrated chemicals.

Here are some common substitutions for vegan cooking:

- Milk: For the closest replacement, use soy milk, rice milk, or almond milk. If the creaminess doesn't matter, vegetable broth or water will work.
- Cream: Soy milk or soy creamer are lighter alternatives. You can also use "cashew milk"—blend together equal amounts of raw cashews and hot water in a blender. It sounds weird, but it makes a rich liquid that's a perfect creamy base in soups or other savory dishes.
- Butter: Olive oil and canola oil are the healthiest fat options. Olive oil works in cooking but not in baking because of its strong flavor. Canola oil, which is milder, works better in cakes and sweet things. Margarine is also an option—but read the label and look for a brand that doesn't contain hydrogenated oils or trans fats. Alternately, if you want to cut the fat content, any oil in a bread, cake, or cookie can be replaced with an equivalent amount of applesauce. It will give the dish a lighter, fruitier, and less rich taste.
- Sour cream or yogurt: Depending on the circumstance, soy milk or blended-up tofu may work. Plain soy yogurt (available at health food stores) is another option.
- Cheese: There are vegan cheeses. Actually, cheese takes a little bit of label reading. If the ingredients include rennet, the cheese isn't even vegetarian: rennet is the lining of a calf's stomach. If it's a soy cheese or other cheese alternative, it is probably vegan, unless the ingredients include casein; casein is a dairy protein. Tofu may also work as a cheese substitute.

- Honey: Brown sugar is the most common replacement. However, many vegans do not eat refined sugar because animal bones are used in processing it. Alternative sweeteners include nonrefined (turbinado) sugar, beet sugar, molasses, maple syrup, and stevia extract.
- Eggs: There are many different ways to replace eggs. All of the following equal one egg:
  - ¼ cup blended banana. Whip it with a hand mixer or blender until it is good and frothy, so it doesn't weigh the dish down. This works only in baking or in sweet dishes—you will be able to taste the banana! It does work with French toast—blend the banana with soy milk and cinnamon.
  - I tablespoon flaxseeds, boiled in 3 tablespoons water. Flaxseeds provide omega-3 fatty acids, which most American diets lack. You can buy flaxseeds at almost any health food store and at many general grocery stores. You can grind up the seeds in a coffee grinder or leave them whole, but grinding them makes it easier for your body to access the oils. Bring the seeds and water to a boil until they start to congeal into a gluey paste, then add to your mix. You won't be able to taste the seeds if you leave them whole, but when ground up, they add a distinctive nutty flavor. Ground seeds work particularly well in baking bread.
  - If all the water boils off while you are boiling the seeds, you may need to add a tablespoon or two of water per "egg" to your dish to keep it from being too dry.
  - Flaxseeds don't absorb oil like eggs do, so decrease the oil content by a tablespoon per cup of oil. That is, if the recipe calls for half a cup of oil and you're using flax, subtract half a tablespoon of oil.

- ¼ cup blended tofu. This is good for recipes that require lots of eggs, such as quiches.
- ¼ cup mashed beans, mashed potatoes, or peanut butter will also work, if the flavors don't interfere with your recipe. Oddly, mashed potatoes can even work in cookies since the potatoes don't have much flavor.
- 2 tablespoons water plus I tablespoon oil plus 2 teaspoons baking powder. This is useful because it doesn't require any unusual ingredients—you can do it when you don't have anything else on hand.
- 2 tablespoons cornstarch plus I tablespoon water. Whisk the cornstarch into warm water until there are no lumps before adding to the mixture.
- I ½ teaspoons Ener-G Egg Replacer plus 2 tablespoons water. This product comes in a box and can be found in health food stores. It is basically potato starch and tapioca flour. It can be whipped into foam just like real egg whites, so it's useful if you need to make a light and fluffy dish, such as pancakes. The box is covered with recipe ideas for everything from muffins to quiches. This is our favorite alternative.

Any of these options may take a little experimentation depending on the recipe you're using, but have no fear! You'll figure it out.

SEASONINGS

A crucial step to becoming a good cook is learning what flavors work well together and how to season different types of food. The more you cook, the more examples you'll encounter, and you'll begin to develop a knack for it. Soon you'll know what flavors work together best, even in unlikely combinations.

When using fresh herbs, such as cilantro or parsley, wait until the last moment

A lot of people don't believe I'm a vegetarian. I guess I don't fit the normal
profile. People seem to have a stereotype of vegetarians as skinny girls.

Sometimes people ask me if I miss
meat. But I like the taste of stuff better without meat. There's more variety
in a vegetarian diet, it's better than
burgers and fries every day. There's not
as much greasy stuff, the food is leaner.
It made it easier to lose weight for
wrestling—I was able to lose about
thirty pounds! Plus there are cholesterol
problems on both sides of my family.

I cook whenever I get the chance,
maybe three times a week during the
school year. I like Mexican stuff a lot.
That's an easy way to cook: toss stuff
in a pan and stir-fry it. Asian takes a
little more work to get the ingredients.
Mediterranean food is pretty good,
depending on the spices.

I know more now about how to get
protein than I did when I started. Some
of my favorite usual foods are tofu,
beans, peanuts, and dairy stuff.

onions, and garlic in the oil until you can
smell them cooking and then add the harder
veggies, such as carrots, to give them a little
head start in cooking time.

Here's a quick reference guide to what
seasonings produce certain flavors in familiar
foods.

- **Asian:** Asian food is very subtly flavored. The
natural flavors of vegetables, rice, and soy are
enhanced with peanuts, ginger, sesame oil, miso
(a fermented soy paste), and tamari. Tamari,
also called shoyu, is similar to soy sauce, but
much healthier. It is naturally fermented,
lower in sodium, and lacks the corn syrup and
other unhealthy ingredients of soy sauce.
- **Cajun:** Spicy Cajun cooking features white
pepper, black pepper, cayenne pepper, chili
powder, paprika, garlic, and salt.
- **Desserts:** The sweet spices that we associate
with apple crisp and pumpkin pie are cinnamon, nutmeg, cloves, allspice, and ginger.
Occasionally these are incorporated into
savory dishes as well.
- **French:** France has the most renowned cuisine
of western Europe, although flavoring is similar in many countries in that area. Typical seasonings include dill, bay leaf, rosemary, tarragon, and thyme. In the spice aisle at the grocery store, you may see a bottle labeled
"Herbs de Provence"—a standard French
blend that you can make yourself:
    - 3 tablespoons marjoram
    - 1 teaspoon rosemary
    - 3 tablespoons thyme
    - ½ teaspoon sage
    - 3 tablespoons savory
    - ½ teaspoon fennel seeds
    - 1 teaspoon dried basil
- **Greek:** The blend of spicy and savory makes
Mediterranean cuisine unique. Typical flavors
include cinnamon, garlic, mint, oregano, and
lemon. This Greek seasoning mix adds a kick
to any dish:
    - 2 teaspoons salt

to add them to your dish. When using dried
herbs, you can add them at any time. Generally, use one and a half parts fresh herbs to
one part dried herbs. That is, if a recipe calls
for two tablespoons of dried basil and yours is
fresh, use three. To bring out the flavor in
dried herbs, it helps to sauté them for a few
minutes in hot oil. A tasty way to start off
most dishes, from soups to burgers, is to chop
up some onions, garlic, and whatever vegetables you're going to use and to start a little oil
sizzling in the frying pan. Toss the seasonings,

- 2 teaspoons oregano
- 1½ teaspoons onion powder
- 1½ teaspoons garlic powder
- 1 teaspoon black pepper
- 1 teaspoon dried parsley flakes
- ½ teaspoon ground cinnamon
- ½ teaspoon ground nutmeg

- **Indian:** Curry powder is a blend of the most common Indian spices, which include cumin, coriander, turmeric, ginger, cardamom, and mustard seed. Fenugreek, fennel, cinnamon, and red chilies complement these flavors as well. Coriander, cumin, and turmeric work best together, in a ratio of 1 to 2 to 4. To bring out their flavor, add these spices to any dish as the onions are sautéing.

- **Italian:** Basil, oregano, thyme, garlic, bay leaf, lemon, sage, anise, fennel, and rosemary all turn up in Italian food. For emergency spaghetti sauce, add these seasonings per cup of plain tomato sauce:
  - 2 teaspoons basil
  - 2 teaspoons marjoram
  - 2 teaspoons oregano
  - 1 teaspoon sage

- **Mexican:** Cumin, or *comino*, is the foundation of that delicious Mexican flavor. Mexican oregano—slightly different from the more common Italian oregano—along with cilantro, lime, cayenne, hot peppers, garlic, paprika, and salt round out the flavor.

Peppers

Bell peppers are not spicy at all. They are large and roundish and come in many different colors. The most common color is green, but if allowed to ripen longer, green peppers turn yellow or red. The colored varieties are sweeter than the green ones. They are all crisp and have a watery flavor.

Banana peppers are not spicy at all. They are bright yellowish green and often at least six inches long. They are long and narrow and taper to the tip.

Anaheim peppers are very faintly spicy, but easily overwhelmed by other seasonings. Their shape is similar to that of banana peppers, but they are a more grassy green in color.

Poblano peppers are somewhat spicy; their heat can build up if eaten in large quantities. They are very large, sometimes as big as bell peppers, but longer and more pointed. They are very dark green, sometimes almost black.

Serrano peppers are fairly spicy. They are tiny and thin, about the width of a finger but not as long. They are medium green in color.

Jalapeño peppers are quite spicy. They are the same color as serrano peppers, but they are fatter at the top and taper slightly.

Habañero peppers are extremely spicy and only to be used by the bravest of the brave. They are bright yellow, red, and orange and are small and roundish, sometimes flat and wrinkled. They are often placed in their own container at the grocery so they won't get mixed up with other peppers by accident.

Planning Meals

Planning meals in advance may help you get all the nutrients you need on the table. See chapter six (page 123) to determine what requirements your meals should meet.

VEGETABLES

Ask a classroom of American students their favorite food, and the most popular answer will probably be pizza, with a variety of junk foods and fast foods bringing up the rear. But that's unfair to the ignored and maligned vegetables of the world. Veggies can be just as yummy and far more healthful. More tasty too, once you've lost your taste for animal fat. Yes, a well-cooked veggie dish can make you whimper with satisfaction. Here are some tips to make sure they turn out right.

- Use fresh ingredients. In terms of health and taste, fresh vegetables are infinitely better than canned or frozen. Frozen is preferable to canned, but nothing compares to a good, fresh vegetable. When buying vegetables, look for crisp and firm produce that is without spots or bruises.

- A little salt is okay, and often enhances flavor. Except for beans, vegetables should be salted while they are still cooking. This way the salt dissolves and is absorbed by the food, which makes it easier for your body to process.

- It does matter how you cook vegetables. Some methods leach out nutrients, while others preserve the vitamins and minerals in the food. No matter what method you use, it's best to cook vegetables slowly, on low heat, still in their skin. You can remove the skin later, if you wish, but it helps trap nutrients inside during the cooking process.

  - **Steaming** is better than boiling. If you don't have a steamer, it's no problem: just run some water in the bottom of a big pot and set a colander inside the pot. Then put your veggies in the colander—they shouldn't be touching the water—and put the lid on the pot. Simmer the water over medium heat and the vapor will steam the veggies. The time will vary depending on what you're cooking.

  - **Sautéing** gives the vegetables more flavor than steaming. To sauté means to lightly cook with a little oil in a frying pan. To sauté anything, heat up a tablespoon or so of oil in a frying pan over medium heat. Add any spices to the oil and then the vegetables. For best results, cook slowly on medium-low heat and cover with a lid, lifting occasionally to check and stir.

  - **Stir-frying** is similar to sautéing. The main difference is to use slightly more heat—a touch above medium—and to cook the vegetables more quickly. When done, the veggies should be tender, but still a little bit crisp.

- **Roasting** vegetables takes the least effort, but the most time. Lots of veggies, especially big ones such as eggplants, squash, and turnips, can be baked whole in the oven, then sliced. Just put the vegetables in a baking dish with a little water or oil to prevent scorching and bake at 400°F for about 30 minutes, or until tender. The time will depend on the size of the vegetable. You may cut them in half to decrease baking time.

- **Grilling** vegetables is delicious and easy. In particular, thinly sliced eggplant, bell peppers, onions, squash, corn, asparagus, artichokes, carrots, and potatoes turn out wonderfully. Brush the veggies with a simple marinade—half tamari, half olive oil works nicely—before putting them on the grill. Root vegetables, such as potatoes, should be boiled until almost cooked before grilling.

GRAINS

Choose Whole Grains If You Can

First of all, choose whole grains whenever you can. Grains are seeds and they have several parts. The outer layer is the husk, or hull, which is tough and inedible. Inside lies the bran, which is another protective layer, sometimes called the seed coat. Inside the bran or seed coat is the germ, or plant embryo, which holds lots of nutrients, and the endosperm, which is starchy food for the embryo, should it sprout.

Highly processed grain products, such as white flour or white rice, have everything but the endosperm removed. This process makes them softer and easier to cook but strips away all the nutrients and leaves only the starchy part. Whole grains, on the other hand, have only the hull removed, which leaves all the fiber and nutrients of the bran and germ. Therefore, they're much better for you.

We have a poster in our kitchen displaying color photographs of at least forty different kinds of delicious, nutritious grains from around the world. And yet how many of these grains do we commonly eat? Wheat, corn, rice, oats, sometimes barley ... that's about it. You might be surprised to learn about the variety of grains that are commonly used in other countries—we were. In Mexico, they make cookies and crackers out of tiny grains of amaranth that are then sold on the streets and eaten at weddings. In West Africa, they pound and boil millet into a thick porridge called *toh*. And right here in North Carolina, adventurous school cafeterias serve a supergrain called quinoa (KEEN-wah), native to the Andean mountains.

If they can do it, you can too. One trip to the health food store will reveal products you've never dreamed of: steel-cut oats, wheat berries, and triticale, just to name a few. If you're tired of eating plain old rice day after day, you're in luck—your boredom ends here. Welcome to the wild world of nutritious grains!

Okay, so I'm getting a little carried away. But really, grains can make or break a meal.

—Sara Kate

1 cup of	Water (cups)	Cooking time (minutes)	Yields (cups)
Amaranth	3	20	2
Barley, pearl	3	45	3
Buckwheat	2	15	2½
Bulgur wheat	2	20	3
Couscous	2	10	3
Grits (hominy)	4	25	3
Millet	3	35	3½
Oats, rolled	2¾	10	3
Oats, steel-cut	2	10	2
Rice, basmati	2¼	20	4
Rice, brown	3	45	4
Rice, white	2	20	4
Wheat berries	3½	90	2

Types of Grains

Amaranth

Centuries ago, amaranth was a staple food of the Aztecs. Among other uses, they mixed it with honey and the blood from human sacrifices to make idols, which were eaten as a ceremonial food. The Spanish conquistadores were perturbed by this and banned amaranth (as if that would solve the problem!). The grain might have disappeared altogether, but fortunately, its high nutritional content and extreme usefulness motivated at least a few people to keep growing it on the sly.

Today amaranth is making a comeback. Very popular in Latin America, amaranth is now used in the United States in numerous ways. It can be cooked as a hot cereal, ground into flour, popped like popcorn, sprouted, or toasted. These tiny seeds can also thicken other whole grains, stir-fries, soups, and stews.

When overcooked, amaranth turns into

Some things classified as grains, such as amaranth and quinoa, aren't really grains. But to keep things simple, we'll include them here.

Storing and Cooking Adventurous Grains

To keep grains from sprouting or spoiling, store them in completely dry, airtight containers in a cool, dark place. There is no need to wash them before cooking, unless they're obviously dirty, and even then use only cold water. To cook any grains, simmer over medium low-heat—with a pinch of salt if you wish—for the indicated time or until they are soft and seem done.

a sticky goo. This is gross if you're trying to eat it as porridge, but useful if you need it to stick something together. For this reason, it is a great "glue" for holding together homemade veggie burgers.

Barley

Barley is an extremely satisfying food due to its unusual texture. Even when fully cooked, it retains a slightly bouncy, poppy feeling in your mouth, more chewy than rice. It's commonly used in soups, but it is delicious on its own as well. It can also be mixed with vegetables, beans, or other foods.

There are several varieties. Pearl barley, which has most of the germ and bran polished off, is the easiest to cook and has the most pleasing texture. Hulled barley—also known as pot barley and Scotch barley—has the hull and part of the bran removed; it takes a long time to cook. For emergencies, there is instant barley, which takes only ten minutes to cook, but it barely resembles barley at all. It's been completely flattened and feels like rolled oatmeal in your mouth.

Buckwheat

Buckwheat is not a grain, it's a fruit! You'd never know from looking at it, though: it comes in the form of crunchy little brown triangles. Also known as kasha, buckwheat originated in Central Asia, where it is traditionally eaten as a porridge or ground into flour.

Corn

From grits and cornbread to tortillas and tamales, corn has a great legacy across the Americas. It is generally eaten as whole kernels or ground into cornmeal.

We eat whole kernels mostly in creamed corn, ears of corn, succotash, and Latin American dishes, such as *pozole*. When ground into coarse chunks, corn becomes hominy, or grits, the popular breakfast staple of the American South. When ground slightly finer, it becomes cornmeal, the basis for cornbread, tortillas, and many other dishes.

Most cornmeal, labeled "degerminated" or "bolted," has the nutritional equivalent of white flour; it has had all the nutritional parts removed, leaving only the starchy endosperm. Stone-ground cornmeal, however, is a more nutritious whole food. The color of a particular cornmeal—it can be white, yellow, blue, or red, depending on the corn it was made from—doesn't affect its nutritional content.

Cornmeal can be added to breads or other baked dishes. It is also a useful replacement for bread crumbs.

Masa harina is an especially finely ground cornmeal that is treated with lime. It is used for making tortillas and other Latin dishes.

Millet

Although it is a nutritious whole grain, millet's lack of texture and flavor keep its popularity in check. When boiled, it forms a grainy goo, much like amaranth. To improve its texture, toast it a little before boiling. Pour the grains on a skillet on medium heat and stir them frequently as they heat for a few minutes. You can do this on a dry skillet or with a little oil. Teff is an African grain that is similar to millet and may actually be related. Teff, millet, and amaranth are generally interchangeable in recipes.

Oats

The oats we're all familiar with—the kind you eat for breakfast—are rolled oats. They are steamed and then flattened by rollers, which makes them cook quicker. I used to think oats were naturally as flat as a piece of paper! But if you buy other kinds of oats, such as the steel-cut variety—also known as Scottish or Irish oats—you'll see that their normal shape is actually roundish. All kinds of oats are delicious and healthy, though instant oatmeal is really pushing it. After the steaming and rolling procedure that rolled oats are subjected to, instant oats are also pulverized, partially cooked, dried, and overpackaged. If those little envelopes of apple–flavored instant oatmeal are your only acquaintance with this food, you owe it to yourself to go buy some good oats right now!

Oatmeal as we know it is usually served as a breakfast dish, but steel-cut oats are a fiber-rich substitute for rice or noodles. Rolled oats can also be added to bread, cookies, or any baked dish for added nutrition.

Quinoa

This ancient food is the sacred mother grain of the Incas. Like amaranth, it's not really a grain, technically speaking, and it also has a dramatic history. When the Spanish conquered the Andes, they forbade the growing of quinoa and promoted the consumption of meat instead. But fortunately for us, a few daring and determined Incan farmers kept their plants growing and so we still have it today.

Quinoa is amazingly rich in protein as well as other nutrients. It's light and fluffy, like white rice, and doesn't take long to cook. Even without seasonings, quinoa tastes delicious, as long as you soak it in cold water before cooking—this rids the grains of a bitter-tasting natural chemical that the plant produces to deter hungry animals.

Rice

Basmati rice is usually a form of white rice, but it is possible to find whole-grain basmati. A staple of Indian cuisine, basmati rice has a unique, delicate flavor that will amaze you if you've never eaten it before—or even if you have. The grains are long, thin, and drier than the white rice we're used to.

Brown rice is the same variety as white rice, but it is a whole grain, with the bran and germ intact. It has more fiber, protein, and nutrients than white rice and is somewhat less sticky.

Short-grain white rice, like basmati rice, has had the bran and germ removed and is therefore the starchy endosperm of the rice grain. It cooks quickly, is almost flavorless, and is quite sticky. It is a basic staple of Asian cooking, as well as Italian.

Wild rice is not actually rice at all. It is the seed of a grass that grows in the Midwest and was traditionally eaten by many indigenous tribes.

Triticale

Triticale (pronounced tri-ti-KAY-lee) is a cross between wheat and rye. It was developed with the hope that it would be a wonder grain, cultivated and eaten all over the world, but so far, it has failed to catch on.

Wheat

Wheat is a versatile grain that leaves all other grains in the dust. It is highly nutritious and can be used in so many different ways that it'll make your head spin. In the United States, we usually consume wheat as white flour, pasta, and bread. Not surprisingly, these are the least healthy options of a dazzling array of possibilities.

All whole grains are really seeds. Brown rice grains are the seeds of the rice plant, kernels of corn are corn seeds, and so on. Wheat berries are the seeds of the wheat plant and can be cooked just like rice or barley, only they're more fun to eat than either of those two. Wheat berries that you buy in a grocery or health food store have not been milled—they are whole grains. They are chewy and, like barley, have a slightly poppy texture. They can be cooked like brown rice, for close to an hour, until soft enough to chew comfortably. They're very good and versatile, with a slightly nutty taste. When ground up, they make a good base for veggie burgers and other dishes that need to stick together. When left whole, they make great stuffings and grain salads.

Topped with butter or margarine, they are a spunky little side dish.

Cracked wheat is produced by cracking dried whole wheat grains (wheat berries) into small pieces, like a very course kind of cornmeal. The bran and germ are not removed, so it's still considered a whole grain. Cracked wheat needs about fifteen minutes of cooking with water before it can be eaten. As a hot breakfast cereal, it has the consistency of a heavily textured oatmeal. Topped with soy milk and honey, maybe some fruit, it's good and very filling. Not knock-your-socks-off good, but good enough that I used to eat it every morning. For general purposes, cracked wheat can add fiber and substance to breads, chilis, casseroles, and so on.

Bulgur is cracked wheat that has been parboiled, dried, ground into particles, and sifted into distinct sizes. Much of the bran is lost during this process, so it is not a whole grain. But it has one advantage: because it has been precooked during processing, it can be softened for eating just by soaking. You're most likely to run into bulgur in the United States in the form of tabouli, a popular vegetable-and-grain salad.

Couscous is really just pasta in tiny balls. Its fluffy yet slightly sticky texture makes it a very useful base for many dishes. It is also flavorful and easily seasoned, and it cooks in less than five minutes, making it a very quick and handy side dish.

Farina is a coarse wheat flour, also known as Cream of Wheat. It is not a whole-grain product.

Pasta is made from a wheat flour called semolina. Spaghetti, angel hair, macaroni, bow tie, rotini, couscous, and almost all the pasta we eat (with the exception of egg and rice noodles) come from wheat. Most pasta is made from white flour, but many grocery stores offer at least one brand of whole wheat pasta. Whole wheat pasta is rich in protein

and fiber and has more flavor and texture than the white kind. Whole-grain noodles with a bean or tofu sauce make a very healthy meal.

Wheat bran and germ are the parts of the grain that are discarded in the process of making white flour. (Oddly, people buy white flour and then buy wheat bran and wheat germ and mix back in the parts they just paid to have taken out. Strange.) Both wheat bran and wheat germ are incredibly nutritious. You can use them in any baking recipe by substituting a portion of the flour for bran or germ. It will make the product denser, heavier, and heartier. Both bran and germ can be used in place of bread crumbs for coating fried foods. They can also be added to granola, oatmeal, cereals, and casseroles—an easy and subtle way to boost their nutritional content. Both should be kept in the fridge to preserve nutritional content.

White flour is made from the endosperm of the wheat grain, meaning it's not a whole grain. It has a finer texture and is easier to bake with than whole wheat flour, but it has very little nutritional content.

Whole wheat flour is the healthier option, but because it contains bran and germ, it is more ornery than white flour. It's a bit more unpredictable in baking and it makes heavier breads and baked goods. However, it's much heartier and much better for you nutritionally. In recipes that call for white flour, try substituting whole wheat flour for half the white flour before going 100 percent whole wheat; it may change the final product significantly.

BEANS

A hearty burrito stuffed with black beans, veggies, and salsa ... Steaming lentil soup, topped with freshly chopped tomatoes and cilantro ... Spicy, creamy hummus, spread atop soft pita bread ... Lightly steamed soybeans, salted and ready to be popped out of their crisp shells ... Chunky refried-bean dip, topped with

More info on the most promising grains:

Grain	Whole grain?
Amaranth	Yes
Barley, pearl	No
Barley, instant whole grain	Yes
Bulgur wheat	No
Cornmeal	No
Cornmeal, stone-ground	Yes
Couscous, white	No
Couscous, whole wheat	Yes
Millet	Yes
Oats, rolled	Yes
Oats, steel-cut	Yes
Quinoa	Yes
Rice, basmati	No
Rice, brown	Yes
Rice, white	No
Triticale	Yes
Wheat, cracked	Yes
Wheat berries	Yes
Wheat bran	Yes
Wheat germ	Yes
Whole wheat flour	Yes

Beans are a dietary staple in almost every country in the world, and, believe me, over the last few thousand years, people have found ways to make them interesting. And now you're going to serve them—mashed or fried, spiced or curried, mixed or plain—to your family, and they are going to like them. *You* are going to like them.

Before you go running to the kitchen, there are a few bean rules of thumb that will make your dishes a success.

> **Student Voice:**
> **Alan, Age 18**
>
> A lifetime of hamburgers and French fries is not easily forgotten. But nothing of value is easy. If the effort is made to change to a healthier diet, then soon the beauty will be in the salad and not the salmon, the beans and not the burger.

Buying Beans

Most Americans buy beans in cans. This is very convenient because they're already cooked—all you've got to do is open, rinse, and dump. However, it's not the best option—it creates a lot of waste, and it's relatively expensive.

Dried beans are a cheaper and more efficient option. One bag of dried beans costs about the same as a can but yields about fifteen times as many beans. We prefer to use dried beans when possible; however, they do take longer to prepare, so it's good to have a few cans on hand for emergencies. You know, bean emergencies ... they happen all the time.

Frozen bags of beans are also an option. These don't take as long to cook as dried beans, but are a bit cheaper than canned beans. It may be worth keeping a bag or two on hand.

jalapeños and scooped up in tortilla chips ...

Notice anything about these dishes? They're making me hungry! Well, yes, but did you notice they're all *beans*?

Beans get a bad rap. Many people—meat eaters and vegetarians alike—complain about beans. They don't have any flavor, they say, or their texture is weird, they're boring, and so on. Well, we're here to change that.

Preparing Beans

Canned beans are quick to prepare. Open the can and dump the beans into a colander or bowl, where you can rinse off the liquid from the can. Then you're ready to roll with your recipe.

With dried beans, you have a couple of options. If you're way ahead of schedule, you can soak the beans overnight. To do this, check over the dried beans and pick out any rocks, twigs, or dried and wrinkled beans. (These may be older and will not cook as well.) Place the beans in a bowl or saucepan and cover with three times as much water for soaking (for example, three cups of water for one cup of beans). Remove any beans that float; they could have an air pocket with mold in it. The next day, pour out any remaining water. Then add water according to the package and cook on low medium-low until they're soft—it will take at least an hour. If you don't have the package, add at least four times as much water as beans and check the water level frequently while cooking.

More realistically, if you don't decide that far in advance what you're going to cook, here's a shortcut. Put the beans in a saucepan with about six times as much water. Bring to a boil on high heat, boil for about a minute, and then turn them off. Cover the pot and let it sit for an hour. Then simmer the beans on medium-low heat for an hour and a half or until they're soft. A common mistake is not to cook beans long enough—make sure they're really soft, soft enough to mash easily. If they're still hard at all, they'll make for some unpleasant eating.

SUGGESTION

If you use dried beans, you can soak the beans overnight as soon as you buy them, then drain them and freeze them in plastic bags. This way, when you want to boil them, all you've got to do is open the bag and they're ready to go.

Here are a few tips for cooking beans:

- Don't use salt. Never put anything salty or acidic in your beans while they are soaking or cooking. This includes salt, lemon juice, tomato products, vinegar, and the like. These toughen the skins of the beans and prevent them from absorbing water.
- Rinse the beans well before cooking, especially canned beans. This reduces their content of oligosaccharides, the compounds that result in the notorious gas caused by beans.
- If you need to add extra water to the pot, heat the water before adding it to the beans; suddenly dumping in a cup of cold water interrupts the cooking process.

Type of Bean	Soak?	Cooking time (hours)
Adzuki	Yes	1
Black	Yes	1 to 1½
Black-eyed peas	No	1 to 1¼
Cannellini	Yes	1 to 1½
Chickpeas	Yes	2½ to 3
Fava	Yes, at least 12 hours	3
Great northern	Yes	1½ to 2
Kidney	Yes	1 to 1½
Lentils	No	30 to 45 minutes
Lima	Yes	1 to 1½
Mung	No	1
Navy	Yes	2½
Peruvian	Yes	2
Pinto	Yes	1½ to 2½
Soy, fresh	No	5 minutes
Soy, dried	Yes, at least 24 hours	3 to 4
Split peas	No	30 minutes

- One cup of dried legumes makes a little less than 2 ½ cups cooked. Cook the beans in about six times as much water. That's 6 cups of water for every cup of dry beans.

Types of Beans and Legumes

Adzuki Beans
Adzuki beans are tiny and red and usually accompany white rice in Asian cuisine. They are also used to make red-bean ice cream.

Black Beans
Black beans, also called turtle beans, are one of the most common and versatile beans in the Americas. They are used in everything from soups to burritos to hummus. They are black, as their name suggests, and relatively small.

Black-Eyed Peas
Black-eyed peas, also called cowpeas, pigeon peas, and field peas, are named for the black dot on their side. These beans are traditionally eaten in the South as good-luck food on New Year's Day. They also turn up in Caribbean, French, and African cooking.

Cannellini
Cannellini are the dried seeds of green beans. They are most often used in Italian cooking, particularly in dishes from the region of Tuscany.

Chickpeas
Chickpeas, also called garbanzos, are like pale little peaches in both their color and their shape, although only slightly bigger than green peas. They are a common feature in salad bars and are also the traditional base for hummus and other Middle Eastern, Indian, and Mediterranean dishes.

Fava Beans
Fava beans look like giant lima beans: flat and curved. They are sometimes served fresh and are the basis for unusual dishes, from breakfast spreads in Egypt to creamy soups in Mexico. They must be cooked very thoroughly to avoid allergic reactions in some people.

Great Northern Beans
Great northern beans are white, smallish, and fairly bland. They originate from Brittany, a region of northern France.

Kidney Beans
Kidney beans are long and slightly curved, somewhat in the shape of a kidney. They are usually red, though occasionally white or brown. They are extremely popular through-out the Americas, Europe, and India. You'll recognize them from dishes such as chili.

Lentils
Lentils come in three varieties: brown, red, and green. They are tiny and shaped like small, flat disks. They are delicious in everything from salads to curries to soups. Lentils are one of the most flavorful and versatile of all legumes.

Lima Beans
Lima beans, also called butter beans, are flat and disklike, usually pale green in color. Although they were named for Lima, Peru, they are commonly eaten in China and Africa as well. In the United States, lima beans are most often served on their own as a side dish, though in other countries, they are incorporated into a variety of different dishes.

Mung Beans
Mung beans are most commonly encountered as raw sprouts on salad, but they are also cooked like lentils when in their bean form.

Navy Beans

Navy beans are small and white. They got their name in the 1800s, when they were served frequently to the Navy. They can be interchanged with cannellini, great northern beans, or any other white bean.

Peruvian Beans

Peruvian beans are not common in the United States, but their unique and subtle flavor makes them absolutely the best bean for making refried beans and other Latin American dishes. Small and light brown, they can be found in Latin groceries under the name *frijoles peruanos*.

Pinto Beans

Pinto beans are a staple throughout the Americas, often used to make refried beans. They are small and pinkish brown, with a marbled coloring that disappears when cooked.

Soybeans

Soybeans, also known as *edamame*, are bizarrely useful. They have even been used to make car parts, though their supreme nutritional content makes them most useful as a food. They are (we think) the only plant food that all alone contains a complete protein. Soybeans are usually processed into other forms, such as soy milk, tofu, tempeh, soy flour, soy grits, and so on. Roasted, they also make a delicious lightly salted snack, either in the pod and popped open or already removed like salted peanuts. The latter are often called soy nuts.

Split Peas

Split peas are yellow or green and the size of lentils. When cooked, they disintegrate completely, making a thick porridge. They taste nothing like green peas.

SOY PRODUCTS AND OTHER SOURCES OF PROTEIN

Tofu

"Aeeoo, killer tofu, ooeeoo, killer tofu!" sing The Beets on the Nickelodeon television show *Doug*.

"Oh no, not again!" moan Jason, Paige, and Peter as their mother serves up a plate of tofu in *Foxtrot* in the Sunday comics.

With media coverage like that, it's no wonder that everyone's afraid of tofu. It can indeed be unappealing when it's not cooked properly. Confused cooks, mashing and squashing and poking their tofu, treating it like a cross between cheese and meat gone terribly, terribly wrong, are responsible for tofu's bad name.

In reality, tofu is an incredibly versatile and healthful food, high in complete proteins and low in fat. It is soft, with the consistency of slightly squishy cheese. Made from soybeans and often called bean curd, tofu has a very mild, slightly nutty flavor. It's easy to cook with, when you know how to treat it right.

Storing Tofu

Fresh tofu usually comes in a little plastic tub of water. Silken tofu is purchased in a foil juice box–like package. Both kinds must be refrigerated and stored in water after opening in order to stay fresh. Place the block in a container with cold water and store it in the fridge. If you change the water every day or every time you use some tofu, it should last for up to a week after opening.

Texture of Tofu

Tofu comes in three forms: firm or extra firm, which is best when you want it to hold its shape; soft, which is ideal for blending up in sauces; and silken, which has a smooth, custardlike texture and disintegrates very easily.

Freezing tofu is an interesting way of changing the texture. Freezing and thawing makes it denser, chewier, and more meatlike. If you want to add tofu to a casserole or a stir-fry as you would ground beef, freezing it is a good option. Just cut the tofu into chunks or slices, toss them into a bowl or plastic bag, and let them freeze overnight. In the morning, take them out to thaw, running hot water over them to speed the process. Try breaking a thawed piece in half and you'll see that it's full of air pockets, like a kitchen sponge. Also like a sponge, the tofu will have absorbed a great deal of water while freezing. Squeeze it gently and gently pat with a towel to remove extra water before cooking.

Adaptable Tofu

Tofu crumbles, slices, dices, and fries easily and absorbs the flavor of whatever you cook it with. It can be used in almost any dish as a substitute for beans or meat or served up on its own.

Pressing Tofu

Tofu is usually saturated with water when you buy it. Whether you put it in a sauce or fry it, it soaks up other flavors better if you press the water out before cooking. To do this, cut it into slabs about ¼-inch thick. Put these slices between two cloths and press them gently. Don't squash the tofu—it's not Play-Doh! It should maintain its form, but you should feel the towel getting wet beneath your hands. When your cloth is wet, move the tofu to a dry spot and press again until not much water is coming out. The tofu should still feel damp to the touch, but it shouldn't drip when you pick it up.

Tofu in Sauces

You can dice a block of tofu into small pieces and toss it into a sauce, stew, chili, soup, or salad; it will make the dish heartier and healthier. If you press the water out first, it will absorb more of the flavor of the dish, but if you don't have time, you can skip the pressing.

Tofu in Spreads

If you squeeze a block of tofu in your hands, you can turn it into a chunky paste with the consistency of egg salad. To do this, break the block into four large chunks. Squeeze the chunks one by one, like a handful of mud, so that tofu squirts between your fingers. Then you can add seasonings, mustard and/or mayo, or finely chopped salad vegetables to make a sandwich spread.

Tofu in Marinades

After slicing and pressing your tofu, you can lay it in a pan and pour a marinade sauce over it. Let it sit for at least an hour, or better yet overnight, during which it will soak up the flavors and juices of your sauce. Then fry it, grill it, bake it, or dice it and sprinkle it over a salad.

Scrumptious Golden-Fried Tofu

If you go to an Asian restaurant, you will likely be served crispy, golden, delicious tofu. If you've never eaten tofu before, this is a wonderful way to be introduced to it. However, upon returning to your own kitchen, you may be disappointed: the white blob lying on your counter bears no resemblance to the tasty dish in your mind. What do you do? Here's how to avoid some common mistakes when frying tofu.

- Pressing all the water out of the tofu is an absolute must for frying, otherwise all that water has to evaporate before you can begin to hope for sizzling deliciousness.
- When you fry tofu, you need to take it by surprise. Don't slap it in the pan, sling the pan on the burner, and wait for it to heat up like a can of soup. The tofu will stay mushy and boring that way. Instead, heat the oil first.

Pour a little olive oil in a skillet, just enough to cover the bottom of the pan, and turn the heat on medium. Wait a minute or two and then try flicking a few droplets of water onto the pan. If they sizzle, the oil is ready for you to drop your chunks or slices of tofu into the oil.

- It takes a while for tofu to fry. If you rush it and turn up the heat, it will burn, so you have to be patient. Keep an eye on it, but it may take several minutes for one side to get golden and crispy. When it does, flip the tofu over and let the other side brown. When it has browned on both sides, it's done.

- Once your tofu is hot and steaming, a little bit crispy and a little bit crunchy, it looks so good. You can eat it like this, but it's still not going to taste like much—it certainly won't be as flavorful and mouthwatering as the tofu you ate in the restaurant. For a little more excitement, try adding in some spices or chopped onion and garlic during the last few minutes of frying. Or drizzle a little tamari, hot sauce, or sesame seed oil over the top after it's done; the tofu will soak the flavor right up. Or cut the tofu into little chunks and toss it into spaghetti sauce. Its firm, post-frying texture will help it hold its shape in the mixture.

Thawed Tofu

If you've frozen and thawed your tofu as described above, it will behave differently, but it has the same versatility. It can be ripped into pieces and added to any sauce or soup, just like any other tofu.

Textured Vegetable Protein (TVP)

Tofu is amazing, but it's not the only useful soy product. Textured vegetable protein, or TVP, despite sounding like some kind of airplane, is actually a very healthy and useful food. It doesn't fry well, but it is great for making soups, chili, sauces, burgers, stir-fries, and so forth. It's a great substitute for meat in these recipes, both in terms of texture and protein. It comes in dried little chips, looking a bit like dried oatmeal. Some varieties come in little fragments no bigger than a cornflake; others are chunks bigger than a quarter. Both can be found at health stores in the bulk food section. It's also supercheap—only a couple of dollars for a bulging bagful.

TVP needs to be reconstituted before it can be used. That just means soaking it in water. Just stir one cup of TVP into 1 ½ cups of hot water and let it sit for 10 minutes or until the TVP feels soft. That's all there is to it. And you don't even have to do that. If you're cooking a pot of chili, for example, that has too much water in it, just stir in some TVP, let it sit for a few minutes, and the TVP will absorb a lot of the extra liquid.

Like tofu, TVP has very little flavor and takes on the taste of whatever you cook it in. For this reason, soaking it in vegetable broth instead of water gives it a little more kick. However, unlike tofu, its texture is pretty much unchangeable. It is rougher and chewier than raw tofu—more like frozen tofu. It has more protein than an equal volume of tofu.

Tempeh

Tempeh (TEM-pay) is a fermented soy product. Unlike tofu and TVP, it has a strong taste of its own and is dark brown in color. It's firmer than tofu and a bit tougher. It can be cooked like meat: crumbled, sliced, or chopped. If you're going for texture, it's the most meatlike of the three.

Seitan

If you've ever eaten fake meat in a restaurant—an imitation chicken patty or fake duck stir-fry—then you've probably eaten seitan (SAY-tan). Unlike the three Ts—tofu, TVP, and tempeh—seitan is not a soy product; it's actually made from wheat. It's possible to wash the carbohydrates out of wheat dough, leaving behind a dense, chewy tangle of proteins. That's what seitan is. It is very meatlike in texture, even down to the threadlike arrangement of fibers. Just like tofu or tempeh, it can be sautéed and mixed into any variety of foods or eaten on its own.

Substitutions and Conversions

Even the most prepared cook occasionally runs out of an ingredient. The more you cook, the more you will learn about how spices and other ingredients interact in dishes and which ones imitate and complement each other. Until then, here are some ways to substitute for things you don't like or don't have.

Ingredient	Amount	Substitution
Allspice	1 teaspoon	$\frac{1}{2}$ teaspoon cinnamon plus $\frac{1}{2}$ teaspoon cloves
Baking powder	1 teaspoon	$\frac{1}{4}$ teaspoon baking soda plus $\frac{1}{2}$ teaspoon cream of tartar
Chives	1 teaspoon	1 teaspoon green onion tops, finely chopped
Cornstarch	1 teaspoon	2 teaspoons flour
Egg	1	See page 171
Garlic	1 clove	$\frac{1}{8}$ teaspoon garlic powder or 1 teaspoon prechopped garlic
Ginger root	1 teaspoon	$\frac{1}{8}$ teaspoon powdered ginger
Herbs, fresh	1 tablespoon	1 teaspoon dried
Ketchup	$\frac{1}{2}$ cup	$\frac{1}{2}$ cup tomato sauce plus $\frac{1}{4}$ cup sugar plus 1 tablespoon vinegar
Lemon juice	1 teaspoon	$\frac{1}{2}$ teaspoon apple cider vinegar or lime juice
Mustard powder	1 teaspoon	1 tablespoon yellow mustard
Onion	1 medium, chopped	1 tablespoon onion powder
Pumpkin pie spice	1 teaspoon	$\frac{1}{2}$ teaspoon cinnamon plus $\frac{1}{4}$ teaspoon ginger plus $\frac{1}{8}$ teaspoon allspice plus $\frac{1}{8}$ teaspoon nutmeg
Sugar, brown	1 cup	1 cup white sugar plus 1 teaspoon molasses or 1 cup honey (decrease other liquid in recipe by $\frac{1}{4}$ cup)
Sugar, white	1 cup	1 cup powdered sugar or 1 cup brown sugar
Yogurt, plain	1 cup	1 cup milk plus 1 teaspoon vinegar

Standard Shorthand and Equivalents

Tricky abbreviations and conversions can be a thorn in the side of any cook. The manner of writing recipes varies from book to book and cook to cook, but below are some handy standards.

Abbreviations

t.	=	teaspoon
T.	=	tablespoon
c.	=	cup
pt.	=	pint
qt.	=	quart
gal.	=	gallon
mL	=	milliliter
dL	=	deciliter
L	=	liter
oz.	=	ounce
fl. oz.	=	fluid ounce

Weight Conversions

1 ounce	=	28.3 grams
1 pound	=	454 grams
1 kilogram	=	2.2 pounds

American measurement	Equals	Fluid ounces	Metric
1 teaspoon	$1/3$ tablespoon	$1/6$	5 milliliters
1 tablespoon	3 teaspoons or $1/16$ cup	$1/2$	16 milliliters
1 cup	16 tablespoons or $1/2$ pint	8	225 milliliters
1 pint	2 cups or $1/2$ quart	16	450 milliliters
1 quart	2 pints or $1/4$ gallon	32	0.95 liter
1 gallon	4 quarts	128	3.79 liters

British measurement	American measurement	Metric
1 U.K. full ounce	0.96 U.S. full ounce	31 milliliters
1 teaspoon	1 teaspoon	5 milliliters
1 dessertspoon	2 teaspoons	10 milliliters
1 tablespoon	$15/16$ tablespoon	15 milliliters
1 teacup	I cup plus 1 tablespoon	190 milliliters
1 breakfast cup	$1^1/4$ cups	281 milliliters
1 U.K. pint	$2^1/2$ cups	570 milliliters (5.7 deciliters)

Cans to Cups

Can size	Cups
5 ounces	$^5/_8$ cup
8 ounces	1 cup
$10^1/_2$ to 12 ounces	$1^1/_4$ cups
12 ounces	$1^1/_2$ cups
14 to 16 ounces	$1^3/_4$ cups
16 to 17 ounces	2 cups
1 pound 4 ounces or 1 pint 2 full ounces	$2^1/_2$ cups
1 pound 13 ounces	$3^1/_2$ cups
46 ounces	$5^3/_4$ cups

Oven Temperatures

°Fahrenheit	°Celsius	Gas mark	Description
225	105	$^1/_4$	Very cool
250	120	$^1/_2$	
275	130	1	Cool
300	150	2	
325	165	3	Very moderate
350	180	4	Moderate
375	190	5	
400	200	6	Moderately hot
425	220	7	Hot
450	230	8	
475	245	9	Very hot

Recipes

Breakfast

ALL-IN-ONE SUPER BREAKFAST SANDWICH

This sandwich is huge! It can feed two people if you aren't starving.

1. In a greased skillet, cook **2 strips of veggie bacon** according to package instructions. When crispy, remove from heat and set aside.
2. Over medium-high heat, crack **1 egg** into the skillet and heat until the yolk is firm.
3. Meanwhile, slice and toast **1 sprouted wheat bagel**.
4. When the bagel is toasted, stack in this order
    the bagel bottom
    a few leaves of spinach
    1 slice pepper jack cheese
    the egg
    2 wedges of tomato
    the strips of veggie bacon
    ketchup, black pepper, and **salt**, to taste
    a handful of alfalfa sprouts
    the bagel top
5. Slice in half and enjoy! Serves 1 (or 2).

AVENA (CINNAMON OATMEAL)

Oatmeal. You're thinking of a dull, sludgy bowl of tasteless gray goop. Are we right? Or maybe those little packets of pulverized oatmeal bits, flavored like candy.

Well, that's gotta change. Oatmeal has a lot of potential. It's rich in fiber and protein, low in fat and sugar, and can be very tasty. In Latin America, avena is a creamy dish served at breakfast or even for dinner.

1. Bring **1½ cups water** to a rolling boil.
2. Reduce heat to medium-low, stir in **1 cup rolled oats**, and return to a boil. When the oats have cooked for half the time listed on the package (it will vary depending on the type of oats), stir in
    1 cup milk
    1 teaspoon cinnamon
    2 tablespoons brown sugar
    and continue cooking on low heat for the allotted time.
3. Cover and allow to thicken for 2 minutes. It will be thinner than plain oatmeal, like a sweet and milky soup.
4. Stir in **½ cup blueberries** or **sliced banana**, if desired, and serve. Serves 2.

SUGGESTIONS
- To keep this dish healthy, use **soy milk** or **skim milk**. **Vanilla soy milk** is particularly yummy.
- For a healthy dose of omega-3 fatty acids, stir in **1 tablespoon walnuts** or **ground flaxseeds** into the oatmeal just before serving.

BEANS FOR BREAKFAST

On my first morning in Mexico, I rose at 6:00 to join the hungry household at the breakfast table. Delicious smells came wafting up the stairs and I could hardly wait to eat. As I poured myself a glass of water and slipped into my seat at the table, I wondered what I would be served. Pancakes? Cereal? Fruit? A moment later, my host mother bustled forth bearing a steaming bowl of … refried beans.

Although I was a little shocked that first morning, I soon grew used to eating beans before the sun came up. In fact, it quickly became one of my favorite ways to start the day. I was dismayed to return to the United States and realize that my school cafeteria served eggs only at breakfast and beans only at lunch—how could I ever re-create this dish on my own?

—Sara Kate

This is a heavy meal, packed with protein. It will keep you full if you're on the go for many hours after breakfast with no time for a snack. It's also very quick to make if you're in a rush.
Cook first! Have ready ½ **cup refried beans** per person.

1. Crack **2 eggs** into a bowl. Whip them vigorously until the yolks and whites are blended together.
2. Heat **1 tablespoon canola oil** in a skillet over medium heat. When hot, pour in the eggs. As they cook, scrape and chop them with the spatula.
3. When the eggs are almost done, add in ½ cup refried beans, stirring them around the frying pan until the mixture is hot. Remove from heat.
4. Meanwhile, toast **2 slices of French bread.**
5. Scoop the eggs and beans generously on top of the bread. Top with your favorite **salsa** and eat as an open-faced sandwich. Mmm! Serves 1.

GALLO PINTO

This is the most popular dish in Costa Rica, often served with fresh avocados and tortillas for breakfast. Although it's usually made with white rice, we use brown rice for a healthier version. It is also traditionally seasoned with a local sauce, called Lizano, but this seasoning combination is a reasonable estimation.
Cook first! Have ready

1 cup cooked black beans with ½ cup extra cooking water
2 cups cooked brown rice

1. Mince ½ **onion.** In a deep skillet, sauté the onion in **1 tablespoon canola oil** until caramelized (brown).
2. After 2 minutes, add 1 cup cooked black beans and ½ cup extra cooking water. (If using canned beans, rinse first, but add ½ cup water.)
3. Add
    1 teaspoon cumin
    1 teaspoon coriander
    ½ teaspoon ginger
    2 tablespoons vegetarian Worcestershire sauce
    ½ teaspoon black pepper
    ½ teaspoon salt
4. Stir well and add this mixture to 2 cups cooked brown rice. Serves 4.

HOMEMADE GRANOLA

Although we think of granola as a health food, commercial granola is actually very high in sugar and fat. Your own mix will be fresher, yummier, and tailored to your own tastes. This recipe is very easy and fast to make and it's amazingly delicious.

1. Preheat oven to 325°.
2. If your wheat germ is untoasted (it should say so on the container), it must be toasted first. Place I cup wheat germ in a dry skillet over medium heat and stir frequently for about 5 minutes, or until it begins to brown. Remove from heat.
3. In a mixing bowl, add 4 cups rolled oats to the wheat germ. Pour ¼ cup honey over the grains and stir thoroughly.
4. Add
   2 teaspoons vanilla
   I teaspoon cinnamon
   I cup chopped walnuts
   I cup raisins
5. Transfer to an oven-safe dish and bake for 10 to 15 minutes, stirring frequently. Remove when some of the grains begin to turn brown. The granola will not be crunchy as long as it is hot, but it will get crunchier as it cools. For especially crunchy granola, stir in **2 tablespoons canola oil** before baking. Serves 6 to 8.

> SUGGESTIONS
> For higher fiber cereal, mix in ½ **cup wheat bran.**
> For other flavors, try
> ♦ **molasses** or **maple syrup** instead of honey
> ♦ **pecans, almonds, sunflower seeds**, or **peanuts** instead of walnuts
> ♦ **dried apples, apricots,** or **cranberries** instead of raisins
> ♦ **ginger** or **nutmeg** instead of cinnamon

KENNY'S WHOLE WHEAT PANCAKES

I grew up eating these pancakes. My dad served them not only for breakfast, but for lunches, dinners, and even occasionally with ice cream when my mom was out of the house! Accustomed to their steamy wholesomeness, I was shocked the first time I encountered a white-flour Bisquick pancake. Even now, I don't regard those flimsy yellow things as *real* pancakes. *This* is a real pancake.

—Sara Kate

The trick to making these pancakes turn out correctly is to sift the flour at least once and to beat the egg whites to within an inch of their life. If you do both of those things, the pancakes will turn out light and fluffy.

1. Sift
   2 cups whole wheat flour
   I tablespoon baking powder
   I teaspoon salt
2. Separate **3 eggs**, placing the yolks in one bowl and the whites in another.
3. Beat the yolks, and stir in
   2 cups milk
   ⅓ cup canola oil
   I tablespoon honey
4. Using an electric mixer, whip the egg whites until they are frothy and foamy.
5. Stir the liquid mixture into the flour mixture.
6. At the last minute, stir the egg whites into the main mixture. Stir this as little as possible to keep as much air as possible beaten into the batter.
7. Heat a greased skillet to medium and wait a few minutes. When droplets of water flicked onto the pan sizzle, pour 2 scoops of batter onto opposite sides of the hot skillet.

8. Watch the raw top of the pancakes for bubbles. When many air bubbles start to appear, peek under the edge. If they're looking brown and crisp, flip the cakes and let the other side cook for a few minutes.
9. Repeat until you've used all the batter. Serves 4 to 6.

SUGGESTIONS
- For **Kenny's Whole Wheat Waffles**, reduce the milk to **1¼ cups**, and make sure to grease the waffle iron.
- Use **Ener-G Egg Replacer** instead of eggs. Beat well.
- Use **soy milk** or **blended fruit** instead of milk.
- Add **blueberries**, **chunks of apples**, **banana slices**, or **sunflower seeds**.
- Serve with **jam**, **fresh fruit**, **honey**, **yogurt**, or **maple syrup**.

TOAD IN THE HOLE

This is a good cooking experiment for beginners.

1. Using a knife, cookie cutter, or a cup with a thin rim, cut a circle about 2 inches in diameter out of the center of **1 slice of bread**. Lift out this piece.
2. Lightly brush both sides of the bread with either **butter** or **canola oil**.
3. Place the bread on a greased skillet over medium-high heat. As the bread becomes brown and crispy, crack **1 egg** into the hole in the center. The white will run out, but the yolk should stay trapped in the hole. Continue to fry for a minute, until the egg begins to solidify.
4. Flip the bread once—be careful not to send the egg flying! Cook until the egg is solid and the bread is crispy and fried on both sides. Serves 1.

WINTER MORNING PORRIDGE

In addition to oatmeal, there are many other hot cereal options. Steel-cut oats, cream of wheat, and grits are popular and delicious, as are mixes of your favorite grains. You can cook extra grains at suppertime the night before, then at breakfast all you have to do is mix and heat them.

Any grain combination should be cooked according to the cooking times listed in the Grains section of this book (pages 174–178). Many have similar cooking times and can be cooked together—for example, wheat berries and barley, or oats, quinoa, and amaranth.

1. Bring **2 cups water** to a rolling boil.
2. Stir in
   ⅓ cup rinsed quinoa
   ⅓ cup amaranth
   ⅛ teaspoon salt
3. Reduce heat and simmer for 15 minutes.
4. When the cereal begins to thicken, remove from heat and stir in
   1 tablespoon maple syrup
   ¼ cup chopped pecans
   1 teaspoon vanilla
5. Serve immediately. Serves 2.

SUGGESTIONS
Experiment with other combinations of grains or single grains on their own. For a **Summer Breakfast Mix**, try equal parts **toasted millet**, **brown rice**, and **steel-cut oats**.
For other flavors, try adding
- **yogurt**, **cottage cheese**, or a splash of **milk**
- slices of **fresh apple** or **banana**
- **dried fruit**, such as **raisins**, **dates**, or **cranberries**
- **walnuts**, **almonds**, or **sunflower seeds**
- **wheat germ**
- **freshly ground flaxseed**

Breads

FIRESIDE SPICE MUFFINS

These flavorful muffins are great for breakfast or for a snack any time of day.

1. Preheat oven to 400°.
2. In a large mixing bowl, combine
   2 cups whole wheat flour
   2 teaspoons baking powder
   1 teaspoon salt
   ½ teaspoon cinnamon
   ½ teaspoon cardamom
   ¼ teaspoon cloves
   ¼ teaspoon nutmeg
   ¼ teaspoon ginger
3. In a separate bowl, beat
   1 egg
   ¼ cup oil
   ⅓ cup honey or **molasses**
   1½ cups milk
4. Combine wet and dry ingredients and mix well.
5. Spoon into greased or lined muffin tins and bake for 20 minutes. Makes 24 muffins.

HANDMADE CORN TORTILLAS

Masa harina is a specially ground type of cornmeal. You must have it; do not use ordinary cornmeal or this will not work. Most small Mexican groceries carry it, as well as many large grocery chains, particularly those with a lot of Latino customers.

You can make extra tortillas and, after they are rolled and ready, refrigerate them until you want to cook them. They cook up in a second.

1. Mix together
   1 cup masa harina
   ½ cup water (add more—up to ¾ cup—if dough is impossibly crumbly)
   The dough will be very dry, but if you squeeze a handful, it should clump together pretty well.
2. Separate the dough into 8 balls.
3. Take 1 ball and place it on the counter or another flat surface. Cover it with a sheet of plastic wrap and mash it as flat as you possibly can. Think of store-bought tortillas—this is what you are aiming for. Rolling it with a rolling pin or a glass may help.
4. Trim the edge with a knife to make it an even circle.
5. Repeat this with the remaining balls.
6. To cook, do not grease the skillet; these are not supposed to be greasily fried. Depending on the size of your pan, place the tortillas in 1, 2, or 3 at a time.
7. On medium heat, cook for about 1 minute per side, then flip. Continue doing this, flipping back and forth, until they begin to look opaque white instead of raw. They may get dark brown spots here

193

and there, but they should not be entirely brown. Cooking each tortilla should take no more than a couple minutes.

8. Stack the cooked tortillas together and wrap them in a cloth to keep them hot until you're ready to serve them. The tortillas will be somewhat thicker and stiffer than what you buy in a store, but more authentic. Makes 8 small tortillas.

> SUGGESTION
> If you don't mind your tortillas a little thicker, here's an easier way to flatten them out. Place the ball of dough on a small saucer. Using your fingers, mash down the dough until it thinly covers the surface of the plate. Gently remove it with a spatula and toss into the skillet.

SOUTHERN DROP BISCUITS

These "baking powder biscuits" are traditionally made with white flour only, but some whole wheat flour can be used without sacrificing their light, fluffy texture.

These taste good with jam or honey, or even veggie bacon.

1. Preheat oven to 400°.
2. In a mixing bowl, combine
   ½ cup whole wheat flour
   ¾ cup all-purpose flour
   2 tablespoons granulated sugar
   1 tablespoon baking powder
3. Add **6 tablespoons cold butter**. Stir aggressively with a fork until the mixture resembles large crumbs.
4. Stir in **½ cup milk**.
5. Drop large spoonfuls of batter 1 to 2 inches apart on a greased cookie sheet and bake for 15 to 20 minutes. Makes about 15 biscuits.

TEX-MEX CORN BREAD

The trick to good corn bread is in how you prepare the pan. Before you put the batter in the pan, it must be greased and heated until the oil is sizzling. Then, when you pour in the batter, it immediately fries a little bit, giving the bread a deliciously crunchy edge.

1. Preheat oven to 375°. Grease an 8-inch by 8-inch glass pan or an iron skillet.
2. Chop and sauté
   1 medium onion
   ½ bell pepper
   in **2 tablespoons olive oil**
3. When the vegetables are almost cooked, add **1 cup corn** and continue sautéing for 2 minutes. Remove from heat.
4. In a large bowl, blend
   1 egg
   1 tablespoon honey
   1 cup milk
5. Add
   1 cup white flour
   1 cup yellow cornmeal
   1 tablespoon baking powder
   ½ teaspoon salt
   and mix well.
6. Stir in the corn mixture. Be sure to use all the oil. Add **¾ cup grated cheddar cheese**. Mix.
7. Place the greased, empty pan in the oven until the oil is melted and sizzling.
8. Carefully remove the hot pan, then pour in the batter.
9. Bake for 30 minutes, or until the bread pulls away from the sides. Serves 8.

WHOLE-GRAIN BANANA BREAD

1. Preheat oven to 350°.
2. Beat well **2 eggs**, and blend in
    ½ **cup canola oil**
    ½ **cup brown sugar**
    2 cups mashed banana
3. In a separate bowl, mix together
    2 cups whole wheat flour
    I teaspoon baking soda
    ¼ **teaspoon salt**
4. Stir the banana mixture into the flour and add ½ **cup walnuts** (optional).
5. Pour into a greased glass casserole dish and bake for 50 minutes, or until a knife inserted in the center comes out clean. Serves 12.

> SUGGESTION
> For **Indian Banana Bread**, in Step 4, omit walnuts and add ½ **cup raisins**, **I cup shredded coconut**, and **2 teaspoons curry powder**. It's slightly spicy and strangely scrumptious!

WHOLE WHEAT BISCUITS

1. Preheat oven to 425°. Grease a cookie tray.
2. Mix together
    2 cups whole wheat flour
    2 teaspoons baking powder
    I teaspoon salt
3. In a separate bowl, combine
    ¾ **cup milk**
    ⅓ **cup canola oil**
    I tablespoon honey
4. Combine the two mixtures and stir well.
5. Pinch the dough into chunks a little smaller than a golf ball. Roll between your palms to form balls and place them on the tray at least I inch apart.
6. Bake for 15 minutes. Makes 12 biscuits.

> SUGGESTIONS
> ◆For **Hearty Biscuits**, substitute ½ **cup wheat germ**, **oat bran**, or **barley flour** for an equal amount of flour.

> ◆For **Fluffy Biscuits**, add ¾ cup grated cheese and leave out the honey.
> ◆For **Sweet Biscuits**, use ⅔ **cup milk**, ⅓ **cup honey**, and **I** ½ **tablespoons cinnamon**. Pat the biscuits into flat ovals.

ZUCCHINI BREAD

This delicate, sweet bread doesn't taste like you're eating vegetables. It's a moist and delicious twist on the classic quick bread.

1. Preheat oven to 350°.
2. Grate **I** ½ **cups zucchini** and set aside.
3. Sift together
    I ½ **cups whole wheat flour**
    ½ **teaspoon baking soda**
    ½ **teaspoon baking powder**
    ½ **teaspoon salt**
    I ½ **teaspoons cinnamon**
4. In a separate bowl, beat **2 eggs** well and stir in
    ½ **cup oil**
    ½ **cup brown sugar**
    I teaspoon vanilla
5. Combine the egg mixture and zucchini. Pour into the flour mixture and stir well.
6. Add (optional)
    ½ **cup raisins**
    ½ **cup chopped walnuts**
7. Bake in a loaf pan for 45 to 60 minutes.

> SUGGESTION
> For a healthy alternative to carrot cake, try **Carrot Bread** by substituting I ½ **cups carrots** for the zucchini.

Salads and Side Dishes

CARROT-FRUIT SALAD

1. Shred **6 large carrots** (about 4 cups).
2. Peel **I orange** and cut into small chunks.
3. Finely chop **⅓ cup walnuts**.
4. Drain **I cup crushed pineapple**.
5. Combine carrots, oranges, nuts, and pineapple in a bowl with
   ⅓ cup raisins
   I cup vanilla yogurt
   ¼ teaspoon cinnamon
6. Stir well and serve chilled. Serves 8.

CHINESE GREEN BEANS

1. Snap and string **4 cups fresh green beans**. Steam until almost tender—just a few minutes. Rinse in cool water and set aside.
2. Meanwhile, mince
   3 cloves garlic
   2 teaspoons fresh ginger
   4 scallions
3. In a small bowl, combine
   ½ cup vegetable stock (or **water**)
   2 tablespoons tamari

½ teaspoon sesame oil
4. Very slowly stir in **1½ teaspoons corn-starch**, until the mixture is smooth.
5. In a skillet on medium-high, heat **2 table-spoons cooking sherry** and the minced garlic and ginger. Stir for a few seconds. Add the green beans and stir for I minute.
6. Add cornstarch mixture and stir. Reduce heat to medium-low and cook for three minutes, or until the sauce has thickened.
7. Stir in the scallions and serve. Serves 8.

FAMILY'S FAVORITE SWEET-POTATO CASSEROLE

We aren't allowed to come to Christmas dinner unless we bring this dish. As delicious as dessert but twice as healthy, you'll never want your sweet potatoes any other way!

1. Preheat oven to 350°.
2. Roughly quarter **2 to 3 large sweet pota-toes** and simmer until soft—about 20 minutes, depending on the size of the chunks.

3. Drain and rinse with cool water. Remove the skins, which will now come off easily, and mash the potatoes in a large mixing bowl. You should have about 4 cups.
4. Add and mix well
   ¼ **cup milk**
   1½ **teaspoons salt**
   ⅛ **teaspoon cloves**
5. Spread the potato mixture in a glass casserole dish.
6. In a saucepan over low heat, melt
   ½ **cup butter**
   ½ **cup brown sugar**
   stirring constantly until the butter is barely melted.
7. Pour the butter mixture over the potatoes and sprinkle with **1 cup pecans.**
8. Bake for 30 minutes. Serves 8.

SUGGESTION
For **Southern Sweet Potato Pie**, cut this recipe in half and bake, following the same directions, in a **Single Whole Wheat Piecrust** (page 226).

HOLIDAY STUFFING

After watching the traditional stuffing being scooped right out of the turkey's hind end, you may want to take this dish to your family's next Thanksgiving dinner.

1. Preheat oven to 350°.
2. Tear **10 slices whole wheat bread**, crusts and all, into small shreds. Place the shreds in a large casserole dish and bake for about 15 minutes, until the bread is well toasted.
3. Meanwhile, thinly slice
   1 medium onion
   3 stalks celery
   2 large carrots, peeled
   and sauté in **2 tablespoons canola oil** until the onion is translucent.
4. Remove the bread from the oven and add the onion mixture, as well as
   3 tablespoons raisins

1 diced Granny Smith apple (or other tart apple)
   ¼ **cup chopped walnuts**
   ¼ **cup chopped pecans**
and stir.
5. Sprinkle with
   ¼ **cup chopped fresh parsley**
   1 tablespoon thyme
   2 teaspoons sage
   1 teaspoon marjoram
   1 teaspoon rosemary
   ¾ **teaspoon salt**
   ¼ **teaspoon black pepper**
6. Drizzle with 1½ **cups vegetable stock** and toss gently.
7. Bake uncovered for 25 minutes. Toss and serve. Serves 12.

ITALIAN ARTICHOKE SALAD

1. Drain **2 cans artichoke hearts** and slice each artichoke into quarters.
2. In a large bowl, combine
   ¼ **cup chopped fresh basil**
   3 tablespoons oregano
   ¼ **cup balsamic vinegar**
   ¼ **cup apple cider vinegar**
   ½ **cup olive oil**
3. Pour over artichokes and let marinate for at least an hour, but preferably overnight.
4. Serve on a bed of fresh spinach leaves. Serves 4.

MASALA POTATOES

1. Roughly chop **6 white potatoes** (or **3 peeled baking potatoes**) into chunks. Simmer until soft, around 15 minutes if the chunks are small.
2. Meanwhile, mince **1 teaspoon ginger** and cut into long, thin strips
   ¾ **red onion**
   ½ **bell pepper**
3. In a pan with tall sides, sauté the onion in

1 tablespoon olive oil. Add the ginger and pepper about 1 minute before the onions are done. Stir in

    1 tablespoon coriander
    ½ teaspoon turmeric
    ¼ teaspoon salt

4. Add the potatoes and **½ cup water**. Cook and stir over medium heat until the water evaporates and the dish is dry.
5. Add **1 tablespoon lemon juice** and remove from heat. Serves 6.

> SUGGESTION
> Serve with **Dal** (Indian split peas) (page 207) or **chapattis** (Indian flat bread), or use as a filling for **stuffed peppers** or **eggplants**.

MOM'S HOME FRIES

1. Cut **2 large potatoes** into eighths and boil until soft, about 15 minutes. Drain.
2. Cut the cooked potatoes into small cubes. Place them in a bowl and drizzle with **2 tablespoons tamari**. Toss until they are well coated in sauce. Set aside.
3. Chop
    ¼ onion
    1 clove garlic
and sauté in **1 tablespoon olive oil** for less than 2 minutes.
4. Add the potatoes to the sauté, stirring frequently.
5. After 5 minutes, add **¼ cup peanuts**. Add another **1 tablespoon oil** if the potatoes are sticking to the pan. Continue cooking for another 5 minutes and serve hot. Serves 4.

NANCY'S TIME-SAVING GREEN BEANS

These green beans are ready in a jiffy and too delicious to turn down.

1. Snap and string **2 cups fresh green beans**.
2. Steam for a few minutes, until tender but still slightly crunchy. Remove from heat.
3. Meanwhile, slice in half
    ¾ cup cherry tomatoes
    ½ cup black olives
4. When the green beans have cooled, mix the vegetables together. Dress with crumbled **feta cheese** and **Italian dressing** to taste. Chill before serving. Serves 4.

ONE-DISH VEGGIES

This is a simple, tasty alternative to a side salad. The vegetables used and the amounts of them are entirely up to you; these are merely suggestions. You can use a bag of frozen vegetables to save time, if you like.

1. Chop
    1 large carrot
    1 stalk celery
    ¼ onion
    3 cloves garlic
    4 cups fresh spinach
2. In a skillet, heat
    2 tablespoons olive oil
    1 tablespoon tamari
    ½ teaspoon black pepper
    1 teaspoon rosemary
3. Add carrot and celery. Sauté for a minute or two, until they begin to get soft.
4. Add onion and garlic. Stir frequently until the onion is almost translucent.
5. Add **2 tablespoons water**, the spinach, and cover. Stir and re-cover every 30 seconds, until the spinach is cooked. Serve hot. Serves 4.

> SUGGESTION
> Stir in **2 cups cooked wheat berries** or **brown rice** for a more filling dish.

ONE-MINUTE SOUTHWESTERN CORN

Cook first! Have ready **1½ cups cooked black beans** and **1½ cups cooked corn.**

1. In a mixing bowl, combine
   1½ cups fresh corn
   1½ cups cooked black beans
2. Season with
   2 tablespoons olive oil
   2 tablespoons red wine vinegar
   ¾ teaspoon cumin
3. Serve chilled, with **pepper jack quesadillas.** Serves 4.

SESAME ASPARAGUS

1. Bring a saucepan of salted water to a rolling boil.
2. Trim ends off **1 pound fresh asparagus.**
3. Simmer for 4 minutes. Drain and rinse in cool water.
4. In a small bowl, mix
   2 tablespoons sesame oil
   ¼ cup apple cider vinegar
   ¼ cup tamari
   1 tablespoon sugar
   until the sugar has dissolved.
5. Pour over the asparagus and marinate for at least 1 hour. Sprinkle with **2 tablespoons sesame seeds** before serving. Serves 6.

   SUGGESTION
   For **Sesame Tofu**, when the asparagus is ready to serve, pour off and save the marinade. Slice and pat dry **half a block of tofu** and soak the slices in the marinade overnight. The next day, sauté the tofu in the marinade and serve over brown rice sprinkled with sesame seeds.

SMOKY GRILLED VEGETABLES

If your family is grilling meat outside, you need not go hungry!

1. Peel and slice as thinly as possible
   1 small eggplant
   1 large potato
2. Cut in thick wedges
   1 sweet yellow onion
   1 green bell pepper
   1 red bell pepper
3. Place these vegetables as well as **1 cup cherry tomatoes** in a baking dish with sides. Drizzle with
   ¼ cup olive oil
   ¼ cup tamari
   and flip a few times until all pieces are thoroughly coated.
4. Skewer the veggies on kebabs, or place them individually on the grill. Watch very closely to prevent burning—different vegetables and different sized pieces will vary widely in cooking time. Serves 4.

   SUGGESTIONS
   ♦ Serve as a side to **grilled veggie burgers** and **tofu dogs**, or make the veggies the centerpiece.
   ♦ For **Grilled Veggie Pizza**, arrange the veggies on 1 or 2 **whole wheat pizza crusts** and lightly sprinkle with your favorite **cheese.** Bake until the crust is done and the cheese is melted.

TABBOULI

This fresh Middle Eastern dish is a great way to get to know bulgur wheat. It will also give you a new respect for parsley.

1. Bring **1½ cup water** to a boil. Remove from heat and stir in **1 cup dry bulgur wheat.** Set aside.
2. While the bulgur soaks, mince
   1 clove garlic
   1 scallion (more if you like raw onions)
   1 bunch (about **1½ cups**) **fresh parsley**
3. Chop
   1 large cucumber
   2 large tomatoes
4. When the bulgur wheat has absorbed all the water and is soft and chewy, stir in
   ¼ cup lemon juice
   ⅓ cup olive oil
   1 teaspoon salt
   ½ teaspoon black pepper
   Add the vegetables, mix well, and chill before serving. Serves 6.

WHERE'S-THE-CHICKEN SALAD

Freezing and thawing tofu gives it a rougher, spongier texture. While freezing is not necessary, it does alter the consistency of the final product.
Cook first! Have ready **1 block tofu**, frozen and thawed.

1. The night before, remove 1 block of tofu from the package. Immerse it in water in a bowl or sealed Ziploc bag and put it in the freezer. The next morning, run the tofu under hot water to get the ice off, and then let the block soak in a bowl of hot water until it is thawed. This will take several hours.
2. When you are ready to begin, break the thawed tofu into a few large chunks. Squeeze these pieces as you would a sponge, to get out as much water as possi-

ble, then crumble in a mixing bowl. Next, chop
   ½ bell pepper
   1 stalk celery
   2 scallions
   and add them to the crumbled tofu.
4. Add
   ⅓ cup nutritional yeast
   1 teaspoon basil
   ½ teaspoon turmeric
   ½ teaspoon black pepper
   ¼ teaspoon salt
   1 tablespoon tamari
   ¾ cup soy mayonnaise
   and squeeze the mixture through your fists until it is well mixed.
5. Serve on toasted **whole wheat kaiser rolls** with leaves of **fresh lettuce** and slices of **red bell pepper.** Serves 8.

WILD WHEAT BERRY WALDORF SALAD

This is a chewy, fiber-rich twist on the good ol' Waldorf salad.

1. Bring **2 cups water** to a boil, then add **½ cup dry wheat berries** and simmer until soft, about 45 minutes. Drain and let cool.
2. Meanwhile, chop **2 apples** and sprinkle with **1 tablespoon lemon juice** to prevent browning.
3. Chop and set aside
   2 stalks celery
   ¼ cup walnuts or **sunflower seeds**
   ½ cup mandarin oranges
4. When the wheat berries are cool, combine all the ingredients in a bowl. Add
   ½ cup vanilla yogurt
   ½ cup raisins
   ¾ teaspoon cinnamon
   Serves 8.

Main Dishes

ASIAN STIR-FRIED RICE

1. Bring **2 cups water** to a boil.
2. Add ¾ **cup dry brown rice**, reduce heat, and simmer for 30 minutes.
3. When the rice is done, remove from heat and stir in
   3 tablespoons tamari
   2 teaspoons sesame oil
   ½ teaspoon white pepper
4. While the rice is cooking, cut ½ **block tofu** into small cubes and pat dry.
5. Finely chop
   6 scallions
   3 stalks celery
   1 cup mushrooms
   ½ bell pepper
6. In a large skillet, heat **2 tablespoons canola oil**. Add tofu and stir-fry for 10 minutes, or until tofu begins to turn golden.
7. Add the vegetables listed above, as well as
   1 can mixed stir-fry vegetables (water chestnuts, baby corn, mung bean sprouts), drained
   ½ cup pineapple (fresh or canned)
   ¼ cup dry-roasted peanuts
   Continue cooking for 2 more minutes.
8. Add the cooked rice and cook for 2 more minutes, or until the mixture is hot and well blended. Serves 4.

   SUGGESTIONS
   ◆Before adding the rice in Step 8, add **1 to 2 eggs**, well beaten, to the pan. Scramble them in the oil, then add the rice when the eggs are almost cooked.
   ◆Serve with **Ginger Sauce** (page 219), **Spicy Peanut Sauce** (page 220), or **Japanese Marinated Tofu** (page 210).

BAINGAN BHARTHA (ONE-DISH EGGPLANT CURRY)

I became acquainted with eggplants in my school cafeteria as soggy, spongy brown lumps, so I wasn't exactly excited about cooking it on my own. But my love of Indian food wouldn't let me rest easy. As it turns out, this is now one of my favorite quick meals.

—Sara Kate

1. Preheat oven to 375°.
2. Slice **1 eggplant** in half. Place it on a greased baking sheet and brush the skin lightly with oil to prevent scorching. Bake for approximately 25 minutes, or until tender. Remove from heat and allow to cool.
3. When the eggplant is cool enough to touch, gently peel away the bitter-tasting skin. Cut the soft insides into thin slices as best as you can.
4. While the eggplant is cooling, thinly slice **1 onion** and finely chop
   1 teaspoon ginger
   2 cloves garlic
   1 tomato
   1 jalapeño pepper
5. Sauté the onion in **1 tablespoon canola oil**, with
   1 teaspoon cumin
   1 tablespoon curry powder
6. Reduce heat to medium-low and add the ginger, garlic, and tomato. Cook for 1 minute.
7. Stir in the minced jalapeño and
   ½ teaspoon salt
   ½ cup plain yogurt
8. Add the slices of eggplant, turn heat to medium, and cover. Cook for 10 minutes, adding water if necessary to prevent scorching.

9. Remove the lid, reduce heat to low, and cook for 5 more minutes. Garnish with **chopped fresh cilantro** (optional). Serves 4.

> SUGGESTIONS
>
> If the oven isn't available, peel the raw eggplant and slice into the thinnest possible slices. Place these slices in a bowl of salty water for a few minutes and heat **3 tablespoons olive oil** in a skillet. Sauté the eggplant slices until soft and well cooked. Remove from the skillet and proceed, beginning with Step 4. Serve with **brown basmati rice** or your favorite grain.

BARLEY-MUSHROOM SOUP

This soup is very easy, yet wholly satisfying, especially on chilly winter nights.

1. Simmer ½ **cup dry barley** in **1½ cups water** until soft, about 45 minutes.
2. Meanwhile, chop
   - ½ **yellow onion**
   - **2 cloves garlic**
   - **1 pound fresh mushrooms**
   - **6 cups fresh spinach** (or **1 block** thawed and drained frozen spinach)
3. Sauté the onion and garlic in **1 tablespoon olive oil**. After 2 minutes, add the mushrooms and ¼ **cup water**. Cover.
4. When the mushrooms are soft and well cooked and the barley is done, combine the two dishes, making sure to scrape in all the oil from the sauté. Stir in the spinach.
5. Add
   - ¼ **cup tamari**
   - ½ **teaspoon black pepper**
   - **2 teaspoons basil**
   - **2 teaspoons tarragon**
   - **water to cover**
6. Simmer on low heat for 20 minutes. Serve with crusty bread. Serves 4 to 6.

BEANY BASIL PASTA TOSS

Cook first! Have ready **2 cups cooked kidney beans.**

1. Thinly slice ½ **red onion** and mince **4 cloves garlic.** Sauté both in **1 tablespoon olive oil.**
2. In a separate pot, boil **8 ounces whole wheat fusilli pasta** in salted water for about 10 minutes, or until done. Drain.
3. Add the onion and garlic, with 2 cups cooked kidney beans, to the drained pasta.
4. Mince
   - ½ **cup fresh basil**
   - ¼ **cup fresh parsley**
   and add to the pasta.
5. Mix in
   - **3 tablespoons nutritional yeast**
   - **1 teaspoon black pepper**
   Serves 4.

> SUGGESTION
>
> For **Beany Basil Florentine**, after Step 3, stir in **1 cup steamed spinach.** Adjust seasonings to taste.

BERRYBROOK BLACK BEANS

> In the restaurant where I work, this recipe invariably causes stampedes of hungry customers. They clamor rapturously, "What is that delicious smell? When's it going to be ready?"
>
> Even after three years, I *still* haven't gotten tired of this mouthwatering dish!
>
> —Sara Kate

These beans make an excellent burrito filling. They can also be eaten on their own or scooped onto tortilla chips. Cook first! Have ready **2 cups black beans.**

1. Mince **2 cloves garlic**.
2. Heat **2 tablespoons olive oil** in the bottom of a large pot. Add the garlic, as well as
   - **I teaspoon oregano**
   - **I teaspoon basil**
   - **I teaspoon thyme**
   - **½ teaspoon salt**
   - **½ teaspoon pepper**

   Heat until the oil is sizzling and the garlic is cooked but not brown.
3. Add 2 cups cooked black beans. Stir until coated with oil, then warm over medium heat, stirring often.
4. When the beans are hot, remove from heat and mash until they stick together in a thick paste. You may need to add a little water if the mixture is too dry.
5. Serve wrapped in **whole wheat tortillas**. Top with (optional)
   - salsa
   - lettuce
   - olives
   - avocado
   - onions
   - grated cheese

   Serves 4 to 6.

- **2 bay leaves**
- **½ teaspoon salt**
- **½ teaspoon pepper**
- **4 cups cooked black beans**

5. Reduce heat to medium-low and simmer a few minutes, until beans are hot and soft.
6. Remove the bay leaves. Pour the mixture in the blender and blend until there are hardly any whole beans. You will have to do this in stages.
7. In a dry skillet on medium heat, brown **I tablespoon whole wheat flour**. Stir frequently to prevent burning. After a few minutes, stir in
   - **I tablespoon canola oil**
   - **I tablespoon lemon juice**
   - **I teaspoon apple cider vinegar**
   - **I teaspoon honey**
   - **½ teaspoon mustard powder**

   and mix well. Add to the blended bean mixture.
8. Stir in the spinach and continue simmering. Add more salt and pepper to taste.
9. Serve topped with the chopped fresh tomato and dollops of **sour cream** (optional). Serves 4 to 6.

BLACK BEAN AND SPINACH SOUP

This is a thick, satisfying soup. The blended beans make a hearty base, which is lightened by the sour cream and tomato. It's particularly good when served with hot Tex-Mex Corn Bread (page 194).

Cook first! Have ready **4 cups cooked black beans**.

1. Chop
   - **I bunch scallions**
   - **I tomato**
2. Thaw and drain **I block frozen spinach** (or steam **6 cups fresh**).
3. Bring to a boil **2 cups vegetable stock** (or **water**).
4. Add the scallions, as well as

BLACK-EYED RICE

This dish has a fresh, sharp taste, very different from most rice-and-bean dishes.

Cook first! Have ready **I cup cooked black-eyed peas**.

1. Simmer **¾ cup dry brown rice** in **2 cups water** for 30 minutes, or until done.
2. While the rice cooks, slice
   - **½ cup black olives**
   - **½ cup green olives**
   - **½ green pepper**
   - **4 scallions**
3. In a mixing bowl, whisk together
   - **2 tablespoons olive oil**
   - **2 tablespoons apple cider vinegar**

I teaspoon tarragon
I teaspoon lemon juice
¾ cup fresh parsley
½ teaspoon pepper
½ teaspoon salt

4. When the rice is done, add I cup cooked black-eyed peas, the sliced vegetables, and the whisked mixture. Stir thoroughly and serve hot or cold. Serves 4.

CARIBBEAN TEMPEH WRAPS

Cook first! Have ready **2 cups cooked black beans** and **I cup cooked corn**.

1. Preheat oven or toaster oven to 300°.
2. Cut ½ **block tempeh** into strips, no more than an inch or two long and not very thick. Place them on a baking tray and drizzle with
   I tablespoon olive oil
   I tablespoon tamari
3. Turn them over once, so that both sides are coated, and bake for 10 minutes.
4. Chop and mix together
   2 tomatoes
   ½ red bell pepper
   I clove garlic
   3 tablespoons fresh basil
5. Combine the tomato mixture with
   2 cups cooked black beans
   I cup cooked corn
   2½ tablespoons lime juice
   ½ teaspoon black pepper
   ¼ teaspoon red pepper flakes
   ¼ teaspoon salt
6. Cut ½ **cucumber** into long strips. On **whole wheat tortillas**, arrange a few leaves of **fresh spinach**, then a couple tempeh strips. Top with a big scoop of the tomato and bean mixture. Arrange a couple of cucumber strips on top. Fold up like a burrito. Serves 6.

SUGGESTION
For **Caribbean Bean Salad**, begin with Step 4. Add an extra **I cup black beans** to the bean and tomato mixture. Dice the cucumber and mix it in. Serve as a chilled salad on a bed of **fresh spinach leaves**.

COUNTRY BAKED PASTA

1. Preheat oven to 400°.
2. Slice ½ **block tofu** into thin slabs. Press and cut into very small cubes. Brown in **2 tablespoons canola oil** over medium heat, if you wish, or add directly to **I jar pasta sauce**.
3. Boil **8 ounces whole wheat rotini noodles** (half a box) according to package instructions, or for about 10 minutes.
4. Meanwhile, chop
   2 zucchinis
   I cup broccoli
5. Two minutes before the noodles are done, add the zucchini and broccoli to the boiling water.
6. When the noodles are done, remove from heat and drain well. Stir into the tofu and pasta sauce mixture.
7. Transfer the pasta mixture into a large casserole dish. Sprinkle with
   ¾ cup grated cheese
   2 tablespoons wheat germ
8. Cover with aluminum foil and bake for 15 minutes. Remove the foil and bake an additional 10 minutes. Let stand 5 minutes before serving. Serves 6.

COWBOY CASSEROLE

Our family has called this dish by this name for as long as we can remember, but no one knows why. As far as I can tell, it has very little to do with actual cowboys, but it's delicious just the same. If you're afraid of grits, this is a good way to get to know them.
Cook first! Have ready **2 cups pinto beans**.

1. Preheat oven to 350°.
2. Prepare **1 cup dry grits** according to package instructions. Cooking time will vary, depending on type. When grits have reached a sticky, porridgelike consistency and no longer feel hard and gritty, they're done. This will take only a few minutes.
3. Meanwhile, chop and mix together
    ½ **red bell pepper**
    ½ **green bell pepper**
    ¼ **red onion**
    1 block thawed and drained frozen spinach (or **6 cups raw**)
4. Add the spinach and the pepper mixture to the grits. Stir in
    1 cup corn
    2 cups cooked pinto beans
    ½ **cup shredded cheddar cheese**
    1 tablespoon chili powder
    1 tablespoon cumin
    1 teaspoon oregano
    ½ **teaspoon red pepper flakes**
    ½ **teaspoon salt**
5. Sprinkle the top with an additional **1 cup cheese**.
6. Bake for 25 minutes or until cheese is melted and edges are bubbly. Serves 8 to 10.

CRAZY SUCCOTASH CHOWDER

Cook first! Have ready **1½ cups cooked lima beans**.

1. Chop **1 large potato** into small cubes. Place in a large saucepan with just enough water to cover. Simmer until soft, probably less than 10 minutes, depending on the size of the chunks.
2. Meanwhile, chop
    ½ **red onion**
    1 clove garlic
   and sauté over medium heat in **1 tablespoon canola oil**.
3. When the onion is almost translucent, add
    1½ teaspoons coriander
    1 teaspoon cumin
    ¼ **cup diced green chiles** (2 fresh minced chiles or 1 small can)
    3 cups corn (fresh or frozen, *not* canned)
   Stir and continue sautéing.
4. Chop
    1 large tomato
    ½ **bell pepper**
   and add to the corn. Stir.
5. Add to the potatoes, without draining them,
    1⅓ cups milk
    1 teaspoon salt
    ¾ **teaspoon pepper**
   followed by the corn mixture. Mix well.
6. Scoop 4 cups of the soup mixture into the blender and blend until smooth. Return it to the saucepan and stir constantly. Dairy products scorch very easily!
7. Add 1½ cups cooked lima beans while stirring continually until the soup is hot.
8. If desired, stir ½ **cup grated cheese** into the soup just before serving. Serves 4 to 6.

SUGGESTION
If you don't like spiciness, use **2 tablespoons or less** of the **green chiles**.

DAL (INDIAN SPLIT PEAS)

This easy dish is a staple of Indian cuisine. After the peas are cooked, it takes almost no time to prepare. It should turn out very thick and porridgelike.

1. Bring **4 cups water** to a boil.
2. Add **1½ cups dry yellow split peas** and reduce heat. Simmer for 30 minutes, or until they are soft but have not lost their shape entirely. Check often and add hot water as needed to prevent scorching, but there should be very little water left over, similar to mashed potatoes.
3. Meanwhile, chop
   1 onion
   ½ bell pepper
   and sauté in **1 tablespoon olive oil** over medium-high heat.
4. When the onion is transparent and the peas are cooked, combine the two dishes, along with
   1½ tablespoons lemon juice
   1 cup milk
   1 teaspoon salt
   1 tablespoon turmeric
   ½ teaspoon curry powder
5. Serve hot or cold, alongside **chapattis** (Indian flat bread) or over **brown basmati rice**. Serves 4.

ELEGANT PASTA CURRY

1. In a dry skillet over medium heat, toast ½ **cup pine nuts**. Stir constantly to prevent burning for 5 minutes, or until the nuts are brown and toasty. Remove from heat and set aside.
2. Prepare **8 ounces** (half a box) **whole wheat linguini noodles** according to package instructions.
3. Meanwhile, warm **1 cup sour cream** in a saucepan on medium-low heat, stirring constantly.
4. Stir in

2 teaspoons cumin
½ teaspoon fenugreek
½ teaspoon turmeric
⅛ teaspoon nutmeg
⅛ teaspoon ginger

5. Stir sour cream mixture into cooked and drained noodles. Add toasted pine nuts and **½ cup chopped dried apricots**. Mix well and serve hot. Serves 4.

FIVE-LAYER POLENTA-IN-A-POT

The success of this dish depends on the kind of polenta you use. If you buy premade polenta, make sure to buy a brand you know you like.

1. Chop
   1 tomato
   4 cups fresh spinach (or **thaw and drain 10 ounces frozen spinach**)
2. Grate **1 cup cheese**.
3. In a dry skillet on medium heat, brown ¼ **cup pine nuts** (or any nut) for 5 minutes, stirring constantly to prevent burning, until the nuts are toasted.
4. Open a **16-ounce package of polenta** and place in the skillet on medium heat. It will probably be quite stiff. Mash it with a fork, stirring in up to ½ **cup vegetable stock** if necessary, until it has the consistency of grits.
5. When the polenta is warm, reduce heat to low. Spread the polenta flat in the pan.
6. Pour **1 cup pasta sauce** over the polenta and spread evenly. Don't stir.
7. Next, spread out the spinach, followed by the tomato, the cheese, and then the nuts.
8. Cover the pan. Let simmer on low heat until the spinach has steamed and the cheese has melted—probably about 5 minutes. To serve, scoop onto plates, similar to serving lasagna. Serves 4.

GAZPACHO TAPATÍO

This spicy, chilled soup is a perfect summer treat served with a fresh salad.

1. Dice
   - 3 tomatoes
   - 1 cucumber
   - 2 avocados
   - 1 clove garlic
   - ¼ red onion
   - ½ bell pepper
2. Add and stir well
   - 1 cup corn
   - 4 cups spicy tomato juice (such as V8)
   - 1 tablespoon warm honey
   - 1 tablespoon apple cider vinegar
   - 1 tablespoon fresh basil
   - 2 tablespoons fresh parsley
   - 1 tablespoon fresh cilantro
   - ¼ cup lime juice
   - 1 tablespoon lemon juice
   - 1 ½ teaspoons cumin
   - ½ teaspoon red pepper flakes
   - ¼ teaspoon salt
   - dash of cayenne
3. Adjust seasonings to taste and serve cold. Serves 8.

GRAIN BURGERS

These burgers can be made out of any grain: wheat berries, couscous, bulgur wheat, even rice. You can also substitute lentils for half the grains for higher protein. Cook first! Have ready **3 cups wheat berries** (or other grain of your choice).

1. While wheat berries are cooling, preheat oven to 350°. Heavily grease a baking tray with olive oil.
2. Mix in a cake or pie pan and set aside
   - ½ cup wheat germ
   - ½ cup wheat bran (or oat bran or bread crumbs)
3. Finely chop
   - 2 stalks celery
   - 2 carrots
   - ½ bell pepper
   - ½ cup fresh parlsey
   and sauté for 2 to 3 minutes in 1 tablespoon olive oil. Let cool for a few minutes.
4. Mix the vegetables and cooled grains.
5. Add
   - 1 tablespoon wheat germ (or toasted whole wheat flour)
   - ½ cup peanut butter
   - ½ teaspoon salt
   - ½ teaspoon black pepper
   and mix thoroughly.
6. The mixture should stay clumped together if you squeeze a handful in your fist. If it doesn't, add a bit more wheat germ and peanut butter.
7. Separate the mixture into 6 equal balls. Squeeze and mold each ball into a patty.
8. Press each patty into the pan of wheat germ and bran. Flip to coat on both sides.
9. Do the same thing in the oily pan—it's important to get oil on both sides of the patty so it will brown nicely.
10. Bake for about 30 minutes. You may flip them, but it's not necessary. Serves 6.

SUGGESTION

If your burgers don't hold together well, try running the wheat berries through the food processor or blender for just a few seconds.

GREEK PITA SANDWICHES

Cook first! Have ready **2 cups cooked kidney beans.**

1. Chop
   - ½ **sweet onion**
   - I **clove garlic**
   - I **tomato**
2. Heat ½ **cup water** in a skillet on medium heat. Whisk in **I teaspoon cornstarch,** dissolving any lumps, followed by
   - I **teaspoon salt**
   - 2 **teaspoons oregano**
   - I½ **teaspoons onion powder**
   - I½ **teaspoons garlic powder**
   - I **teaspoon black pepper**
   - I **teaspoon dried parsley**
   - ¼ **teaspoon cinnamon**
   - ¼ **teaspoon nutmeg**

   and then the onion, garlic, and tomato.
3. Let cook for a few minutes. Add the cooked kidney beans and simmer.
4. Meanwhile, wash and shred **I cup lettuce** and slice ½ **cucumber** into strips.
5. Toast **4 pitas** in the oven at 200° for 5 minutes.
6. Serve by slicing open the pitas, tucking in a few pieces of lettuce and cucumber, and heaping in the bean mixture. Top with **sour cream** (optional). Serves 4.

GREEK TOFU SALAD

1. Cut **I block tofu** into small chunks the size of dice. Press the chunks gently with towels or cloths to absorb any excess water.
2. Whisk together in a bowl
   - ⅓ **cup olive oil**
   - ⅓ **cup wine vinegar**
   - I **tablespoon basil**
   - ½ **teaspoon black pepper**
   - I **teaspoon oregano**
   - I **teaspoon salt**
3. Pour this marinade over the tofu and let

sit for at least an hour, or up to overnight.
4. Meanwhile, chop
   - 2 **small tomatoes**
   - I **cucumber**
   - ¼ **red onion**
   - I **cup black olives**

   Stir them into the tofu mixture and toss.
5. Serve as a salad on its own or atop a bed of **fresh spinach leaves.** Serves 6.

   SUGGESTION
   For **Greek Tofu Bake**, cut the tofu into thin slabs instead of cubes. Prepare the marinade as directed above. Lay the slabs on a baking tray, cover with marinade, and bake at 350° for 25 minutes, flipping once. Cut into strips and serve over **salad** or in **whole wheat tortillas.**

HOMEMADE PESTO

This sauce is so easy and so good!

1. In a blender, combine
   - I **cup fresh basil leaves**
   - ½ **cup fresh parsley**, with the stems removed
   - ½ **cup grated Parmesan or Romano cheese**
   - ¼ **cup pine nuts**
   - I **clove garlic**, roughly chopped
   - ¼ **teaspoon salt**
2. Cover and blend, stopping often to scrape the mixture off the sides and back down toward the blades.
3. When it is well blended, remove the lid and slowly drizzle in ¼ **cup olive oil.** Continue blending until the mixture is a smooth paste.
4. Serve on **whole wheat noodles.** Serves 4 to 6.

   SUGGESTION
   For an **Open-Faced Pesto Melt**, spread pesto over slices of **French bread.** Top with slices of **fresh tomato** and sprinkle with **mozzarella cheese.** Place on a baking sheet and broil for 3 minutes, or until cheese melts.

JAPANESE MARINATED TOFU

1. Mince and mix together
   5 scallions
   6 cloves garlic
   2 tablespoons fresh ginger
2. Combine in a saucepan
   ⅔ **cup tamari**
   ⅔ **cup water**
   ¾ **cup rice wine** (or **sake**)
   ½ **teaspoon powdered ginger**
   and add the three minced items. Bring to a boil and simmer for 10 minutes.
3. Meanwhile, slice **a block of tofu** into ¼-inch strips. Press and place in a dish with sides. When the sauce has simmered, pour it over the tofu and let stand at least 1 hour, or up to overnight.
4. To cook, heat **2 tablespoons olive oil** on medium heat. Cook the slabs of tofu—as many as will fit in the pan at once—for about 10 minutes per side, or until they are browned and crispy.
5. After all the tofu is cooked, remove it from the pan. Pour the remaining marinade into the empty skillet.
6. On medium-high heat, steadily stir the sauce and slowly sprinkle in ¾ **tablespoon cornstarch**.
7. Continue stirring for about 3 minutes, until the sauce begins to thicken. Spoon over the tofu.
8. Serve over **sticky rice** or **Asian Stir-Fried Rice** (page 202). Serves 4.

JULIE'S ALMOST-PESTO ROTINI

Nothing makes my friend Julie happier than a box of tricolor rotini. I'm not sure why, but there is something imminently satisfying in those curly, bouncy multicolored noodles.

This dish tastes very similar to pesto, but it takes only a few minutes to prepare.

1. Simmer **8 ounces of tricolor rotini** in boiling salted water for about 10 minutes.
2. Meanwhile, finely chop **3 large tomatoes**.
3. Mince
   ¼ **cup fresh basil**
   1 clove garlic
4. Drain the pasta and sprinkle with
   1 tablespoon olive oil
   ¼ **teaspoon salt**
   ½ **teaspoon black pepper**
   ⅓ **cup grated Parmesan cheese**
5. Add the tomatoes, basil, and garlic and mix well. Serve with **crusty bread** and a **tossed salad**. Serves 4.

LENTIL LOAF

So much better than meat loaf! You'll actually enjoy eating this.
Cook first! Have ready **5 cups cooked lentils** (2 cups dry).

1. Preheat oven to 350°.
2. Boil **2 cups water** and pour over **1 cup dry bulgur wheat**. Set aside.
3. Grate **3 carrots**, and chop
   1 onion
   1 clove garlic
4. When the bulgur has absorbed the water and is fluffy, add the carrots, onion, and garlic, followed by
   5 cups cooked lentils
   1 egg, beaten
   1 cup wheat bran, **wheat germ**, or **bread crumbs**
   1 tablespoon ketchup
   1 teaspoon thyme

2 teaspoons oregano

I teaspoon tarragon

½ teaspoon salt

½ teaspoon pepper

5. Mix well, using your hands if necessary.

6. Pat mixture into a greased 9-inch loaf pan. Bake for about 40 minutes, until firm but not dry. Let cool for 15 minutes before serving. Serves 4 to 6.

LENTILS WITH 'MATERS AND 'TATERS

Tomatoes and potatoes perk up these versatile legumes.

1. Prepare **2 cups cooked lentils.**

2. While the lentils simmer for half an hour, chop **I potato** into very small cubes and boil or steam until soft, for no longer than 10 minutes.

3. Meanwhile, finely chop

I red onion

I stalk celery

I carrot

½ bell pepper

I tomato

I tablespoon fresh basil

4. Sauté the onion, celery, and carrot in **I tablespoon olive oil.** After 3 minutes, add the bell pepper.

5. After 2 minutes, add the sautéed mixture to the cooked lentils. Stir in the chopped tomato and basil as well as the cooked potato and

2 tablespoons white wine vinegar

2 tablespoons lemon juice

I tablespoon thyme

¾ teaspoon salt

I teaspoon black pepper

6. Sprinkle with ½ **cup feta cheese** (optional) and serve hot or cold. Serves 6.

MARTY'S CURRIED LENTIL SOUP

This soup is savory, simple, and ready in no time flat. It's perfect for busy evenings.

1. Chop

I medium onion

I clove garlic

I bell pepper

2 large carrots

2. Sauté the chopped vegetables in **2 table-spoons olive oil.** As the onions soften, stir in **2 tablespoons curry powder.**

3. As the vegetables cook, dice **2 medium tomatoes.**

4. Transfer the sauté mixture to a saucepan. Add the chopped tomatoes as well as

4 cups vegetable broth

I cup dry lentils

½ teaspoon salt

½ teaspoon black pepper

5. Simmer for 45 minutes, or until lentils are done. Serves 4.

NEW ORLEANS JAMBALAYA

It's no wonder Emmylou Harris sings about jambalaya— this spicy Cajun dish will make you warm and warbling to the tips of your toes!

1. Chop

I large onion

2 bell peppers

and sauté for 10 minutes in **2 tablespoons olive oil.**

2. Meanwhile, mince **2 cloves garlic** and add to the sauté, as well as

2 tablespoons dried parsley

I tablespoon oregano

I teaspoon thyme

3 bay leaves

I teaspoon cayenne pepper

3. Chop **2 medium tomatoes** and place in a saucepan. Add the sautéed mixture.

4. Stir in

211

1 tablespoon tomato paste
2 cups uncooked dry brown rice
⅓ cup uncooked dry lentils
6 cups water
2 teaspoons salt

5. Increase heat to medium-high and stir thoroughly. When the mixture comes to a boil, reduce heat and simmer for 25 minutes.
6. Stir in
    1½ cups corn
    1 cup olives
7. Let cook for another 5 to 10 minutes, until the lentils and rice are well done. Season with black pepper and serve piping hot. Serves 8.

NO-CHICKEN AND RICE

This is a familiar, comforting dish that's perfect for snowy winter days or when someone's sick.

1. Bring **2½ cups water** to a boil.
2. Add **1 cup dry brown rice**, reduce heat, and simmer for 30 minutes.
3. In a separate saucepan, bring **1 cup veggie stock** to a boil.
4. Add ¾ cup **dry TVP chunks** and simmer on medium-low until the TVP is soft and the liquid is absorbed. This will only take a few minutes.
5. Meanwhile, chop
    2 stalks celery
    2 carrots
    1 medium onion
    2 cloves garlic
    ½ **cup fresh parsley**
    and sauté all except the parsley in **2 tablespoons canola oil**.
6. Combine the cooked rice, vegetables, and TVP, including any extra veggie stock.
7. Stir in the parsley, and season with **salt** and **pepper**. Serves 4 to 6.

SUGGESTION
For **No-Chicken Soup**, add an extra **2 cups veggie stock**. Adjust seasonings to taste.

PALAK PANEER (SPINACH AND CHEESE)

Indian food is so exquisite, I never imagined it could be so easy to create in your own kitchen. This recipe is simple, but a dead ringer for a restaurant dish. It is very good as a hot main dish, and equally delicious as a cold lunch spread.

This recipe is traditionally made with paneer, *a kind of firm cheese. You may be able to find it at ethnic markets, but tofu as a substitute is nearly indistinguishable in the finished product.*

1. Cut **1 block tofu** (or **1½ cups paneer**) into tiny cubes, smaller than dice. Press to remove excess water.
2. Heat **3 tablespoons olive oil** in a skillet and sauté tofu over medium heat for at least 10 minutes, or until golden brown.
3. Meanwhile, mince
    2 cloves garlic
    2 teaspoons fresh ginger
    ½ **jalapeño pepper**
    ¼ **onion**
4. When tofu is done, set aside and sauté garlic, ginger, jalapeño, and onion for 3 minutes.
5. Reduce heat to medium-low and stir in
    1 cup sour cream
    1 tablespoon cumin
    1 teaspoon coriander
    2 teaspoons turmeric
    ½ **teaspoon salt**
6. Add **3 pounds fresh spinach**, handfuls at a time, until it is cooked down. (Or add **2 blocks frozen spinach, thawed and drained**.) After the spinach is well cooked, remove from heat and allow to cool slightly.
7. Meanwhile, wash and quarter **1 large tomato**.

8. Pour the spinach mixture into a blender and blend, followed by the tomato, 1 chunk at a time. Return to the skillet and add the tofu cubes (or cheese). Stir, then simmer for 10 minutes on low heat.
9. Serve hot, tucked into **chapattis** or **pitas**, or cold, spread on **crackers** or **bread**. Serves 6.

PESTO PIZZA

This is one of our family's favorite dishes. We always make two pizzas—one is never enough.

1. Preheat oven to 425°.
2. Open a **premade whole wheat pizza crust.** These are available at most grocery stores, in brands such as Mama Mary's.
3. Spread ½ **cup pesto sauce** evenly over the crust.
4. Thinly slice **3 tomatoes** and arrange them on the crust.
5. Grate **2 cups Monterey Jack cheese.** Spread over the pizza.
6. Sprinkle ½ **cup black olives** atop the cheese and dust with ¼ **teaspoon black pepper.**
7. Bake for 15 minutes, or until cheese is melted and tomatoes are soft. Serve hot. One pizza serves 2 to 3.

   SUGGESTION
   For individual pizzas, use **whole wheat English muffin halves** or **whole wheat tortillas** instead of a single large crust. Place on a baking tray and bake for 10 minutes.

QUINOA PEANUT WRAPS

1. Rinse **1 cup dry quinoa** thoroughly (to rid it of bitter-tasting saponins, a natural chemical that prevents grazing by wild animals). Bring **2 cups water** to a boil and simmer the rinsed quinoa for about 15 minutes, or until light and fluffy.
2. Meanwhile, shred **1 large carrot** and finely chop
   1 teaspoon fresh ginger
   1 scallion
   1 clove garlic
   ¼ **cup dry-roasted peanuts.**
3. Mix these into the quinoa, along with
   1 teaspoon red pepper flakes
   ½ **teaspoon salt**
4. Whisk together
   1 tablespoon olive oil
   1 tablespoon honey
   3 tablespoons lemon juice
5. Stir this mixture into the quinoa and put it in the fridge to chill. To serve, spread a thin layer of **peanut butter** over a **whole wheat tortilla.** Scoop quinoa into the middle and roll it up like a burrito. Serves 4 to 6.

   SUGGESTION
   For **Quinoa Veggie Wraps**, in Step 2, add **an extra large carrot**. Slice ½ **cucumber** into thin strips. Place **2 lettuce leaves** and 2 cucumber strips inside each wrap before adding the quinoa.

ROASTED VEGGIE TOSTADAS

Cook first! Have ready **1 cup refried beans.**

1. Preheat oven to 450°.
2. Cut into thin strips or chunks
   4 Roma tomatoes
   1 yellow squash
   1 onion
   2 bell peppers
3. Spread the vegetables in a baking pan.
4. In a bowl, combine
   2 tablespoons olive oil
   1 teaspoon chili powder
   ½ teaspoon cumin
   ½ teaspoon oregano
   Drizzle over the vegetables and toss until thoroughly coated.
5. Bake for 15 minutes, or until peppers and onions are tender but still crisp.
6. Meanwhile, warm 1 cup refried beans over medium heat.
7. In the toaster oven, or in the main oven after the veggies have come out, toast 8 **whole wheat tortillas** at 400°. Do not stack. Watch them carefully to make sure they don't puff up and burn, and remove them when they start to brown. They should be crunchy and stiff, similar to tortilla chips.
8. Spread a very thin layer of beans over the top of the tortillas, then heap with roasted veggies. If desired, top with **hot sauce** or **salsa** (optional). Pick up the entire tostada and eat it like a slice of pizza. Serves 6 to 8.

SKINNY'S EGGPLANT PARMESAN

This version is a simpler, healthier take on the deep-fried traditional recipe.

1. Set oven to "Broil."
2. Peel **1 medium eggplant** and slice it into ¼-inch disks.

3. Place the slices in a greased baking dish and broil for 10 minutes, flipping once.
4. Meanwhile, mix together
   ½ cup grated Parmesan cheese
   2 teaspoons olive oil
   ¼ cup toasted wheat germ
   ½ teaspoon oregano
   ½ teaspoon basil
5. Sprinkle crumb mixture over eggplant slices. Flip them once to get some crumbs on both sides. Top with **1 cup grated mozzarella cheese** and broil for 2 minutes, until cheese is melted.
6. Meanwhile, heat **1 cup marinara sauce** (or other pasta sauce) on the stove.
7. Spoon the sauce over the eggplant slices.
8. Serve atop your favorite **whole wheat pasta.** Serves 4 to 6.

SONDRA'S ITALIAN COUSCOUS

You'll be surprised by how tasty this simple dish is. It's best of all in the summer, with fresh tomato and basil from the garden.
Cook first! Have ready **1 cup cooked chickpeas.**

1. Cook **1 cup dry couscous** according to the package—about 5 minutes.
2. Chop ½ cup **sweet yellow onion** and stir it into the couscous.
3. Add
   1 cup cooked chickpeas
   ⅔ cup diced tomatoes
   1 tablespoon fresh basil
   1 teaspoon black pepper
   ½ teaspoon salt
4. Serve hot or cold over steamed greens. Serves 4.

SOUTHERN STIR-FRY

This is a colorful dish with a variety of tastes and textures. The creamy grits contrast pleasantly with the crunchy vegetables and the soft TVP.

1. Shred **1 cup pepper jack cheese**. Set aside.
2. Chop
      2 banana peppers (or ½ **bell pepper**)
      1 tomato
      ½ onion, into thin slices
      1 carrot, into very thin slivers
      4 cups strung and snapped green beans
   Place each ingredient in a separate bowl or cup.
3. Heat **1½ cups water**. When it boils, remove from heat, add **1 cup TVP flakes**, cover, and set aside. The TVP should become soft after 10 minutes or so. All the water should be absorbed—if not, pour the remainder off.
4. Steam the green beans until tender but still firm. Add the carrots and continue steaming for 1 minute.
5. Meanwhile, sauté the onion in **1 tablespoon olive oil** until translucent.
6. When the onion is mostly cooked, reduce heat to medium-low and add the soft TVP. Stir.
7. Next, boil **3 cups water** with a little **salt**.
8. When the water boils, add **1 cup grits** and cook for 5 minutes (or according to package instructions).
9. Add the green beans and carrots to the onions and TVP. Stir.
10. After the grits have been cooking for 5 minutes, add the 1 cup of pepper jack cheese **and ½ teaspoon black pepper**. Set aside.
11. Add to the vegetable mixture
      ½ teaspoon salt
      ½ teaspoon black pepper
      2 tablespoons chopped fresh parsley
   and stir. Remove from heat.
12. Serve immediately—grits topped with the veggie mixture. Sprinkle the chopped tomato and raw banana peppers over the top. Serves 6.

SPINACH BURRITOS

1. Preheat oven to 350°.
2. Shred **2 cups cheddar cheese** and set aside. Also set aside
      6 whole wheat tortillas
      ¾ cup salsa
3. Chop
      ¼ onion
      2 cloves garlic
   and sauté in **1 tablespoon olive oil** until tender.
4. Add
      1 block frozen spinach, thawed and drained (or **6 cups fresh**)
      ¼ teaspoon black pepper
5. Cook for 3 minutes, stirring often.
6. Remove the spinach mixture from heat and divide into 6 equal heaps.
7. Place 1 heap of spinach atop each tortilla. Top with a spoonful of salsa and a spoonful of cheese.
8. Roll each tortilla into a burrito and arrange them side by side in a casserole dish. Sprinkle with the remaining salsa and cheese.
9. Bake uncovered for 20 minutes, or until the sauce is bubbly and the cheese is melted. Serves 4 to 6.

   SUGGESTION
   For a heartier dish, in Step 4, add **1½ cups black beans** to the spinach mixture.

SUMMER TOFU

This dish's light, tangy flavor is refreshing on a hot summer day. Serve over whole wheat couscous (or other grain of your choice).

   As for the pepper, choose your own according to desired spiciness (see the Cooking Tips section of this book, page 169). If you use a bell pepper, use only one-third of it.

1. Preheat oven to 400°.
2. Roughly chop
   I large tomato
   I hot pepper
3. Place them in a baking pan and drizzle with **2 tablespoons olive oil**. Bake for 20 minutes, or until soft.
4. Transfer the tomato and pepper to the blender. Add
   ½ **cup orange juice**
   ¼ **cup lime juice**
   and blend.
5. Thinly slice **I block tofu** and press until dry. Place in a pan with sides.
6. Pour the sauce over the tofu and marinate for at least I hour, or up to overnight.
7. After marinating the tofu, heat **I table-spoon olive oil** in a skillet on medium-high. Place half the tofu in the pan and spoon some sauce over it. Cook, flipping periodically, for at least 20 minutes, until the tofu starts to brown. Repeat this with the rest of the tofu. When it has all been cooked, return it all to the pan to heat for a minute before serving. Serves 4.

TEN-MINUTE TACOS
Cook first! Have ready
   I½ **cups pinto beans**
   I½ **cups kidney beans**
   I½ **cups black beans**

1. Mince
   ½ **red onion**
   I **clove garlic**
   and sauté in **I tablespoon olive oil** in a deep skillet over medium heat.
2. Add pinto, kidney, and black beans. Stir well. Warm gently while stirring often.
3. Meanwhile, roughly chop

   I **large tomato**
   2 **packed cups lettuce**
   I **avocado**
   and place in a large mixing bowl.
4. Add
   2 **tablespoons vinegar**
   2 **tablespoons olive oil**
   I **tablespoon chili powder**
   I **teaspoon cumin**
   I **teaspoon salt**
   ½ **teaspoon pepper**
   and the bean mixture, and mix well.
5. Serve in **taco shells** or on **whole wheat tortillas** toasted until crisp and crunchy.
6. Top with (optional) **sour cream**, **salsa**, and chopped **cilantro**. Serves 6 to 8.

TOFU TEMPURA
This is the tastiest tofu possible. It's not much more diffi-cult than cooking plain tofu and should win over even the most anti-tofu meat eater. The tofu chunks can be tossed over a salad or mixed into a stir-fry or other cooked dish.

1. Cut ½ **block tofu** into bite-sized chunks and pat dry. Set aside.
2. In a wide bowl or cake pan, combine
   ½ **cup whole wheat flour**
   2 **tablespoons wheat germ**
   ½ **teaspoon thyme**
   ¼ **teaspoon black pepper**
   ¼ **teaspoon garlic powder**
   ¼ **teaspoon dill**
   and mix well.
3. In a separate bowl, beat
   I **egg**
   I **tablespoon milk**
   dash of hot sauce
4. In a skillet, heat **2 tablespoons canola oil** over medium-high heat. Meanwhile, dip each piece of tofu into the egg mixture, then roll it in the flour mixture. Drop it in the hot oil and sauté for 5 minutes, or until lightly browned.

5. Serve with **Ginger Sauce** (page 219) or **Spicy Peanut Sauce** (page 220) over **rice**, or as part of a **vegetable stir-fry**. Serves 4.

TOMATILLOS AND ANGEL HAIR

This dish is spicy and simple.
Cook first! Have ready **2 cups black beans**.

1. Boil **8 ounces whole wheat angel hair pasta** (half a box) according to package instructions.
2. Meanwhile, mince **2 cloves garlic** and sauté until tender in **1 tablespoon olive oil**.
3. Before the garlic begins to brown, stir in
   1 small can tomatillo salsa
   1 tablespoon cumin
4. Mix well, and stir in 2 cups black beans. Cook for 5 minutes, or until thoroughly hot.
5. When the pasta is done, drain and place 1 serving on each plate. Arrange the noodles into a nest shape and, in the center, place a generous dollop of the black bean mixture. Top with **sour cream** (optional) and sprinkle with **fresh cilantro leaves**. Serves 4.

TWO-BEAN CHILI
WITH BULGUR WHEAT

This dish is so hearty, it'll satisfy even the staunchest eater. And with both beans and bulgur, it provides a complete protein all in one dish.
Cook first! Have ready
   2 cups cooked kidney beans
   2 cups pinto beans

1. Bring **3 cups water** to a boil and pour over
   1 cup dry bulgur wheat
   ½ cup dry TVP
Stir well and set aside.

2. Chop
   4 cloves garlic
   1 medium onion
   3 stalks celery
   3 medium carrots
   1 bell pepper
   2 large tomatoes
3. Heat **3 tablespoons olive oil** in a skillet and sauté the garlic and onion. After 1 minute, add the celery and carrot, and after 2 minutes, add the bell pepper. Cook until tender but still firm.
4. Combine the sautéed vegetables with the chopped tomatoes and the bulgur mixture. Then add
   2 cups cooked kidney beans
   2 cups pinto beans
   2 teaspoons lemon juice
   1 tablespoon cumin
   2 teaspoons basil
   1 tablespoon chili powder
   1 teaspoon salt
   1 teaspoon black pepper
   1 cup tomato paste
5. Heat on the stove over medium heat, stirring often, until mixture is hot. Adjust spices to taste and serve sprinkled with **1 cup grated cheddar cheese** (optional). Serves 10.

Spreads, Sauces, and Dips

BABA GHANOUJ
(BAKED EGGPLANT DIP)

This is a delicious, creamy Mediterranean spread. It's similar to hummus, but with a smoother, creamier texture. It's great for taking to potlucks or for keeping on hand in the refrigerator. Serve on pita bread or use as a dip for carrots, cucumber slices, and celery sticks.

1. Preheat oven to 375°.
2. Slice **1 eggplant** in half. Place it on a greased baking sheet and brush the skin lightly with oil to prevent scorching. Bake for about 25 minutes, or until tender. Remove from oven and allow to cool.
3. When the eggplant is cool enough to touch, gently peel away the bitter-tasting skin. Place the soft insides in a mixing bowl and mash thoroughly.
4. Add
   2 tablespoons tahini
   2 minced cloves garlic
   2 tablespoons lemon juice
   ½ teaspoon salt
   1 teaspoon olive oil
   ½ teaspoon cumin
5. Mix well and chill for at least half an hour before serving. Makes 2 to 3 cups.

SUGGESTION

For **Chickpea Hummus**, a high-protein variation on this spread, skip Steps 1 through 3. Begin the recipe by mashing or blending **1½ cup cooked garbanzo beans** with **2 tablespoons hot water**. Then continue with Step 4, increasing **tahini** to ¾ **cup**.

FIVE-MINUTE MARINADE

1. Mince **2 cloves garlic**.
2. Place in a small bowl and add
   2 teaspoons tamari
   1 tablespoon brown sugar
   1½ teaspoons mustard
   2½ tablespoons apple cider vinegar
   2 tablespoons lime juice
   1 tablespoon lemon juice
   2 tablespoons olive oil
   1 teaspoon black pepper
3. Pour over vegetables, beans, tempeh, tofu, TVP, or seitan and allow to marinate for at least an hour, up to overnight. Makes ¾ cup.

SUGGESTIONS

◆For **Marinated Chickpea Salad**, pour marinade over **2 cups cooked chickpeas**. After marinating, sprinkle over a **spinach salad** for added protein.
◆For **Marinated Tofu Sizzlers**, slice **1 block tofu**

into thin slabs and pat dry. Soak in the marinade for at least an hour. Sauté the tofu in the marinade in **2 tablespoons olive oil** for 15 minutes, or until golden brown. Slice into bite-sized cubes and scatter over a **green salad** or stack on **bread** with **sliced tomato** and **cucumbers** for a hearty tofu sandwich.

GINGER-PEANUT SPREAD

This slightly spicy spread is light and airy, due to the tofu, but also rich and creamy, thanks to the peanut butter. It is best spread on crunchy toast or crackers. With strips of cucumber and carrot, it can fill a tasty sandwich.

1. Chop **I block tofu** into small cubes and blot dry. Set aside.
2. Mince **4 teaspoons fresh ginger.** Set aside.
3. In a small saucepan over medium heat, combine
    6 tablespoons peanut butter
    5 tablespoons water
    I tablespoon tamari
   and stir into a smooth sauce. Remove from heat.
4. Stir in the ginger, followed by the tofu. Stir with a fork, mashing slightly, until it forms a crumbly and chunky spread. Makes 2 to 3 cups.

    SUGGESTION
    For **Thai Tempeh:** prepare the sauce as above, but in Step 1, add **I block tempeh** instead of tofu. Cut it into cubes; do not crumble. Add ½ **cup finely chopped celery** and serve hot over **brown rice.**

GINGER SAUCE

This sauce perks up an ordinary vegetable or tofu stir-fry. It can also be used as a marinade.

1. Mince **I tablespoon finely minced ginger** and place in a small saucepan.
2. Add
    6 tablespoons rice vinegar

I½ tablespoons sugar
½ cup water
2 tablespoons tamari

3. Bring to a boil. Reduce heat to medium-low and simmer, stirring occasionally, for 5 minutes.
4. Meanwhile, in a small bowl, slowly blend **I tablespoon cornstarch** into ¼ **cup water.** Add to ginger mixture and stir until the sauce is thickened and clear. Remove from heat. Makes I⅓ cup.

OLIVE-NUT SPREAD

> This spread is so good, it taught me to like olives. The first time I ate it, I couldn't stand olives, but somehow I couldn't stop eating it just the same. I got used to their flavor that way, and now I love olives in any dish.
>
> —Sara Kate

This dish is an excellent source of healthy oils from both the olives and the walnuts.

1. In a blender or food processor, combine
    I cup green olives
    I cup black olives
    ⅔ cup walnuts
    2 chopped cloves garlic
    I tablespoon thyme
2. Blend until the spread is mostly smooth. Add a little **olive oil** if it is too chunky to blend. Makes about 3 cups.

    SUGGESTION
    For **Mediterranean Subs,** spread on **toasted whole wheat sub rolls** and heap with **Italian Artichoke Salad** (page 197), **leaves of lettuce, strips of red bell pepper,** and **slices of red onion.**

RASPBERRY VINAIGRETTE

Raspberry and garlic may seem like a strange combination, but it really is good. This is one of the few dressings I never get tired of.

1. Mince **2 cloves garlic**. Combine in the blender with
   - **¼ cup apple cider vinegar**
   - **¾ cup balsamic vinegar**
   - **2 tablespoons raspberry jam**
2. As the mixture is blending, slowly drizzle in **1 cup olive oil**. It will turn a lighter, frothy brown. Use on your favorite salad. Makes about 2 cups.

SASSY SOY SPREAD

This spread is good on crackers, chips, or even in sandwiches. It's a good dish for a party or a potluck.

1. Shred **2½ cups soy cheese** (or dairy cheese with a mild flavor).
2. Rinse **1 cup green olives** and mince finely.
3. Mix cheese and olives together and add
   - **1½ teaspoons mustard**
   - **½ teaspoon garlic powder**
   - **½ teaspoon black pepper**
   - **½ cup soy mayonnaise**

   Mash with your hands if necessary to achieve a spreadable consistency. Makes about 4 cups.

SAVORY REFRIED BEAN DIP

This one-pot dish is very versatile. Topped with salsa or sour cream, it makes a great addition to a party or picnic. Inside taco shells, it's a quick and easy meal.

1. Heat **3 cups refried pinto beans** in a saucepan over medium heat, stirring and adding water if necessary to prevent sticking.
2. Add
   - **¼ cup diced green chiles** (one small can)
   - **1 teaspoon chili powder**
   - **1 teaspoon cumin**
   - **1 teaspoon oregano**
   - **1 teaspoon garlic powder**
   - **dash of hot sauce**
   - **salt and pepper to taste**
   - **2 cups grated cheese** (optional)
3. Serve wrapped inside whole wheat tortillas, as a taco filling, or scooped on top of tortilla chips. Serves 6.

SPICY PEANUT SAUCE

This sauce perks up the dullest vegetable side dish: it adds protein and heartiness in addition to delicious peanut flavor. It can also be added to a stir-fry, sauté, or sandwich, or used as a dip for chips or spring rolls.

1. In a small saucepan, heat **1 cup milk** on medium-low heat.
2. Not allowing the mixture to boil, stir in **¼ cup peanut butter** and mix vigorously until the mixture is uniform.
3. Stir in
   - **3 tablespoons plain yogurt**
   - **¾ teaspoon oregano**
   - **¾ teaspoon red pepper flakes**

   and continue stirring until the sauce is smooth. Remove from heat. Makes 1½ cups.

SPRING TOFU SPREAD

1. Chop very finely
   - ½ **red onion**
   - **2 stalks celery**
   - ⅔ **cup walnuts**
2. Place them in a bowl and add
   - **1 tablespoon dill**
   - **2 teaspoons celery seed**
   - **2 tablespoons nutritional yeast**
   - ⅔ **cup sweet pickle relish**
   - ¾ **cup soy mayonnaise**
3. Break **1 block extra firm tofu** into chunks and add it to the bowl. Mash the mixture around with your hands, squeezing it through your fists until it is thoroughly mixed and broken up.
4. Serve on **whole wheat Kaiser rolls** with **fresh lettuce** and **sliced tomato**. Makes about 4 cups.

Desserts

BANANA BIRTHDAY CAKE

*This cake is sumptuous on its own, but **Easy Cream Cheese Frosting** (page 223) makes it fancier for special occasions.*

1. Preheat oven to 350°.
2. In a mixing bowl, combine
   2 cups whole wheat flour
   I teaspoon baking soda
   I teaspoon salt
3. In a separate bowl, cream
   ½ cup softened butter
   ½ cup granulated sugar
   ¾ cup brown sugar
4. Beat in
   2 eggs
   I teaspoon vanilla
   ½ cup milk
5. Stir in **I cup mashed ripe banana**.
6. Combine the sugar mixture and flour mixture.
7. Stir in ½ **cup chopped walnuts** (optional).
8. Bake 25 to 30 minutes in a greased square glass casserole dish. Serves 8 to 10.

BLUEBERRY PIE

Any berry is delicious in this easy fruit pie—in the summer, we use the black raspberries that grow in our garden. But nothing beats good old-fashioned blueberry, topped with vanilla ice cream.

Have ready I **Double Whole Wheat Piecrust** (page 226).

1. If using frozen fruit, set out **2½ cups frozen blueberries** to thaw. If using fresh, simply rinse and begin with Step 2.
2. When the fruit is partially melted, stir in
   3 tablespoons quick-cooking tapioca
   ½ cup granulated sugar
   ⅛ teaspoon salt
   2 tablespoons melted butter
   or canola oil
3. Let the fruit mixture stand for 15 minutes. Meanwhile, preheat the oven to 450°.
4. Scrape the berries into the prepared bottom crust. Remove I sheet of wax paper from the top crust and place it, paper side up, atop the berries. Peel off the second sheet of wax paper, leaving the crust draped over the pie.
5. Use your fingers and a fork to tamp down the edges of the crust, forming a seal

around the edge of the pie. With a knife, cut a few slits in the top crust so that steam can escape.

6. Tear aluminum foil into 2-inch-wide strips and fold these around the very edges of the crust so it doesn't burn.

7. Bake at 450° for 10 minutes. Reduce heat to 350° and bake for 40 minutes, removing the foil after 20 minutes.

8. Let stand 15 minutes before serving. Serves 8 to 10.

CHOCOLATE CHIP "PUMPCAKES"

These cupcakes are so good, it's worth sacrificing a little whole wheat nutrition in favor of cake mix. Keep the recipe on hand because everyone will be demanding it.

1. Preheat oven to 350°.
2. Mix together
   1 package spice cake mix
   1 cup canned pumpkin
   ⅔ cup water
   2 eggs
   2 cups chocolate chips
3. Divide the dough among 24 greased or lined muffin tins.
4. Bake for 20 to 25 minutes, or until golden. Makes 24 muffins.

CHOCOLATE PECAN PIE

> I once baked two of these pies in order to entice my housemates to attend an important house meeting. The meeting began at 10:00, the first pie came out of the oven at 10:02, and it was gone by 10:06. Thank goodness there was another one on the way or I might have lost a finger or two!
>
> —Sara Kate

Not only is this pie decadent and delicious, but it doesn't contain corn syrup as most pecan pies do.
Cook First! Have ready **1 Single Whole Wheat Piecrust** (page 226).

1. Preheat oven to 375°.
2. Stir together
   ½ cup granulated sugar
   1 cup brown sugar
   1 tablespoon flour
3. In a separate bowl, beat **2 eggs**.
4. Stir into the eggs
   2 tablespoons milk
   1 teaspoon vanilla
   ½ cup melted butter
   1 cup pecans
5. Stir the sugar mixture into the egg mixture.
6. Sprinkle **1 cup chocolate chips** over the prepared piecrust. Pour in the filling mixture.
7. Bake for 40 to 50 minutes. Serves 8 to 10.

EASY CREAM CHEESE FROSTING

1. Beat together
   ½ cup cream cheese
   ¼ cup softened butter
   1½ teaspoons milk
   1½ cups powdered sugar
   ½ teaspoon vanilla
2. Stir until smooth. When the cake is cool, spread over top. Makes 2¼ cups.

FRESH FRUIT SMOOTHIES

These smoothies taste better than any you can buy in a bottle, and they're better for you too. The trick to a good smoothie is to freeze your fruit—otherwise you have to use ice, which waters down the drink. Many commercial smoothies counter this problem with fake fruit syrup. Yuck! These drinks, on the other hand, are as delicious as ice cream and as healthy as a fruit salad.

For all smoothies, freeze the fruit ahead of time, at least a day in advance. Always peel bananas before freezing. Rinse berries and fruit slices and place them on a tray, covered with plastic wrap.

When it's well frozen, chop the fruit into bite-sized pieces and toss it in the blender. If the mixture is too thick to blend, add a little more liquid. Soy milk can always be substituted for yogurt. This will make the smoothie less sweet, so you may want to add a dab of honey.

Orange Push-Up

Ever tried one of those creamy push-up pops? This tastes just like an orange one—tangy, sweet, creamy, and cold.

½ cup orange juice
½ cup pineapple, frozen
1 cup peaches, frozen
⅓ cup vanilla yogurt

Lazy Afternoon

The contrast between the rich soy milk and refreshing fruit flavors makes this smoothie both light and satisfying.

¾ cup soy milk
⅓ cup orange juice
1 banana, frozen
1 cup strawberries, frozen

Nutty Buddy

This smoothie seems so indulgent, it's as good as dessert.

For variety, try strawberries or raspberries instead of blueberries, or walnuts or pecans instead of almonds.

1 cup vanilla yogurt
1 banana, frozen
1 cup blueberries, frozen
⅓ cup almonds

Maple Dream

The richness of the walnuts and maple syrup makes this concoction very different from most fruit smoothies. It's also a great source of omega-3 fatty acids.

1 cup soy milk
2 bananas, frozen
¼ cup walnuts
2 teaspoons maple syrup

Banana Sundae

Vanilla, chocolate, banana, and peanut—this is an ice cream parlor treat you can drink with a straw. And just think, it's actually good for you!

1 cup vanilla yogurt
1½ bananas, frozen
⅓ cup peanuts
¾ tablespoon cocoa or carob powder

Summer Squeeze

This is a refreshingly tangy and sweet citrus drink. It's infinitely better with fresh-squeezed fruit, but bottled juice will do in a pinch. There's no need to blend up the ice cubes entirely, just let the blender knock them around for a minute.

⅔ cup orange juice
½ cup grapefruit juice
2 tablespoons lemon juice
2 teaspoons maple syrup
3 ice cubes

FUDGE BROWNIES

These brownies are not healthy in any way, but they are unspeakably delicious. We would be doing the entire world a disservice if we did not include this recipe. They're wonderful when hot, and possibly even better after they've cooled. They have a thick, fudgelike consistency.

1. Preheat oven to 350°. Grease a 9-inch square casserole dish.
2. In a saucepan on medium heat, melt
     4 ounces unsweetened baking chocolate
     ¾ cup butter
3. Stir constantly and watch closely to keep from burning or bubbling. When the chocolate has melted, remove from heat.
4. Stir in
     2 cups granulated sugar
     3 eggs
     I teaspoon vanilla
   and mix well.
5. Stir in
     I cup white flour
     I cup chocolate chips
6. Spread the batter into the casserole dish and bake for 35 to 40 minutes, or until a toothpick inserted in the middle comes out with moist crumbs. Cool in pan. Serves 10 to 12.

   SUGGESTIONS
   ◆If you add **½ cup chopped walnuts**, then at least you'll get some omega-3 fatty acids.
   ◆For tart, sweet **Raspberry Marble Brownies**, stir in **I cup fresh or frozen raspberries** in Step 5.

GRANDMA EDITH'S APPLE CRISP

This fast and easy version of apple pie is best with Granny Smith or other tart apples. Serve it steaming hot, topped with vanilla ice cream. (For you vegans, vanilla Tofutti won't let you down.)

1. Preheat oven to 350°.
2. Wash and thinly slice **8 medium tart apples.** No need to peel them.
3. Place the apples in a bowl, and sprinkle with
     2 tablespoons lemon juice
     ⅓ cup water
     ½ cup raisins
     2 tablespoons brown sugar
     2 teaspoons cinnamon
     I teaspoon nutmeg
4. Toss until the apples are evenly coated. Pour into a 9-inch by 13-inch casserole dish and set aside.
5. In a mixing bowl, combine
     I¼ cups rolled oats
     I cup wheat germ or **wheat bran**
     ½ cup whole wheat flour
     ½ cup honey
     ½ cup canola oil
     2 teaspoons cinnamon
     ½ teaspoon allspice
     ½ teaspoon nutmeg
6. The oats mixture should be clumpy but fairly dry. Sprinkle it over the apples evenly.
7. Bake for 30 to 40 minutes, until the apples are soft. Serves 8 to 10.

LOG CABIN PEANUT BUTTER COOKIES

1. Preheat oven to 375°.
2. In a large mixing bowl, combine
   2½ cups flour
   ½ teaspoon salt
   1½ teaspoons baking soda
   1 teaspoon baking powder
3. In a small bowl, beat together
   2 eggs
   2 teaspoons vanilla
4. In a third bowl, combine
   ¾ cup melted butter
   1 cup creamy peanut butter
   1 cup granulated sugar
   1 cup brown sugar
5. Bit by bit, gradually stir the egg and flour mixtures into the sugar mixture. Mix thoroughly.
6. Place heaping spoonfuls of dough on an ungreased cookie sheet. Flatten each ball somewhat into a patty, making crosshatch marks on its top with a fork. Sprinkle each flattened cookie with a dusting of **granulated sugar.**
7. Bake for about 10 minutes. Makes about 4 dozen cookies.

WHOLE WHEAT PIECRUST

If you're expecting a fluffy white flour crust, you may be surprised by this one. A whole wheat crust is not as light and flaky; instead it is crumbly, dense, and satisfying. We're betting you'll get used to it pretty quickly once you try a bite.

Single

The following recipe is for a bottom crust only.

1. Combine
   2 cups whole wheat flour
   ½ teaspoon salt
   ½ cup canola oil
   ¼ cup cold water
2. Stir with a fork until well blended. Roll into a ball with your hands and place into a greased 9-inch pie dish.
3. Using your hands, mash the dough into a thin layer, coating the pie dish. Flatten it out as thinly as possible until it evenly covers the entire dish. If it is too crumbly, add a little more oil. You may have a little leftover.

Double

The following recipe is for a bottom and top crust.

1. Combine
   3 cups whole wheat flour
   1½ teaspoons salt
   ¾ cup canola oil
   ⅓ cup cold water
2. Stir with a fork until well blended.
3. Form 2 large balls of dough with your hands. Set one aside and place the other in a greased 9-inch pie dish.
4. Using your hands, mash the dough into a thin layer coating the pie dish.
5. Flatten it out as thinly as possible until it evenly covers the entire dish. Set aside.
6. If that ball of dough was very crumbly, you may need to add a little extra oil to the second ball before proceeding. Place the second ball between 2 sheets of wax paper and flatten it with a rolling pin. Set aside until you are ready to top the pie. See Step 4 in the **Blueberry Pie** recipe (page 222) for tips on placing the top crust.

Endnotes

CHAPTER 1

[1] Kurtz, Barbara, "The Environmental Case for Vegetarianism," *The Indy* 1 no. 1 (4 October 2001), http://indy.pabn.org/archives/104envir.shtml (accessed 4 July 2005).

[2] Robbins, John, *The Food Revolution: How Your Diet Can Help Save Your Life and the World* (Berkeley, Calif.: Conari Press, 2001), 236–237.

[3] U.S. Census Bureau, "World Population: 1950–2040," *World Population Information* (International Database, April 2005), http://www.census.gov/ipc/www/img/worldpop.gif (accessed 4 July 2005).

[4] Cunningham, William, and Barbara W. Saigo, *Environmental Science: A Global Concern* (Boston: McGraw-Hill, 1997), 125.

[5] Fox, Lewis, and Jonah Sachos, *The Meatrix* (New York: Global Resource Action Center for the Environment, Inc., 2003), www.themeatrix.com/information/index.html (accessed 4 July 2005).

CHAPTER 2

[1] Robbins, John, *The Food Revolution: How Your Diet Can Help Save Your Life and the World* (Berkeley, Calif.: Conari Press, 2001), 209.

[2] Brower, Michael, et al., *The Consumer's Guide to Effective Environmental Choices: Practical Advice from the Union of Concerned Scientists* (New York: Three Rivers Press, 1999), 85.

[3] Robbins, *The Food Revolution*, 236.

[4] Nelson, Jeff, "8,500 Gallons of Water for 1 Pound of Beef," VegSource Interactive, Inc. (30 April 2004), http://www.vegsource.com/articles2/water_stockholm.htm (accessed 4 July 2005).

[5] Pollan, Michael, "Power Steer," *New York Times Magazine* (31 March 2002): 72.

[6] "The Browning of America," *Newsweek* (22 February 1981): 26.

[7] Miller, G. Tyler, *Environmental Science: Working with the Earth* (Pacific Grove, Calif.: Brooks/Cole, 2003), 337.

[8] Ibid., 336.

[9] Ibid., 294.

[10] Browner, Carol, et al., "Environmental Assessment of Proposed Revisions to the National Pollutant Discharge Elimination System Regulation and Effluent Limitations Guidelines for Concentrated Animal Feeding Operations" (Washington, D.C.: U.S. Environmental Protection Agency, 2001), 2-1, 2-2. www.epa.gov/region08/water/wastewater/cafohome/cafodownload/cafodocs/EnvAssessPt1of2.pdf (accessed 19 July 2005).

[11] Stith, Pat, Joby Warrick, and Melanie Sill, "Boss Hog: North Carolina's Pork Revolution," (Raleigh, N.C.) *News and Observer*, 19, 21, 22, 24, and 26 February 1995, www.pulitzer.org/year/1996/ public-service/works/about.html (accessed 19 July 2005).

[12] Burkholder, JoAnn M., et al., "Impacts to a Coastal River and Estuary from Rupture of a Large Swine Waste Holding Lagoon," *Journal of Environmental Quality* 26 (1997): 1451–1466. and Mallin, Michael A. 2000, "Impacts of Industrial Animal Production on Rivers and Estuaries," *American Scientist* 88: 26–37.

[13] Stith, Warrick, and Sill, "Boss Hog."

[14] Browner, "Environmental Assessment," 2-17.

[15] Joe Rudek, Ph.D., senior scientist, Environmental Defense, Raleigh, N.C., phone conversation and e-mail with the author, 6, 7, 24, 25 January 2005 and 6, 7, 8 July 2005.

[16] United States Environmental Protection Agency, "Rivers and Streams," ch. 2 in *2000 National Water Quality Inventory*, http://www.epa.gov/305b/2000report (accessed 7 July 2005). and Browner, "Environmental Assessment," ix.

[17] Shore L. S., D. L. Correll, and P. K. Chakraborty, "Relationship of Fertilization with Chicken Manure and Concentrations of Estrogens in Small Streams," in *Animal Waste and the Land-Water Interface* (Boca Raton, Fla.: Lewis Publishers, 1995), 155–162.

[18] Browner, "Environmental Assessment," 2-15.

[19] Union of Concerned Scientists, "Hogging It!: Estimates of Antimicrobial Abuse in Livestock," www.ucsusa.org/food_and_environment/antibiotic_resistance/page.cfm?pageID=264 (accessed 7 July 2005). and Mellon, M., C. Benbrook, and K. L. Benbrook, *Hogging It — Estimates of Antimicrobial Abuse in Livestock* (Cambridge, Mass.: Union of Concerned Scientists Publications, 2001).

[20] Florini, Karen, senior attorney, Environmental Defense, "Comments on the Proposed Effluent Guidelines for Concentrated Animal Feeding Operations, EPA Docket Number OW-00-27" (30 July 2001): 6, www.keepantibioticsworking.com/new/

resources_library.cfm?refID=36256 (accessed 19 July 2005).

21 Merryman, Terri, "UTI News Brief," *WSMV Nashville Evening News*, NBC TV 4, 6 January 2005, www.keep antibioticsworking.com/new/news.cfm?refID=37764 (accessed 19 July 2005).

22 Chapin, Amy, Ana Rule, Kristen Gibson, Timothy Buckley, and Kellogg Schwab, "Airborne Multi-Drug Resistant Bacteria Isolated from a Concentrated Swine Feeding Operation" (Baltimore, Md.: Johns Hopkins Bloomberg School of Public Health), www.keep antibioticsworking.com/new/resources_library.cfm?ref ID=37560 (accessed 7 July 2005).

23 JoAnn Burkholder, Ph.D., professor of botany, North Carolina State University, conversation with the author, 18, 29, 31 January 2005.

24 Natural Resources Defense Council, "America's Animal Factories: How States Fail to Prevent Pollution from Livestock Waste. Policy Recommendations," http:// www.nrdc.org/water/pollution/factor/exec.asp (accessed 5 July 2005).

25 Durning, Alan, "Cost of Beef for Health and Habitat," *Los Angeles Times*, 21 September 1986, V3.

26 Miller, *Environmental Science*.

27 Ibid.

28 Belsky, A. J., A. Matzke, and S. Uselman, "Survey of Livestock Influences on Stream and Riparian Eecosystems in the Western United States," *Journal of Soil and Water Conservation* 54(1999): 1, 419–431.

29 Rainforest Action Network, "About Rainforests: By the Numbers," http://www.ran.org/info_center/ about_rainforests.html (accessed 5 July, 2005).

30 Ibid.

31 Myers, Norman, *The Primary Source: Tropical Forests and Our Future* (New York and London: W. W. Norton, 1984), 127, 142.

32 Durning, Alan, and Holly Brough, "Taking Stock: Animal Farming and the Environment," *Worldwatch Paper 103*, July 1991.

33 Environmental Defense, http://www.environmental defense.org (accessed 19 December 2004).

34 Miller, *Environmental Science*, 304.

35 "Global Warming Nears Danger Point," *The New Zealand Herald*, posted 5 July 2005, http://www.nzherald .co.nz/index.cfm?c_id=2&ObjectID=10334302 (accessed 7 July 2005).

36 Lovgren, Stefan, "Warming to Cause Catastrophic Rise in Sea Level?" *National Geographic News*, 26 April 2004, http://news.nationalgeographic.com/ news/2004/04/ 0420_040420_earthday.html (accessed 7 July 2005).

37 Egan, Timothy, "Global Warming Is a Costly Reality in Alaska," *The New York Times*, http://www.NY Times.com (accessed 7 July 2005 via Global-Warming.net: http://www.global–warming.net/ acostlyrealityinalaska.htm).

38 Union of Concerned Scientists, "Global Environment. Global Warming," http://www.ucsusa.org/global_ environment/global_warming/index.cfm?pageID=27 (accessed 7 July 2005).

39 Ibid.

40 Ibid.

41 Ibid.

42 Floyd, Mark, "Atlantic Current Shutdown Could Disrupt Ocean Food Chain," (Corvallis, Ore.: OSU News & Communication Services), 12 April 2005, http://oregonstate.edu/dept/ncs/newsarch/2005/ Apr05/plankton.htm (accessed 6 July 2005).

43 AccuWeather.com, "Florida: The Mean Season," http://www.accuweather.com/promotion.asp?dir=aw &page=florida (accessed 6 July 2005).

44 Lovgren, "Warming."

45 Union of Concerned Scientists, "Global Environment."

46 Blakemore, Bill, "A New Report about Global Warming," WSOC Charlotte, *World News Tonight with Peter Jennings*, ABC-TV, 8 November 2004.

47 Strom, Ken, "Population and Habitat in the New Millennium" (Boulder Colo.: National Audubon Society and the Global Stewardship Initiative, 1998).

48 Miller, *Environmental Science*, 464.

49 Ibid., 461.

50 Raven, Peter, "World's Biodiversity becoming Extinct at Levels Rivaling Earth's Past 'Mass Extinctions'," (St. Louis, Miss.: International Botanical Congress, Canadian Conservation Network, 2 August 1999), http://www.rbg.ca/cbcn/en/news/archive/press_ibc 2.htmlBotanical.

51 Miller, *Environmental Science*, 464.

52 Myers, Norman, "The Biodiversity Crisis and the Future of Evolution," *The Environmentalist* 16 (1996): 37–47.

53 Ibid.

54 Arms, Karen, *Environmental Science* (Austin, Tex.: Holt, Rinehart, and Winston, 2000), 255.

55 "The Demographic Facts of Life," *Population Connection*, http://www.populationconnection.org/Communica tions/ED2002WEB/demfactsf.PDF (accessed 5 July 2005).

56 "Population and the Environment," *Population Connection*, http://www.populationconnection.org/Communica tions/ED2002WEB/PopEnvFactSheet2002.pdf (accessed 5 July 2005).

CHAPTER 3

[1] Chapin, Amy, et al., "Airborne Multi-Drug Resistant Bacteria Isolated from a Concentrated Swine Feeding Operation," *Environmental Health Perspectives* (November 2004), http://www.factoryfarm.org/ docs/Airborne Bacteria_JH_1104.pdf (accessed 4 July 2005).

[2] Schlosser, Eric, *Fast Food Nation: The Dark Side of the All-American Meal* (New York: Perennial, 2002), 172.

[3] Ibid., 169–172.

[4] Pollan, Michael, "Power Steer," *New York Times Magazine*, 31 March 2002.

[5] Grace Factory Farm Project, "Hogs: Information & Resources," http://www.factoryfarm.org/topics/ hogs/ (accessed 7 July 2005).

[6] Robbins, John, *Food Revolution* (Berkeley, Calif.: Conari Press, 2001), 202.

[7] Napolean, Burt, "Perioperative Pain Management in Newborns," *eMedicine* (30 November 2004), http://www.emedicine.com/ped/topic2856.htm (accessed 8 July 2004).

[8] Kempster, A. J. and D. B. Lowe, "Meat Production with Entire Males," in *44th Annual Meeting of the European Association for Animal Production* (Arhus, Denmark, 1993), 2.1.

[9] Singer, Peter, *Animal Liberation* (New York: Ecco, 2002), 141.

[10] Ibid., 126.

[11] Ibid., 126.

[12] Temple Grandin, Ph. D., professor of animal science, Colorado State University, telephone conversation with author, 7 July 2005.

[13] Singer, *Animal Liberation*, 98.

[14] United Egg Producers, "United Egg Producers Animal Husbandry Guidelines for Animal Care Certified U.S. Egg Laying Flocks" (Alpharetta, Ga.: United Egg Producers, 2004), 10. http://www.animalcarecertified .com/docs/UEPanimal_welfare_guidelines.pdf (accessed 5 July 2005).

[15] Ibid., 8.

[16] Ibid., 5.

[17] Ibid., 6–7.

[18] Temple Grandin, Ph.D., professor of animal science, Colorado State University, telephone conversation with author, January 2005 and 7 July 2005.

[19] BBC Online Network, "Change of Diet Could Defeat Killer Bug," 11 September 1998, http://news.bbc.co .uk/1/hi/health/169255.stm (accessed 11 November 2004)

[20] Union of Concerned Scientists, "Hogging It!: Estimates of Antimicrobial Abuse in Livestock," www.ucsusa .org/food_and_environment/antibiotic_resistance/ page.cfm?pageID=264 (accessed 7 July 2005). and Mellon, M., C. Benbrook, and K. L. Benbrook, *Hogging It — Estimates of Antimicrobial Abuse in Livestock* (Cambridge, Mass.: Union of Concerned Scientists Publications, 2001).

CHAPTER 4

[1] Robinson, Jo, *Why Grass-Fed Is Best: The Surprising Benefits of Grass-Fed Meat, Eggs, and Dairy Products* (Vashion Island, Wash.: Vashion Island Press, 2000).

[2] "Health Benefits of Pasture Raised Food," *Sustainable Table*, http://www.sustainabletable.org/issues/ pasture/pastured2.html (accessed 4 July 2005).

[3] Robinson, Jo, *Pasture Perfect: The Far-Reaching Benefits of Choosing Meat, Eggs, and Dairy Products from Grass-Fed Animals* (Vashon Island, Wash.: Vashon Island Press, 2004).

[4] "Eat Wild: The Clearinghouse for Information about Pasture-Based Farming," www.eatwild.com (accessed 11 July 2005).

[5] Salatin, Joel, *Holy Cows and Hog Heaven: The Food Buyer's Guide to Farm Friendly Food* (Staunton, Va.: Polyface, Inc., 2005).

[6] Bower, Michael, Ph.D., and Warren Leon, Ph.D, *The Consumer's Guide to Effective Environmental Choice: Practical Advice from the Union of Concerned Scientists* (New York: Three Rivers Press, 1999), 50–53.

[7] Sierra Club, "Going Grass Fed," http://www.sierra club.org/e-files/grassfed.asp (accessed 10 July 2005).

[8] Nijhuis, Michelle, "Rethinking Organics," *Grist Magazine* (12 November 2003).

[9] Bower, Michael, Ph.D., and Warren Leon, Ph.D, *The Consumer's Guide to Effective Environmental Choice: Practical Advice from the Union of Concerned Scientists* (New York: Three Rivers Press, 1999), 50–53.

CHAPTER 5

[1] Sligh, Michael and Carolyn Christman, "Who Owns Organic? The Global Status, Prospects, and Challenges of a Changing Organic Market" (The Rural Advancement Foundation International USA, 2003), 18, www.rafiusa. org/pubs/organic report.pdf (accessed 4 July 2005)

[2] Nijhuis, Michelle, "Rethinking Organics," *Grist Magazine* (12 November 2003).

CHAPTER 6

[1] Ronco, Alvaro, Eduardo De Stefani, Maria Mendilaharsu, and Hugo Ronco-Pellegrini, "Meat, Fat and Risk of

Breast Cancer: A Case-Control Study from Uruguay," *International Journal of Cancer* 65 (26 January 1996): 3, 328–331, http://www.findarticles.com/p/articles/mi_m0887/is_n3_v15/ai_18194856#continue (accessed 4 July 2005).

[2] Jenkins, David J. A., et al., "Effects of a Dietary Portfolio of Cholesterol-Lowering Foods vs. Lovastatin on Serum Lipids and C-Reactive Protein," *Journal of the American Medical Association* 290 (23 July 2003): 4, http://jama.ama-assn.org/cgi/content/abstract/290/4/502 (accessed 4 July 2005).

[3] McCarthy, Colman, "Dioxin Burgers," *The Washington Post*, 24 September 1994. and Robbins, John, *Diet for a New America* (Walpole, N.H.: Stillpoint Publishing, 1987).

[4] United States Department of Agriculture, "Steps to a Healthier You," http://www.mypyramid.gov (accessed 8 July 2005).

[5] Harvard University School of Public Health, "The Nutrition Source: Food Pyramids: Healthy Eating Pyramid,"www.hsph.harvard.edu/nutritionsource/pyramids.html (accessed 8 July 2005).

[6] National Center for Nutrition and Dietetics, The American Dietetic Association, "Food Guide Pyramid for Vegetarian Meal Planning," www.utexas.edu/depts/he/ntr/NTR311pyramidpage5.htm (accessed 8 July 2005).

[7] Nestle, Marion, *Food Politics: How the Food Industry Influences Nutrition and Health*, (Berkeley, Calif.: University of California Press, 2002).

[8] Department of Health and Human Services (HHS) and the Department of Agriculture (USDA), "Chapter 5 Food Groups to Encourage," *Dietary Guidelines for Americans 2005*, www.health.gov/dietaryguidelines/dga2005/document/html/chapter5.htm (accessed 8 July 2005).

[9] "About the National School Lunch Program," *USDA Food and Nutrition Service* (December 2004), http://www.fns.usda.gov/cnd/Lunch/AboutLunch/NSLPFactSheet.htm (accessed 4 July 2005).

[10] "Recalled Meat in School Lunches Only Tip of the Iceberg, Say Doctors," *Physicians' Committee for Responsible Medicine*, 21 October 2002, http://www.pcrm.org/news/health021021.html (accessed 4 July 2005).

[11] Robbins, John, *Food Revolution*, (Berkeley, Calif.: Conari Press, 2001), 236–237.

[12] Lappe, Frances Moore, *Diet for a Small Planet*, 20th anniversary ed. (New York: Ballantine Books, 1991), 445–446.

[13] "The National Outreach Program: Customer Brochure," *USDA Agricultural Marketing Service*, April 2002, http://www.ams.usda.gov/nop/Consumers/brochure.html (accessed 4 July 2005).

[14] USDA, "Labeling and Marketing Information, National Organic Program," http://www.ams.usda.gov/nop/FactSheets/LabelingE.html (accessed 18 July 2005).

[15] "Free Range," *The Consumers Union Guide to Environmental Labels*, 2002, http://www.eco-labels.org/label.cfm?LabelID=111&mode=text (accessed 11 June 2005).

[16] "Top Ten Reasons to Buy Organic," promotional poster from *Delicious Living Magazine*.

[17] National Center for Nutrition and Dietetics, The American Dietetic Association, "Food Guide Pyramid for Vegetarian Meal Planning," www.utexas.edu/depts/he/ntr/NTR311 pyramidpage5.htm (accessed 8 July 2005).

[18] Havala, Suzanne, *Being Vegetarian for Dummies* (New York: John Wiley & Sons, 2001).

Glossary

Aerosolize: To become a gaseous suspension of fine particles

Amino acid: Any of a class of organic compounds that are the building blocks of proteins

Ammonia: A nitrogenous product of the decomposition of animal wastes that has a caustic, penetrating odor and contributes to both air and water pollution

Animal Feeding Operation (AFO): A term used in government and environmental documents to refer to a farm or other place that raises livestock

Antibiotic: A drug or substance that kills or suppresses bacteria and is used to prevent and treat bacterial diseases

Aquifer: An underground layer of permeable rock, sand, or gravel that contains water. The water can move aboveground into springs, lakes, and streams.

Bacteria: Single-celled organisms present on skin, in soil, air, water, and almost every environment. Some cause diseases; others are helpful to humans and other living things.

Barrow: A male hog that has been castrated

Battery cages: The long rows of attached cages in which egg-laying hens are kept

Beak trimming: The practice of using a hot blade to cut off the end portion of chickens' beaks to keep them from pecking each other in crowded housing. In the past, both the top and bottom of the beak was cut, but today sometimes only the top is cut.

Boar: A male hog that has not been castrated

Boar taint: A pork industry term referring to the taste of pork from mature male hog that has not been castrated. The taste is caused by male hormones.

Bovine: Noun: A member of the genus *Bos* (cattle); Adjective: Of or relating to a ruminant of the genus *Bos*

Bovine Growth Hormone (BGH): A nonsteroid hormone that increases milk production in dairy cows. It is injected approximately every two weeks once milk production has begun to wane.

Bovine Somato-Tropin (BST): Another name for the dairy-cow hormone BGH (See entry above.)

Brand: Noun: The scar created by a branding iron; Verb: To press a red-hot piece of iron against the hide of a cow or other livestock animal for several seconds for the purpose of creating a distinctive scar used to identify the animal as belonging to a particular ranch. The iron is called a branding iron.

Breeder: A female farmed animal kept for the purpose of laying fertile eggs or giving birth to additional animals or a male farmed animal kept for the purpose of mating with female breeders. Breeders typically live much longer than animals raised for meat, and on factory farms, they are housed only with other breeders.

Broiler: A chicken raised to an age of seven to eight weeks then sent to a processing plant to be packaged as fresh breast cuts, thighs, and legs

Buttresses: Supporting structures at the base of tropical trees that resemble fins on a spaceship. They keep the trees from blowing over in strong winds.

Carbohydrate: A broad category of sugars, starches, fibers, and starchy vegetables that the body converts to glucose, the primary source of energy. Sugars are simple carbohydrates and are absorbed by the body very quickly. Complex carbohydrates include starches and fiber found in whole grains and beans; they take longer to digest and provide more nutrients than simple carbohydrates.

Carnivore: An organism that consumes mostly flesh

Carrying capacity: The maximum number of individuals of any particular species that a given environment can sustain for a long period of time without depletion or degradation of resources

Castrate: To remove an animal's testicles. Castration causes infertility and can also affect the animal's behavior, weight gain, and appetite, as well as the taste of its flesh.

Cattle: A group of bovines including at least one male

Chemical fertilizer: Chemical compounds such as nitrates and phosphates that are synthesized in factories and then applied to soil to provide nutrients for plants

Cholesterol: A compound present in animal cells and body fluids that functions as a precursor to some hormones and is used in the construction of cell membranes. Cholesterol is carried through the bloodstream in lipoproteins of two types: low-density lipoproteins (LDL) and high-density lipoproteins (HDL). (See entries below for "LDL" and "HDL.") As a component of LDL, cholesterol can clog blood vessels by forming plaques on the inner walls of the vessels. Eating saturated fats can increase the amount of cholesterol in the blood.

Community-supported agriculture: Farming that is financially maintained by the marketing of the farm products to the neighboring community. This term usually applies to farms that use humane and environmentally sustainable methods that are valued by their neighbors, who may be willing to pay higher prices for local goods.

Complete protein: A full complement of all nine or ten essential amino acids. A meal may be said to have "complete protein" if it supplies all of the essential amino acids.

Complex: In corporate chicken farming, a complex is a geographical hub surrounded by about 200 chicken farms, all of which are operated by farmers under contract to the corporation. At the central hub are a hatchery, a feed mill, and a processing plant to slaughter and package the chickens. All the facilities at the hub are owned by the corporation, which may have dozens of complexes throughout the country.

Concentrated Animal Feeding Operation (CAFO): A term used in government and environmental documents to refer to a feedlot, a factory farm, or a dairy farm with several hundreds or thousands of animals

Confinement: On a factory farm, a farming practice in which animals are kept in crowded quarters indoors and are often fed by automation

Contract: In the context of this book, a contract is a written legal agreement between a farmer and a corporation that allows the farmer to raise animals that are owned by the corporation but housed in the farmer's buildings. As a verb, to contract means to enter into such a legal agreement.

Corporation: In the context of this book, a corporation is a large company or business, usually operating in many states, that contracts with farmers to raise animals and that owns and operates a large number of meatpacking plants.

Cow: In the meat and milk industry, a mature bovine female that has had at least one calf

Cud: Food brought up into the mouth from the first stomach of a cow and chewed again

Debeak: To trim the beak of a chicken (See entry for "beak trimming.")

Desertification: The transformation of land that was previously forest or grassland into desert by removal or trampling of the vegetation and subsequent erosion of the topsoil

Developed countries: The countries of the world whose residents have a high standard of living due to industrialization and economic development, including the United States, Canada, Japan, Australia, New Zealand, and western Europe

Developing countries: A country whose standard of living, infrastructure, and economy are inadequate to meet the growing needs of the population or a country which is in a rapid state of development. Most are in Africa, Asia, and Latin America.

Ecosystem: Communities of interdependent species interacting with one another and with the physical and chemical environment around them

Environmental Protection Agency (EPA): A federal agency in charge of protecting human health and the natural environment through research, law, and administration

Erosion: The removal of topsoil by runoff following rain. Erosion often follows the removal of natural vegetation and can be aggravated by overgrazing and trampling by livestock.

Essential amino acid: One of the nine or ten amino acids that the human body needs and cannot synthesize; they must be acquired through food consumption.

Essential Fatty Acids (EFAS): Fatty acids that our bodies cannot produce, yet which are required for vital metabolic functions. Linolenic acid, the shortest chain omega-3 fatty acid, and linoleic acid, the shortest chain omega-6 fatty acid, are essential fatty acids.

Estuary: The junction between a river and the ocean where marine and freshwater mix

Eutrophication: The depletion of oxygen in a lake, estuary, or slow-flowing stream that is caused by runoff of nitrates and phosphates and the resulting bloom of algae can cause fish kills

Factory farm: A rural operation that houses tens of thousands or even hundreds of thousands of animals in one location with automated feed and water dispensers

Farrowing: The birthing of a litter of pigs by a sow

Feeder pigs: Pigs three to four months of age that are ready to enter the finishing stage of production (See entry for "finishing.")

Feedlot: A flat outdoor area of several acres that is divided into fenced compartments and is used to confine beef cattle in the second half of their fourteen-month-long life as they are fed corn and grown for slaughter

Finishing: The final stage of a hog's twenty-five-week-long life in which it is fattened for slaughter

Food chain: A sequence of living things in an ecosystem through which energy is transferred by one organism feeding on another. The beginning plant or producer is consumed by an herbivore, which is consumed by an omnivore or carnivore, which may in turn be consumed by another omnivore or carnivore, and so on.

Food pyramid: A drawing of a triangle showing classes of foods in recommended proportions. In the base of the triangle are foods to be eaten most often, with rarely eaten foods at the top.

Food web: A network of interconnecting food chains

Forced molting: In factories with caged layers, this is a common practice of depriving hens of food for several days in order to cause a physiological change that prolongs egg-laying and induces feather shedding.

Free trade: The buying and selling of goods across international borders without tariffs and taxes to discourage it. This is a factor that facilitates globalization.

Globalization: The increased connectedness and interdependence of international markets and businesses as a result of increased mobility of goods, services, labor, technology, and money throughout the world. Economically, globalization is often harmful to workers in developing nations and helpful to corporations in industrialized nations.

Grass farmer: A farmer who raises livestock in pastures and spends a large proportion of his time and attention on raising a mix of the most wholesome grasses and clovers for maximum nutrition of his animals.

Grass-fed: A farmed animal fed a diet of grasses, usually in pastures, instead of grain

Groundwater: Water under the surface of the earth that feeds springs, wells, and sometimes rivers

High-Density Lipoprotein (HDL): Considered the "good cholesterol." An HDL level of 60mg/dL or higher in the blood helps protect against heart disease. Scientists think that HDL may carry cholesterol away from the arteries and back to the liver. Some believe that HDL even removes cholesterol from plaque in arteries, thus preventing blockages.

Heifer: A female bovine other than an older, mature one

Herbicide: A chemical applied to agricultural fields to kill weeds

Herbivore: An animal that eats only plants

Hormone: A substance produced by cells in the body that causes a change or activity in cells or tissues located elsewhere in the body. Manufactured hormones can mimic natural hormones and can be taken orally, implanted under the skin, or injected.

Hybrid: A plant or animal that has parents of two different species, breeds, or varieties

Hydrogenated oil: A fat or oil that has had hydrogen added so that it becomes solid at room temperature, such as a stick of margarine. Foods made with hydrogenated oils should be avoided because they contain high levels of trans-fatty acids, which are linked to several diseases, including heart disease and cancer. (See entry for "trans-fatty acids.")

Induced molting: See entry for "forced molting."

Industrialized countries: See entry for "developed countries."

Integrator: A meatpacking corporation that pays farmers under contract to raise the animals that are slaughtered and processed in its meatpacking plants. Also called a vertical integrator

Lagoon: A large, deep pool or settling basin on a factory farm that is used for storing livestock manure until it can be sprayed onto agricultural fields

Layer: A hen that lays table eggs

Low-Density Lipoprotein (LDL): The "bad cholesterol" that can clog blood vessels. An LDL level of less than 100 mg/dL is the optimal level.

Legume: A plant in the family *Leguminaceae* that produces seeds in pods; commonly called beans or peas.

Litter: The mixture of sawdust and feces that covers the floor of a poultry building on a factory farm

Logging: The cutting of trees for lumber

Macrobiotic diet: A diet consisting mainly of whole grains, vegetables, and fish

Manure: The feces of livestock, often mixed with urine

Mineral: Inorganic ions such as calcium, magnesium, and phosphorus that are required in very small amounts for the maintenance of hormones, enzymes, strong bones and teeth, and fluid levels in the body

Molting: In birds, molting is the periodic shedding of old feathers to make way for new feathers. In hens that perpetually lay eggs, molting induces a period of more frequent egg-laying.

Monounsaturated oil: The healthiest type of fat or oil to eat, it helps to lower blood cholesterol if used in place of saturated fats. Olive oil, canola oil, and peanut oil are composed mainly of monounsaturated fats.

Nitrate: A compound containing nitrogen that is found in chemical fertilizers and in animal wastes. Nitrates are one of the main pollutants of water in the United States, causing illness in humans and fish kills in nature.

Nitrogen: An element that is a primary component of nitrates

Nursery: In the meat industry, a nursery is a series of indoor compartments for housing newly weaned piglets from the age of three weeks to three to four months, when they are transferred to the finishing stage of production.

Old-growth forest: A forest that has never been logged or cut by humans. Also called a primary or virgin forest

Omega-3 fatty acid: An essential polyunsaturated fatty acid that may help lower LDL cholesterol and triglyceride levels. It is found in some fish, flaxseeds, walnuts, and a few other foods.

Omega-6 fatty acid: An essential fatty acid; linoleic acid is the primary type. Some medical research has suggested that excessive levels of omega-6 acids relative to omega-3 acids may increase the risk of a number of diseases.

Omnivore: An animal that eats both plants and animals

Organic: In chemistry, this term applies to any molecule whose structure is based on carbon atoms. In the food industry, it refers to food grown without the use of pesticides or chemical fertilizers.

Ovo-lacto-vegetarian: A person who eats eggs, dairy products, and plant foods, but no meat

Partially hydrogenated oils: Oils that have had some hydrogen added so that they will stay solid but still soft at room temperature, such as margarine in a tub. Foods made with partially hydrogenated oils should be avoided because they contain high levels of trans-fatty acids, which are linked to heart disease and a number of other diseases. (See also the entry for "trans-fatty acids.")

Pasture-based agriculture: The raising of livestock in pastures on a diet of grasses and a few other nutritious plants

Pastured: An adjective describing farmed animals that are raised in pastures rather than in buildings or feedlots

Pesticide: A chemical applied to crops or agricultural fields to kill pests, usually insects or other invertebrates

Pfiesteria: A one-celled dinoflagellate that periodically increases in numbers in estuaries causing fish kills and health problems in humans. *Pfiesteria* appears to increase in response to nitrate and/or phosphate pollution from agricultural runoff and human sewage.

Phosphate: A compound containing phosphorus that is found in chemical fertilizers and in animal wastes. Phosphates are considered pollutants in water, causing algal blooms that can kill massive numbers of fish.

Phosphorus: An element that is a primary component of phosphate

Polyunsaturated oil: A type of fat or oil that is more healthful for blood cholesterol levels than saturated fat, but not as beneficial as monounsaturated oil. The oils from corn, soybeans, safflower, and sunflower are mainly polyunsaturated oils.

Potash: Any of several chemical compounds containing potassium, especially a strongly alkaline material from wood ashes that is added to chemical fertilizers

Prairie: An ecosystem in which the dominant plant forms at maturity are grasses and other nonwoody plants. A broad area of flat or rolling grassland

Protein supplement: In the meat industry, this is an addition to the diet of confined livestock that may consist of chicken feathers, chicken litter (sawdust and feces), or other animal parts or animal products.

Protein: Any of a large group of complex organic compounds composed of amino acids that are essential to all living things for the building and repair of cells, tissues, enzymes, and hormones

Pullet: A young hen that has not yet begun laying eggs

Rain forest: An ecosystem characterized by abundant rain and lush plant growth. Tropical rain forests are home to a very high proportion of the planet's wildlife and plant species.

Revlar: A hormone commonly implanted under the soft skin behind the ear of feedlot cattle for the purpose of increasing weight gain

Riparian zone: The ecosystem along the margins of streams containing many distinctive plant and animal species that are less common or absent in other ecosystems

Roundup: The brand name of a group of herbicides produced by the American chemical company Monsanto and widely used on agricultural crops. It is the world's single most popular herbicide. It is effective only on actively growing plants. There is debate about the toxicity of Roundup.

Roundup Ready crops: Crops that are genetically engineered to be tolerant to Roundup and are grown from seeds produced by Monsanto. Such crops allow farmers to spray Roundup on both weeds and crops. Current Roundup Ready crops include soy, corn, cotton, canola, and alfalfa.

Rumen: The first stomach of a ruminant animal such as a cow. Food from the rumen is moved back up into the mouth and chewed again, at which point the food is called the "cud."

Saturated fat: Fat that is solid at room temperature, such as butter and lard, because its molecoles are loaded, or saturated, with as many hydrogen atoms as possible. Fats from animal sources, including dairy products, are highly saturated. Some vegetable oils such as coconut and palm oils also contain saturated fats. Saturated fats can increase blood levels of LDL, the type of cholesterol that causes heart disease.

Seasonal food: Food that is naturally abundant during a certain part of the year, such as peaches in summer or pumpkins in autumn. Seasonal consumption means buying food during the season in which it naturally grows.

Secondary growth forest: Forest that has regrown after having been logged

Sediment: Fine soil particles carried in moving water. Sediment is the largest water pollutant in farming states such as North Carolina, causing serious environmental problems.

Seitan: A vegetarian protein source often used to make imitation meat. Made from wheat proteins, seitan has a chewy texture and mild flavor. It can be handmade or purchased in health food stores or Asian grocery stores.

Shed: On a factory farm, a building that houses thousands or tens of thousands of animals

Silent forest: A term used by environmentalists to describe a forest that looks intact but, as a result of overhunting, is devoid of all animal life. The term usually refers to tropical forests that have recently been stripped of animals by using modern guns, often automatic weapons. Logging roads often provide access for commercial hunters.

Sow: A mature female pig

Steer: A male bovine that has been castrated

Surface water: Water in rivers, streams, lakes, ponds, or elsewhere aboveground; water that is not groundwater

Sustainable: A practice that can be maintained indefinitely into the future. The term applies to agriculture or other human activities that do not deplete limited resources and do not pollute beyond the environment's ability to eliminate the pollutants.

Tempeh: A fermented vegetarian protein source made from cooked soybeans mixed with a type of mold called *Rhizopus*. As the mold grows, it binds the soybeans together into a solid cake that can be sliced or crumbled. Tempeh is firmer than tofu and has a stronger taste.

Textured vegetable protein (TVP): A high-protein meat substitute. Made from soy flour that has had the fat removed, it comes in the form of small, dried bits that are reconstituted in water before eating.

Topsoil: The fertile top layer of soil, usually rich in material from decomposed plants and animals

Trans-fatty acids or **trans fats:** Fats created when an unsaturated fat such as vegetable oil is hydrogenated or partially hydrogenated to make it a solid at room temperature, as in the case of margarine. Trans-fatty acids can raise blood levels of LDL, the "bad cholesterol," and lower levels of HDL, the "good cholesterol." They are implicated in a variety of diseases,

including heart disease, cancer, diabetes, and more. Trans-fatty acids are found in fried foods and almost all packaged convenience foods. Of all the fats, trans-fatty acids are the most unhealthy.

Tropical: Pertaining to the region between the tropic of Cancer and the tropic of Capricorn where the climate is usually warm and humid

United States Department of Agriculture (USDA): A department of the federal government that oversees programs related to agriculture, food, and drinking water. Its purported goals are to promote agricultural production and research, meet the needs of farmers and ranchers, protect natural resources, and ensure the safety of American food and water. Areas ranging from national forests to school lunches fall under its jurisdiction.

Vegan: A person who avoids consuming meat, eggs, dairy products, and all other animal products

Vegetarian: The term is flexible, but it generally refers to a person who does not eat meat but may eat eggs or milk.

Vitamin: Any of various organic substances essential in minute amounts for normal growth and activity of the body

Volatile: Evaporating faster and more easily than water

Water table: The highest limit of an area of underground rock, sand, or gravel that is completely saturated with water

Glossary

Bibliography and Suggested Reading

Books:

Brower, Michael, and Warren Leon. *The Consumer's Guide to Effective Environmental Choices: Practical Advice from the Union of Concerned Scientists*. New York: Three Rivers Press, 1999.

Halweil, Brian, et al. *The State of the World*. New York: W.W. Norton & Co., 2004.

Harrison, Ruth. *Animal Machines*. New York: Ballantine Books, 1964.

Kennedy, Robert F., Jr. *Crimes Against Nature: How George W. Bush and His Corporate Pals Are Plundering the Country and High-Jacking our Democracy*. New York: Perennial, 2005.

Lappe, Frances Moore, and Anna Lappe. *Hope's Edge: The Next Diet for a Small Planet*. New York: Putnam, 2003.

Lyman, Howard F., and Glen Merzer. *Mad Cowboy: Plain Truth from the Cattle Rancher Who Won't Eat Meat*. New York: Scribner, 2001.

Mason, Jim. *An Unnatural Order*. New York: Lantern Books, 2006.

Mason, Jim, and Peter Singer. *Animal Factories*. New York: Three Rivers Press, 1990.

Mason, Jim, and Peter Singer. *Food Matters: The Ethics of What We Eat*. New York: Rodale, 2005.

Nestle, Marion. *Food Politics: How the Food Industry Influences Nutrition and Health*. Berkeley: University of California Press, 2002.

Robbins, John. *Food Revolution: How Your Diet Can Help Save Your Life and the World*. Berkeley, Calif.: Conari Press, 2001.

Schlosser, Eric. *Fast Food Nation: The Dark Side of the All-American Meal*. New York: Perennial, 2002.

Scully, Matthew. *Dominion: The Power of Man, the Suffering of Animals, and the Call to Mercy*. New York: St. Martin's Griffin, 2003.

Singer, Peter. *Animal Liberation*. New York: HarperCollins, 2002.

Speth, James Gustave. *Worlds Apart: Globalization and the Environment*. New York: Island Press, 2003.

Web sites:

The American Dietetic Association. "Food Guide Pyramid for Vegetarian Meal Planning." http://www.utexas.edu/depts/he/ntr/NTR311pyramidpage5.htm.

Animal Rights International. http://www.ari-online.org.

Animal Welfare Institute. http://www.awionline.org/farm.

Conservation International. http://www.conservation inter national.org.

The Consumers Union Guide to Environmental Labels. "Free Range." http://www.eco-labels.org/label.cfm?LabelID=111&mode=text.

Earth Day Network. http://www.earthday.net.

EarthSave International. http://www.earthsave.org.

Eat Wild: The Clearinghouse for Information about Pasture-Based Farming. http://www.eatwild.com.

Ecological Footprint Lifestyle Calculator. http://www.bestfootforward.com/footprintlife.htm.

Environmental Defense. http://www.environmental defense.org.

Farm Sanctuary. http://www.farmsanctuary.org.

Grace Factory Farm Project. http://www.factoryfarm.org.

Grandin, Temple. http://www.grandin.com.

Harvard University School of Public Health. "The Nutrition Source: Food Pyramids: Healthy Eating Pyramid." http://www.hsph.harvard.edu/nutrition source/pyramids.html.

Humane Farming Association. http://www.hfa.org.

International Vegetarian Union. http://www.ivu.org.

The Jane Goodall Institute. http://www.janegoodall.org.

Keep Antibiotics Working. http://www.keepantibiotics working.com.

The Meatrix. http://www.themeatrix.com.

Natural Resources Defense Council. http://www.nrdc.org.

The Nature Conservancy. http://www.nature.org.

People for the Ethical Treatment of Animals. http://www.peta.org.

Population Connection. http://www.population connection.org.

Rainforest Action Network. http://www.ran.org.

Redefining Progress. http://www.redefiningprogress.org.

The Sierra Club. http://www.sierraclub.org.

Sustainable Table. http://www.sustainabletable.org.

Union of Concerned Scientists. http://www.ucsusa.org.

U.S. Census Bureau International Data Base (IDB). http://www.census.gov/ipc/www/idbnew.html.

U.S. Census Bureau. "World Population: 1950–2040." International Data Base, April 2005 version. http://www.census.gov/ipc/www/img/worldpop.gif

U.S. Department of Agriculture. "Chapter 2, Profiling Food Consumption in America." *2002 Agriculture Factbook.* http://www.usda.gov/factbook/chapter2 .htm.

U.S. Department of Agriculture. "National Agricultural Statistics." http://www.usda.gov/nass.

U.S. Department of Agriculture. National Organic Program. http://www.ams.usda.gov/nop/FactSheets/ LabelingE.html.

U.S. Department of Agriculture. "Steps to a Healthier You." http://www.mypyramid.gov.

U.S. Department of Health and Human Services (HHS) and the U.S. Department of Agriculture (USDA). "Chapter 5 Food Groups to Encourage." Dietary Guidelines for Americans 2005. http://www.health .gov/dietaryguidelines/dga2005/document/html/ chapter5.htm.

U.S. Environmental Protection Agency. "2000 National Water Quality Inventory." http://www.epa.gov/ 305b/2000report.

Waterkeeper Alliance. http://www.waterkeeper.org.

On-Line Seafood Guides for a Healthy Body and Healthy Planet:

The following Web sites have guides to choosing fish for consumers who are concerned about chemical pollutants in fish and dwindling fish populations. Each has a link on the home page.

Audubon's Living Oceans. Seafood Lover's Guide. http://www.seafood.audubon.org.

Environmental Defense. http://www.environmental defense.org.

Oceans Alive. http://www.oceansalive.org.

Articles

(articles in the Endnotes are generally not repeated here):

Barrett, Bruce. "Livestock Don't Need Routine Antibiotics." Madison, Wis: *The Capital Times,* 4 December 2004.

Burkholder, J. M. "The Lurking Perils of *Pfiesteria.*" *Scientific American* (August 1999).

Butler, Pat. "Appetite for Success: Dangerous, Low-Paying Meat Plants Fuel Hispanic Growth." Columbia University Graduate School of Journalism. http://www.jrn.columbia.edu/events/race/thestate/ migrant6.html.

Casau, Armelle. "When Pigs Stress Out." *New York Times,* 9 October 2003.

Chee-Sanford, J. C., et al. "Occurrence and Diversity of Tetracycline Resistance Genes in Lagoons and Groundwater Underlying Two Swine Production Facilities." *Applied Environmental Microbiology* 67 (2001): 4, 1494–1502.

Connor, J. "Air in Your Shed a Risk to Your Health." *Poultry Digest* (December–January 1987/88): 14–15.

Gentle, M. J., and Hunter, L. H. "Neural Consequences of Partial Toe Amputation in Chickens." *Research in Veterinary Science* 45 (1988): 374–376.

Grady, D. "Scientists See Higher Use of Antibiotics on Farms." *New York Times,* 28 January 2001.

Grandin, Temple. "2000 McDonald's Audits of Stunning and Handling in Federally Inspected Beef and Pork Plants." http://www.grandin.com/survey/2000 McDonalds.rpt.html.

Grandin, Temple. "Corporations Can Be Agents of Great Improvements in Animal Welfare and Food Safety and the Need for Minimum Decent Standards." Paper presented at *National Institute of Animal Agriculture,* 4 April 2001. http://www.grandin.com/welfare/ corporation.agents.html.

Grandin, Temple. "Environmental Enrichment for Confinement Pigs." *Livestock Conservation Institute 1988 Annual Meeting Proceedings.* http://www.grandin.com/ references/LCIhand.html.

Greenhouse, Steven. "Rights Group Condemns Meatpackers on Job Safety." *New York Times,* 26 January 2005.

Henry, Fran. "Big Farms, Big Problems? Manure from Large-Scale Dairies Creates Environmental Issues." Cleveland, Ohio *Plain Dealer,* 1 August 2004. http://www.greenlink.org/public/hotissues/manure1 .html.

Kaufman, Marc. "Cracks in the Egg Industry." *Washington Post,* 30 April 2000.

Kilman, Scott. "Iowans Can Handle Pig Smells, but This Is Something Else." *Wall Street Journal,* 4 May 1996.

Mallin, Michael, J. M. Burkholder, et al. "Comparative Effects of Poultry and Swine Waste Lagoon Spills on the Quality of Receiving Streamwaters." *Journal of*

Environmental Quality 26 (1997): 6, 1622–1631.

Mallin, Michael, J. M. Burkholder, et al. "North and South Carolina Coasts." *Marine Pollution Bulletin* 41 (2000): 1, 56–75.

McNamee, P., et al. "Study of Leg Weakness in Two Commercial Broiler Flocks." *The Veterinary Record* 143 (1998).

Mlot, Christine. "The Rise in Toxic Tides: What's behind the Ocean Blooms?" *Science News* 152 (27 September 1997): 202–204.

Montgomery, David. "Not Quite a Slice of Poultry Heaven." *Washington Post*, 24 November 2000.

Myers, Norman. "The Biodiversity Crisis and the Future of Evolution." *The Environmentalist* 16 (1996): 37–47.

National Research Council of the National Academies. "Air Emissions from Animal Feeding Operations: Current Knowledge, Future Needs." Washington, D.C.: The National Academies Press, 2003. http://www.epa.gov/ttn/chief/ap42/ ch09/ relatednrcanimalfeed_dec2002.pdf.

Pollan, Michael. "Power Steer." *New York Times Magazine* (31 March 2002).

Satchell, Michael. "The Cell from Hell." *US News & World Report* (28 July 1997).

Schildgen, Bob. "Who Grows Your Food? And Why It Matters." *Sierra* (November/December 2004).

Scully, Matthew. "Fear Factories: The Case for Compassionate Conservatism — for Animals." *The American Conservative* (23 May 2005).

Stith, Pat, Joby Warrick, and Melanie Sill. "Boss Hog: North Carolina's Pork Revolution." Raleigh, N.C. *News and Observer*, 19, 21, 22, 24, and 26 February 1995. http://www.pulitzer.org/ year/1996/public-service/works/about.html.

Sustainable Agriculture Network. "Profitable Pork: Strategies for Hog Producers." Sustainable Agriculture Research and Development. http://www.sare.org/ bulletin/hogs.

Union of Concerned Scientists. "Global Environment. Global Warming." http://www.ucsusa.org/ global_environment/global_warming/index.cfm.

Vorman, Julie. "Feces, Vomit on Raw Meat a Growing Risk." *Reuters News Service*, 6 September 2000.

Weeks, C. et al. "Comparison of the Behaviour of Broiler Chickens in Indoor and Free-Range Environments." *Animal Welfare* 3 (1994): 179–192.

Wolcott, Jennifer. "'Cage-Free' Eggs: Not All They're Cracked up to Be?" *Christian Science Monitor*, 27 October 2004.

Index

Index of Recipes

♦For general information on preparing various ingredients, refer to the Subject Index.

About the Authors

Sally Kneidel, Ph.D., has cultivated a lifelong passion for the natural world. With a Ph.D. in biology from the University of North Carolina, she has taught biology and writing in colleges and public schools for more than fifteen years. Her interests in animal behavior, ecology, and wildlife photography have driven her repeatedly to the tropical forests of Costa Rica, where she and her ecologist husband occasionally take student groups for rain forest field studies. While her first ten books deal strictly with zoology and botany, *Veggie Revolution* is her first examination of how human behavior and social responsibility impact the natural environment.

An activist, feminist, and Quaker, **Sara Kate Kneidel** earned a B.A. in Spanish and women's studies from Guilford College in 2005. Currently coordinating a community-development program in Guadalajara, Mexico, she plans to travel, farm, and write her way from Spain to West Africa before returning to her native North Carolina. Writing, she believes, is an effective means of raising public awareness of political issues and social concerns. *Veggie Revolution* is her first book.